M000317976

epic

epic

FORM, CONTENT, AND HISTORY

Frederick Turner

Transaction Publishers

New Brunswick (U.S.A.) and London (U.K.)

Library of Congress Catalog Number: 2012016759
ISBN: 978-1-4128-4944-9
Printed in the United States of America

Library of Congress Cataloging-in-Publication Data

Turner, Frederick, 1943-
    Epic : form, content, and history / Frederick Turner.
        p. cm.
    Includes bibliographical references and index.
    "A bibliography of epic texts": p.   .
    1. Epic literature—History and criticism. 2. Myth in literature. 3. Human behavior in literature. 4. Literature and society. 5. Literary form—History. I. Title.
    PN56.E65T87 2012
    808.8'015—dc23
                                                        2012016759

Contents

In Memoriam

A few days after my last email conversation about this book with Irving Louis Horowitz, Editorial Director of Transaction Publishers, I heard that he had died. His extremely useful suggestions and edits have been incorporated into the text. I thank him not only on my own behalf but also on behalf of the social sciences, which he did so much to create and serve.

Frederick Turner

Introduction

The Monster that Won't Stay Dead

If modernity has ever agreed on any one thing, it is that epic is dead. Historians today like to date modernity all the way back to the Renaissance, a practice that deprives us of some useful if impressionistic language for historical periods.[1] In these terms, Giambattista Vico (1688–1744)[2] is already a modern thinker, and he is already, by his famous categorization of history into the age of gods, the age of heroes, and the age of men, implicitly consigning epic to the respected but dismissed childhood of the race. In his footsteps, almost every sober sensible theorist of history has classified epic as the product of a naïve and barbarous era, defining "now" as "not like that."

The tone of that dismissal has changed over the last few centuries. Edward Gibbon and Jean-Jacques Rousseau regret the passing of a nobler and simpler heroic age. Nineteenth- and twentieth-century literary scholars like W. P. Ker and C. S. Lewis see epic as having decayed into romance or sophisticated itself from the robust old "primary epic" into the self-conscious "secondary epic" and thence into extinction. The novel was to replace the epic; the novel was, in the words of the Marxist scholar John Lukacs, "a typical product of the Bourgeois Age"—our own era—and was in turn slated for revolutionary replacement. "History begins in novel and ends in essay," wrote Macaulay, implying that history had not even begun at all in the prior age of the epic.[3] Lukacs agrees with him, and quotes Ortega y Gasset:

> The novel and the epic are precisely poles apart. The theme of the epic is the past as such: it speaks to us about a world which was and which is no longer, of a mythical age whose antiquity is not a past in the same sense as any remote historical time . . . the epic past is not *our* past.[4]

1

Mikhail Bakhtin was probably the most influential theorist of the novel's triumph over the epic.[5] He argued that while the novel was, like clay, adaptable and suitable to a world of change and evolution, the epic was marble—fixed, hierarchical, sacred, fit only for a static society, with a hero who is perfect and exists only in his external actions. The novel was "dialogic"—it could contain many different and even conflicting voices; the epic was "monologic." This book will demonstrate the error of this view, its ignorance of the actual texts and their historical context; but it is to a large extent the contemporary view of the matter.

Some on the left have suggested that the virtues of the novel—its individualism, its power to engage the emotions on behalf of the characters, its acceptance of the social status quo even while pushing for incremental social reform, its dialogical acceptance of different truths—make it a reactionary bourgeois form, an instrument of sentimental "false consciousness." Perhaps instead, epic could be dragged out of the dustbin of history and put to work for the revolution. As Walter Benjamin put it:

> Epic man is only at rest. In the epic, the people rests after the day's labor; it listens, dreams, and collects. Nothing contributes more to the dangerous silencing of the human spirit, nothing stifles the soul of narration more thoroughly than the shameless expansion that the reading of novels has undergone in all of our lives.[6]

Benjamin called for an "epic leftism," using the monologic of epic to weld the people into an instrument of heroic class struggle. After all, he argued, the fascists were already, in Wagnerian Nuremberg style, co-opting the old heroic meta-narratives—they were weapons that should rightly belong to the leaders of communist struggle. Berthold Brecht devised an "epic theater" for the same purpose, eschewing the easy identification of audience with bourgeois hero or heroine, reviving the stern clarity of the ancient tribal storyteller. If epic was, as they believed, dead, it might be revived for the sake of the people's revolution. But this view would leave epic in the hands of the perpetrators of the Gulag, the Cultural Revolution, the Killing Fields.

Postmodern critics, however, their hopes for revolution dashed by the collapse of world socialism, rejected all such "grand narratives." Jean-François Lyotard, the coiner of the phrase, left open the possibility of many little narratives, culture-worlds that could not claim a utopian general truth[7] (an idea developed by Michel Foucault in his theory of distinct incommensurable epistemes, local regimes, or hegemonies of power and knowledge[8]). Perhaps, though Lyotard and Foucault are not specific, epic could find its place among these local regimes, but only if shorn of its grand pretensions to universality. Epic would be another picturesque and picaresque tale told around some local campfire. Jean Baudrillard goes further:

> The end of history is, alas, also the end of the dustbins of history. There are no longer any dustbins for disposing of old ideologies, old regimes, old values. Where are we going to throw Marxism, which actually invented the dustbins of history? (Yet there is some justice here since the very people who invented them have fallen in.) Conclusion: if there are no more dustbins of history, this is because History itself has become a dustbin. It has become its own dustbin, just as the planet itself is becoming its own dustbin.[9]

In other words, because the Marxist grand narrative has failed us, all grand narratives must be rejected. All we have left is simulacra. But there is a small ray of hope even here for epic as grand narrative: if the planet itself is a dustbin of narratives, then maybe we must live in that dustbin and make some kind of home there, and the making of that home might be a fairly grand story in itself. And maybe that was what epic was all along, but this is to anticipate one of the conclusions of this book.

One result of these developments in cultural and political theory has been a relative absence of serious literary critical attention to epic as a world literary genre for at least the last sixty years.[10] If one thinks of the critical attention to the novel, the lyric poem, the diary, the autobiography, and the drama, the contrast is obvious. W. P. Ker's *Epic and Romance*[11] was published in 1897; J. R. R. Tolkien's lecture "The Monsters and the Critics" was delivered in 1936[12]; C. S. Lewis's *A Preface to Paradise Lost*, the last comprehensive defense of epic as a serious literary form, came out in 1942.[13] Gregory Nagy's excellent *The Best of the Achaeans* confines itself to the Greek epics, with glances at Virgil.[14] Scholars in the classical critical tradition have illuminated important aspects of the European epic,[15] and insightful scholarly articles have appeared in the classical journals dealing with fine points of linguistic and textual detail in Homer and Virgil.[16] There have been some excellent introductions to individual epics in non-European traditions, such as Dennis Tedlock's important preface and notes to his translation of the *Popol Vuh*.[17] But there is nothing to match the enormous output of material in the literary field on other subjects, including really ephemeral texts in the popular media. Here we have a major genre, surely as important as the novel, the lyric poem, or the tragic drama, that has been profoundly neglected.

There are reasons for this neglect other than the consignment of epic to the dustbin of history. One is that classicists and conservative literary scholars have tended, as we have seen in the case of Ker and Lewis, to set a very high and narrow bar for what constitutes epic at all. Epic, some seem to imply, is a creation of certain high (Western) civilizations like Greece, Rome, Italy, France, Germany, and Britain, not naked savages or oriental despotisms. This territorial tactic (the obverse of that of the Marxist historicists, who regarded epic as admirably barbaric but passé) was to rebound upon its perpetrators' heads when deconstruction, feminism, and postcolonial studies set out to undermine and dismantle the imperialist male western canon. If epic is the "high" "Western" genre par excellence, the grand narrative of oppression, essentialism, and the marginalization of the subaltern, then it presents a ripe target for dismissal.[18]

Modern academic specialization largely concealed from the literary dismissers the fact that an enormous variety of "nonwestern"[19] societies also have works that, if construed without slavish adherence to European classical rubrics, are unmistakably epic. The postmodern literary critics of modernity had already accepted the modernist categories that divided the West from all other cultures, "us" from the "other." They wanted to reverse the "Western" valorization of the former, but had swallowed the distinction itself. When, as the result of the renewed (and very welcome) interest in nonwestern cultures that was one good result of the postmodernist movement, literary academics started to pay attention to the larger nonwestern texts, they had lost the taste and criteria by which they could have recognized some of those texts as epic and placed them in the company of Homer and Virgil.

In my own experience of teaching and writing epic over at least forty years, I have run across an extraordinary variety of reasons why my literary colleagues reject epic as a proper subject of study and try to put it away in a definitional cage (even if the cage differs radically from one critic to another). They try to cage it to make the world safe—safe for reason, for prose, for the novel, for the lyric poem, for democracy, for the marketplace, for revolution, for nonwestern traditional wisdom, for non-narrativity, for nonlinearity, for the hermeneutic incommensurability of local epistemes, for little narratives, for women's stories, for minorities, for unmediated existential experience, for an undamaged natural environment, and for many other endangered causes.

Beyond these reasons for the literary dismissal of epic as a legitimate object of critical study is a pervasive sense that epic is for children (or "young adults"), especially boys, and may bring out the worst in them at that, like war toys. Perhaps, in a skeptical and self-critical time, we are embarrassed by the emotions and partisanships aroused by the half-remembered nobility and grandeur of the old stories. We are so much more conscious, self-aware, and disillusioned than that now.

Outside literary studies as such there are fields of scholarship that still pay attention to the material of epic. The six most important ones are folklore, oral tradition studies, religious studies, anthropology, mythology, and evolutionary psychology (or sociobiology). Here the perverse incentives against the study of epic qua epic work in a different way.

Folklorists are often faithful to the "low" oral culture, defining themselves as champions of the cultural underdog, and are ambivalent about letting literary high-culture types lay claim to their material by means of such markers as epic. The study of oral tradition, a closely related field, has taken a similar position. Felix Oinas' pathbreaking collection of scholarly essays on what he calls "folk epic" (1978), though valuable, suffers from what I regard as too rigid a distinction between oral epic and literary epic, and an implicit prejudice against the latter, as not being truly of the folk.[20] Where this distinction breaks down is in two respects. The first is that written and oral versions of the epic stories have often coexisted for decades or centuries, exchanging material and ideas, such as the stories of Rama, the Volsungs, the Nibelungs, Roland, King Arthur, Cuchulainn, the Mayan hero twins, Alexander, Rostam, and Sundiata. Certainly epic cannot be studied adequately without a McLuhanesque attention to its medium.[21] But as in many other ways epic always and constitutively stands at the borders, it does so also between different media and modes of communication and commemoration. It "always already" implies some kind of fall from an ancient mythic world to a legendary and even historical one, and it generally marks one of the many transitions in media that go along with that fall—from one kind of orality to another (e.g., iconic or ritual to narrative or moralistic), from the oral to the written, from the written to the printed, from the classic language to the vernacular, from verse to prose. We will discuss this issue in detail at a later point.

The other consideration that makes the "oral vs. literary," "folk vs. individual," and "popular vs. courtly" distinctions, so loved by folklorists, not always useful in understanding the epics themselves, is the matter of the audience. Literary epics can be just as popular, just as much of a folk phenomenon, as oral epics. Scholars and gentlemen are not the only people who read and love literary epic. Consider the popularity of the *Mahabharata* in India, the written text of the Homeric epics in Greece, the *Divine Comedy* in Italy—the folk culture of those nations is not just shaped by those works, but even constituted by them, so that it would be inconceivable without them. And on the other hand, the implication that the oral poets were not scholars, not conscious of themselves, not individuals, and not conversant with courts and schools, is itself of course an illusion. The folk did not compose epic—particular poets did. The professional modesty of the oral performer—they usually say "this is how I heard it from the old griots, my fathers" or something of the kind—should not deceive us, any more than should similar protestations from the folk-singers of our own mountains. Certainly the oral poets were in close touch with their market, and possessed a deep intuition into the fundamentals of human nature—if they did not, they would fail. But it is in their individual conscious voice, fully capable of "meta" analysis, that the folk—or rather the human—themes are articulated.

One might cite as a counter to the general critical neglect of epic studies the hugely important work of Milman Parry and Albert Lord in uncovering the techniques of oral epic composition and reproduction, and pointing out the relationship between ongoing Balkan oral practice and the Homeric epics.[22] Their work came out to the general audience in 1960 with the publication of Lord's *The Singer of Tales* and spawned a whole field of oral epic studies.[23] But the effects of their discoveries in some ways unintentionally undermined the serious literary consideration of epic. For literary "theory" it further confined epic to a premodern world of mysterious skills and techniques inaccessible to the modern consciousness and irrelevant to contemporary socioeconomic conditions. For lovers of the folk tradition it had a different effect, to cast doubt on the authenticity of any epic *not* composed and disseminated by the old methods. Literary epic became a fake antique, so to speak. At worst, it was an artificial form, using an ancient patina to give credence to the political and social concerns of the author's class.

The demonstration of the compositional differences between oral and literary epic gave weight to Lewis's distinction between primary and secondary epic, downgrading the importance of shared epic content, deemphasizing the commonalities in composition and form among epics in general, and thus helping to undermine the integrity of the term "epic" itself. This book seeks to recover that integrity, both by reestablishing the continuity between folk epic and literary and other forms of epic, and by turning the focus from differences of compositional technique to profound commonalities in epic content. Though the earliest epics must by necessity have been composed and preserved by means of the techniques that Parry and Lord described, epic composers used the new forms—of writing, printing, and so on—as soon as they were available. And—an ingenious twist—they *celebrated* the transitions in form as themselves part of the epic story of our evolution. In Chapter 11, "A New Medium of Communication," we will explore this epic feature with special reference to works like *Gilgamesh*, the *Mahabharata*, the *Popol Vuh*, the *Heike*, *Paradise Lost*, and *Mwindo*, all of which explicitly explore the relationship between oral performance and writing.

This is not to underestimate the great importance of contemporary scholarship in the oral epic. John Miles Foley, a giant in the field, gives a splendid list of current and recent textualizing projects in his review of Lauri Honko's fine translation of Gopala Naika's *The Siri Epic*:

> ... the Manas epic and Wilhelm Radloff, the Mohave epic and Alfred Kroeber, the South Slavic epic and Milman Parry and Albert Lord, the Sunjata epic and Gordon Innes, the Anggun Nan Tungga epic and Nigel Phillips, the Annanmaar epic and Brenda Beck, the Palnaadu epic and Gene Roghair, the Son-Jara epic and Charles Bird and John Johnson, the Siirat Banii Hilaal epic and Susan Slyomovics, and the Paabuujii epic and John Smith.[24]

This work is providing a whole new wealth of stories for the enrichment of our perhaps over-refined stock of narrative, and will perhaps be material for epics of the future. The irony is that these very efforts themselves represent the ancient epic event in which the oral and the literate meet and merge and turn back to examine the transition itself. And scholarship of this kind, specialized as it must be (except in the synthesizing work of Foley himself) cannot yet afford to broaden its purview to include the canonical literary epics, and ask itself the meaning of all the remarkable underlying commonalities in epic across the globe.

Similar barriers to a truly comprehensive view of epic exist also in the academic field of comparative religion. Religious studies scholars naturally focus their attention on the priestly caste—whether brahminical, scribal, and mandarin or mystical, shamanic and ascetic—and pay less attention to the worldview of the warrior-ruler caste, the knights, kshatriyas, and samurai, whose exploits are so large in epic.[25]

In anthropology there is a traditional split between sociocultural and physical (evolutionary) anthropology that has tended to paralyze epic studies. This book will argue that epic is basically *about* human evolution—that is, epic is the traditional way we have explained to ourselves as a species our emergence from nature and the stresses within our own nature that result from that emergence and our look back at it. But in the quarrel between sociocultural constructionist anthropologists and naturalist evolutionary anthropologists, this fundamental theme of epic is lost.

It is lost on one side because cultural and social anthropologists tend to believe that we are more or less what Steven Pinker calls a "blank slate" to be inscribed by social and cultural norms. There is an honorable history to this view, for it is the easiest and most comprehensive rebuff to the scientific racism of much early anthropology. There is also, perhaps, a less admirable subtext, which is that since each society and subculture to be studied is a unique world unto itself, unconstrained by human universals, there will always be significant new material for anthropological fieldwork. So epic, with its powerful myths of the natural underpinnings of our social practices, would seem to imply an essentialist naturalization of unjust status roles, and would look much like the enemy of the egalitarian ethic of humanistic anthropology. Epic's cultural universality would both unify a field of study that temperamentally prefers radical diversity, and suggest that the "West" (usually the villain of the piece) is not the only tribe that has fought, conquered, ordered the world, and subjugated nature.

On the other side, the naturalist evolutionists, who like to look underneath social and cultural conventions and practices to the deep survival drives that have preserved our species, tend to dismiss such cultural genres as religion, art, and epic poetry as "spandrels"[26] in the evolutionary edifice, pretty but insignificant by-products of the interplay of inherited neural and behavioral traits that confer adaptive advantages. Thus the idea that epic composers may have already second-guessed the evolutionists and conducted their own rather penetrating analysis of how we got to be human would be a little humbling, and turn what were the raw materials of scientific study into equal collaborators in it.

And if epic composers and their audiences have known about our evolution all along—in traditional symbolic and narrative terms to be sure, but rather useful ones—then who knows how our analysis of underlying evolutionary motives and behavioral drives may have been compromised and nullified by conscious resistance to them or enlistment of them for cultural, strategic, or ideological ends? After all, anthropological evolutionists themselves often justify their analysis of human behavioral predispositions on the basis that if we understand them we can—if they lead to racism or the oppression of women or an unwholesome appetite for sweet things, for instance—control them by social policy. But if the participants in the human drama of evolution were always already canny observers of it, the clarity of the evolutionists' subject and method would suddenly give way to a complex, colorful, and subtle set of puzzles and branching pathways, like the world of epic itself.

Of course, I am here exaggerating the anthropological rift and the extremes to which its participants have gone. Most anthropologists have a more mixed and nuanced view. But the ideological rifting has been enough to leave epic in the resulting limbo between the sides.

The field of myth studies, like those of oral, folk, and religious literatures, has its own resistance to epic. Mythologists prefer their mythemes and deep structures unmediated and unadulterated by the artistic ambitions, rational reductionism, and ideological biases of courtly epic composers. The pursuit of mythemes and root myths, and the attempt to clear away editorial accretions that obscure the beautiful logical structures of myth, can all too easily bypass the epic narrative that links them together as a later, consciously ideological distraction. The present study is at least as interested in the synthesizing imagination that makes epic epic as in the mythological material it often organizes.

Nevertheless, the reader may well be wondering at this point about how this book is related to the concept of the monomyth, as proposed by Joseph Campbell,[27] and indeed to the whole tradition of mythology including the work of James Frazer, Carl Jung, Jessie Western, Robert Graves, Georges Dumézil, Karl Kerenyi, and others.[28] The search for the "Key to All the Mythologies," in the ironic words of George Eliot,[29] is not new. The literary academic culture has for many years regarded that tradition with suspicion, consigning it to newly subaltern categories such as "Western," "patriarchal," "unscientific," "impressionistic," "mystical," etc., and preferring more mainstream and hard-headed structuralist, poststructuralist, sociological, feminist, postcolonial, or political approaches to the material. Recent work in humanistic anthropology, under the banner of a multiculturalist depriviling of "Western" epistemes,[30] has to some extent reinstated *ritual* as more than just an epiphenomenon of economic and power relations; but this work has not yet brought a friendlier eye to the *myths* that often serve as the scripts to ritual performance. One welcome exception to this tendency to dismiss myth is the work of Wendy Doniger, whose feminism prefers to understand myth than to chastise it.[31]

Though Joseph Campbell's work, like the epic impulse itself, has survived in the broader culture, its claims of universality have been widely challenged in the academy. As academic attention swung toward postmodern and poststructuralist concepts of cultural untranslatability and incommensurability, closed hermeneutic circles, hegemonic regimes of power and knowledge, social construction and moral relativism, Campbell fell out of fashion and began to be suspected of the old "Western" device of "essentialism," and of claiming as natural and universal its own local conception of what is properly human. This book is in some respects a defense of Campbell's claims of universality and naturalness. It does so through a close and meticulous documentation and analysis of hundreds of parallels among epics in widely separate cultures and periods, amounting, I claim, to proof of the disputed proposition of epic's human universality. In a modest, various, and messy way there is a human essence that is worth recognizing and preserving. This book thus also maintains that there are grounds for a genuine reassertion of the old dream of human siblinghood and solidarity.

One of Campbell's most cogent critics is the brilliant and thoughtful science-fiction author David Brin, who (despite the heroic archetypes that cannot help emerging in his own fiction) claims that the old epic myths are a pernicious drag on human well-being. A self-confessed advocate of the Enlightenment, modernity, free markets, progress, reason, and democratic equality, he regards the old heroic stories as cloaks for the maintenance of aristocratic or priestly privilege, mystical obscurantism, superstition, and obsolete technologies. Though I share much of Brin's general view, I believe he sells epic short. Modern humans have been around for about two hundred thousand years, and our current achievements are based on an enormous accumulation of skills, knowledges, actions, and sacrifices, most of which we do not notice at all because we take them for granted. Each achievement—the control of our own bestial nature, the mastering of other species, the exploration of the planet, the transcendence of the family or tribal unit, the creation of language, the recognition of our own special nature, the bloody political struggle to create cities and nations, the emergence of law and ethics, the survival of natural disasters, the development of technology and trade, the preservation of history—was a desperately heroic adventure, achieved in the teeth of huge unknown dangers, pathetically short lifetimes, and tragic misunderstandings. Epics tell that story, the greatest story in the world. Our current technological and organizational advances are only the cap on a huge history of discovery and invention. We did not waste any time getting here, and our failures were all necessary. Our current enlightenment (if such it is, with the Gulag and the Holocaust in living memory) is deeply indebted, and we should acknowledge that debt. More, we need the heroic story as inspiration and advice for our own future and the challenges we will certainly face.

Campbell's work (like all coherent and useful works of scholarship) is built upon a paradigm that both constrains and empowers its meanings. That paradigm is basically psychological, and the psychology is basically Jungian, taking on something like that valuable but risky assumption, the human collective unconscious. This present book prefers the more provable unity of our common human evolutionary history to the rather mystical or telepathic unity of the collective unconscious, synchronicity, and the deep subconscious. It takes its spirit from Edward O. Wilson's bold and exciting concept of consilience.[32] Its basic paradigm is the biological and social evolution of the human species, as seen by the species itself as it evolves. And, partly because of its special interest in epic, this book takes the psychoanalytical perspective as only one of its lenses. The great poets who composed epic, like us, were coming to terms with myth in a historical and civilizational context, and therefore they—and this book—are equally concerned with natural science, history, society, technology, economics, law, ethics, philosophy, and language.

Despite the shadow that has fallen over myth studies, the work of Campbell especially has been hugely effective in the culture at large, inspiring mass phenomena like the *Star Wars* films, the TV miniseries as a genre, and computer role-playing games. Clearly, Campbell did identify common elements in many human narratives across the world, prompting important questions that undermine any purely sociopolitical constructionism. If very different cultures and economies produce the same tales, perhaps there is much that is universal, fundamentally human, or even biologically or psychologically *given* about storytelling.[33] If the principles of myth work in the highly competitive and consumer-driven crucible of Hollywood scriptwriting, and survive the iconoclasm of one liberationist assault on tradition after another—and if the results are eagerly viewed on screen in Nigeria, Korea, Indonesia, Bolivia, and New Guinea—then perhaps they should be reexamined for their universality.

Given the importance of myth, how does this book's approach and subject differ from that of, say, Campbell's *Hero with a Thousand Faces*?

The focus of this book is both narrower and wider than that of Campbell's. It is narrower in that it concentrates on epic as such, rather than on mythic elements in tales, narrative fragments, exegeses of ritual cycles, and stories of all kinds. Epic is what very conscious and thoughtful people have made of large bodies of myth from different sources once they have the equivalent of a city of their own to do it in, records of the past, and ways of recording their syntheses for the future. In Chapters 8, 9, and 11 we will look closely at those elements that set off epic from myth in general—city-founding, the epic continuity of myth with historical fact, and the deep awareness of the communication medium itself.

But the focus of this book is also wider. We stand on the shoulders of giants. There has been a torrent of good scholarship since Campbell's work in 1949 that has brought to light the narratives of dozens of formerly obscure cultures and nations. We now have a much wider choice of examples of both myth and epic, and thus correctives for over-emphases that are the result of small sample size, and confirmations of hypothetical universality. Moreover, we now have the benefit of at least two frames of reference that have deepened our understanding of myth. One is the structuralist analysis of Claude Lévi-Strauss; the other is the study of the source and enactment of story in ritual, as explored by Victor W. Turner.[34] There also exists an accumulating body of good scientific evidence and analysis concerning the evolutionary history of *Homo sapiens*. Thus there is a basis for estimating the real accuracy of epic—if epic is, as this book claims, the history in symbol and story of the human species itself.

The thesis of this book, then, is that epic is not beneath serious critical attention, nor even just another legitimate literary form, but the most fundamental and important of all literary forms. It is the *fons et origo* of all the others, the frame within which any literature is possible at all, and a live genre whose reawakening may stimulate a fresh burst of creative literary activity. It is not just a "Western" genre. It is not just an outdated historical relic. The mission of this book is to begin to repair the great gaps in the literary understanding that have been created by the absence of epic studies—and perhaps offer a permission to future epic writers and composers. Perforce the body of this work must be a close and also wide-ranging analysis of specific passages, themes, plot elements, and symbols in epics from across the globe, which will be the only possible proof of the pudding.

This book explores the proposition that epic is the basic story that the human species tells to itself about itself and, using its own narrative and symbolic and folk-science terms, an accurate description of the evolution of the human species seen from the inside and half-remembered in the most graphic and intuitive language. It is a record of the emergence of language itself, and a way to understand the formation of new words and the process of definition and referentiality. In making these assertions, this book cannot ignore such disciplines as cultural, genetic, and linguistic archeology, evolutionary anthropology, ecology, climatology, and neuroscience; we must look at the historic and prehistoric records of the earliest roots of human civilization.

One method that I will use is to read the recurring epic themes in the light of what is known of the evolution of the human species. If epic is our best subjective memory of the childhood of our species, we can check its accuracy by how it fits the objective evidence as various disciplines now reveal it. (And perhaps in turn check our interpretation of the scientific evidence against the "inside story" as told by epic.) This project immediately involves an ongoing and vigorous debate about the relative strengths of culture and genes in the new humanistic field of biopoetics or bioesthetics. Since my own exploratory work in *Natural Classicism: Essays on Literature and Science* and *Beauty: The Value of Values* in the 1980s and the pathbreaking magisterial work of Leda Cosmides and John Tooby,[35] there has been a torrent of research on the study of human aesthetic, literary, and artistic practices, and a lively controversy about how that research is to be interpreted. Much of that controversy is already implicit in *Biopoetics: Evolutionary Explorations in the Arts*, edited by Brett Cooke and myself,[36] with essays by such major players in the field as Edward O. Wilson, Daniel Rancour-Laferriere, Joseph Carroll, Nancy Easterlin, Kathryn Coe, Alexander Argyros, Ellen Dissanayake, Nancy Aiken, and Koen DePryck. Robin Fox's book *The Tribal Imagination: Civilization and the Savage Mind*[37] contains a characteristically trenchant account of the parallel debate that was going on in the social sciences.

Many in today's humanistic academy would argue that human beings do not have a nature, commonsense to the contrary notwithstanding. In some academic and artistic circles, both right and left, it is even argued that nature itself is an ingenious fiction made up—"socially constructed"—by authorities self-constituted as such by their social, political, or economic power, in pursuit of their own interests, or as a rationalizing justification for their power and past actions. But those authorities are themselves puppets of the politico-economic system. In this view, our actions are determined by the society we live in.

Others, both past and present, have taken an opposing view: that we are simply animals—very sophisticated ones, to be sure—whose selfish genes control us. Thus our whole superstructure of social norms, morality, and aesthetics is just a cloak for our drive to survive and reproduce. Needless to say, in this perspective our sense of freedom and autonomy is an illusion, our noble motives merely strategic demonstrations to others of our trustworthiness and our potential as partners in profitable and reproductively promising enterprise.

These two positions about what we are and how we relate to the world around us may be summarized in this way: is a human being basically a unit of society, or basically an evolved animal? Are we socially or biologically determined? Depending on the answer to these questions—*and on whether we take these questions to exhaust the possibilities*—we will come to very different conclusions about the core issues of human responsibility, governance, ethics, and aesthetics. If we adopt either position, the study of epic becomes an irrelevance, as we have already seen in the fields of critical theory, folklore, comparative religion, anthropology, and mythology. Epic, I will argue to the contrary, with its branchy plotlines and its large role for human action and freedom, is in fact our traditional way of grappling with precisely these same problems that now present themselves to us in the terminology of the humanities and the sciences.

New work on human genetics, individual development, and the translation of genes into actual cells and organs resoundingly confirms this "branchiness" in the field of human heredity. The field of epigenetics shows that instead of having one gene per behavior, we have hundreds of sets of genes for various behavioral strategies that can be turned on or off depending on our experience and our own actions: we can change ourselves. A whole level of self-organization, the proteome as it is called, lies between the gene and the cell, again subject to life experiences and our own responsive choices. This malleability is such that the moral sentiments of love, sympathy, justice, mercy, faith, curiosity about what is true, spiritual aspiration, mystical communion, and so on can readily become instincts of their own, equipped with their own internal pleasure rewards. As such they are well able to compete with the older more atavistic drives to individual survival and reproduction embodied in the passions of covetousness, greed, laziness, revenge, envy, lust, and jealousy. We even have the passion of shame to actively suppress our selfishness and self-assertion. We have lived in and been domesticated by societies for the whole of our existence as a species, and the speed of our epigenetic malleability has given us ample time to develop the noblest and more spiritual of instincts along with the old temptations to force, fraud, and rape.

Thus if "construct" means "necessitate" or "compel" or even "require," both social and natural constructionism are profoundly wrong. Certainly things and social systems are constructed by nature and society, and the constructions are not empty of meaning: but they are affordances, tools, opportunities, offerings, gifts, choices, far more than they are tyrants. Paradoxically we make them tyrants only when we persuade ourselves that they are so and that we can do no other than what they dictate. Epic is always a protest against that tyranny. It is encouraging that the new fields of developmental genetics and epigenetics confirm the epic protest.

Beyond the various disciplinary and theoretical obstacles to the present project that I have cited, there are also practical difficulties that stand in the way of a fair, updated, and comprehensive assessment of the value of epic. The problem of academic specialization has already been mentioned; scholars often seem unaware of the rich variety and wide extent of the epic literature, partly because of their confinement within the literary, mythological, folkloristic, comparative religionist, or anthropological worlds, partly because if one is studying a particular culture one is relatively unaware of others. More immediately to the point, though there are many epics in the world, there are few in any given language; most cultures are blessed with only one or two (if any) that have received the true epic response of a popular audience. Thus a new student of epic must choose to work with translations if any real scope and a good sample of the genre is to be attempted, and even an experienced multilingual scholar will have access to only a small fraction of the literature in the original, often in archaic forms of the language at that. Time and tenure will not wait for the linguist, and the canons of scholarship are contemptuous of work with translations. This book must perforce ignore such cautions and obstacles, but there are good reasons for doing so, as I hope I will show.

Despite all these discouragements (from Vico onward) in the secondary academic world of theory, commentary, and criticism, the epic impulse continued unabated through modernity within the primary arena of creative art and literature. Wordsworth's *The Prelude* explicitly and implicitly invites the designation "epic," arguing that the history of the individual soul is worthy of epic treatment. Tolstoy's *War and Peace* is plainly epic in conception. Herman Melville's *Moby Dick* adopts the epic rhythms of Christopher Marlowe, William Shakespeare, and John Milton into its prose, and Melville's ambition was arguably more to create the great American epic than the great American novel. Joyce's *Ulysses* reprises Homer. Ezra Pound evoked the great classical epics in his *Cantos* and, in *The Waste Land*, Eliot created a marvelously mutilated and condensed mini-epic based on the matter of Parzifal. The epic work of the major American poet Julia Budenz, *The Gardens of Flora Baum*, has just been published, an enormous poem in five books that invokes the ghosts of Virgil and Tasso.[38] The science fiction genre is lavishly epic in scope, inspiration, and action, taking on the ancient themes of world-creation, sacrificial heroism, death and immortality, nature and human nature, without embarrassment. Arthur Clarke's *Childhood's End*, Asimov's *Foundation* trilogy, Kim Stanley Robinson's Mars series, to name just a few examples, have epic scope and many epic elements. But the avant-garde literary world since the postmodern movement emerged has been largely dismissive of epic.

A new generation has, however, grown up without the prejudices against epic that accompanied the revolt against grand narrative. Even when their elders are content with the novel's elegant little narratives of suburban divorce and private existential struggle, the young are unashamedly epic in their tastes. The very word "epic" is now a live term in their vocabulary for something that is big, exciting, and cutting-edge.

The cultural genres of Marvel Comix, gothic, anime, manga, multi-user dungeon gaming, summer superhero movies, Civil War reenactments, Renaissance Faires, etc., reprise all the epic themes and motifs, sometimes consciously, but sometimes as a natural human tropism toward a real human need. Consider *The Wizard of Oz, Star Wars, Star Trek, The Lord of the Rings, Lost, The Matrix, Superman, Harry Potter, Narnia, Batman*, and even Lady Gaga's *The Monster Ball*: here we find the epic beast-man, the miraculous birth of the hero, the creation myth, the founding of the city, the quest journey, the descent into the land of the dead, the monsters, the trickster, the mystery woman, and all the other epic elements that I shall analyze in greater detail in later chapters.

A Loose List of Epics

But perhaps at this point the question has been begged—what actual works are we calling epic, and on the basis of what defining characteristics do we so name them? Here the problem for the epic scholar is like that of the taxonomist. Does one present as confirmation the best specimens of the species one seeks to claim and name—in which case how does one make the choice of specimens? Or does one give one's criteria for describing the species, and then pick specimens to fit one's definition?—in which case one stands in danger of imposing an abstract and arbitrary unity and uniqueness on a set of unrelated hand-picked individuals. If one claims king penguins as a species on the basis of a collection of specimens, how does one avoid the charge that one just picked, for instance, large, long-beaked Adélie penguin individuals?—and if one defines the king penguin as being warm-blooded, marine, air-breathing, and predatory, one could end up with dolphins, whales, walruses, otters, and plesiosaurs as all variants of king penguins. I shall here adopt, as the beginning of a confirmation process, the first strategy, which relies on a strong intuitive sense of family resemblance[39] in choosing a reasonably canonical group of representatives of the genre. Given the fact that I make no appeal to traditional literary authority beyond the use of the term "epic" itself, I beg the reader's provisional assent to the classification, pending later analysis of the features shared by the group, exclusion of nonmembers of it, and confirmation of the category's organic necessity.

This "fresh start" is, I believe, necessary because so many new candidates for the epic canon have emerged through international scholarship that the criteria for admission need to be looked at with an unbiased eye. We may end up with a kind of classicism—but it will not be a European or "Western" one, and it may be very much more exciting and useful than the old one.

In order to illustrate the cultural universality of epic, across multiple remote geographical locations, historical eras, ethnic and linguistic groups, and levels of technological and economic development, I shall classify my proposed list of epics by geographical area, but in no special chronological order.[40]

Africa
Sundiata (Mali)
Mwindo (Congo)
Tambuka (Kenya)
Taghribat Bani Hilal (Egypt)

Asia
Gilgamesh (Mesopotamia)
Enuma Elish (Mesopotamia)
The Iliad (Asia Minor)
The Odyssey (Asia Minor)
Mahabharata (India)
Ramayana (India)
Shahnameh (Persia)
Book of Genesis (Palestine)
Book of Exodus (Palestine)
The Tale of the Heike (Japan)
The Journey to the West, or Monkey (China)
The Three Kingdoms (China)
King Dongmyeong of Goguryeo (Korea)
King Gesar (Tibet)
Silappathikaram (Tamil India/Sri Lanka)
Manimekalai (Tamil India/Sri Lanka)
David of Sassoun (Armenia)
The Book of Dede Korkut (Turkey)
Battalname (Turkey)
Manas (Kyrgyz Turkey)
The Secret History of the Mongols (Mongolia)
Antar (Arabia)

Europe

Works and Days (Greece)

The Oresteia (Greece)

The Aeneid (Italy)

The Divine Comedy (Italy)

The Liberation of Jerusalem (Italy)

Orlando Furioso (Italy)

The Song of Roland (France)

The Saga of the Volsungs (Scandinavia/Iceland)

The Elder Edda (Scandinavia/Iceland)

The Poetic Edda (Scandinavia/Iceland)

Njal's Saga (Iceland)

Laxdala Saga (Iceland)

The Peril of Sziget (Hungary)

Toldi (Hungary)

Kalevala (Finland)

The Poem of My Cid (Spain)

Don Quixote (Spain)

The Cattle Raid of Cooley (Ireland)

Parzifal (Germany)

Faust (Germany)

The Song of the Nibelungs (Germany)

Beowulf (England)

Sir Gawaine and the Green Knight (England)

The Morte d'Arthur (England)

The Faerie Queene (England)

The Henriad (Shakespeare's Richard II, Henry IV parts 1 and 2, Henry V) (England)

Hamlet (England)

Paradise Lost (England)

The Prelude (England)

The Lord of the Rings (England)

The Kossovo Epic (Kossovo)

The Lusiads (Portugal)

Lacplesis (Latvia)

Americas

Popol Vuh (Mesoamerica)

Omeros (St. Lucia, West Indies)
The Gaucho Martín Fierro (Argentina)
Hiawatha (USA)
Moby Dick (USA)
Clarel (USA)
The Cantos (USA)
Paterson (USA)
Davenport's Version (USA)
The Gardens of Flora Baum (USA)
The Alamo (USA)
Genesis, an Epic Poem (USA)
The New World (USA)

It would be easy to argue with both the inclusions and the exclusions in this list. Why leave out Apollonius' *Argonautica*, Lucan's *Pharsalia*, or for that matter Joel Barlow's *Columbiad*? If Ariosto, why not Boiardo? Why exclude current film and TV work in the popular media that might qualify as epic? Should recent small-press poems such as John Gery's *Davenport's Version* and Budenz's *The Gardens of Flora Baum* be included—or other works with rather small audiences like Michael Lind's *The Alamo* and my own *The New World* and *Genesis: An Epic Poem*? What about Wordsworth's *Prelude* and Pound's *Cantos*? Shouldn't they be excluded?—the former could well be called an extended autobiographical lyric, the latter a collection of cultural reflections without a central narrative. The *Eddas* are more collections of epic myths than epics in themselves, but they seem to belong to the list. The *Kossovo Epic*, like *The Book of Dede Korkut*, could be said to be a cycle of epic tales rather than a coherent epic per se. Some of the Asian works may be better classified as king lists or chronicles, especially the *Shahnameh*. Wu Cheng-En's *The Journey to the West*, Lo Kuan-Chung's *The Three Kingdoms*, the Icelandic sagas, *The Cattle Raid of Cooley*, the *Morte d'Arthur*, *Moby Dick*, and *The Lord of the Rings*, among other works, are in prose—and if we are to include Aeschylus' *Oresteia*, Shakespeare's *Henriad* and *Hamlet*, and Goethe's *Faust*, what about other large-scale heroic plays? Where would we put Ossian?

I have left out the great mock-epics, such as Pope's *Dunciad*, on the grounds that mock turtle soup is not made of turtles, a brilliant photograph of the Grand Canyon is not the Grand Canyon, and even an exquisitely written critique of a play is not a play. But I keep *Don*

Quixote (though I have largely left commentary on it to its many superb critics and appreciators), despite the fact that it is among other things a satire on the western European epic tropes and content. It is on the list because the knight of La Mancha is a not unheroic figure, and his exploits and quests are real ones even if they do not take place in the world that the Don thinks they do.

A further problem suggests itself. How do we establish the canonical texts of these works, when so many of them, like the *Mahabharata*, the Old Testament books, *Gilgamesh*, the *Popol Vuh*, the Tamil versions of the *Ramayana*, and the *Kalevala*, are manifestly palimpsested compilations, summaries, abridgements, translations, or what Albert Lord called "multiforms"? My practice in this book is to treat the more composite texts (as opposed to "signed" final versions like *The Aeneid* or *Paradise Lost*) as musicologists treat folksongs or as internet users treat corrigible collaborative texts like Wikipedia. The variants, whether as different retellings, like the various versions of the Mio Cid story, or as included in the same text, like the J, P, and E texts in the biblical Book of Genesis, or as translations or abridgements, or as embedded annotations and interpretations like those of the *Mahabharata*, will be treated as legitimate elements of the work, contradictions included.

Some traditions, like those of the classical Greeks, Romans, and Chinese, and those of modern Europe, seem to like to keep the text, once established, as fixed, and then generate around it a body of commentary, imitation, and interpretation; others, like those of the Hebrews, the Indians, and medieval Europe, prefer to grow a text collectively around an armature or core. Criticism and discussion of such live evolving verbal organisms will call on some of the techniques of the theater critic or the anthropologist of ritual performance. But I will reserve the right to concentrate on the vital earlier text where the author has gone back to a work of his own that had already entered the public imagination and censored it for ideological correctness, as was the case, for instance, with Tasso's *The Liberation of Jerusalem* and Wordsworth's *Prelude*.

Both types of traditions—those that keep the ur-text pure, and those that lovingly ornament it—attest to the recognition by the culture of the epic's special place at the heart of its system of meanings, and its openness to amendment by interpretation and translation at least. Even the distinction between textual purists and textual amenders begins to blur on closer inspection. *The Aeneid*, for instance, might have been burned had Virgil's last will and testament been obeyed; can we treat even this most exquisitely wrought and contrived and polished of poems as a "final" text? And given the fact that the European languages have been significantly changed by the allegorical and symbolic interpretations given to Homer and Virgil over the ages, can we possibly read them as they might have been read in their own time? Both the *Popol Vuh* and the *Shahnameh*—and others less explicitly—present themselves simultaneously as records of a defeated civilization and inspirations to cultural survival and resurrection. If the Mayans ever attain some measure of self-government, the *Popol Vuh* will become an enshrined and sacred text, but will be read very differently than it can be read today. And if Iran becomes a secular democracy, the *Shahnameh*—which ends with the tragic eclipse of Persian civilization by a puritanical Arab version of Islam—will arise as a new text even if its wording is untouched. Borges' joke about Pierre Menard, the postmodern author of *Don Quixote*, is more than a joke.

Further objections to my list might legitimately be raised. Where are Oceania and Australasia in this picture? Why are some great civilizations, like ancient Egypt, absent from the list, and others, like China and much of Latin America, rather thinly represented—while England and Italy are given plenty of candidates? Why did some cycles of story material—the Pele myths of the Hawaiians, the Chishimukulu stories I heard as a child growing up among the Ndembu people of Zambia, the Gjeto Basho Muji hero legends of Albania, or for that matter the Arthurian round table—never quite cohere into the definitive epic narrative?

I believe these questions are all relevant and legitimate, but far from being true objections they are an indication of the richness and value of the epic category itself, and an invitation for rewarding readership and scholarly debate. My own ignorance, and that of the literary world, in general, is surely to blame for some omissions, and the cultural suppression of epic texts and oral traditions—and whole languages—by conquering aliens may have deprived us of many great works. The survival of the *Popol Vuh*, one of the purest and most comprehensive epics in the canon, containing almost all the essential epic elements, was something of a miracle—probably written down in the Mayan hieroglyphics, it was lost (or destroyed by the Spanish with many other Mayan texts), and exists only because a Franciscan friar made a handwritten copy in the 1700s.

But the point is that the very idea that an epic is strangely missing in a great culture—that it might be buried somewhere, or that, on the other hand, it was there all the time but we did not recognize it as such—is a powerful research hypothesis. Further, it may make us think more deeply about epic, in ways that will help us reinterpret the existing canon. Are the Australian songlines actually the Aboriginal version of epic, for instance? Most epics incorporate story explanations of place-names like Mount Moriah in the Book of Genesis, or Misenum in *The Aeneid*, named after the drowned sailor, or Thorgeir's Ford in *Njal's Saga*, named for Thorgeir Otkelsson, one of Gunnar's unfortunate victims whose floating body ended up at that location. The list of place-names in *The Cattle Raid of Cooley* is surely reminiscent of Aboriginal songlines. Could it be that instead of epic merely *containing* place-name stories, it *is* a place-name story, and the Aborigines have the purest, most fully enacted, and most graphic version of it, its meter here the footsteps of the walkabout? In these terms the Hoares' great garden of Stourhead in Wiltshire, which compels the visitor to symbolically reenact the journey of Aeneas around its exquisite artificial lake, may itself be a walkabout, a sort of epic performative text.

The absence of ancient Egypt from the list perhaps constitutes another critique of our classification. Ancient Egypt surely had the time and stability to produce a poet who could integrate into an epic tale the rich body of myth and story that constitute the soil of any human culture. There are two Egyptian candidates for possible inclusion in our list: the Egyptian creation myth in one of its versions (from Thebes, Heliopolis, Hermopolis, or Memphis), and the *Egyptian Book of the Dead*. Neither incorporates what one might call an epic hero story. The latter is almost a "how to" book for negotiating the underworld. But the former bears comparison with the Mesopotamian *Enuma Elish* and Hesiod's *Works and Days*, and the latter obviously with Dante's *Divine Comedy* and the underworld journeys in many epics across the world. If the Aborigines' songlines argue that epic is essentially place-naming, the Egyptians seem to be arguing that epic is basically a preparation for death, which requires a theology of creation if one is to know whom one is meeting in the afterlife. Perhaps the landscape and architecture and history and funerary ritual of Egyptian civilization were so epic in themselves that no heroic epic was necessary. Again, such issues are more indications of the richness and fertility of the epic category than a refutation of it—if the category provokes questions of great analytical power, then it is worth keeping.

I have included a few contemporary literary works of critically acknowledged quality even though they have not yet won large popular audiences. The reason has more to do with intention: works like Budenz's *The Gardens of Flora Baum*, Gery's *Davenport's Version*, Walcott's *Omeros* and my own epic poems explicitly and with serious scholarship claim a place in the canon, and I give them the benefit of the doubt. *The Lord of the Rings* apparently makes a lesser claim—as a fairy tale for children—but deserves consideration as being in some ways an exemplary example of the epic genre, and should be given a special place to plead its case where its author was too modest to do so. Frederick Feirstein's *Manhattan Carnival* is of equal or higher literary quality in comparison with the contemporary epics I have listed, but is more a verse tale in the tradition of Chaucer or Shakespeare's narrative poems than an epic as such.

Epics until now have been largely rooted in the idiom and culture of their composition, though their subject is, as I will argue, the emergence of the human race itself. But without a second list, against which we can cross-reference the first—a list of the basic themes, elements, and plot structures of epic, the habits, gifts, and mannerisms, so to speak, by which we recognize the epic family, our list of epic candidates remains only a hypothesis. And to this second list we will now turn.

Elements of Epic: The Super-Attractor

This book proposes an expanded definition of epic, not as focused upon a single attractor, such as W. P. Ker's fine but limited formula, "the defense of a narrow place, against odds,"[41] but as tending in its many iterations to fill out the form of a beautiful, shapely, but intricately rich and complex "strange attractor." The proof of the pudding is in the eating, and in later chapters I hope to show how useful to the "eating," or reading, of the great tales this new definition can be.

In the academy, epic has increasingly come to be defined in terms of its composition and form, and as we have seen this emphasis has tended to fragment the concept epic and weaken the term itself. The stress in this book is on the content, subject, and meaning of epic, what its story is and what it is about. If form and compositional method define epic, either literary epics are not really epic, or orally composed epics are not. In the view of this book, form and compositional technique should be seen as serving, rather than determining, the content and genre.

The definition I propose is expanded in two senses. One is that it literally takes in works from all over the world, without narrow classicizing boundaries of space or time, as we have seen in our first list.

The other is that it includes a much larger range of elements, especially in the realm of content and subject, than have been proposed to date. If the choice of examples from so extensive a range would tend to loosen the term "epic," blur its boundaries, and erode its usefulness, the corresponding expanded specification of epic elements that are demonstrably common and shared will tend to restore the sharpness and value of the word's meaning. Here, then, is the proposed second list, with some important subheadings.

1. The Epic Storyteller

The prayer or invocation
The appeal to tradition
Frame tales
Blindness and memory
The retrieval of the story as itself an epic theme

2. The Creation Myth

Does it need to be explicit?
The dividing of the primal unity
Creation by word
The rules of recombination
False starts
The great flood

3. The Hero

Miraculous birth
Obscure origins
Blazing the trail: the hero as representing but transcending the cultural norm
The heroic code
Heroic leadership and its dangers

4. The Quest

The question
The journey
Obstacles and enemies
Monsters, natural and divine; our own monsterhood
Magical helpers, weapons, and talismans
Games, rituals, and trials

The great battle
The noble death or return

5. Kinship and Kinship Troubles
Kinship in human evolution
Succession and nepotism
Adultery
Youthful rebellion and oedipal conflicts
Hero twins and male bonding
The dangerous woman
In-law troubles, bad gifts, and bloody feasts
The burning house and tragic kin-slaying

6. The Fall of Natural Man
The beast-man
The Fall: awareness of death, moral knowledge, and self-consciousness
Sex
Clothes and shame
Drugs
Technology, invention or shamanic revelation of new technology
Mobility, the loss of the home place
Loss of one kind of strength, gain of another
Domestication of animals
Agriculture

7. The Descent into and Return from the Underworld
The dead companion and the need for funeral
Funeral games
The hero, the shaman, and the animal spirit guide
The guardians and lords of the realm of death
The protecting talisman
The conversation with the dead
The prophecy
The commission: the assignment of the task or duty
The return to the land of the living
Time anomalies

8. The Founding of the City
The idea of home

The building of the walls and gates
Sacrifice and commutation of sacrifice
Origin of present rituals, food laws, taboos, mutilations, etc., distinguishing ingroup from others
Genealogies of gods and humans
The establishment of a civic language
Orientation in space and time: place-names, the cosmological center, boundary markers, the calendar
The code of laws

9. The History of the People
From myth to history
War
Singled out by the gods
Faults and flaws of epic nations: epic hero versus epic ruler
National destiny

10. Setting an Example—Definitions of Core Values
Building a value language
Good–bad
Right–wrong
Elevated–base
Admirable–despicable
Firstness–secondness
Meso–meta
Pure–impure
Playful–serious
Natural–artificial
Wise–foolish
Sacred–profane
Venerable–ridiculous
Tragic–comic
Honest dealing–trickery
Beautiful–ugly
Contradictions and choices in the application of these values

11. The New Medium of Communication
From mute to spoken
From oral to written

From written to printed
From print to new media
New record-keeping institutions
Unification and fixing of national language
Economic changes in the media of exchange
A new religion

12. Epic Form and Epic Content
Meter and mnemonics: the epic lyre
Epic content: the human narrative
Epic magnitude

The first objection to this list might be that it has bundled into one category several entirely different kinds of things—creation myths, hero tales, national histories, magical romances, religious scriptures, etc. Here I shall invoke Wittgenstein's term, "family resemblance," for the second time.[42] In the family not everyone has grandfather Edwin's nose, though most do. Young Tom's stammer only seems to occur once or twice in a generation. Great Aunt Ruby has that odd smile, that shows up unmistakably in several cousins, some of whom have Edwin's nose and some do not. When you know the family well, a newly met member of it is easy to spot. I would argue that the second list is the set of basic epic features, not all of which occur in all epics, but which stamp a work as epic if there is a sufficient critical mass of them—the way to spot whether some work is a member of the epic family. Of special value to the critic and reader is that sometimes one of those family features may be present in a subtle or hidden form, the recognition of which will produce a cascade of insight into a difficult text. Sometimes an epic element is significantly lacking, either because of a special cultural suppression of it, or because of the author's intent to make a statement, as when a composer omits an allegro movement or chooses not to make a pause between two movements.

Though the *Mahabharata*, for instance, is not ostensibly a creation myth (like the Book of Genesis and the *Enuma Elish*), nor does it make a special point of a journey to the land of the dead, nor give prominence to the "beast-man" theme, all three elements are present in relatively brief episodes. The churning sea of milk creation story becomes a microcosm of the creative process of the whole poem. The underworld vision that Yudhishthira experiences in a dream, of Duryodhana enjoying the afterlife while the Pandavas languish in darkness, is a significant critique of easy moralistic interpretations of Karma, and is an important complement to the paradoxes of the *Bhagavadgita* episode.

The story of the horned forest child Rishyasringa, who is so natural, ignorant, and holy that he does not recognize as female the girl who is sent to lure him from the wild, is just a tale told by Yudhishthira to entertain his brothers. But in that it is the wild man whose capture restores the rain to a drought-ridden civilization, the story is an important commentary on the healing and fertility that the Pandava brothers bring back from their sojourn in the forest—a theme that now casts light on the forest exile of Rama in the *Ramayana*, and exactly parallels the great myth of the fall of Enkidu from natural innocence in *Gilgamesh*; it illuminates the meaning of the shaggy nakedness of Odysseus when he emerges from his bed of leaves on the shore of Phaeacia (he resembles a "mountain lion"), and the transformation of the half-brothers of Hunahpu and Xbalanque into monkeys exiled to the forest. Meanwhile, the *omission* of the "wild man" theme in *The Aeneid* (explicitly signaled by Aeneas' prudent decision to leave Polyphemus and the Cyclopes alone) is plainly meant by Virgil—who knows what the theme means—to indicate that his poem is *not* about the transition from wild nature to human nature, but about the transition from human nature to lawful civilization. But natural man in this brief episode is still present, "*sous rature*" as Derrida would say.[43]

Some cultural traditions suppress certain epic themes. Creation myths are scarce, except by remote inference, in the great Christian hero epics of Roland, Parzifal, the Arthurian world, and the Crusaders, but that is because the Christian creation story was the canonical and unchallenged possession of the Church. The proto-Christian epic of Beowulf gives Grendel a provenance not, as we might expect, among the ice-giants, but in the Genesis account as a descendant of Cain. The pagan saga of the Volsungs, which preceded the later northern works and supplied them with story material and heroes, begins explicitly right in the midst of the old Nordic creation myth, but that part is omitted from the Christian sagas (though traces of the old creation myths remain in the Icelandic prose sagas, whose subtext is the transition from pagan polytheism to Christianity). The creation theme returns in full theological garb in *Paradise Lost*, Milton having found a way to accommodate the rich material of pagan creation myths as tropes and imagery, carefully criticized for their relative correspondence with Christian truth.

Some cultures, perhaps, have been so disturbed and divided by economic, political, or ecological change that there simply has not been time enough for their proto-epic ingredients—creation myths, trickster tales, funeral rites, heroic tales, animal spirit lore, etc.—to cohere into a single large story. Had the unification of the Hawaiian island chain by King Kamehameha been followed by a couple hundred years of consolidation and the emergence of a bureaucratic script for record-keeping, no doubt some courtly maker would have told the great story in fitting language, incorporating ancient legends of the arrival at the islands and the myth cycle of Pele.

If certain clusters of story elements were unique to specific cultures, another argument might be made against the validity of the epic category as suggested in expanded form here. That is, if hero tales only occurred in one culture, creation myths in another, and so on—if quests, tricksters, underworld journeys, wild men, etc., were exclusive inventions of particular nations—then the coherence of the epic classification would be in doubt. But though many epics lack significant elements, there are enough epics in widely different locations and times that contain almost all of them for us to be sure that the differences among such works are not differences of kind but choices within a single menu. For instance, as I have already pointed out and will demonstrate later in detail, the *Popol Vuh* contains almost all of the major elements—the creation, the hero tale, the founding, the quest, the journey to the land of the dead, the wild man or beast-man, the trickster, the wrong woman (Egret Woman), the national history, the gods, the genealogy, the placenames, etc. Other epics with a fairly full complement include the *Sundiata* of Mali, the Nyanga *Mwindo*, *The Odyssey*, the *Mahabharata*, the Tibetan *Epic of King Gesar*, and *Paradise Lost*.

If one considers the scope of the story the epic composer sets out to tell—as I argue in this book, "How we got to be human"—and then reflects on the list of epic elements I have sketched, it becomes clear that a huge and purely technical challenge faces the storyteller. How to fit everything in? The variety of narrative strategies found in epic begins to make sense in the light of this question. Does one make perhaps the most obvious choice—the life of one's nation's greatest king, like Gilgamesh, King Dongmyeong, or King Gesar? Or its fiercest warrior, like Achilles or Cuchulainn or Martín Fierro? Or its founder, like Aeneas or Moses? Or its wisest man, like Rama, Njal, or Odysseus? Or its dragon- or bear-slayer like Beowulf or Lacplesis? Or its greatest explorer, like Vasco da Gama? Or its liberator, like Sundiata or Liu Pei or David of Sassoun? Or, ingeniously, its greatest tragic evildoer, like Kiyomori in the *Heike*? If one chooses such a story, then somehow the other elements of the Grand Story must be worked in, through shamanic journeys into the past and future, epic similes or allusions, stories within the story (a great device of the Indian poets of the *Mahabharata* and the *Ramayana*), or episodes in which the missing bits such as the creation, the founding of the city or the beast-man are briefly introduced, and so forth.

Homer uses the sea adventures of Odysseus, especially the extended tale of the hero's encounter with Polyphemus, to deal implicitly with the theme of the beast-man, the Fall, and the foundations of Greek technology and culture. The land of the dead comes into *The Saga of Burnt Njal* in the form of ghostly appearances, especially that of Gunnar. The history of the community is told in prophecy by Anchises in *The Aeneid*, Melissa in *Orlando Furioso,* and Michael in *Paradise Lost.* In a reversal of this device, a future poet recounts the historical events of the next few centuries in my own *The New World* and *Genesis: An Epic Poem.* Tasso uses the enchanted forest and the island of Armida to introduce the land of the dead and the beast-man themes into the basic hero-story. Opportunities for a recounting of events earlier than the life of the hero can be created by genealogies of the hero, poetic descriptions of old temples, conversations with ghosts, explanations of the aetiology of a gift, or the introduction of ritual objects like the Bead Strand Box, one of the three sacred objects of the Japanese imperial family in the *Heike*.

A less obvious strategy is to tell the whole history, or at least the early legendary part of it, in terms of a king-list or a dynasty of leaders. The *Saga of the Volsungs*, the *Shahnameh*, and the Book of Genesis are the clearest examples of this choice, though it also plays a part in *Sundiata, King Dongmyeong,* the *Popol Vuh,* the *Song of the Nibelungs* and others. Obviously the artistic problem now becomes one of coherence—how to prevent the story from fragmenting into episodes or becoming a chronicle? Genesis solves the problem by making every episode revolve around the immortal figure of Elohim, and by making the whole into the progressive unfolding of the moral law. The *Shahnameh* solves it by the iteration of tragic themes: the failure of the regnant king to maintain his royal *farr* (his mana, charisma, mandate of heaven), his conflicts with his loyal but wiser and nobler followers, and the contradictions between maintaining the heartland and extending its power and culture by intermarriage with foreign princes and princesses. The *Saga of the Volsungs* unifies the episodes with a single tragic trajectory, rising to a climax with the story of Sigurd and Brunnhild and ending with the holocaust in the house of Atli and the deaths of the last of the Volsungs.

Another strategy is called for if the epic author conceives that there is not just one way of being the true hero of his people. Here we get the epic that is confined to one time period but features many heroes. The *Mahabharata* is a beautifully handled example of this strategy. Certainly Arjuna takes precedence, but Karna, Yudhisthira, Krishna, Vyasa, and even Duryodhana, together with several other figures, play heroic roles in their own stories. The Turkish *Dede Korkut* paints a series of action portraits of various highly differentiated Oghuz heroes, unified by a single system of honor and courage. For modern tastes, the plethora of heroes we find in *Orlando Furioso* and *The Faerie Queene* may dissipate the focus, but the opportunity now exists for a typology and ecology of heroes and a more complex moral landscape. In *Parzifal*, Eschenbach compromises by giving us two main heroes, Gawan and Parzifal himself, together with supplementary heroes, so to speak, all in some way deriving from the more traditional heroism of Parzifal's father Gahmuret.

The pair of heroes—the classic "buddy" tale—is another favorite strategy. It is the choice of the oldest epic of all, *Gilgamesh*. This device, from a purely dramatic point of view, gives the heroes someone to talk to; it can also outline two different kinds or aspects or origins of heroism. The hero twins of the *Popol Vuh* are another example, likewise Martín and Cruz in *Martín Fierro*, Monkey and Tripitaka, Krishna and Arjuna, Roland and Oliver.

An epic can concentrate on one of the epic elements only and bring in the others obliquely. The Book of Genesis is the Fall writ large, the *Divine Comedy* the journey to the land of the dead, *The Iliad* is the great battle, *The Aeneid* the city founding, and the *Shahnameh* the history of the people. The *Enuma Elish* focuses on the creation story, Wordsworth's *Prelude* concentrates on the epic storyteller, the *Lusiads* on the journey, *Beowulf* on the monster-slaying, and the *Nibelungenlied* on kin strife.

Some ingenious composers of epic manage to combine the epic elements in a balanced and seamless way. Here the *Popol Vuh* stands out: a creation story, a hero tale (with two central individuals who are "buddies," and other major heroes), and a history of the people are all cunningly superimposed in a story that is also a descent into the land of the dead, a Fall, a quest, a moral typology, a battle, a founding, an investigation of the epic storyteller, an astrological cosmology, and a classic study in narrative form of the means of communication themselves.

The kind of community for which and about which the epic is composed can vary: it can be the citified tribe (the Quiché in the *Popol Vuh*), the city-state (*Gilgamesh*), the ethnic nation (*Sundiata*, the Homeric epics), the theocracy (the Biblical epics), the nation-state (Shakespeare's Henry plays, the *Lusiads*), the empire (*The Aeneid*), the federal republic (*Moby Dick*), the inhabited solar system (*Genesis: An Epic Poem*), and the human race itself (the *Divine Comedy, Paradise Lost*). Here again narrative possibilities for recombining and extending the epic elements offer themselves to the epicist.

In so characterizing these works—as if they were retellings of a story mysteriously known to the poets already, retellings modified by local concerns, I am introducing a method whose validity will need to be proved. Part of the purpose of this book is to do so. I would add, however, an unverifiable but to me compelling observation drawn from my own experience of having composed two narrative poems of epic length and several more of lesser magnitude, and thus having been compelled to invent plot details and symbolic and thematic material to flesh out the story. When my intent was to tell a grand narrative, it was as if episodes, plot points, bones of contention, and situations sprang in full detail to my mind as I proceeded, linking up with each other in a fashion like the architect Christopher Alexander's "pattern language"[44] and guided by an organic sense of rightness. In chaos theory parlance, I was being drawn into certain preexistent basins of attraction.

When this happened I often found later, upon reading an epic from the canon for the first time, that I had reproduced exactly an episode that had been composed hundreds or thousands of years before and in two or three different and in their time unconnected parts of the world. Perhaps I was composing clichés, but these were very peculiar clichés if so, since I had not heard them before. Indeed one could argue, as would proponents of the social construction of the self, that I had picked them up as part of my local episteme from forgotten conversations or reading; or, on the other hand, agree with the evolutionary psychologists that I was simply reporting my innate psychological hardwiring. But if those memes are so pervasive or the genes are so persuasive that poets will naturally seek such basins of attraction, then epic is indeed a real category, a super-attractor composed of many such preferred spots in the topology of the human phase space.

Notes

1. Lawrence Besserman, ed., *The Challenge of Periodization: Old Paradigms and New Perspectives*, (New York: Routledge, 1996). See Chapter 1 for an overview of the postmodernist position on periodization.

2. Giambattista Vico, *The New Science of Giambattista Vico*, trans. Thomas G. Bergin and Max H. Fisch (Ithaca, NY: Cornell University Press, 1968).

3. Thomas Babington Macaulay: review of Henry Neele's *The Romance of History. England* in *The Miscellaneous Writings and Speeches of Lord Macaulay* (London: Longmans, Green & Co., 1889), 133.

4. John Lukacs, *Historical Consciousness: The Remembered Past* (New Brunswick, NJ: Transaction Publishers, 2004), 118.

5. M. M. Bakhtin, "The Epic and the Novel: Towards a Methodology for the Study in the Novel," in *The Dialogic Imagination*, ed. Michael Holquist (Austin, TX: University of Texas Press, 1981).

6. Walter Benjamin, "The Crisis of the Novel" (review of Alfred Döblin's *Berlin Alexanderplatz*, 1930), in *Selected Writings*, vol. 2, ed. Michael Jennings (Cambridge, MA: Belknap Press, 2003), 301.

7. Jean-François Lyotard, *La condition postmoderne: rapport sur le savoir* (Paris: Minuit, 1979)..

8. Michel Foucault, *The Archaeology of Knowledge*, trans. A. M. Sheridan Smith (London and New York: Routledge, 2002).

9. Jean Baudrillard, *The Illusion of the End* (Palo Alto, CA: Stanford University Press, 1994), 263.

10. There are honorable exceptions, for instance, *The Epic Cosmos*, edited by Larry Allums (Dallas, TX: The Dallas Institute Publications, 1992).

11. W. P. Ker, *Epic and Romance* (Charleston, SC: Bibliolife, 2009).

12. J. R. R. Tolkien, *The Monsters and the Critics* (New York: HarperCollins, 1997).

13. C. S. Lewis, *A Preface to Paradise Lost* (Oxford: Oxford University Press, 1961 [1942]).

14. *The Best of the Achaeans* (Baltimore, MD: Johns Hopkins University Press, 1980, 1997).

15. See C. M. Bowra, *From Virgil to Milton* (London: Macmillan & Co. Ltd, 1948) and *Heroic Poetry* (New York: St Martin's Press, 1966); Dennis Kratz, *Alexander the Great in Literature and Legend: a Handbook* (London: Taylor and Francis, 1994); Maurice B. McNamee, SJ, *Honor and the Epic Hero* (New York: Holt, Rinehart and Winston, Inc., 1960); Michael Murrin, *The Allegorical Epic* (Chicago and London: The University of Chicago Press, 1980); David Quint, *Epic and Empire, Politics and Generic Form From Virgil to Milton* (Princeton, NJ: Princeton University Press, 1992).

16. Clifford Weber's work on Virgil is a good example, e.g., "Metrical *Imitatio* in the Proem to the *Aeneid*," *Harvard Classical Review*, http://www.jstor.org/pss/311408, 1987.

17. Dennis Tedlock, trans., *Popol Vuh: The Definitive Edition of The Mayan Book of The Dawn of Life and The Glories of Gods and Kings* (New York: Touchstone, 1996).

18. Virgil Nemoianu's *Postmodernism and Cultural Identities: Conflicts and Coexistence* (Washington, DC: Catholic University of America Press, 2010), a remarkable summing-up and critique of recent cultural trends, has a profound discussion of global canons in Chapter XI, "Literary Canons and Social Value Options," 168–98.

19. I put "Western" in quotation marks here and by implication throughout this book, because any term that includes the worldviews of thirteenth-century Spanish shepherds, Des Moines businessmen, Finnish housewives, aging black California hippies, American colonial frontiersmen, Budapest rabbis, Emily Dickinson, Czech UN soldiers, William Blake, Florentine ballerinas, sixteenth-century French Carthusians, and Glasgow neuroscientists—or has no criteria for excluding any of them—must necessarily be treated with much caution and taken as an ideological marker rather than a sober and responsibly usable classification.

20. Felix Oinas, *Heroic Epic and Saga: An Introduction and Handbook to the World's Great Folk Epics* (Bloomington, IN: Indiana University Press, 1979).

21. Marshall McLuhan, *Understanding Media* (New York: Routledge and Kegan Paul, 1964).

22. Milman Parry, *The Making of Homeric Verse* (New York: Oxford University Press, 1987); Albert Lord, *The Singer of Tales* (Cambridge, MA: Harvard University Press, 2000).

23. E.g., David Rubin, *Memory in Oral Traditions: The Cognitive Psychology of Epic, Ballads, and Counting-Out Rhymes* (Oxford: Oxford University Press, 1995).

24. John Miles Foley, "Experiencing the Siri Epic," Folklore Fellows Communications, http://www.folklorefellows.fi/comm/rev/reviewffc264-266.html, 1999.

25. As in the hugely important work of Mircea Eliade, for instance.

26. Steven Jay Gould and Richard C. Lewontin, "The Spandrels of San Marco and the Panglossian Paradigm: A Critique of the Adaptationist Programme," *Proc. Roy. Soc. London B* 205 (1979), 581–98.

27. Joseph Campbell, *The Hero with a Thousand Faces* (Princeton, NJ: Princeton University Press, 1968).

28. James George Frazer, *The Golden Bough* (Old Saybrook, CT: Konecky & Konecky, 2010); Carl Jung, *The Portable Jung* (Penguin, 1976); Jessie Western, *From Ritual to Romance* (Mineola, NY: Dover, 1997); Robert Graves, *The White Goddess* (London: Faber & Faber, 1999); Georges Dumézil, *Mythe et Épopée* (Bibliotheque des sciences humaines) (Paris: Gallimard, 1995), *Archaic Roman Religion* (Baltimore, MD: Johns Hopkins University Press, 1996), and *Gods of the Ancient Northmen* (San Jose, CA: University of California Press, 1977); Karl Kerenyi, *Gods of the Greeks* (New York: Thames & Hudson, 1980).

29. *Middlemarch* (Oxford: Oxford University Press, 2008). The key to all the mythologies is the goal of the plodding pedant Casaubon in her novel.

30. See, e.g., the periodical *Anthropology and Humanism*.

31. E.g., Wendy Doniger O'Flaherty, *Other Peoples' Myths: The Cave of Echoes* (Chicago, IL: University of Chicago Press, 1995) and *Splitting the Difference: Gender and Myth in Ancient Greece and India* (Chicago, IL: University of Chicago Press, 1999).
32. Edward O. Wilson, *Consilience: The Unity of Knowledge* (New York: Vintage, 1999).
33. See also Brian Boyd, *On the Origin of Stories* (Cambridge, MA:. Harvard University Press, 2009).
34. Claude Lévi-Strauss, *The Raw and the Cooked* (Chicago, IL: University of Chicago Press, 1983), *From Honey to Ashes* (New York: HarperCollins, 1973), and *The Savage Mind* (Chicago, IL: University of Chicago Press, 1968); Victor W. Turner, *From Ritual to Theater: The Human Seriousness of Play* (New York: PAJ Publications, 2001), *The Ritual Process: Structure and Anti-Structure* (New Brunswick, NJ: Aldine Transaction, 1995), and *The Forest of Symbols* (Ithaca, NY: Cornell University Press, 1967).
35. Frederick Turner, *Beauty: The Value of Values* (Charlottesville, VA: University Press of Virginia, 1992) and *Natural Classicism: Essays on Literature and Science* (New York: Paragon House Publishers, 1986). Reprinted in paperback, Charlottesville, VA: University Press of Virginia, 1991; Leda Cosmides and John Tooby, *The Adapted Mind* (Oxford: Oxford University Press, 1992).
36. New York: Paragon House, 1999.
37. Cambridge, MA: Harvard University Press, 2011.
38. Julia Budenz, *The Gardens of Flora Baum* (5 volumes) (Chelmsford, MA: Carpathia Press, 2012).
39. In the sense of Ludwig Wittgenstein, *Philosophical Investigations* (Princeton, NJ: Prentice Hall, 1999).
40. Bibliographical details for these texts are given in the bibliography of epic texts at the back of this book. Except when otherwise noted, quotations are taken from, and references are given to, the first text cited for each epic work.
41. Ker, *Epic and Romance*, 7.
42. Ludwig Wittgenstein, *Philosophical Investigations* (Princeton, NJ: Prentice Hall, 1999).
43. Jacques Derrida, *Of Grammatology* (Baltimore, MD: Johns Hopkins University Press, 1967).
44. *A Pattern Language: Towns, Buildings, Construction* (New York: Oxford University Press, 1977).

1

The Epic Storyteller

I have chosen to group together various elements under the general topic of the epic storyteller: the self-referential prayer or invocation, the appeal to tradition, the use of frame tales, the mnemonic theme of the blind poet, and the plot device of the carrying of the tale itself to our ears. Because these elements are so closely bound up with each other both in the narrative logic of epic and in every example of the genre, I shall not attempt to separate them into subtopics, but deal with them together.

Almost every "Western" epic in the classical tradition begins with, and returns often to, a direct reference to the author, narrator, or singer of the tale. But this reference is highly complex in implication. Often it is in the form of a second-person prayer to or invocation of the muse. And the actual singing voice is insisted upon. "Sing in me, Muse," says Homer; "Arms and the Man I sing," says Virgil; "I sing of war, of holy war," says Tasso; "Sing, heavenly muse," says Milton. The author then, at the same time, asserts the fact that this is a story told by someone, and disclaims credit for it. (There are a few exceptions to the initial self-introduction—*The Song of Roland* refers only indirectly to the author at the beginning, in characterizing Charlemagne as "our" emperor, but "signs" the poem at the end with "Turoldus," his name.)

The muse is a spirit of invention, of fiction, but she is also a god, and is authorized by God or at least the other gods to communicate truths to the poet. The story that the poet tells is also vouched for by tradition and ancient sources, and is acknowledged to be part of the accepted knowledge of the past—the Trojan War, the liberation of Jerusalem, the fight in Attila's hall, the Fall of Man. But the "fourth wall" is decisively breached at the outset—the poet looks us in the eye, and his throat and tongue quiver with the live intention of a human presence. The whole poem, then, is already in quotes, so to speak.

Of course, as Thoreau reminds us at the beginning of *Walden*, every book is written in the first person, so it is more honest to admit that one is doing the crowing oneself than to pretend that one's dunghill is Mount Sinai; but epic somehow manages both, by claiming something like a fit of possession. If I possess my words, they are mine, but if the god possesses me, maybe the words are free for anyone's possession. The quotes in epic are double quotes—one set for the poet, one set for the muse. If quotes—"scare quotes"—tend to negate the veridical objectivity of what is quoted, double quotes would tend to negate the negation, and to give us something that is "not untrue." And maybe the kind of truth that has gone through this double filter is deeper and more reliable than mere fact.

Many genres—textbooks, histories, manuals, treatises, etc.—do not have (or admit they have) such quote marks. Many others—lyric poetry, drama, the non-epic storyteller, etc.—have explicit single quotes. One of the distinguishing marks of epic—Western classical epic, at any rate—seems to be that it is in double quotes (at least). Many epics in this tradition are not content to merely open the poem with this disclaiming claim (or hugely assertive disclaimer). Homer gives us not one, but two, inspired blind court poets in *The Odyssey* (Phemios and Demodocus) as self-portraits and stand-ins to remind us of the quotes, and then throws in Odysseus himself, a consummate storyteller—and not always a truthful one—for good measure. He even advises us in the episode with Eumaios, the swineherd, how we should "read" such stories. He starts oddly to refer to Eumaios as "my" swineherd, thus identifying himself with Odysseus, who is Eumaios's only master; and addresses him, as he is addressing us, in the second person. Then he tells the story of the forgotten cloak, which Eumaios, playing the part of the intelligent audience (ourselves), correctly interprets as a hint to give his guest (Odysseus/Homer) a cloak to keep out the night's cold.

Dante is even more present in his epic, and he is being scolded again and again: first by Virgil and then by Beatrice, for his human moral blunderings and misapprehensions of what he sees. The double quotes now become an amazing guarantee of the truth—or at least the allegorical truth—of what he tells us. We can trust the scientist who tells us that his experiment failed. The author surrenders his own trustworthiness to the truths about which he has been mistaken.

Milton, too, does not settle for one initial invocation and confession. He returns in Book III to give his passionate plea for light in his blindness (thus identifying himself, in this amazing hall of mirrors, with Homer himself and again deflecting any merely autobiographical interpretation). More subtly he insists all along that we must read him with suspicion, for after all he is seeing Paradise with fallen "eyes," prone to make fallen that which is not yet so—and even shows us Eden first through the eyes of Satan, the only fallen being there present.

Eschenbach begins his epic of Parzifal with an elaborate argument justifying his own strange crabbed metaphorical style. Here the self-mockery wins us to him and makes us the more ready to take in the beautiful details, the mystery of Trevrizent's initial but necessary lie to Parzifal about the guardians of the Grail being lost angels, the ugliness of the wise guide Sigune, and the odd encounter with the fisherman on the second approach to Munsalvaesch.

Wordsworth outdoes all in the tradition by making the invocation/confession into the whole poem. As the poem depicts the accumulating self-consciousness of the poet, each time there is a new viewpoint, a new insight, a new frame-tale emerges. The poet sees the poem with fresh eyes as "I" the subject turns to "me" the object, and the poem itself is taking so much time to compose that a large part of the poet's increasingly reflexive identity is being forged by the poem itself. Here there is a multiple ventriloquism—the older poet throwing his voice into the mature poet, the mature poet into the youthful poet, the youth into the child. And yet it is the child's voice that is animating all those voices:

> Six changeful years have vanished since I first
> poured out (saluted by that quickening breeze
> which met me issuing from the City's walls)
> a glad preamble to this Verse: I sang
> aloud, with fervour irresistible
> of short-lived transport, like a torrent bursting
> from a black thunder-cloud, down Scafell's side
> to rush and disappear. (VII.1–8)

So one could argue that in addition to the epic being the story of a people and of the universe, it is also a gigantic form of lyric; but in response to the likes of Bakhtin, the epic is far more "dialogical" than any novel, since its Gödelian questioning of its own premises leaves its story utterly free for anyone's possession. Epic is always already post-modern in this sense, but it has not had to concede any of its veridical power in the process. Its truths stand for themselves.

But is this characteristic, of the constitutive self-reference (and its humbling by the possessing muse) borne out in epics from other times and parts of the world? The answer is that if anything, the first person (and its negation by the claim of ventriloquism) is even more pronounced outside the "West," the double quotes more multiplied. The *Popol Vuh* is insistent:

> This is the beginning of the Ancient Word, here in this place called Quiché. Here we shall inscribe, we shall implant the Ancient Word, the potential and source for everything done in the citadel of Quiché, in the nation of Quiché people.
>
> And here we shall take up the demonstration, revelation, and account of how things were put in shadow and brought to light . . .

The poet is saying what he is going to say. Tedlock's translation is evidently laboring to convey the simultaneity of the acts of naming, of demonstration, of revealing, of picture-drawing, of planting (as corn), and of creation itself. These first self-referential and self-validating words are echoed throughout the story itself. The point is that if such words as these were never uttered, coherent and probative language itself could not exist, for it would have no axioms for itself to be based upon. And if the whole course of creation be taken (as for instance some contemporary quantum cosmologists suggest) as the emergence of coherent naming systems that are able to observe what was previously only potential into actual being, then this account is not just descriptive but prescriptive. What is being emphasized—even more clearly than in the book of Genesis, which St. John's glosses as "In the beginning was the Word"—is that the very words that the *Popol Vuh* storyteller uses at this moment performatively and retroactively create the world. Like the pronouncement of the rules for a new game, like the words "I do" in the marriage ritual, like the signing of a bill into law, and like the words of a Catholic priest consecrating the host, the epic storyteller's speech act makes a new reality come into being.

In a more playful but equally profound way, the *Mahabharata* opens with an explicit act of self-reference and self-validation. But like everything else in the *Mahabharata*, this act is multiplied, mirrored, and elaborated into a delightful and bewildering game, so that the poem itself is enclosed by multiple frame tales, multiple quote marks. Vyasa the poet has dictated his poem to the god Ganesha, who adds an account of his own origins, as a sort of password key to the written text. This text has been taught by Vyasa to his disciple Vaisampayana, who recites it to three hearers—the king Janamejana, grandson of the poem's hero Arjuna, to Sauti, and to Vyasa himself. Sauti later recites the poem (with its verifying provenance) to Saunaka, from whom, presumably, we readers get it in turn. Is Vyasa, who is alive at the time this "final" version is performed, responsible for the transmission of the frame tales and implied certification, as well as the main tale? We are reminded of the way classic Chinese scroll paintings are certified by the chops of successive emperors, which also certify the previous chops. We might also recall the old joke:

> One dark and stormy night, three men sat round a fire. And one said to another: 'Jake, tell us a tale.' And this is the tale he told: "'One dark and stormy night, three men sat round a fire. And one said to another: "Jake . . . "'"

More confusing still, one of the first events to be recounted, after the creation of the universe, is the miraculous birth of Vyasa himself; and Vyasa is to play an important part in the action of the main story of the Pandavas, a participant-observer. (The tricks of postmodern fiction are not new.) In mathematical terms, Vyasa as poet is the set of all the sets in the poem; but he is also one of the sets. Is he a member of the set of all sets that are members of themselves, or the set of all sets that are not members of themselves? Can he contain himself in the poem, who contains the poem that contains him? If he is an inventor of fictions, can he be one of the fictions? This Cretan has truly lied himself into existence as lying Cretan, retroactively turning the lie into the truth. We trust him because he is there before us, lying to us. The world, after all, itself lies to us, and therefore, qua veil of maya or illusion, it exists. Nonexistence could not lie; the veil of illusion is a real veil of illusion, and Vyasa claims no more for it than that. "The poet," says Philip Sidney, "nothing lieth, for he nothing affirmeth."

This is Russell's paradox—the village barber shaves everyone in the village who does not shave himself: who shaves the barber? Analysis of this paradox led in the history of mathematical logic to Gödel's incompleteness theorem, which states that because such statements as "This statement is unprovable" are legitimate, unprovable, and true, there must be truths that preexist proof.[1] Only if some axioms are simply assumed on faith—or performatively enacted by speech act—can one reason (mathematically or logically) at all. To even state Gödel's paradox in words requires, if one unpacks the adjective "this," an infinite set of nested quote marks: "this statement: 'This statement:

"This statement: 'This statement ... is unprovable' is unprovable" is unprovable' is unprovable." Perhaps the supreme unforgettable oddity of all basic creation myths is a signal that we are not to take them as reasoning within a preexisting set of grammatical, lexical, and logical rules, but a specification of the rules themselves. "This piece looks like a horse and moves one square orthogonally and one diagonally, and can jump other pieces" is not a good move in Chess.

Though the *Mahabharata* resembles many other epics in its framing devices, it adapts this general device to its specific cultural practice—as indeed the others do too. The Vedic disciplines of meditation require a similar dizzying hall of mirrors, in that the process of cleansing one's mind of distraction itself provokes distractions that must in turn be cleansed, so that the illusion of the self as a fixed thing dissolves in the activity itself to lay bare the inner soul or Atman as a dynamic of subject–object rather than as an object viewable by a subject. One discipline, recommended in the *Upanishads*, is the repetition of a mantra. The periodicity of that repetition is the same as the periodicity of the eye's response to an ambiguous gestalt image like the faces–vase illusion, the rabbit–gull illusion, or the Necker cube. Every three seconds or so—the length of the chant line—the visual system finds itself unable to maintain one interpretation of the illusion, and must switch to the other. The concentric squares, circles, and other geometrical figures that enclose the inner space of the mandala serve a similar psychological purpose: the figure–ground or frame–reality distinction is disrupted, leading to a state of *chairos* where the subject–object duality disappears.

By the same basic logic as the Gödel theorem the *Mahabharata* is claiming to be a set of unprovable but true axioms upon which a world can be created or, in mythological terms, churned out of the original sea of milk by the play of dialectical opposites. And the storytelling situation itself is a sort of proof or demonstration of the originary validity of the speech act that performs the poem, with its interpretive and epistemological universe, into being.

In the *Heike*, the self-referential framing is much more muted (as befits Japanese minimalist aesthetics) than is the case with the *Mahabharata*'s postmodern pyrotechnics. The storyteller is modest and self-effacing, but he is no less definitely *there*, even when he comments, in some scene of agonizing pathos, that one can scarcely imagine, nor can words express, the suffering of the victim. His most frequent means of meta-commentary is his characteristic device of drawing a parallel between an incident in the struggle and an ancient classical story from China, both pointing a moral and dignifying the heroic stature of the story. Roman writers—Virgil and Plutarch of course, but all the others too—used Greek stories for the same purposes; Renaissance writers used classical Roman stories. When the narrator speaks for himself he cloaks himself during his frequent commentaries and editorials by avoiding the first-person singular and substituting what McCullough translates as "one," in the English fashion; that is, the impersonal persona of the cultured sympathetic observer or devout follower of the Buddha or pious public-spirited disciple of Confucius:

> Most touchingly, the children also picked sprays of blossoms and scooped holy water to pray for their father in the other world.

> Thus do times change and things depart; even as the Five Signs of Decay herald the deaths of heavenly beings, so must change come to mortals in this world. (84)

> One wonders if the author might have composed it [a poem] because he remembered that the Great Teacher Dengyo had prayed to the Buddhas of all-encompassing wisdom when he founded the temple long ago. It was an elegant gesture.(88)

> It would have been correct for such men to make enlightenment their sole concern after having rejected this transitory world for the path of truth, but it is only human nature to admire good government and deplore injustice.(173)

Whatever the philosophical or emotional timbre of the commentary, it is always deeply aesthetic in its basic orientation. For the Japanese sensibility, it is the realm of aesthetics that properly houses the infinite complexity and self-reference of the mysteries of creation, expressing epistemological and logical complication in sensory and experiential simplicity. Often the *Heike* author quotes the exquisite tropes of Tang Chinese poetry:

> Already the passing days had interposed mountains and rivers between the travelers [the Heike court in exile] and the capital, which now lay far behind the clouds. They seemed to have reached the limits of the earth, the point at which all had ended save their endless tears. A flock of white birds on the waves evoked pathetic thoughts. (255)

In the language of the *Heike* storyteller, one can clearly see a landscape scroll-painting, with its layers of cloud representing perspective distance, and the brushstrokes of the flock of birds. And one can hear the soft shriek of the performer's flute, the exquisite pathos of the *biwa* lute as it enters the mode of *origoe*, the "broken voice melody." The storyteller has in mind, perhaps, such poems as Du Fu's "At Night Far From Home He Unburdens His Heart":

> A light wind in the thin grass of the shore,
> A boat at night, tall-masted and alone;
> The stars hang over a vast open plain,
> The moon swims in the mighty river's stream.
>
> So, do my writings make a famous name?
> This sick old officer should just resign.
> Adrift, adrift, what kind of thing am I?
> A lone white gull between the earth and sky.
> (My translation)

The aesthetic distance implied by this constant editorializing serves the same self-referential framing function as do the more explicit devices of the *Popol Vuh* and the *Mahabharata*. The impersonal collective viewpoint with which the narrator, Kakuichi, identifies himself is, finally, that of the Buddha himself: the whole huge epic begins and ends with the boom of a temple bell: that of the Gion Shoja at the beginning, and the Jakko-in at the end:

> The sound of the Gion Shoja bells echoes the impermanence of all things; the color of the *sala* flowers reveals the truth that the prosperous must decline.[2]
>
> Presently, the boom of the Jakkoin bell announced nightfall, and the evening sun set in the west.[3]

It is scarcely necessary to point out the national as well as cosmic symbolism of the second quotation.

Significantly, the *Heike* was traditionally performed by a caste of blind storytellers, of whom Kakuichi was one, called *biwa hoshi*. They performed with the *biwa* lute, an instrument similar to the Chinese *pipa*, from which it got its name. Were they following the example of blind Homer with his lyre, of whom they almost certainly could not have heard in the 1180s? Could blind Milton have known of the *biwa hoshi*? What about Louad Dall, the Irish blind bard? Or Roukadi, the blind poet of Samarkand, or Banzoumana Sissoku, the blind griot, or blind Filip Visnjc of Kosovo, or Surdas of India? Were all these

44

in their different times and places part of some continuous cultural fashion? Or is this archetype, of the blind epic poet, another signal of the human universality of the epic form, and its claim to an inner truth undistracted by the sensory eye of local fact?

The theme of the blind seer clearly indicates a special kind of vision, needed for the epic poet. Not that a sighted poet would have to blind him or herself (like Oedipus) to take on the epic task—though in an age of reading and poor lighting the task of acquainting oneself with the needed cultural and scientific knowledge might well endanger one's sight, as it may have done in Milton's case. The meaning of the blindness of Teiresias, the one-eyedness of wise Odin, the Asian legends of blind martial arts masters and sages, is that the fleshly eye may distract us from the inner sight of memory and anticipation—the poet must learn to see in time rather than in space. In my own martial arts school of Shotokan one common exercise is to shut one's eyes during close sparring practice, and rely on the ear (which has a faster reaction time than the eye) and the other senses. Oddly, to do so is to experience a certain liberation, as if another world of cause and consequence and temporal flow were opened up in place of the flashy but superficial surprises of the visual world. Even if an epic poet is blind, he must shut his eyes to see the inner light.

Perhaps the clearest and most explicit version of the storyteller's role and special place in the self-legitimizing frame of the epic can be found at the beginning of the *Sundiata*:

> I am a griot. It is I, Djeli Mamoudou Kouyaté, son of Bintou Kouyaté and Djeli Kadian Kouyaté, master in the art of eloquence. Since time immemorial the Kouyatés have been in the service of the Keita princes of Mali; we are vessels of speech, we are the repositories which harbour secrets many centuries old. The art of eloquence has no secrets for us; without us the names of kings would vanish into oblivion, we are the memory of mankind; by the spoken word we bring to life the deeds and exploits of kings for younger generations . . . every name has a meaning, a secret import . . . I teach kings the history of their ancestors so that the lives of the ancients might serve them as an example, for the world is old, but the future springs from the past.
>
> My word is pure and free of untruth . . . we are the depositories of oaths which the ancestors swore.[4]

This set of claims is remarkably sophisticated in its understanding of the relationship between epistemology and ontology, knowledge and power, in its clarity about the role of the interpretive frame, and in its grasp of the odd legitimacy that can arise out of self-validation itself. The oaths of the ancestors are their performative speech-acts, and their continued fulfillment and memory by the griots is the very continuity of time itself. The author is not boasting, but putting himself on the line, vouching with his own life's meaning for the validity of his words.

Even the most ancient of all epics begins in the same way. The Gilgamesh poet starts his poem in the first person: "I will proclaim to the world the deeds of Gilgamesh," and goes on, rather like the *Popol Vuh* poet, who often seems to be explicating ancient pictorial images, with a second-person imperative guided tour of the monumental record of the story:

> In Uruk he built walls, a great rampart, and the temple of blessed Eanna for the god of the firmament Anu, and for Ishtar the goddess of love. Look at it still today: the outer wall where the cornice runs, it shines with the brilliance of copper; and the inner wall, it has no equal. Touch the threshold, it is ancient. Approach Eanna the dwelling of Ishtar, our lady of love and war, the like of which no latter-day king, no man alive can equal. Climb upon the wall of Uruk; walk along it, I say; regard the foundation terrace and examine the masonry: is it not burnt brick and good? The seven sages laid the foundations.[5]

The city is the house of the gods; the hero has built the city; the city is built of burnt brick, upon which material the story of the hero is engraved in cuneiform. So the poet's truth is vouched for by the gods whose city this is; the poem itself is the inscription on the city's fabric that constitutes the city's meaning. At the end of the poem these words are repeated, but now in the hero's own voice, when after his return from his great tragic journey he shows off his home city, his only form of immortality, to the boatman Urshanabi. So hero and poet share the same voice, and the power of the gods to make the world meaningful flows from that union.

Four thousand years later, a gaucho poet in the pampas of Argentina begins his own epic poem with an invocation of divine powers, the plucking of his musical instrument (symbolizing the technology of memory, predecessor of the inscribed word), a merging of his voice as gaucho-poet with the voice of his gaucho-hero, a quest for a homeland, and a self-referential frame tale:

I sit me here to sing my song
To the beat of my old guitar;
For the man whose life is a bitter cup,
With a song may yet his heart lift up.
As the lonely bird on the leafless tree,
That sings 'neath the gloaming star.

May the shining Saints of the heavenly band,
That sing in the heavenly choir,
Come down and help me now to tell
The good and ill that me befell,
And to sing it true to the thrumming strings:
For such is my desire.

Come down ye Saints that have helpèd me
In many a perilous pass;
For my tongue is tied and my eyes grow dim,
And the man that calls, God answers him
And brings him home to his own roof-tree
Out of many a deep morass.[6]

Martín Fierro is almost as remarkable as the *Mahabharata* in its use of a complex chiastic system of enclosed quotes and frame tales. During the account that Martín's friend Cruz gives of his own life, for instance, the poet is speaking in the generalized voice of the gaucho, quoting the autobiographical memoir of Martín, in turn quoting the words of Cruz, who himself quotes the folk wisdom of the gaucho on the subject of the faithful and unfaithful wife. And Cruz is speaking here for Martín himself, who has been too hurt and ashamed to go into detail about his own wife's desertion of him.

One of the most remarkable features of world epic is the astonishing uniformity of the epic poet's social role across the globe. The Celtic bard, the Malinese griot, the Anglo-Saxon scop, the Kyrgyz manaschi, the Japanese biwa hoshi, the Tibetan babdrung, the Mayan ajq'ij, the Norse skald, the Hindu pandit, the Balkan guslar, and the Greek poietes all have an identical role and typical biography in their different societies. All seem to be chosen mysteriously, experience a kind of possession, learn from their dreams, have divinatory or healing powers, perform in a communal context with food and drink, use a musical instrument to punctuate their recitation, and are rewarded by gifts; many, as we have seen, are blind.

Epic's preoccupation with the tale as tale and the role of the storyteller often extends even further, to include the story of how the story itself comes to us. *The Odyssey*, with its many episodes in which stories of the siege of Troy and its aftermath are retold, embroidered, falsified, graphically represented, and used as a currency of exchange and a language of civility, can be well described as "how we got the news from Troy." Virgil follows Homer in this as in many things—Aeneas' telling of the Troy story to Dido is what wins her love and propels the subtext of the poem, Rome's future struggles with Carthage and later with the other African queen, Cleopatra. Aeneas literally carries on his back the Lares and Penates, the household gods, together with his father Anchises, when he flees Troy, symbolically preserving Rome's mythic patrimony and legitimation as he does so.

The very subject of Wu Cheng-en's *The Journey to the West* (or *Monkey*, in Waley's good retelling) is the carrying of the sacred Buddhist scriptures across the Himalayas from India to China—and the story itself is one of those scriptures. In my own epic poem, *Genesis*, the carrying of the Lima Codex, the genetic archive of all Earthly life-forms to Mars, is the central subject, and it stands also for the transfer of the epic tradition itself into the future. One of the myths for this transfer in both *The Aeneid* and in my *Genesis* is the old Greek story of Alpheus and Arethusa—the love-smitten river-god Alpheus pursues the shy fountain-nymph Arethusa all the way under the salt ocean from ancient Arcady in the Peloponnese to the fertile valley of Enna in Sicily where they mingle their waters, a sweet myth of the renaturalization of wellsprings and the making of a new home.

The return of the hero twins from the deathland of the Lords of Xibalba in the *Popol Vuh* enables the story itself to be brought to the human world, and the story-bringing, reenacted in the retelling we hear, is simultaneously the dawn of the first day, the beginning of corn cultivation, and the birth of the Quiché people. Sundiata's return from exile brings the vital information about the secret spells of the wizard Soumaoro that enables Mali to be free. And the whole story of the Passover and the wanderings in Sinai is the story of how Jahweh's law and covenant get carried back to the promised land.

The theme of the horn blast in *Roland* that tells the main army of the outnumbered plight of the hero and his men, or the lone survivor who escapes to tell the tale—Sanjaya in the *Mahabharata*, Ishmael in *Moby Dick*, Charles (the Danish knight who brings back the news of the defeat of the Danes by Solyman) in *The Liberation of Jerusalem* (Canto 8), Kari in *Njal's Saga*—is another version of the same idea. We cannot go where the hero goes, and sometimes the hero does not come back. Somebody, or some message, must carry the vital knowledge back from that dark event-horizon, the edge of our world. As the poet says at the end of *Gilgamesh*:

> He was wise, he saw mysteries and knew secret things, he brought us a tale the days before the flood. He went on a long journey, was weary, worn out with labour, and returning engraved on a stone the whole journey.[7]

So the epic begins with a grand paradox: it is invented at this moment, yet it is an ancient truth; it is sung and composed by a man, but dictated by a god; it is a personal voice singing a universal history; it is a quotation, but also a direct statement and even injunction; and it is both the tale and the tale of how the tale comes down to us. Any thought that the self-consciousness of European classical epic is unique must surely be dispelled by the examples of these six non-western epics, from pre-Columbian Mesoamerica, from ancient India, from medieval Japan, from twentieth-century sub-Saharan Africa, from prehistoric Mesopotamia, and from nineteenth-century Argentina.

Modern epics continue to find ingenious and epistemologically interesting uses for storyteller self-referentiality. Julia Budenz, the flesh-and-blood author, was a character in a poem that her heroine, Flora Baum, is composing, referring to herself in the third person. John Gery's *Davenport's Version* contains an elaborate scholarly account of how the text came to the author's hands. My own *Genesis* was dictated to me, I claim, by the future poet who, sacrificially, is erasing his own future timeline by giving the warning that is implicit in its plot.

Notes

1. Kurt Gödel, *On Formally Undecidable Propositions of Principia Mathematica and Related Systems* (Mineola, NY: Dover edition, 1992).
2. McCullough text, 23.
3. Ibid., 436.
4. *Sundiata*, 1. (I shall be using here the Niane/Pickett text of this epic, based on the retelling by Kouyaté, for the sake of simplicity. There are, however, many other versions, as the story still exists in the oral tradition.)
5. Sandars, 61–62.
6. Owen, 1–2.
7. Sandars, 117.

2

The Creation Myth

Does It Need to Be Explicit?

The creation myth is one of those "family features" of epic that are not often found in a fully expressed form, but which seem to specially characterize the genre. Hints of its underlying presence are everywhere in epic, not necessarily in an overt and full treatment, but more explicitly, consciously, and centrally than is the case in other genres of a given culture.

As I have already suggested, epic often omits the creation story if it already exists in a more or less canonical form. There is no need for the *Iliad*, *Odyssey*, and *Aeneid* to include a creation myth, because Hesiod has already done the job. The Book of Exodus need not recapitulate the Book of Genesis (though the parting of the Red Sea and the striking of springs from the rock recall the Flood of Genesis); nor need the *Ramayana* repeat the many Vedic accounts of origin.

Even when creation accounts already exist in a satisfactory and standard form, epic will sometimes go over the same material for special reasons. The *Mahabharata* summarizes the story of Mount Mandara (or Meru in other texts) and the churning of the ocean of milk, because it wants as its premise this particular version of the creation, with its dialectical tension of opposites, rather than the other Vedic versions, such as the division of the primal man or the act of ascetic sacrifice. The *Heike* alludes often to the fundamental Japanese creation myths because, although the epic story is set in a period long past the dawn times, the destruction of Japan that it describes involves also the holy shrines and sacred objects—the sword, the mirror, the Bead Strand Box, the imperial inheritance from the sun god—that go back to and draw their power from the creation itself.

The creation myth is typically not omitted if it has itself reached its full articulation, or emerged politically as the union of previous national or tribal myths, at the same time that the epic is composed,

51

but is not yet written down. In the epic, then, it is given its accepted shape in the context of the rest of the narrative. The Book of Genesis, the *Popol Vuh*, and the *Enuma Elish* are themselves canonical creation texts as well as being epic stories.

Some epics will include the human part of the creation story—most often the later part, since the physical world is usually created before its inhabitants—as a way to indicate how the hero story is to be taken. The saga of the Volsungs begins in creation times and segues from creation myth into historical legend. *Gilgamesh* includes the flood story, part of the creation, as a flashback that illuminates the important role of Utnapishtim as the paradigm of human immortality. *Beowulf* explains who Grendel is in terms of the Genesis story of Cain.

The *Shahnameh*, whose context at the time of its writing was that the ancient Zoroastrian civilization had been recently defeated by Arab Muslim invaders, provides as much of the old cosmogony as it can without trespassing on the fundamental theology of Islam. "What," the author asks pointedly at the very beginning, "does the Persian poet say about the first man to seek the crown of world sovereignty? No one has any knowledge of those first days, unless he has heard tales passed down from father to son. This is what those tales tell . . ." Ferdowsi is obviously avoiding any mention of the Koran's account of creation, while at the same time distancing himself from the original authorship of the tales he will tell; but he is also, as we have already seen in other epics, taking on the authority of the tradition. He *is* the Persian poet, while at the same time representing the Persian poet as a generic entity. He goes on to give a fascinatingly detailed and highly evolutionary account of the emergence of humankind, its separation of itself from the life of the beasts, the invention of the technologies of clothing, fire, smelting, agriculture, textiles, hygiene, navigation, and so on.

Monotheism tends at the beginning to reject any natural creative capacity and thus to disenchant the physical world, because its main competition is local gods and natural spirits. The universe must be God's handiwork and his alone. Zoroastrian monotheism leaves some room for an animist view of the world, but Islam leaves almost none at all. Ferdowsi, like all poets, sees the world as basically alive and sentient; only thus can we make live metaphors, which depend on a kind of empathy or *Einfühlung* with the physical world. Poets are born animists! Though he cannot, because of his religion, describe the world as the dismembered but still vital body of a god or goddess, he compensates by filling his poem with as many of the djinns and demons and talking beasts as orthodoxy permits, and he alternates between Ahriman and Satan, the Zoroastrian and Islamic names for the enemy of humankind.

Other reasons also prompt a reopening and explicitation of the creation myth underlying the epic story. In *Paradise Lost* part of Milton's intention is a full unification of classical humanist thought with Christian truth. He thus hugely elaborates the biblical creation account so as to bring it into harmony with Romano-Greek classical poetry, art, and philosophy. He finds a place for the Greek and Roman gods as denizens of Hell or symbols of the angelic powers, and incorporates metaphorically the myth of the Titans' defeat and the ascendancy of the Olympians. He is also, like his acquaintance Galileo, concerned to show that there is no contradiction between contemporary Renaissance science and sacred scripture, and so his creation account, without departing from the letter of Genesis, gives the emerging universe a much more spontaneous and naturalistic flavor. Thus the plants and animals are not passively manufactured in some kind of divine workshop; rather, they burst from the earth almost as if by a natural generative (or even evolutionary) impulse, called forth rather than constructed or pushed into existence.

A similar intention also prompts the inclusion of a creation account in my own poem *Genesis*. Here the author has the good luck of being present at the emergence of a new creation story, that of the Big Bang, the evolution of the physical universe, and the origins of the biological species through heredity, variation, genetic recombination, selection, and the adaptive attraction of potential ecological niches. The transformation of a (relatively) dead planet, Mars, into a living one provides the perfect setting for a full poetic and literary version of the new creation myth, one which need no longer exclude the full range of moral, spiritual, teleological, aesthetic, and sacred values.

The Dividing of the Primal Unity

If the creation story does appear in an epic, it has many fairly universal and standard features. It begins with a primal, featureless, undifferentiated, chaotic, and usually liquid unity.

> When above the heaven had not been named,
> Below the earth had not been called by a name;
> Apsu primeval, their begetter,

Mummu, and Tiamat, she who gave birth to them all,
Still mingled their waters together,
And no pasture land had been formed and not a reed marsh was
to be seen . . . [1]

In the beginning God created the heavens and the earth. The earth
was without form and void, and darkness was upon the face of
the deep; and the Spirit of God was moving over the face of the
waters.[2]

Of old was the age when Ymir lived;
Sea nor cool waves, nor sand there were;
Earth had not been, nor heaven above,
But a yawning gap, and grass nowhere.[3]

Now it still ripples, now it still murmurs, ripples, it still sighs, still
hums, and it is empty under the sky.
Here follow the first words, the first eloquence.
There is not yet one person, one animal, bird, fish, crab, tree, rock,
hollow, canyon, meadow, forest. Only the sky alone is there; the
face of the earth is not clear. Only the sea alone is pooled under all
the sky; there is nothing whatever gathered together. It is at rest;
not a single thing stirs. It is held back, kept at rest under the sky.
Whatever might be is simply not there; only the pooled water, only
the calm sea, only it alone is pooled.
Whatever might be is simply not there: only murmurs, ripples, in
the dark, in the night.[4]

On heavenly ground they stood, and from the shore
They view'd the vast immeasurable Abyss
Outrageous as the Sea, dark, wasteful wild,
Up from the bottom turn'd by furious winds
And surging waves, as Mountains to assault
Heav'n's height, and with the Center mix the Pole . . .[5]

A numb plain spread with stones. A weary steppe
All bleached to tired red with ultraviolet.
Soil crusted, sere; limonite, siderite.
Hard radiation in a waste of cold.
Rocks sucked dry by the near vacuum.
Stunned with the blank math of the albedo
The eye tries to make order of it, fails.
Whatever's here once fell from someplace else.
Sometimes a crag a foot high, or a mile;
Always the sagging tables of the craters,
The precise record of a mere collision.[6]

Whether or not this predawn state is specifically described in epic, it is always present by implication. Epic does not only maneuver among the established pathways, meanings, and definitions of a given society, but also encounters what is radically alien to it—especially that which is prior to it, as with the creation story, but also that which is beyond its ken here and now. Even if there is no explicit creation story, epic will encounter radical otherness in some other way. One way is the journey to the land of the dead, which will be discussed later in this book. Another is the encounter with a cultural disjunction sufficiently radical to put our world in question—the standard device of science fiction. Christian crusader epics like *The Song of Roland* and *The Liberation of Jerusalem* find that radical otherness in the Saracen world, of whose beliefs and culture they are totally ignorant. The otherness serves as a sort of precipice at the edge of our world, a way to indicate the precariousness of the values, meanings, and culture we know, and the need for heroism and even tragedy in their maintenance and defense. It can even serve, as it does in Eschenbach's *Parzifal*, as a mysterious intellectual space where the core myth of the Grail is partly located. That other or prior world is represented in *Martín Fierro* as the domain of the Indians, who hold Martín and his friend Cruz captive for over a year.

Epic, unlike the mainstream bourgeois novel, exists in a world where its writ does not always run, where it encounters always a boundary beyond which our meanings are mute, and chaos and arbitrariness—or some utterly different game rules—prevail. It cannot possess the verisimilitude of the novel, because it is always on the edge of what is in our terms highly unlikely, and must battle in an obvious way to maintain the integrity of the normalcy that makes verisimilitude possible. The fact that epic is usually in verse is both a concession to the criticism that it is fabulous (real people do not speak in verse lines) and a magic charm to reconcile us to its unlikeliness. But the point is that our very existence, and the existence of the universe itself, is highly unlikely as it is, and though the bizarreness of all creation stories is the quickest way to remind us of this fact, it is not the only way. That unlikeliness, that bizarreness, is not the flaw of epic but its point—it is a human story under the sign and threat of its context at the edge of the known world. Myth emerges from muteness as the arbitrary axioms of a game that is justified only by its fruits as a generative system of meanings. Epic is the story of that emergence itself, the transition from myth to story to historical rationality through sacrificial

55

action, containing and harmonizing aesthetically, if not logically, all three.

In order to have a universe, the primal unity must be broken and divided. In the Vedic system of the *Mahabharata* and the *Ramayana* the cosmic egg must be cracked so that time and the multiplicity of things, together with the separation of reality and illusion, may emerge and play. Or in another metaphor, the milk ocean must be churned and clotted, as butter is from milk, into moon, stars, and the physical world. In the Mesopotamian world of the *Enuma Elish* and *Gilgamesh*, the goddess Tiamat is dismembered after her defeat and becomes the land and sea; salt and fresh water are divided and provided with their own gods, and the heavenly bodies separate out, much as Chaos in the Homeric tradition gives rise to Gaia and Eros, and Gaia divides herself to generate Ouranos, who mates with his mother to produce the Titans. In the *Prose Edda*, which gives the background of all the Nordic epics, the world is formed out of the dismembered corpse of Ymir, the first giant. In the Book of Genesis, the first acts of God are to divide night from day, the firmament above from that below, and the upper waters from the lower; and further divide the world temporally into an order of days. Milton and Blake imagine God leaning in with his compasses, dividing chaos and thus giving it order and rationality. In the *Popol Vuh* the same theme of dividing is emphasized:

> Let it be this way, think about it: this water should be removed, emptied out for the formation of the earth's own plate and platform, then should come the sowing, the dawning of the sky-earth . . .
>
> And then the earth arose because of them, it was simply their word that brought it forth. . . . It arose suddenly, just like a cloud, a mist, now forming, unfolding. Then the mountains were separated from the water, all at once the great mountains came forth. By their genius alone, by their cutting edge alone, they carried out the conception of the mountain-plain . . .
>
> The channels of water were separated; their branches wound their ways among the mountains. The waters were divided when the great mountains appeared. (65–66)

Our own cosmological myth, which has experimental and observational support and may be true in its general outline, is nicely in line with these early inspired guesses. According to contemporary cosmological physics, this universe began as a singularity occasioned by the splitting of the vacuum into positive and negative particles defined by a single force, quantum gravity. As the early universe experienced its first sudden inflation, quantum gravity divided up into gravity and a superforce that later split into the strong nuclear force and the electroweak force, which in turn divided into electromagnetism and the weak nuclear force. Matter and energy separated themselves out from the quantum foam, and the universe was under way. (Hydrogen, the basic component of water—oxygen having itself evolved from original hydrogen in the interiors of stars—is the root of all other elements, so the mythographers' guess about water being the primal element is not far off the mark.) Later, organic chemistry divides itself off from inorganic chemistry, living matter from nonliving, animals, plants, bacteria, etc., from early lifeforms, mammals from other species, primates from mammals, and humans from mammals. In my own *Genesis* this branching process is recapitulated:

> Follow the swan's genes back, and there are branches
> Where grebes and petrels, storks and pelicans
> Fork outward from the stem, then distant kin,
> The swifts and passerines; and further back
> The archeopteryxes, and their roots
> Which also fed the undreaming monotremes,
> The platypus, the anteaters, and so
> Turning a moment to climb up the stem—
> Marsupials, the mammals, and ourselves.
> And further down the chordates split again
> To tunicates and dim cephalochords;
> And now the great branch of the arthropods,
> The insects, spiders, and crustacea;
> And the mollusca, with their pearly shells . . .
> Then down the stem again, where rotifers
> And mesozoans branch away; and then
> The radiates and formless parazoa:
> The sponges in their blind communities.
> And down again, to the stromatolites
> Which lived two billion years without change;
> And then to mineral colonies and clays. . . .
> If we could take this path a little further
> We'd find those silicates and carbonates
> To be compacted ash of burnt-out stars;
> The nuclei themselves cooked up inside
> The crushing fusion of their white-white cores;
> Their particles the frozen motes of light
> That burst in nightmare from the primal atom.
> And we would know that moment as the fall
> Of the Uranian Goddess to Her dream.[7]

It is perhaps no coincidence that if one is contemplating the composition of an epic, one must work in much the same way, by dividing, separating, and branching. The state of mind of an author at such a point is one of a sort of vacuous potentiality, peculiarly single in its intent, yet without content. Something happens to divide that general intention into one special act as opposed to everything else—the geste is born. But that geste, the "great action" of Aristotle, must in turn be divided up into subordinate actions, the persons who constitute its *dramatis personae*, the sections, books, cantos of its form, and the thematic motifs that articulate the main subject. Do we naturally gravitate toward cosmologies that match our own mode of large-scale narrative composition, thus distorting nature by our mammalian and primate prejudice? Or do we accurately reproduce in our own mind's function the real original theme of the universe that gave us birth? Luckily we do have observation and experiment to interrogate the world and confirm or deny our hypotheses.

Creation by Word

In the creation passages from the *Popol Vuh* cited above, it takes only the word of the creator to bring about the division in the primal chaos that brings a new entity into being. Creation by word is not clearly distinguished from naming in these stories. In the *Enuma Elish* the gods themselves get their being as they get their names:

> When above the heaven had not been named,
> Below the earth had not been called by a name . . .
> When none of the gods had been brought into being,
> They had not been called by name, destinies had not been fixed,
> Were the gods created within them.
> Lahmu and Lahamu came into being: they were called by names.[8]

In the Book of Genesis, God only has to speak the words "Let there be light" for light to be separated from darkness, day from night. When he gives Adam and Eve the injunction to name the beasts, he is sharing with them his creative power. Milton follows and even amplifies the theme of creation by naming. In the *Mahabharata*, the creation begins with words of command by Narayana.

There is a distinct oddity about this idea, which occurs in only a few of the epics under consideration, but which is strongly consonant with the more common idea of the storyteller's performative power to make a reality come into being. The oddity is that it is unclear whether the creating speaker, divine or human, precedes the act of speech or is constituted or even created by it. Milton, following the evangelist St. John and enlarging upon the Christian doctrine that the Word is the second person of the trinity, identifies God with his coeternal Word and so resolves, or at least sets aside, the paradox as a problem of temporal precedence but leaves it as a paradox of logical transitivity. If the speaker both creates and is created by his utterance, if the axioms, so to speak, can only be stated in language based on the axioms, the logical ground has disappeared.

Perhaps it is too much of a stretch to connect this oddity with the contemporary issue of the anthropic principle in cosmological physics, but the principle is certainly similar. One version of the anthropic principle notes the proven fact that until a quantum particle/wave is measured (or at least registered) by something, it is only a statistical probability, a likelihood or "wave function" without a specific spatial or temporal location. The universe was at an early stage of the Big Bang composed only of such wave/particles, as it was neither big enough nor old enough for anything else to have room to exist. If no qualified observers or "registerers" of real events exist, there is no reason why the universe as a real rather than possible entity should have emerged. The strong version of the anthropic principle states that later observers of the events constituting the Big Bang retroactively collapse its wave function, bringing into being the very conditions that would lead to their own emergence later on.

Current quantum physics has demonstrated the property of entanglement, in which the collapse of the wave function of one member of an entangled pair occasions the simultaneous collapse of the other, raising temporal paradoxes associated with the possibility of faster-than-light transfer of information. The Feynman diagrams of particle interactions are time-symmetric, that is, do not require a particular time direction, and in theory could be run backward in time. But we cannot be allowed to get into a time machine and go back and murder our yet-virgin grandmother. Various "cosmic censors" have been proposed by Stephen Hawking and others to prevent such paradoxes. If we identify the act of observation as theorized by contemporary physics with the "naming" function in traditional epic, we see that we are still perhaps wrestling with the ancient problem of the cosmic egg and the cosmic chicken. The gods speak and see themselves and the world into being, so that they and the world (with its griots) will be around to speak and see them into being.

A related set of problems has bedeviled philosophy for centuries: the issue of epistemology (to what extent is the world constituted by our knowledge of it?), the question of reference (to what exactly does the word "refer" refer?) and, as we have already noted, the oddity of true-but-unprovable axioms. "The limits of my language are the limits of my world," said Wittgenstein. But when we come to know the world better, when a new word is added to the scientific vocabulary, when a child learns a new word, what has happened? Has the world acquired a new identity? Is knowledge part of the world, or not? Is the increase of knowledge an expansion of the universe, a free lunch? The core question in all these issues is "what is time?" leading to the further questions "how did it begin?" and "what kind of *fiat* can begin it?" I would argue that epic is the fundamental way that humanity has chosen to answer these questions.

The first answer, given by the epic creation stories and implied by the relationship between teller and tale, is that there was a primal but null unity that was divided by the word. But it is not enough for a composer of epic, or for a universe or universe-maker, to simply divide the primal unity. How are the pieces to be related and connected, so that we do not just end up with a fresh lot of primal but null unities? It is not enough, for instance, in the little universe-making that we do when we invent a game, to create chess pieces—they must be given moves, the capacity to obstruct and take each other, a board that both holds them apart and locks them together. Do we want our world-game to be closed or open? Causally deterministic, logically deterministic, fated, arbitrary, or free, or some combination of these? What will be our definition of "free"? If logical, is our logic to be two-valued (true or false), multivalued, fuzzy, or open to quantum superposition?

The Rules of Recombination

In a sense the whole of the rest of an epic—beyond its implicit or explicit creation story—is devoted to defining the rules of recombination. It can do so explicitly, in terms of moral principles designed for the human inhabitants of the world, as in the Book of Genesis—by prohibitions such as the forbidding of the fruit of knowledge, statements of consequences such as death, exile, the pain of childbirth, and the division of labor, and condemnations of bad conduct or praises for good conduct. But we should bear in mind that epic creation myths are designed not to reiterate rules already embedded in an understood language, but to establish the rules in the first place, and even the very language that makes them intelligible. By the time we get to outright laws such as the Ten Commandments in Exodus and their elaboration in Deuteronomy and Leviticus, the story logic of such episodes as the lives of Cain, Noah, Lot, Abraham, Jacob, and Joseph has already enlisted our sympathies for certain types of noble behavior, whether as an emerging nation of humans or as a child learning the ancestral lore. Similar sets of precepts can be found *in The Iliad, The Odyssey, The Aeneid, The Mahabharata, The Ramayana, Sundiata, Parzifal, The Liberation of Jerusalem, The Heike, Paradise Lost,* even in the raffish outlaw epic *Martín Fierro*—indeed in all the epics under consideration.

But the rules of recombination are not just for humans. More subtly, epics contain natural taxonomies and classifications, signally in the form of creation stories but also embedded in the characteristic epic lists, itineraries, food laws, taboos, and calendrical notes, and in descriptions of games, banquets, natural landscapes, hunts, and local nature spirits. In creation myths, the classification is often done by the sequence in which things are created or emerge. The sequence implies specifications of natural kinds such as lands, seas, sky, rivers, and mountains, or trees, fishes, birds, domestic and wild beasts. It nominates for special attention the uncanny "betwixt and between" species like snakes, pigs (which have trotters not hooves), coyotes, spiders, monkeys, macaws, and so on that are the exceptions that prove the taxonomic rules.

Genealogies, whether of inanimate entities, animals or humans, also indicate the taxonomic organization of the created world. Gaia (earth) gives birth to Ouranos (sky) who together beget the Titans, the forces of nature. In the *Popol Vuh*, Xpiyacoc and Xmucane, who are the timekeepers of the 260-day cycle of Venus and who represent sexuality and the 260-day term of childbirth, give birth to the first hero twins, One Hunahpu and Seven Hunahpu, who fail in their contest with the lords of death. But before their defeat these first twins have mated with Blood Moon, who is the daughter of one of the death lords, and her offspring are the successful hero twins, Hunahpu and Xbalanque. One Hunahpu, one of the first twins, has meanwhile also married Egret Woman, an animal being; their offspring are defeated by their heroic half-brothers, the second set of twins, whose maternal grandfather is the underworld death-god Blood Gatherer. There is a logic in this genealogy which defines the human descent in terms of natural forces. To be human we need to have natural roots in the childbirth cycle of Venus, but must also have a dash of the infernal, and we must overcome the animal branch of our family in order to conquer death. And we must have the lords of death in our genes in order to do so.

The stories themselves indicate the rules of recombination. Humans cannot be immortal gods. Gilgamesh, however superhuman, is limited to time and mortality by the test of the loaves (having boasted, in his desire to defeat death, that he does not need to sleep, he dozes off for seven days and is shown the stale and rotted loaves he had not eaten meanwhile). Later he is robbed of the herb of rejuvenation by the snake, which changes its skin as it escapes with its prize. The rules of recombination also include definitions by story example of key concepts such as death, sexuality, work and play, consciousness, the avoidable as opposed to the unavoidable, and so on. Male and female are defined by their interactions. Generative processes are distinguished from static or cyclic ones. The success of tricksters defines the nature of conscious intelligence as against mere appetite or animal impulse: consider Odysseus, Hunahpu, and Not Right Now (the first Quiché lord), Jacob, Nana Triban (who reveals to Sundiata the secret fetish of his enemy Soumaoru), Krishna in the *Mahabharata*, Kari in *Njal's Saga*, Shakespeare's Prince Hal, Cruz in *Martín Fierro*, Vainamoinen in the *Kalevala*, Hanuman in the *Ramayana*, and Trevrizent in *Parzifal*. Especially important is the definition through story of the extent and limits of human freedom and responsibility, and the relations among the three categories of power: limitless agency, passive subjection to fate and necessity, and limited freedom—and which of these belong to what or whom.

False Starts

In most accounts, the process of creation involves false starts. In the Book of Genesis there are at least three beginnings: the creation, the fall, and the flood; four if one counts the destruction of the Tower of Babel and diaspora of languages. In the *Popol Vuh* there are five: the initial creation that fails to be sentient, then, in an attempt to produce humans who can name the gods, three unsuccessful attempts, followed by final success. The first attempt is the creation of birds and deer, who prove a disappointment: "They just squawked, they just chattered, they just howled. . . . And so their flesh was brought low: they served, they were eaten, they were killed." The next is the gods' "experiment" of creating people out of mud; but the mud people just dissolve in the water. The final failed attempt is the making of the wood people, carved manikins; like Pinocchio they have no soul and cannot name the gods, so they are scattered by the Mayan version of the great flood, and destroyed by their own implements and domestic animals. For true humans to exist they cannot be merely begotten, but must be brought into being in some other way—and this is the subject of the hero tale. The *Popol Vuh* sees humans as having been "modeled," and "by sacrifice alone, by genius alone, were they made." History is not just what conscious responsible beings do, but also how they are formed in the first place.

False starts characterize the creative process in several other epics. In *The Journey to the West*, Monkey's history tracks the emergence of true human being. He must go through several false starts, in which his power and bumptious energy is again and again rebuffed and brought to nothing: he achieves dominance in both the Taoist and the Confucian worldviews, but he is only liberated from his prison into true *Menschlichkeit*, soulfulness or mindfulness, by the quest for the Buddhist scriptures that forms the body of the story. The mythical early kings of Persia, in the *Shahnameh*, also undergo a sort of trial-and-error process of rebeginning, and the first gods of the *Poetic Edda*, the background of all the Nordic epics, go through several violent revolutions before the present regime of the gods is established. Behind the story of the *Heike* is the Japanese theory of a ten-thousand-year cycle, in which the Buddhist law declines, fractures, and must be renewed. Similarly, in the *Mahabharata*, avatars of Vishnu must appear from time to time in the history of the world to restore the balance of karma in the world when it has failed. The Greek epics are based upon a universe in which the false start of the elder gods has been aborted by the Olympians, but in which the Titans are still capable of insurrection, and there is the prophecy of a third generation of gods possibly heralded by Athena's birth from the head of Zeus.

But these false starts and their often-violent suppression are not just mistakes. They play the same role in traditional cosmologies that extinction plays in Darwinian evolution; they prepare the ground, they reveal creation as a process not a single act, and they open up the conceptual world to revision and narrative. Time itself is being defined by the erection of these great historical ratchets that clang into place behind the wheel of events, preventing return and requiring an open future. When Odysseus, Homer's own hero-storyteller, begins his account of his travels before the court of King Alcinous, he asks: "What shall I say first? What shall I keep until the end?" Anyone who has ever written a story, or even a scholarly book, knows that this is the essential question—how to spin out from the inchoate mass of what one knows the thread or yarn of one's narrative. It is the rejected errors, their extinction—or rather perhaps the setting-by of invalid hypotheses for some other possible use—that constitute the essential sequence of the discourse and the structure of time of which one wishes to convince the reader. In a sense the main body of these epics, usually the hero tale, is a close analysis in symbolic and narrative terms of the necessity for false starts, for adventure itself, for the descent into contingency of any initial necessity if it is to have a future and bear fruit. As we shall see, the epic themes of the beast-man, the fall, the descent into the underworld, the journey, and so on are all ways of elaborating the theme of the terrible but redemptive passage, through false starts and their devastating refutation, into consciousness and freedom.

The concept of the necessity for false starts and dead ends is essential to the human construction of time itself. If the universe is like a perfect and finite equation (even if it is a very large one) with a solution that, as with Laplace's famous calculator containing all the vectors of all the atoms in the cosmos, or Feynman's particle diagrams, can be arrived at instantaneously, there is no need for time. Such a universe is, as they say, time-symmetric: run the movie backwards or forwards in time, no physical laws are violated and perfect determination of every event is preserved. Causality collapses to simple inference; any event is simply the restatement in other terms of any other event. Perfect prediction and perfect memory constitute an eternal present, since there is no difference between the experience of the present state of affairs and the inference of that state at any other moment.

In our own time three discoveries, two in physics and one in mathematics, have decisively refuted the Enlightenment dream or nightmare of the perfect clockwork universe. The increase of entropy over time is one; there is not enough information in an earlier state of the universe to describe a later state. The quantum theory, which postulates the absolute randomness of some events such as radioactive decay, is the second; some events are irretrievable, mathematically or inferentially, from others, and the retrievability of events is time-asymmetric: the universe can remember the past but not the future. The third, the mathematical discovery, was the formalization of the idea of "hardness" in the solution of mathematical problems. Some calculations, like the solution of the "Traveling Salesman" problem, increase in difficulty exponentially with the addition of new variables: it is easy to find the shortest route among three cities, but impossibly hard to find the shortest route among a few hundred. The only dimension that can describe the degree of hardness is that of time: how much time it would take for a theoretically perfect computer to complete the algorithm or method of arriving at the solution. Time, then, seems in our own modern myth system to be constituted, as it is with the myth systems of our epic ancestors, by difficulty, by obstacles, false starts, and dead ends. Only if "you can't get there from here" can time be real.

The Great Flood

The great flood appears in a small number of epics and is an important part of the background of others. The flood is of course central to the Book of Genesis and is reprised literally or symbolically throughout the whole Judeo-Christian epic tradition, in the symbolism of the parting of the Red Sea in Exodus, as an emblem of purification in Dante's *Divine Comedy*, in Michael's account of human history in *Paradise Lost*, and in the "Death by Water" episode in Eliot's *The Waste Land*, for instance.

But the flood is important in many other traditions. We have already encountered the great flood at the outset of the *Popol Vuh* that destroys the Wood Men, when four men and four women are born out of a corn sacrifice ritual after the great flood and give birth to the tribes, including the conquering Quiché. In the *Prose Edda* Ymir the giant is slain by Odin, and his blood overwhelms the world; one giant, Begelmir, and his wife escape the flood in a ship and propagate a new race. At the final battle of Ragnarök the World serpent Jormungandr will arise from the ocean and overwhelm the land with a flood, but a new race of humanity will be born. In the *Mahabharata*, the "Hindu Noah" Manu is advised by a giant fish to build an ark to escape the great flood (the fish is an earlier avatar of the supreme god Vishnu, who later manifests himself as Krishna, Arjuna's friend and charioteer). In the background of the Greek and Roman epics are the floods of Ogyges, Deucalion, and Dardanus, the founder of Troy; that of Ogyges ends the Silver Age, and that of Deucalion ends the Bronze Age. The Hawaiian ancestors, Nu'u and Lili-noe, survive the flood on the summit of Mauna Kea. In my own epic poem, *Genesis*, the first era of the human creation of life on Mars is terminated by the planned impact of an ice moon on the planet, which provides the water and the heat to create oceans and begin the work of generating a breathable atmosphere; the first Martians ride out the impact in orbit.

As well as being the most potent symbol of the false starts and irretrievability that are required to provide time and the historical substance of the creation, the flood serves another purpose, I believe. If epic is, as this book argues, the human story itself, it must grapple with the central feature of human consciousness, the awareness of personal death. The persistent theme in epic of the unsuccessful quest for immortality and the journey to the land of the dead clearly deals with the core experience of the awakening of consciousness in a child or adolescent when he or she first realizes that he or she is going to die. But there is a second experience of death, more terrifying even than personal death, which is the recognition that our whole tribe, our whole species, our whole world could die. It is not a matter of falling off the ship; the *Titanic* itself will go down. One could well argue that if individual adulthood begins with the awareness of personal death, civilization begins with the awareness of collective or universal death. Civilization is the ark within which the two sexes can mate and re-populate the world.

What follows the flood is usually some form of sacrifice, and a covenant. In the traditions deriving from Mesopotamia, the covenant is in the form of the rainbow. Both *Gilgamesh* and the Book of Genesis stress this sequence. The rainbow is an interesting symbol, because it arises, in mythic language, out of an apparent contradiction, between rain and sunlight. It is a bridge between earth and heaven, and it gives us back the white light of the sun in the shape of the colors of the visible world. The Quiché people of the *Popol Vuh* say that "the visible sun is not the real one" (161)—if we could see the sun as it really is, it would look like a blazing person. The rainbow is a sort of compromise, a partial "making visible" of the intentions of the gods. For Genesis it is God's bow, the instrument of punishment that has been put aside. For *Gilgamesh* it is the necklace of Ishtar, the goddess of love, given to her by Anu, the sky-father.

Thus the creation myth, whether as an episode in the hero tale, or as part of the symbolic and ideological framework of the story, or as fully integrated with the whole work as in the *Popol Vuh*, is an important element in the epic account of what it is to be human. By showing the splitting and branching process by which the natural species of the world came about—a thoroughly evolutionary process, one might note—it reconciles the unity of the universe with its diversity and multiplicity. It thus denies both the reductionism of any scientific or philosophical attempt to simplify the world to a single principle, and also the incoherence and relativism of any purely pluralistic account. It also insists on the irreversibility of time and thus its fundamental open-endedness with respect to the future; a branchy timescape is the only assurance of freedom and thus the possibility of meaningful and responsible human action. Its identification of the word itself as possessing the ontological power of creation signals that its world is one in which knowledge and thought are not strangers, and in which naming takes its place among the real creative forces of the world. The myth's taxonomies and the rules of recombination that reconnect the divided elements of the world in a coherent game give a dynamic order to the universe in which the hero will take a crucial part. The creation story's false starts, especially the fall and the flood episode, and their sacrificial meaning, imply that real things are accomplished only through a historical process that provides them with an internal structure of rejected possibilities and chosen alternatives. The formation of a covenant with the divine powers, ratified by sacrifice, initiates a process of language-creation in which the hero's task will constitute a decisive step forward. This topic will require further treatment later on.

Notes

1. *Enuma Elish*, 18. (I have omitted the editor's interpolations, which tend to obscure the identification of being and naming.)
2. The Book of Genesis, 1, 1–2.
3. *Voluspo*, verse 3, from *The Poetic Edda*, Bellows trans., 4.
4. *Popol Vuh*, 64.
5. *Paradise Lost*, VII. 210–15.
6. *Genesis: An Epic Poem*, IV.v. 60–71.
7. V. ii. 62–99.
8. See note 1 above.

3

The Hero

Miraculous Birth

Much has been well said about hero tales by Joseph Campbell, Claude Lévi-Strauss, and others. It remains to distinguish the special meaning given by epic to the archetypal features of the hero, and to point out the ways in which the epic hero perhaps differs from the hero in general. Epic is a second look at myth, from within the mythic world and language, but at the edge of it too as it gathers itself together, so to speak, for civilization, for philosophy, for more explicit psychological understandings, a more conscious and detailed view of history, more inclusive forms of political organization, and new codes of communication, recording, and commemoration. Old and familiar features of myth are pressed into service to make new points; sometimes the old meanings of those features are lost thereby, but in the finest epics the old meanings remain as an enriching background to the new.

This is especially true of a very common plot element in the epic: the hero's strange birth and extraction. Mythological characters often, perhaps nearly always, have strange births, often because their genealogy is an explanation—in the most traditional logical system for human beings, the kinship system—of the conceptual foundations of the tribe. Epic presses into service this familiar feature to indicate the special character of the hero, as opposed to the normal people who appear in the story: one who is on the very edge of the human world, human but beyond human, "above and beyond the call of duty." Gilgamesh is two-thirds god and one-third human, a heredity impossible in the binary system of human kinship. He can thus act both as the mediator between the human and the superhuman, and also as the representative of the human race, as the edge or outline of something acts visually to identify and represent it.

Tripitaka's birth in *Monkey* is a precise allegory of his saintly identity. While his parents are traveling to the capital so that his father can take up an imperial appointment, the father notices that the giant live carp he has bought is looking at him. Thinking that this carp must be special, he releases it into the river. Later the criminal ferryman, lusting after Tripitaka's pregnant mother, murders Tripitaka's father and casts the body into the water. The carp turns out to be the dragon-king of the river, who finds the father's body, reincarnates him as a high official in his own court, and watches over the mother. When she gives birth, the evil ferryman commands her to throw the baby into the river. The river-god at the last moment provides a plank, to which the mother binds the baby; it floats down to the Temple of the Golden Mountain, where the abbot takes the child in and has it named, in Chinese, "River Float."

Readers may have remarked the similarity to the birth of another great founder of religion, Moses, who was also given to the river by a mother under constraint of a tyrant, and whose name—combining Egyptian and Hebrew words in a kind of multilingual pun—also refers to his birth. The Egyptian word "mo" means "water," the Egyptian word "uses" means "to save from the water," and the Egyptian word "mes" or "msy" (transliterated in Greek as "mosis") means "born of (a god)," as in "Tutmosis" or "Rameses." The Hebrew word "mashah," from which the Book of Exodus explicitly derives the name, means "to draw out."

Mwindo, the Bantu hero, is born miraculously, able to speak and walk from birth. His father, Chief Shemwindo, a Herod figure, wishes to kill him as he has killed all his other newborn sons in an attempt to prevent them succeeding him. The chief's councilors lock him in a drum (the shamanic instrument) and throw him into a river to drown. But Mwindo uses his magic powers to travel under water and escape. Parallels with the miraculous birth of Jesus, who is rescued from infanticide and paradoxically takes refuge in Egypt, Moses' birthplace, are obvious.

The extraction of Vyasa, the poet and one of the heroes of the *Mahabharata*, is also oddly similar. His grandfather, a king, dreams of his wife and lets fall a drop of vital fluid on a leaf. On awakening the king summons a hawk to carry the leaf to his queen. But the hawk is attacked by another hawk, and drops the leaf into the river, where it is swallowed by a fish. When a fisherman catches the fish he finds in its belly a baby girl, whom he raises as his own. That girl is Vyasa's mother. All of the heroes of the *Mahabharata* have miraculous births, but Vyasa's is especially significant.

Hunahpu and Xbalanque are conceived and born in a way oddly consonant with the births already described. The first generation of hero twins, inventers of the ball game, and the fathers of the second generation of twins, had failed to distinguish the Lords of Xibalba from carved manikins. After the defeat and slaying of One and Seven Hunahpu, One Hunahpu's head is set on the crotch of a tree. But the tree bears a calabash-like fruit. Later the maiden Blood Moon reaches out to pluck the fruit, but the fruit—which now turns out to be the skull of both brothers—speaks to her and spits on her hand. The speech and the spittle impregnate her, and she gives birth to the second generation of hero twins, Hunahpu and Xbalanque. Though the river theme is not present in the *Popol Vuh*, there is a virgin birth like those of Vyasa's mother and Jesus. The river, however, appears later, at the second birth of Hunahpu and Xbalanque. When they have defeated the Lords of Death in the ball game and chosen their own deaths by leaping into the deathlords' oven, the hero twins' bones are ground up and scattered in the river. There they are resurrected, and appear to the Lords of Death as catfish at first. Later they emerge unharmed, and perform human sacrifices on themselves and each other, returning from death much to the admiration of the Death Gods, who are thus fooled into wanting to be able to do the same thing. Of course the hero twins do not resurrect the first Death God to try it. After that the rest of the Lords of Xibalba bow down to the hero twins and acknowledge them to be the masters.

It is almost as if the *Popol Vuh* has explicated the myth-logic of the other stories, in which the river of generation and of life and death-by-drowning gives birth to beings who by craft and moral virtues transcend the river's power to destroy, and who can step beyond the rules of mere reproduction.

Mysterious births are everywhere in epic. Adam and Enkidu are molded by a deity out of clay. The ancestors of the Quiché people are made out of maize meal. Rama is the incarnation of Vishnu, after his mother Kausalya, wife of the childless Dasaratha, emperor of Kosala, is impregnated with a grain of sacred rice from the sacrificial feast the emperor has held to pray for an heir. Isaac is born to childless overage parents as the result of divine intervention. David of Sassoun, in the Armenian epic, is also born to aged parents as a result of prayer; both his parents die the day he is born. King Gesar speaks to his mother while he is still in the womb, and asks her the way out. The hero Zal

71

in the *Shahnameh*, who is an albino, was exposed on a mountainside, and nourished and raised by the Simorgh, a magic bird, as one of its chicks. Sundiata is the son of Naré Maghan, king of Mali, and Sogolon, the ugly hunchback woman who is the wraith of the Buffalo Woman and the spirit of the buffalo itself; at night she takes her feral shape and the king cannot make love to her until he casts a hunter's spell and threatens to sacrifice her to the Mandingo kings; she faints, and he begets a son. Sundiata as a child eats unceasingly, has a huge head and is preternaturally strong, but cannot walk until at the age of seven he uses an enormous iron staff to stand, and can walk thereafter.

In Malory, King Arthur is conceived in a bed-trick when his father, Uther Pendragon, persuades the magician Merlin to give him the appearance of the Duke of Tintagel so that he can make love to Igraine, the duke's wife. In one version of the Irish story of the cattle-raid of Cooley, Cuchulainn is conceived three times on Deichtine, the daughter of King Conchobar—by the god Lug, by her husband Sualtam mac Róich, and by her own father, Conchobar. Cuchulainn is born in a strange house encountered during a wild bird hunt, a house that vanishes in the morning leaving the hunting party in the wilderness; a mare gives birth to twin horses at the same time. King Dongmyeong of the Korean kingdom of Goguryeo, whose birthname is Jumong, is the son of Hae Mosu, a general and military hero, himself the son of a god, and Yuhwa, daughter of a river god. But like many such originating heroes, he has more than one father. The river god disowns his pregnant daughter, who leaves and becomes the concubine of King Geumwa of Dongbuyeo. She is impregnated by a ray of sunlight and gives birth to an egg. Geumwa's attempts to destroy the egg by feeding it to animals are unsuccessful; the animals do not eat it but protect it. The egg hatches and Jumong is born. The multiple-conception theme may also be present in *The Iliad*. Though Achilles' nominal father is King Peleus, two gods, Zeus and Poseidon, had wooed his mother, the sea-nymph Thetis.

Rostam, the great hero of the *Shahnameh*, is delivered in the first Caesarian birth with the help of feathers from the magical bird, the Simorgh. He grows into a boy in five days, and a man in a few weeks, and is described as a lion cub. Clorinda, the warrior-heroine of *The Liberation of Jerusalem*, is born white to black royal Ethiopian parents; fearing that King Senapo will suspect his wife of adultery, a faithful eunuch exchanges the newborn child for a black child who is raised in her stead as the princess, while Clorinda herself is nursed by a tiger in the wilderness. The theme of association with some animal, perhaps an echo of totemic identification, haunts many of these births.

Volsung is born to the wife of Rerir, who has been unable to conceive a successor and has begged the gods for a child. The goddess Frigg persuades Odin to help, and Odin sends Rerir a wish maiden in the shape of a crow with a magic apple; on eating it, he begets a son. Sinfljotli, another hero in the Volsung saga, is the result of brother–sister incest. Scyld Scefing, king of the Danes in *Beowulf*, is a foundling. But significantly Beowulf himself, though high-born, seems to be not otherwise odd in his origins, perhaps suggesting that the poem is celebrating a different kind of hero, one who is just a man; his death fighting the dragon, and his need for Wiglaf's assistance in slaying it, imply the same thing. A particular epic can use conspicuous departures from the narrative expectations to make its own points.

Obscure and Humble Origins

The miraculous birth theme often has a further implication, developed especially in Eschenbach's *Parzifal*. Parzifal (like Cuchulainn) is raised by his mother in the woods away from human contact, and especially away from knights and knighthood. Herzeloyde does not want her son to follow in the path of his father, who died in battle before his son was born. As a result, Parzifal grows up a naïve bumpkin and is shamed again and again when, against his mother's wishes, he sets out to be a knight. Although his birth is not as odd as that of his half-brother, who is born piebald, son of a white father, Gahmuret, and a black Saracen mother, the theme of a feral or rustic upbringing is very clear here. Heroes often have a humble upbringing, though they usually have a royal ancestry.

In a sense, the oddity of their births can be seen as an explanation of this paradox: If the seed or the resulting baby is somehow spirited away from its parents, then it can grow up in obscurity. People (often including the heroes themselves) do not find out about their royal blood until the time of their revelation by some great deed, such as Arthur's or Sigmund's drawing of the sword from the stone or oak. When the gospel writers want to make an uplifting story of Jesus' origins, they choose the epic mode: he is both a descendant of King David (himself a shepherd/prince) and an obscure dweller in rustic Nazareth, born in a barn between an ox and an ass. The obscurity of the heroes' upbringing can be of two kinds, sometimes conflated: it can be that they grow up in the wild in the company of the beasts, or that they grow up in the house of a poor person or forest hermit, or as an orphan or foundling, a sort of charity case. If the emphasis is on the former, then we are in the territory of another master-theme in epic: the natural man or beast-man (I shall discuss this theme later). If the emphasis is on the latter, we might well ask why the epic poet goes to such lengths—straining the plot to incorporate both royal ancestry and humble beginnings. Why not just make the hero a royal prince or princess? Or why not make the hero a true child of nature or of the common people, with the advantage—so admired today—of needing to have pulled him or herself up by the bootstraps?

A cynical democrat might respond that most real great leaders do come from humble origins, since the aristocratic theory of noble blood is actually false and the human gene pool can produce extraordinary genius from any ancestry at any social level. Traditional societies, such a cynic would argue, find this truth embarrassing and invent the long-lost prince or princess story to explain the stubborn memory of the people that the hero rose from the dirt. It is suggestive that in the *Shahnameh*, Alexander, the historic conqueror of the Persian Empire, is made into the secret grandson of Darab (Darius). If an epic writer is willing to make a successful ethnic outsider into a member of the royal family, why not an energetic usurper risen from the peasantry?

But this political argument does not explain why there is such a universal tropism toward the noble birth/humble origins pattern, even when the epic storyteller is free to invent at his pleasure. The point is again, perhaps, to locate the hero both at the margins of human society and at its center—as both the extreme case and the universal representative. Perhaps an illuminating parallel would be the widespread moral tale of the poor person who is good and hospitable and who takes in a beggar or vagrant, only to find out later that the beggar is a god in disguise, and that they have been blessed with riches. Odin as a one-eyed stranger in a hat, Jove in a thatched hut—and whatsoever ye do unto the least of these my brethren, ye do also unto me.

Victor W. Turner, the anthropologist (and my father), described socially marginal figures—such as beggars, strangers, idiots, gypsies, pregnant women, the extremely old and young—as possessing in many societies the "powers of the weak," which include blessing and cursing. They are the interface between the human world and what lies outside it, and they are therefore both uncanny and sacred. Heroes possess some of those same characteristics—they are left-handers, so to speak, and have something of the almost schizophrenic and visionary character of the shaman. They need to be legitimate leaders, and lawfully in authority; but they also need to have or acquire the mana of the marginal, whether by a feral childhood or a sojourn in the forest, like Rama and the Pandava brothers, or by experiencing beggarhood or even sex-change in disguise, like Odysseus among the suitors or Arjuna disguised as a woman in the court of Virata.

Given the paradoxes of the hero's nature, what is the heroic code? I use the cliché "heroic code" ironically, because it is anything but a code. It is a way of getting beyond a code and adding to and revising it. To explain how this happens requires an analysis that combines linguistic philosophy, literary close reading, semantics, and a sort of universal anthropology. To understand the heroic code we must first understand the metaphor of the blaze.

Blazing the Trail

Among the Ndembu people of northwest Zambia in central Africa the word for a profound metaphor or ritual symbol (roughly equivalent to the Christian term "sacrament"—the outward and visible sign of an inward and invisible grace) is "chinjikijilu" (chinjíki-jílu). A chinjikijilu is literally a blaze—the mark that a hunter or explorer cuts on a tree in order not to get lost in the forest and to enable him to find his way back. When a girl becomes a woman a great coming-out ritual is celebrated for her, centered upon the Mudyi tree, which like a Christmas tree or a Mexican paradise tree is set up in the village center. Its white sap symbolizes mother's milk, male semen, matrilineal inheritance of property, female nurture, the moral qualities of innocence and goodness, and the divine creative principle. The Mudyi Tree is a chinjikijilu. Ndembu people would call the bread of the Christian sacrament a chinjikijilu. A master-metaphor or chinjikijilu blazes a trail from the world that we know to a realm that we do not know and enables us to find our way back. The Greek root for the word "metaphor"—*meta* (beyond), *pherein* (to carry)—to carry beyond—has the same implication. (Note that the word itself is a metaphor, carrying us beyond the known physical action of carrying to the abstract idea it indicates.)

In order to understand the point of this trailblazing or carrying-beyond, we need to understand the philosophical and semantic problem it addresses. Ludwig Wittgenstein's *Tractatus Logico-Philosophicus* was designed to demonstrate the rules by which words could become true pictures of things.[1] The attempt failed, and Wittgenstein spent the rest of his life exploring that failure, and trying to find ways in which language could still be shown to be useful. (For instance, it is not enough to point at something and say its name, because pointing itself is a symbol of a meaning, and how could one point at that meaning without assuming a pointing-meaning already?)

Two of the aphorisms in the *Tractatus* are of special interest here:

> Whereof one cannot speak, thereof one must remain silent.[2]

> The limits of my language are the limits of my world.[3]

At first glance, what these statements mean is that we are forever trapped within our verbal means of understanding and expression. We cannot say what we do not have words to say. There are no true discoveries. The world of nature is for us constructed by our language, and our language is a dictionary, each of whose entries is glossed by other entries, and we are imprisoned within this hermeneutic circle. Since our words only refer to other words, they are meaningless in any deep sense—and this is the fundamental idea of Deconstruction. We live in a play of signifiers, always deferring any final reference to a Signified.[4]

Inside the hermeneutic circle of the known world are all the categories of the reasonable and the familiar—the sayable, the knowable, the logically provable, cosmos, the connected, the ordered, the remembered or recorded past, conscious life, the defined (in terms of all the other definitions in the dictionary).

But hasn't Wittgenstein already referred to that whereof one cannot speak? He himself is doing what his statement declares impossible, precisely by declaring it so. "Whereof one cannot speak" is a noun phrase denoting something, giving a name to the unsayable—but if so, then it's not unsayable! If our language truly had limits, and if limits divide off one area from another, then surely the idea of our language having limits would be unthinkable and unsayable in our language, since we could not even conceptualize what might lie on the far side of the "limits of my language," even in a negative way (because a negative way is still a way). There is an obvious connection with Gödel's little paradox, of the unprovable statement. There is a truth outside the limits that makes what is inside them meaningful. Maybe we could not conceive of death—the boundary of our lives—without conceiving of "something after death," as Hamlet says, something on the other side of "that bourn ['limit', but also, 'river'] from which no traveler returns."

And if what is inside the circle is not what is outside it, we can understand what is outside it in at least a negative way. Recalling our little list of the characteristics of home territory, we can describe what is on the other side as: the unsayable ("whereof one cannot speak"), the unknowable, the unprovable, the irrational, chaos, the disconnected, the future, sleep/dream/death, the undefined. It is into this region that the hero, as the poet's proxy, makes his or her perilous adventure.

So somehow the boundary of our language must be able to be overcome; but this cannot be so, because then the boundary would now include what was previously unsayable. So the boundary of what is knowable must somehow *expand*. And is this not what happens when an explorer cuts a blaze?

Shakespeare may help us to see the deep wisdom of the Ndembu sages. Theseus at the beginning of Act V of *A Midsummer Night's Dream* has just listened to the strange but strangely consistent account of what happened to the lovers in the forest. Was it merely a dream? And are dreams "mere"?

> Such shaping fantasies, that apprehend
> More than cool reason ever comprehends.
> The lunatic, the lover, and the poet
> Are of imagination all compact . . .

They all "carry things beyond" the bounds of good sense.

> The poet's eye, in a fine frenzy rolling,
> Doth glance from heaven to earth, from earth to heaven,
> And as imagination bodies forth
> The forms of things unknown, the poet's pen
> Turns them to shapes, and gives to airy Nothing
> A local habitation and a name . . .

That "turning to shapes" is what the poet/hero partnership does.

Let us pull all these ideas together into a single question: where does it make sense to cut a blaze? Not within the circle of the known world, the expected and comprehensible range of ordinary statements. The explorer still knows where he is at that point—a blaze would be useless. Niels Bohr, the great quantum physicist, once said: The opposite of a true statement is a false statement; but the opposite of a profound truth is another profound truth. The shaping fantasy apprehends more than cool logic comprehends: what it sees is true but not provable. The explorer is not trying to get from one familiar place to another, but is headed into unexplored territory. He is trying to make the leap from honesty to magnanimity, to see the game he has always lived in as just a game. Art that cuts blazes inside the circle can only be pretty or charming or craftsmanlike, but never great or transforming or redeeming—at worst, it is trite.

If it is useless to cut the blaze inside the circle, should he not cut it outside the circle? After all, that is the only alternative, no? But if he cuts it outside the circle he is already lost. The purpose of a chinjikijilu, like the clue (the ball of string) that Theseus unwound as he penetrated the Minotaur's labyrinth, is to show him his way back home. Cutting the blaze outside the circle only helps him find his way from one place where he is lost to another where he is equally lost. One who cuts a blaze outside the circle of the known has already kicked himself loose of the earth, and, as Marlowe says of Kurtz in *Heart of Darkness*, "Confound the man! he had kicked the very earth to pieces."[5] This blazeless "kicking loose" has been the nemesis of much avant-garde art in the last hundred years or so.

There is only one place to cut the blaze—where it is a true blaze—and that is at the exact edge of the circle, just when the explorer crosses into terra incognita. And now something marvelous happens. A new space opens up—whatever is within eyeshot of the blaze. It is neither one side of the line nor the other. And this space is a temporal space. We must now redescribe what is outside the circle by means of the odd little word "yet." It is unsayable *yet*, unknowable *yet*, irrational *yet*, chaotic until now, etc. The present moment, in other words, ceases to be just a demarcation between past and future (the knowable and the unknowable), but takes on a territory of its own. Within that specious present one can go back and forth at will in one's mental and imaginative time machine. That space is the space of art, of new scientific hypothesis, of grace, of moral discovery. It is within the region of the previously unsayable, the unknown, the future, but is within eyeshot of the blaze. It is still in itself unknown and unexplored, but its contents can be located, referenced, and identified by metaphor, that acts as a sort of verbal triangulation or trigonometry, providing their vector and distance, so to speak, in terms of a new relation between fixed points within the known world. This space is Shakespeare's fairyland, his midsummer night's dream, of which Bottom says:

I have had a most rare vision. I have had a dream, past the wit of man to say what dream it was. Man is but an ass if he go about to expound this dream. Methought I was, there is no man can tell what. Methought I was, and methought I had, but man is but a patch'd fool, if he will offer to say what methought I had. The eye of man hath not heard, the ear of man hath not seen, man's hand is not able to taste, his tongue to conceive, nor his heart to report, what my dream was. I will get Peter Quince to write a ballad of this dream. It shall be call'd "Bottom's Dream," because it hath no bottom; and I will sing it in the latter end of a play, before the Duke. (IV.i.204–19)

But note that Bottom does not stay out there in the forest. He comes back to Athens and tries to make a ballad of it, to put it into words, to give to airy nothing a local habitation and a name. Bottom has cut his blaze in the right place, for all his bumbling.

It is well known to etymologists and linguists that languages grow—that is, develop vocabularies for talking about new things and ideas—by means of metaphor. Metaphors—especially grand metaphors—chinjikijilus—create new language for us to think in. The old Scottish *Ballad of True Thomas* or *Thomas the Rhymer*—almost a mini-epic in itself—gives a very clear picture of how this works. He is sitting under a tree at a crossroads[6]—perhaps a crossroads in his life, like Dante's dark wood at the beginning of the *Divine Comedy*—and the queen of fairyland rides by. Mistaking her for the queen of Heaven (Mary) he kneels to her, but she corrects him and offers a kiss, with the proviso that the kiss will make him her slave. Of course he kisses her, and is taken up behind her on her magic white horse. They come to another crossroads, a place where three roads branch off: one is the steep rocky path to heaven, one is the broad, pleasant, well-trodden path to Hell, but the third is something else:

And see ye not yon bonny road
That winds about the fernie brae?
That is the road to fair Elfland,
Where thou and I this night maun gae.

The road to Elfland is explicitly not the legalistic road of moral salvation or damnation, but one that is aesthetic or artistic ("bonny")—one that is essentially free, though it requires specific disciplines. Thomas, like Tamino and Papageno in Mozart's *Magic Flute*, is enjoined to silence in the magic realm. They ride across a river full of the blood of the dead, and through a dawnless darkness, like the darkness Gilgamesh endures in his search for his dead friend Enkidu. Finally they come to a delightful garden, where Thomas serves his mistress. At the end of his indentured servitude, she gives him an apple from the tree in the center of the garden, as his reward, implying that he cannot leave unless he eats it, and telling him that if he does so he must tell the truth always thenceforth. Thomas cavils at this:

> 'I dought neither speak to prince or peer,
> Nor ask of grace from fair ladye!'—
> 'Now haud thy peace, Thomas,' she said,
> 'For as I say, so must it be.'
>
> 'My tongue is my ain,' true Thomas he said;
> 'A gudely gift ye wad gie to me!
> I neither dought to buy or sell
> At fair or tryst where I might be.'

When Thomas is in fairyland he is not permitted to speak—but when he returns, he is given the great, and embarrassing, power to tell the truth always. And he does it in rhyme, and so he gets his other name as well, Thomas the Rhymer. When he returns, even if it seems to him that he has spent but a single night or a single week in fairyland (depending on which version of the ballad one reads), seven or seventy long years have passed. We can now see that this time-dilation is nicely predicted by the operation of the blaze, which expands the present moment. Outside the circle is that whereof one cannot speak—but if one has cut one's blaze, has entered that eternal present, and returned, one is able to make a ballad of one's vision.

There is a structural parallel in this story with the ancient Greek story of Orpheus, who, another poet, likewise goes to the underworld and is able to return. The mysterious prohibition this time is that he must not look back to check to see if his dead wife, Eurydice, is following him—he must not seek perfect certain knowledge here, for this is outside the realm of the provable. When he does look back, he loses his wife forever. And this myth may derive in part from the oldest extant poem in the world, *The Epic of Gilgamesh*. Gilgamesh goes to the underworld to bring back his dead friend Enkidu and find the secret of immortality. He also breaks one of those arbitrary rules (thou shalt not sleep), and comes back empty-handed—but with the gift of new knowledge and enduring words.

The Heroic Code

We can understand the moral import of the hero's journey in terms of a moral taxonomy that identifies four main regions of moral awareness, with two responses to each. Those four regions are naturally dictated by the notion of there being an edge to the known world: they are the region entirely within that world, the region within it but at its edge, the region at its edge but immediately beyond it and in contact with it; and the region outside it altogether.

In the first region, a moral agent is not aware of the rules, laws, constraints, and prohibitions that define the moral world he inhabits. If his intentions are cooperative and empathetic, we call such a person an innocent; if not, we call him bestial—he is no better or worse than an animal.

In the second region, where the limits of our world and language are apparent, we find those who, if their intentions are good, we call honest. They are the good citizens, the honorable and law-abiding conformists. Though they are aware of the rules and laws and prohibitions, the regard them as The rule, The law, The taboo. Their imagination does not stretch to imagining different lawful regimes, different games with different rules. Any other rule is simply wrong, not a true rule at all. If, on the other hand, such a dweller has suborned his own conscience, he is what we call dishonest. Like the honest person, he knows the rules are The rules, but he is happy to break them for his own advantage. Not being able to compare the game he is in with another game with different rules, he is not aware that the rules of the game also create the very values and prizes that might constitute his advantage if he possessed them. He reifies those prizes and steals them or defrauds others of them, like a child who sneaks $500 bills out of the bank in a game of Monopoly, and wonders why the game is not so much fun and a piece of Monopoly money is not as desirable as when you got it fair and square in rent for Park Place. The dishonest car-thief, who envies the pleasure you get from having earned your car and steals it, fences it to get money to buy a car he has not earned.

But if one possesses the imaginative and intellectual power to cross the boundary of one's world and language, the moral situation changes. Such a person can imagine different games, different sets of coherent laws, and can see how their own language-world works by comparison. One who has noble intentions and a good heart looks back at the world-game or language-system or rule-of-law he has left behind and recognizes its beauty, its capacity to generate meanings, values, goodness, intelligible categories, codes of behavior that enable people to live together in peace, cosmic visions that give us hope, and incentive. Though perhaps the $500 Monopoly bill or Chess queen or home run is less alluring, the game of Monopoly or Chess or baseball itself becomes more wonderful, more marvelous as a system, more of a work of art. Such a person we could call magnanimous, both in the sense of being generous to the regime he has transcended, and in the older sense of having—and needing—a great soul, to maintain his goals and values and habits without an external justification. Many heroes are of this kind. His mission, from which he can gain his own motivating suite of desires and hopes and dreams, is often to guard, protect and help regulate the game he came from (if he is a classical hero) or to extend and improve it (if he is a romantic hero). He takes pleasure in playing the game well, and more than fairly, exceeding the commitment of the true believers, giving advantage to those not blessed with a superior vision of the playing-field, helping expose the dishonest while showing them compassion on account of their naïve belief in the system they exploit.

What if one has stepped outside the world, though, and one is not magnanimous, and indeed has the dishonest person's instinct to cheat? We are now dealing with someone very dangerous indeed, far more so than the simple and rather pathetic dishonest person, who is as much of an unconscious supporter of the law as is the honest person. We are dealing with the cynic. The cynic is one who sees all the poor dumb rubes within the law as fair game (including the dishonest who are the ripest targets for the con). He has the intelligence and imagination to see that the rules are basically arbitrary, but does not have the generosity to affirm them nevertheless, as does the magnanimous person. Knowing how the rules work he can break them with impunity—and in principle, not just in their application to himself. Of course the cynic has a problem, since he knows that the pleasures of the world are largely the creation of the rules of the game in which he no longer believes. But the old habits of desire fade slowly, and it can be pleasant to indulge them until the habit has worn off. Nature has given us some very robust pleasures that resist satiety, such as the sensory delights of the table and the hunt, sexual conquest, and power. And there is a certain malicious pleasure in wanton destruction itself, and in the manipulation of those less clever than oneself. The rape and perdition of the innocent is especially piquant. Here we have the main opponent of the magnanimous hero.

Such characters—the magnanimous and the cynic—are still, despite their transcendence of the system, in contact with and concerned with it. Some, however, no longer have that concern and connection. They have detached themselves from the hermeneutic circle and are no longer so tied to the blazes that define and expand its edge. Of them, those who have generosity of spirit and the habit of love can be called the holy. They might be said to have a love beyond even that of the magnanimous—they have fallen in love not just with the decent law-abiding world of the system they were born into, but with the inner principle of goodness and creativity itself that must exist for any system of rules to survive. They are attracted to what Robert Wright calls "nonzero-sumness" itself; they have devoted themselves to God or to the gods who represent and personify that universal goodness. They may even become bodhisattvas or gods themselves, making the realm that lies outside the circle more friendly and hospitable to its expansion as time and history roll on. Though such persons are seldom heroes of epic—Tripitaka is one, Galahad, and perhaps Parzifal achieve such a state—they are frequent inhabitants of the genre, especially the Indian epics, where they are usually of the Brahmin or ascetic castes.

But there is another possible character who has renounced the world: the nihilist. Just as the holy person has turned from the particular instance of rule-governedness and nonzero-sumness represented by the world he has left to the joyful creative principle behind it, the nihilist has turned from that same world, but with a ferocious hatred for its whole pretension of value against the vacuum that is for him the proper ground state of all things. The nihilist's curious honesty is not that of the law-abiding citizen; but like him he takes it that there is a necessary rule: and the rule is (in answer to Heidegger's question, Why is there something rather than nothing?) that there ought to be nothing rather than something. Something, anything, is a blemish upon the perfection of nonexistence. Though the nihilist is not an activist as the cynic often is in pursuit of appetite or power or destruction, he is more thoroughly devoted, in an often ascetic way, to the annihilation of all that pretends to goodness, creativity, order, and reason. He is a sort of personified black hole. It might be said that though the chief danger to the magnanimous hero is the cynic, there is not much of a temptation to the hero to *become* a cynic; but there is a serious danger that the hero, in despair at the obstacles to his path and the thanklessness of the world he protects and extends, could fall into the dark gravitational field of the nihilist and become one himself. Perhaps the most dangerous nihilist of all is the nihilistic idealist, the one who justifies himself morally by an appeal to the injustice of the system he attempts to destroy, and is so justified in the only remaining emotion that is consistent with the nihilist's philosophy, that is, pure hatred. We find many revolutionaries in this category—Robespierre, perhaps; Pol Pot, Hitler, and Osama bin Laden.

Given this moral typology, which emerges naturally from the geography of metaphor as blaze, the trajectory of the hero in any given epic comes into clear focus. *Parzifal* is a good place to start. Parzifal begins as an innocent, and is socialized by the court of Arthur into an honest and honorable man, by being shown the limits of proper behavior. The root of "honest" and "honorable" is "hon," as in the French *honneur* and *honnête*; and it is also cognate with *honte*, shame. The honorable man is the one who is capable of shame; shame is the fear of being cast out of the boundary of the community, of being lost, and is what keeps a man of this kind honest. But Parzifal's learned honor is at a disadvantage with his original innocence in one respect: it makes him unable to cross the world's bourn or boundary when it is needed, that is, when his heroic quest or gest calls him into the realm of the holy, the castle of Munsalvaesche ("Mount Salvation" or "my salvation") where dwells the Holy Grail. Cundrie *la sorcière*, the loathly lady, personifies that shame; her fearsome ugliness and discourteous frankness are the authentic signs of that most painful of emotions. But she is the passage to the truth of Parzifal's condition, which is that his courtesy is inadequate to face the ultimate truths of the world and that he must learn a new kind of innocence if he is to achieve the grail. Parzifal has been trained in good manners by Gurnemanz, and remembering his advice he does not feel it is polite to ask the suffering Anfortas, the Fisher King, why he is in such pain. Simply to have asked would have relieved Anfortas' suffering. Cundrie searingly exposes Parzifal's failure:

> You are so shy of manly honor and so sick in knightly virtue that no physician can cure you. I will swear by your head, if someone will administer the oath to me, that never was greater falsity found in any man so fair. You baited lure! You adder's fang! Your host gave you a sword, of which you were never worthy. Your silence earned

you there the sin supreme. You are the sport of the shepherds of hell. Dishonored are you, Sir Parzifal. Yet you saw the Grail borne before you and the silver knives and the bloody spear.[7]

Worse still, Parzifal's half-brother, Feirefiz the Angevin, even though he is a pagan, has not failed his father's line as Parzifal has, in Cundrie's new definition of true manliness. That new definition involves being as free of the rules as innocence is, but not through unconsciousness of them but through the sense that those rules must yield to the deeper truths that lie outside the hermeneutic circle and world-picture of Arthur's court.

The placement of this episode in Wolfram's epic is deeply significant. The beginning of Book VI, where it occurs, tells how Arthur creates the first principle of the rule of law: that no man can engage in combat without the king's permission. Immediately afterwards Parzifal falls into his famous trance, depicted in many a medieval illustration: Arthur's falcon has struck down a goose, which sheds three drops of blood upon the snow. To Parzifal the three drops remind him compellingly of the body—the *beau corps*—of his beloved wife Condwiramurs ("she who conducts to love"). Though there is a euphemistic explanation (the three drops are her cheeks and her chin), the euphemism is itself significant, being the product of shame. It is plain what the three drops signify, a much more bodily image altogether. So distracted, Parzifal dishonorably fails at first to respond to the challenges of Sir Segramors and Sir Kay. Only the movement of Parzifal's horse, which puts the blood-drops out of sight, restores Parzifal to his senses. Both challengers are unhorsed: and it so happens that Kay is badly injured in the process. Parzifal had long sought to take revenge on Kay for having beaten a lady of Arthur's court, Cunneware de Lalant, for laughing discourteously at the uncouth Parzifal when he first arrived. Now Parzifal has unwittingly succeeded in defending the lady's honor. He is welcomed back into the court, and Arthur sets up his round table, the great symbol of the new rule of equality before the law. It is at this point that Cundrie appears and accuses Parsifal.

But Parsifal accepts her humiliating judgment of him, and resolves to take up again the great adventure of the Grail. In this quest, he must put away knightly glory and study with Trevrizent the hermit. The tale itself diverges at this point, following the exploits of Gawan, who represents the standard of courtesy, the honorable man who, though he is only human (and does not have the strange tinge of the superhuman that Parzifal possesses) represents the best that the courtly world can offer. Gawan stays on this side of the line that divides the known world from the unknown. Only after Gawan's tale is complete do we return to Parzifal, to his harsh retraining, and to his triumphant and mystical approach to the Grail.

So Wolfram's judgment is nicely weighed. Gawan is a true hero, in the sense of being an honest and honorable man of great deeds. He is certainly necessary to the vision of Arthur's court and table; and that vision is the highest political hope of the Middle Ages and even our own times—democracy is a round table. We need that circle, we need that game to keep us from each others' throats. But Wolfram is showing us another way, the path of the magnanimous hero, who carves his blaze and goes out into the waste land. "Waste," by the way, derives from the Latin vastus, empty, and is cognate with words like void, vacuum, vacant, vacation, vanity, vanish, evanescent, vaunt, and want. The blaze here is, I think, the unforgettable symbol of the three drops of blood and Parzifal's seizing of them as the image of his wife. Wolfram throughout this extraordinary passage addresses a series of odes to Love and to Adventure. Love is what enables Parzifal eventually to return from his great quest; the frank sensuality of the image of the blood drops, combined with its pathos and devotion, and its promise of fertility and a future generation—Loherangrin is to be their child—are the warrant that the passage from safe past to free future can happily and naturally be made. Adventure, on the other hand, is what drives him out beyond all knightly seemliness and all rule—and even all narrative coherence in places—into the realm of the holy. The magnanimous man is here the one who is the mediator between the holy, on one hand, and the honest and honorable, on the other: "I will allow myself no joy," says the hero,

> until I have seen the Grail, be the time short or long. My thoughts drive me toward that goal, and never will I swerve from it as long as I shall live. If I am to hear the scorn of the world because I obeyed the law of courtesy, then his counsel may not have been wholly wise.[8]

We can now understand Adventure in a way that may rehabilitate its rather shabby and despised glory. Adventure is in the terms of post-structuralist discourse the transgressive, the holy grail of deconstruction. The "adventure story" is not necessarily juvenile escapist fiction: it is the vital ingredient in any truly groundbreaking text. The word itself has an intriguing etymology, revealing as etymology so often does the collective metaphorical reasoning of its language-community. From the Latin *ad-venire*, to come upon, the word came in French to mean chance or hazard, especially the taking of dangerous chances, and then took on the meaning of exciting risky action and experience that it has today. Thus its roots imply a coming by surprise on an unanticipated contingency outside the logic of one's intended journey.

Looked at in the terms we have been exploring in this chapter—the boundary, the blaze, the moral types that are implied by the approach to and the crossing of the boundary—the characteristics common to epic heroes make lucid sense in the logic of narrative.

Epic heroes inhabit an economic world of gifts and gift-exchange. They almost never exist in the marketplace, because the marketplace, with its logic of exchange, pricing, and compromise is precisely what lies within the circle of a culture. A market is like a dictionary, in the closed sense: the universal mutual definability of words in a dictionary resembles the universal exchangeability and fungibility into money of everything in a market economy. To cross the boundary of the known world is to give up buying, selling, hiring, and being hired. Though some of the Icelandic saga heroes, like Gunnar, Kari, Kjartan, and Bolli engage temporarily in trade or at least contemplate doing so, and Njal is closely involved in property law, raiding and plunder are considered more heroic means of getting wealth. And it is precisely where trading gives way to family relations, and weregild law gives way to bloodfeud, that the epic and tragic characteristics of the heroes get the scope to show themselves. Likewise, Captain Ahab becomes a truly epic hero exactly when he nails the doubloon (his chinjikijilu!) to the mast and interrupts the *Pequod*'s legitimate business venture in mad pursuit of the white whale. Epic heroes do not count the cost. But it is precisely through the transgressions of Gunnar, Njal, and the sons of Njal that the Fifth Court of Iceland is established, the beginning of the true rule of law in Iceland. And it is through the unification of Ahab's crew in the hunt that Melville's vision of a new America of the whole human race, the "joint-stock universe," is articulated.

The ways goods are exchanged in the hero story are by gift-giving, lucky discovery of unclaimed or stolen or lost goods (the dragon's hoard, for instance), inheritance, marriage, violence (appropriation, conquest, or theft), and gambling or wagering. In every case there is an arbitrariness about the heroic economy. This is not a critique of the market, rather a praise of it; epic usually recognizes the existence of a world of trade (one of Odysseus' aliases is as a merchant, and though it is a false one, it is a respectable one), but its concern is with the initial "givens" of any market, with the clearing of the space that is needed for a marketplace.

Related to this heroic characteristic is the hero's paradoxical capacity to lose control of himself, especially in wrath. All epic heroes have a bit of the berserker, even the pious and public-spirited Aeneas, who cannot resist when he sees Pallas' sword-belt on Turnus, but slays his fallen enemy. Of course the greatest of all the heroes of uncontrol is Achilles. In his *menis*, his mania, his wrath, he blazes and burns across the plain of the Scamander in a way that makes his story archetypal as epic even when, as is the case, so many of the standard features of epic are otherwise missing. (Homer makes up for these gaps in *The Odyssey*.) But there are many other instances of the epic hero's ability to fall into a sort of fit or seizure. In *The Liberation of Jerusalem* Rinaldo kills Gernand in such a fury, and Tancred unwittingly slays his beloved Clorinda:

> Savage fight—
> Where Skill is banned, where Strength lies all but dead,
> And in their place mad Frenzy rules outright![9]

In their final battle both Karna and Arjuna burn with that insane hero-light. Skarpheddin of *Burnt Njal* and Egil of *Egil's Saga* have an insane joy in battle; Skarpheddin sings in the midst of the fire that consumes his father's house, to the superstitious (and justified) terror of his enemies. All of the male Volsung line are happy only when they are bloody to the elbow. Cuchullain in his *ríastrad* (the Irish technical term for the berserk state) is beautifully translated by Thomas Kinsella:

> The first warp-spasm seized Cúchulainn, and made him into a monstrous thing, hideous and shapeless, unheard of. His shanks and his joints, every knuckle and angle and organ from head to foot, shook like a tree in the flood or a reed in the stream. His body made a furious twist inside his skin, so that his feet and shins switched to the rear and his heels and calves switched to the front . . . On his head the temple-sinews stretched to the nape of his neck, each mighty, immense, measureless knob as big as the head of a month-old child . . . he sucked one eye so deep into his head that a wild crane couldn't probe it onto his cheek out of the depths of his skull; the other eye fell

out along his cheek. His mouth weirdly distorted: his cheek peeled back from his jaws until the gullet appeared, his lungs and his liver flapped in his mouth and throat, his lower jaw struck the upper a lion-killing blow, and fiery flakes large as a ram's fleece reached his mouth from his throat . . . The hair of his head twisted like the tangle of a red thornbush stuck in a gap; if a royal apple tree with all its kingly fruit were shaken above him, scarce an apple would reach the ground but each would be spiked on a bristle of his hair as it stood up on his scalp with rage.[10]

This image is not unlike the graphic illustrations of the Japanese heroes of the *Heike*, such as Kajiwara, Yomyo Meishu, Benkei, and Kiyomori himself in the throes of wrath. Shakespeare's Harry Hotspur—whose qualities of wrath are to be cropped and absorbed by Prince Hal and fully expressed upon the field of Agincourt—gives us an exact picture of the exhaustion of the adrenals that succeeds the berserk frenzy:

> But I remember, when the fight was done,
> When I was dry with rage and extreme toil,
> Breathless and faint, leaning upon my sword, . . .
>
> I then, all smarting with my wounds being cold,
> To be so pestered with a popingay,
> Out of my grief and my impatience
> Answered neglectingly, I know not what—
> (I.iii.28)

Monkey, in the *Journey to the West*, is another proverbial berserker. The hero twins of the *Popol Vuh* are so given up to the ball-game that they play it with Hunahpu's own head for a ball.

Yet all these heroes are capable of great stoicism and self-control on occasion. Many can conceal their motives and fears, and possess the self-mastery required for successful dissimulation. Though they are huge in their other passions too, they are able, usually with the help of the gods, to master them; Monkey learns restraint from Tripitaka, Aeneas tears himself away from Dido at Mercury's behest. How can we explain the berserkerhood of the epic hero, his apparently beastlike weakness in being unable to resist his rage?

Perhaps we can understand this seeming anomaly in terms of Odysseus' self-control when, disguised as a beggar, and after being insulted by the suitors, he sees his serving-women going off to bed with them.

His heart cried out within him
the way a brach with whelps between her legs
would howl and bristle at a stranger—so
the hackles of his heart rose at that laughter.
Knocking his breast he muttered to himself:
"Down: be steady. You've seen worse, that time
the Kyklops like a rockslide ate your men
while you looked on. Nobody, only guile,
got you out of that cave alive."
                                    His rage
held hard in leash, submitted to his mind,
while he himself rocked, rolling from side to side,
as a cook turns a sausage, big with blood
and fat, at a scorching blaze, without a pause,
to broil it quick . . .[11]

There will be time enough next day in the locked hall with the suitors to eat that sausage. The point is not that he has a lesser capacity for rage than, say, Achilles; his wrath is like a leashed dog, an animal that is dangerous but useful; or more exactly, it is like a bitch who will be perfectly happy to kill or be killed for her whelps between her legs. Odysseus remembers how he pretended to be an animal—a ram—to escape the cyclops' cave. But stranger yet, his wrath is like that delicious sausage, which will not be swelled up tight enough and good to eat until it is hot and fully cooked through. The phallic suggestion is obvious. And when the rain of arrows flies down the hall at the suitors (from a bow that has just propelled a shaft horizontally through twelve axe-heads) that wrath is released and now entirely out of control.

So what is the imagery saying? Here, that the hero must be capable of the joyful ferocity of an animal, that he must have the shaman's gift of *becoming* the totem animal, like the dancing shaman with the deer's head in the stone-age cave-painting. He must know what it is to be an animal, whose desires to eat and mate and protect its whelps are utterly innocent and all-consuming. We only become free within our animal nature when we are able fully to yield ourselves over to it. We can, at need, control it for a while, but it must have its prey. We control it only by rewarding it, as we reward the hunting-dog with a scrap of the kill. But the work of control—the taming, cooking, or disguising of the force of nature in ourselves—does not in these images diminish the potency and brilliant life of passion (as Freud suggested in *Civilizations and Its Discontents*), but intensifies it. That intensification is part of the promise of the epic hero to the culture that it addresses.

The epic hero represents neither control nor frenzied loss of control, but both at the same time.

In other words, the hero must exist not only at the boundary between known and unknown, past and future, but also between the animal and the human—he must embody and recall the moment when the animal became human. And here we begin to see why so many epics contain beast-men, a theme we must keep for another chapter.

Recent work in anthropology, sociology, neuroscience, endocrinology, ethology, and evolutionary psychology has become increasingly concerned with the pivotal role of emotion. The most interesting insight seems to be that as rational calculation is the reason of the individual, emotion is the reason of the species. Emotion by definition makes us do things that our reason would not have us do. But as a social and sexually reproducing species we would not survive unless we were able to override rational self-interest to ensure our reproductive posterity by sexual love, safeguard it by jealousy, police our own conformity to social morality by shame, gravitate toward what is healthy and productive by the love of beauty, make infractions of community solidarity expensive by vengefulness, and improve our collective economic and technological lot by envy. Our very genes, expressed in the neurochemistry and hormones of our bodies, contain an implicit morality, often at war both with the more primitive urge toward individual survival, and the loftier commands of abstract ethics and justice. The emotions named in the seven deadly sins are mammalian virtues, at odds both with the more conservative rules of the selfish gene and the more advanced and speculative ideals of the human experiment. The epic hero inhabits precisely the space where these forces are most powerful, most at odds, and most potentially capable of emergent behaviors and ideas that transcend them.

But why is wrath so singled out as the special passion of the hero in epic? Certainly epic heroes have other emotions that are larger-than-life: Parzifal's shame or fear of shame; Gilgamesh's grief for his friend, so great that he will not let go of his body until the worm seizes upon it; the amorous frenzy of Rinaldo and Tancred in *The Liberation of Jerusalem*; the desire for honor in so many heroes. But wrath seems to trump them all. Why? Wrath is the emotion most deeply associated with the establishment and preservation of the self. Other emotions ensure and safeguard extensions of the self into the realms of sympathy, social standing, and reproduction. Wrath, though, is the emotion perhaps most closely concerned with the greatest mystery of organic life, the self itself—that is, the subjective center that is to itself the focal point of the universe, with its motivational system that makes possible action, the deed, as opposed to mere happening. Wrath is the inner force that maintains against the pressure of the external environment the internal world of the organism. Wrath is what mans the city wall of the cell, the immune system, the individual animal. You hear it in the yell of the healthy newborn baby. Though it is a crude and ugly passion, it has its own joy and beauty—it is akin to what Blake called "energy" and characterized as "eternal delight." Melville's analysis, in the voice of Ahab, nicely catches some of its nuances:

> All visible objects, man, are but as pasteboard masks. But in each event—in the living act, the undoubted deed—there, some unknown but still reasoning thing puts forth the mouldings of its features from behind the unreasoning mask. If man will strike, strike through the mask! How can the prisoner reach outside except by thrusting through the wall? To me, the white whale is that wall, shoved near to me. Sometimes I think there's naught beyond. But 'tis enough. He tasks me; he heaps me; I see in him outrageous strength, with an inscrutable malice sinewing it. That inscrutable thing is chiefly what I hate; and be the white whale agent, or be the white whale principal, I will wreak that hate upon him. Talk not to me of blasphemy, man; I'd strike the sun if it insulted me.[12]

In the passage above, Ahab is defending himself against Starbuck's charge of paranoia—that Ahab is insanely blaming an unreasoning animal. But the implication of Ahab's reply is something like this: to have an authentic living existence at all is to have intention. An intending being maintains its selfhood by resistance to the world about it, and that resistance is emotionally expressed as wrath. Wrath could not exist without the attribution of hostile intention to that against which the anger is directed. Thus, if we are to be selves at all we cannot but attribute intention to the world—to exist as a conscious moral being is to dignify the universe as the purpose of a god or gods, the more inscrutable the more malicious.

One could argue, with Milton, that the more inscrutable the purposes of that god, the more miraculously and generously concerned with the creation and preservation of one's human freedom, and thus the more to be loved. The inscrutability of such a god would be the inscrutability of the good teacher who, when asked by the student what the teacher wants him to say in the term paper ("will that be on the test?"), tells him that he wants to read what the student has to say, and will grade him partly on how much he has managed to surprise his teacher with the unexpected. The student's wrath at this might fuel the emergence of genuine intellectual, moral, and imaginative agency on the part of the student. Milton's Satan certainly isn't buying this argument; Milton's humans do eventually buy it. Ahab does not.

The reader might wonder what has become of wrath in some of the more recent works that I have claimed as epic—notably Wordsworth's *The Prelude* and Eliot's *The Waste Land*. A good objection, and one that might stand as an objection to the whole modern introspective turn in literature. Wordsworth seems so gentle and well-intentioned, and Eliot's Tiresias (or Prufrock, or Gerontion) so beaten down, that wrath seems too big for them. "Do I dare to eat a peach?" But the aggression is still there, even if it is passive aggression. We cannot ignore the underlying viciousness of Wordsworth's ridicule of London life, and the studied insults of Eliot directed at the small house-agent's clerk, the Smyrna merchant, and the Bradford millionaire. They are still slyly striking through the mask.

Heroic Leadership and Its Dangers

The epic hero, as we have seen, is one who transgresses the boundaries—physical, moral, metaphysical, psychological—of his (or her) home world, yet who remains its guardian and chief scout. The many paradoxes that are involved in this, the volatile role of the magnanimous, are entirely consistent. The hero's action is both dutiful and above and beyond the call of duty. The hero is a model of honor but also a scandalous critique of the limits of honor. The hero has superhuman self-control, and superhuman wildness. Where many of these paradoxes gather to a head is in the issue of leadership. The hero is quintessentially an individual, and quintessentially a leader. The hero is blessed by the gods, but in a competition with them that may destroy him.[13]

In the Western classical tradition this matter is an ancient trope of criticism and scholarship. Achilles is a rebel who saves his leader's army; Odysseus is a fine leader who just wants to get home, yet manages to get all his followers killed; and Aeneas abandons his native city to destruction and becomes a very unwilling founder of an empire he never wanted. Critics have often tried to avoid the paradoxes by proposing some kind of theory of social and political progress—upgrading the relative irresponsibility of the Homeric heroes and the relative piety of Aeneas (which is piety to Troy, not Rome!), for instance, to draw sociological distinctions between the city-state and the law-bound empire.[14] But the paradox in the hero's nature of individuality vs. community, opportunism vs. caring leadership, the rebel vs. the shepherd, is constitutive of epic, as can be shown by a larger survey of the genre as we have begun to examine it.

In *Gilgamesh* the hero starts out as an egoist, a tyrant, a bully, and a rapist, and he embarks on his last and most striking adventure absolutely alone. Yet he is also the great leader in the partnership with Enkidu, as the builder of the city's gates, and as the royal king of Uruk. Abraham, the founder of the chosen people, gets his final authority by being prepared to commit (for the Lord) the most monstrous of crimes against human community, the murder of his son—the very person who is to be the ancestor of the chosen people. Jacob becomes Israel through a course of action that seems thoroughly selfish and in violation of the rules of succession and inheritance. In the Book of Exodus, Moses, the archetypal leader of Israel, begins as a rootless individual, a criminal and outlaw and, even after he has been given the mandate of Jahweh, complains that he is no public speaker, must delegate that role to Aaron, and share his staff of office with his much more down-to-earth, unmystical, and unimaginative lieutenant. Rostam, like virtually all the great heroes of the *Shahnameh*, is a loner who must keep a delicate balance between obeying the unwise and unjust commands of his rightful monarch (Kavus, in his case) and doing what he believes to be the right thing. Indeed this tension between the heroic follower and his foolish, weak, mad, tyrannous or corrupt liege lord, the tragic center of the Persian epic, is a major theme in many epics, notably *The Iliad, Mahabharata, The Poem of My Cid, The Song of the Nibelungs*, Shakespeare's *Henriad*, the *Heike, Moby Dick*, and others. Abdiel plays the same role, on a minor scale, in *Paradise Lost*.

To understand the hero's nature is to begin to understand his quest and task. There must be a departure from the circle of the known. There must be a reason for that departure, a reason which can make sense within the known world but which takes on a new meaning once home is left behind. There must be some kind of blaze or mark or gesture that will function as a link to familiar territory. There must be either a return or a failure to return, with a meaningful high-water-mark of the adventure. There must be a home to return to. And there must be a gift with which the hero returns, and a commemoration of the adventure that transmits it to us, the hearers or readers.

Notes

1. Ludwig Wittgenstein, *Tractatus Logico-Philosophicus*, trans. C. K. Ogden (New York: Cosimo Classics, 2007).
2. Prop. 7.
3. Prop. 5.6.
4. Jacques Derrida, *Of Grammatology* (Baltimore, MD: Johns Hopkins University Press, 1967); *Writing and Difference*, trans. A. Bass (New York: Routledge, 1978).
5. Joseph Conrad, *Heart of Darkness* (New York: Simon & Brown, 2010), 82.
6. W. Peacock, *English Verse*, Vol. II (Oxford: Oxford University Press, 1961), 411. Like True Thomas, the hero twins in the *Popol Vuh* must cross a river of blood and pass through a crossroads to get to the underworld. It is the correspondence of such details that is so convincing on the question of whether epic is an artistic form that is natural to the human species.
7. Mustard and Passage, 171.
8. Ibid., 177.
9. *The Liberation of Jerusalem*, Wickert, 12:62.
10. Thomas Kinsella (trans.), *The Táin* (Oxford: Oxford University Press, 1969), 150–53.
11. Fitzgerald, 20:18.
12. Modern Library, 161.
13. See Gregory Nagy, *The Best of the Achaeans* (Baltimore, MD: Johns Hopkins University Press, 1980, 1997), ch. 9, 17.
14. E.g., Agathe Thornton, *The Living Universe: God and Men in Virgil's Aeneid* (Leiden: Brill, 1997).

4

The Quest

The Question

Every epic begins with a question mark. When the literary study of epic confined itself to the European epic tradition, it was common to cite the beginning *in medias res* as a defining feature of epic. A wider study of world epic shows this formal feature to be a local variant, not in itself constitutive of the genre, but it points us toward a more universal element, the initiating question mark. Homer's brilliant device of starting in the middle of things was picked up and exploited by the whole of the Western tradition, by Virgil, Dante, Ariosto, Tasso, Milton, and so forward. But in the allusive and reminiscent value of the technique, perhaps its original meaning was somewhat lost: that epic always, despite being usually set in the remote past, seizes a moment when the present trembles on the precipice of the future.

The *in medias res* technique makes the reader demand "What is going on?", a question that unites him or her at once with the hero or heroine who must decide what to do, what mark or blaze to set upon the inscrutable blank of the future. It chooses a place and time where various outcomes are offered, and where we, and the hero, are posed some great question, whose grammatical openness and inversion ("should I?", not "I should") invites decision and action. The rising tone at the end of a sentence by which many languages signal a question suggests an unfinished trajectory, a spear cast into the future that has not yet come to rest in its yet-unseen target.

The very meaning of the question itself is up for grabs, and the beauty of the *in medias res* device is that this meaning is then determined by the interplay of future action with past flashbacks. The present tense of the opening of an epic is one that is distended, in Augustine's sense when he speaks of our experience of time as a distension of the mind. Aeneas ponders, "to and fro dividing the swift mind"—the hero's present is one which can not only hurl itself into reckless rage but also push and hold apart with its strength the prison-walls of past and future, select items and actions from both, and decide on how to weave them into the best story. The hero's present articulates itself by going both backward and forward in time, taking the dividing-line between past and future and expanding it into a flexible specious present, within which scenarios can be tried out and evaluated, and true freedom can exist.

Perhaps this place is the philosopher's aporia that Socrates praises in the *Meno* and elsewhere. The organic drives of an animal simply fulfill the causal inference of the past, except when its drives oppose each other, as when the territorial urge to defend its personal space conflicts with the sexual urge to union with a mate, and new ritual behaviors emerge. Such behaviors are the instinctual equivalent of reflection in a human lover or hero. The most moving moment in *Parzifal*, when the knight sits paralyzed upon his horse, caught between the recollection of his beloved and the threat of attack, is the point where he can begin the successful conclusion of his quest.

What looks in Homer to be a theoretical obstacle to the clear unfolding of the plot—how did we get here? What's the story so far?—reveals itself as an amazingly economical technique for transforming exposition into action, and giving explanation the spur of urgent suspense. Flashbacks are not just the way a hero recollects and re-members himself, but deeds. Odysseus' stories of Troy are not just backstory—they are crucial acts of diplomacy, persuasion, and even survival.

Epics in other traditions, though, even if they do not avail themselves of this technique per se, manage the function it serves in different ways. The *Popol Vuh*, for instance, begins not in the middle but at the beginning; but this beginning is re-begun, so to speak, at least four times in the poem, with new meaning each time: with the tale of the first hero twins, the tale of the second pair, the history of the pre-dawn tribes, and then the history of the Quiché people. The *Heike* uses a system of historical allusion to perform the same function, paralleling present action with three sets of past events, in the mythical dawn time of the world and in the imperial Japanese and imperial Chinese histories. The *Mahabharata* works this purpose too, but this time by references to the past incarnations of the present heroes, and by the profusion of tale-telling episodes within the larger frame-narrative. In each case, the present moment is defined as the pivot, and the pivot is a question or *quest*.

The Journey

A quest, of course, requires a journey. It need scarcely be pointed out that every single epic in the world canon involves a great journey. If, as I argue here, epic is the story humans tell themselves about how they became humans, the core of that story would seem to be a double journey—an evolutionary journey and a physical journey. Even when, as often, epics emerge from settled and stable societies that have inhabited a homeland for centuries or millennia—take the China of *The Journey to the West*'s composer, Wu Cheng-en, for instance—they still organize themselves around a journey. All humans know, and express in their epics, that we came from somewhere else and our coming itself made us what we are. And the anthropological evidence seems to confirm this basic human intuition.

The picture sometimes given by utopian popularizers of ancestral humanity is often rather misleading. We are portrayed as living for huge stretches of time in the Serengeti plains, small hunting bands in an endless savannah. There is some truth to this picture, but it needs to be radically supplemented by new information about human prehistory—which is very much more dramatic than the arcadian view once held—and about human individual development and maturation. For instance, modern humans evidently originated in Africa, about 190,000 years ago. But they did not stay in one place. Luigi Luca Cavalli-Sforza[1] and other anthropologists have traced humanity's extraordinary migrations across the globe. Humans were present in Australia at the very least fifty-thousand years ago, and some estimates give much older dates. The Americas were colonized not long afterwards.

Almost immediately, humans were walking, and to get to Australia and America they must have walked through wildly different terrains—deserts, tundras, mountains, forests, jungles, ice-floes, marshes, barren, and fertile seacoasts—and navigated across open oceans. Humans are the most efficient walkers on the planet; over very large distances, we can even outpace the horse. Our temperature control system is extremely sophisticated, better even than that of wolves and dogs. We are specialized for getting quickly to very different places. Perhaps we could say with some justice that it was not that humans evolved and then walked and ran, but that we walked and ran, and so evolved into being human—we were forced to grow big brains to deal with the technological and social stresses of moving about.

The sociology and sociobiology of our migrations is itself very interesting. One important key to understanding our migrations is adolescence. Many social species—dolphins, langurs, baboons, and chimpanzees, for instance—go through a significant behavioral metamorphosis during the transition into sexual maturity, leading them to separate from their kin group and seek mates elsewhere. Human adolescence, which builds upon this pattern, has developed into a very remarkable phenomenon, neurologically and hormonally. As the body acquires its full strength, endurance, and sexual readiness, the behavioral pattern changes. The human brain seems to be programmed to rewire itself through puberty and sexual maturation, and delay the establishment of fixed moral habits until after the age of eighteen. A wave of dendritic pruning surges across the cortex from back to front. Simultaneously the adolescent is designed to adopt a different diurnal temporal niche from those of the child and the adult, staying up late at night and sleeping in the morning. There is a profound questioning and rebellious testing of parental and tribal knowledge, and a wanderlust that includes a rejection of childhood companions as mates and a search for exotic sexual partners. At the same time, an urge to identify and bond with and conform to a group of age-mates emerges. Human exogamy and the incest taboo are part of this set of instincts.

To keep the lid on these maturational changes, all human societies have developed systems to suppress or recruit them—male longhouses to discipline boys, rules governing female honor, rites of passage, and so on. But the alternative to joining the older generation and accepting its security and its control is, for humans, always present—to leave the tribe and set up house elsewhere. Langur males form gangs and try to invade the territories and harems of their elders; chimpanzee females leave home and seek exciting males in other troops. In humans both males and females in their teens like to throw over the traces and seek new experiences, often on the other side of the tracks.

Archeology and the observation of modern hunter-gatherer and herding societies seem to suggest a common lifecycle for the human group, based on the challenge and spur of human adolescence. The story might go something like this. A group of young adults accompanied by a few elders disgruntled and politically disempowered in their home village set out down the coast (or into the next valley). They settle down, have children, and are faced with having to teach them the lore of the group, one that will prevent the children from wanting to go back to the old village. They tell an alternate version of the myths and stories, which contains most of the ideational content of the originals, but which reverses key aspects of them or creates mediators in the old binary oppositions to explain the move. Their numbers increase, but while there are still plenty of local resources so that everyone can live comfortably and found lineages, there is no major conflict.

When resources grow scarcer, the adolescents get restive, having to take subordinate positions in established households. Factions arise among the elders; the losing side recruits the support of some of the disaffected young, or talented youngsters choose as mentors those among the old who resist the majority. Some incident occurs, usually involving kinship conflict—between a suitor and the loved one's family, between a wife and her husband's family and friends, between a father and a maternal uncle over the loyalties of a boy, between brothers over an inheritance, or between the blood kin and affines of a young woman, for instance—and triggers a breach. Attempts at ritual resolution of the grudge succeed at first, and finally fail.[2] A group of adolescents, perhaps including eloping couples, leaves the home, accompanied by their allied elders; the home village settles down until it must bud a new group of emigrants. This new group of malcontents must take a different direction from that of the first emigration, or try to join or conquer the new village or the ancestral village, or strike out into the hinterland, evolving its own set of modifications to the traditional myths and rituals, and sometimes reviving the more ancient unrevised versions of them.

Each new version of the old stories encapsulates the traditional knowledge, but also adds a record of its experience, failures, and successes over history. This is a story of continuous branching and spreading, and is consistent with the expansion of humanity across the globe. Myths such as the founding of Rome and Tudor England by Trojan survivors, the founding of Japan by Chinese voyagers, the founding of Israel by Mesopotamian emigrants, the founding of Hungary by the brothers Hunor and Magyar, the founding of the Hawaiian empire by Polynesians, and of course the taming of the Wild West continue the story.

In other species, adaptability is managed mostly by the DNA and RNA and the immune system. The human version of adaptability, like so many human traits, seems to be a complex partnership between innate and learned traits. In our species, culture, with its ability to store and transmit vast quantities of information, takes a full partnership role. Adaptability requires mechanisms for accumulating information about the world and about past successful and unsuccessful strategies for dealing with the contingencies of the world, for recognizing such contingencies as they arise, for triggering those strategies when appropriate, and for recording the results into the future. In other words, for culture to play its full role in supplementing our hardwired biological adaptability, it must be evolutionary in its own operations. It must be able to preserve a rich and various fund of traditions, to recognize departures from the conditions justifying the current set of "toggled" settings, and to use tradition as a way to give new responses to new situations, toggling on new combinations of older settings to meet current needs. In other words, it must be conservative in preserving its heritage of old information, observant in comparing it with the current situation, and imaginatively free in applying the old knowledge.

This model of human adaptability is, it might be noted, markedly different from modernist theories of innovation and originality. Instead of progress emanating from the present, progress is held back by present practice when it encounters new contingencies (including anthropogenic ones like the overcrowding of a coastal village or the environmental stresses of the modern city). Instead of the past acting as the obstacle to progress, the past is the source of progress, an archive of possible strategies and narratives and collective memories to be consulted and recombined to meet the new situation. The most powerful stories are the great myths of exodus and liberation—and they are virtually determined by the creative tension between territorial possession and expanding demographic numbers. What the present says is: "Put up with your bondage"; what the past says is "But your ancestors did not, and they found the Promised Land." And those myths of the past are not just stories, but the beginnings of a true archive of biocultural adaptability.

Epics of course explore every possible modality of the journey. The journey can be a great military expedition, like Charlemagne's or the Cid's liberating invasions of paynim Spain, or the Greeks' war on Troy, or Henry V's invasion of France, or the liberation of Jerusalem, or the Persian conquests in Asia. Or they can be a more exploratory journey, like Da Gama's voyage to India or Satan's to Paradise, or my Chance van Riebeck's to Mars. The journey can be an exile, like Aeneas' from Troy, or Satan's from Heaven, or Eve and Adam's from Eden, or Rama's or the Pandavas' from their respective kingdoms; or perhaps the most moving of all, the long flight of the Heike, the Taira clan, from the imperial capital to the remote islands of southern Japan, pursued by the relentless armies of the Minamoto, anticipated by the pathetic story of Shunkan's exile (immortalized in the great Noh play on the subject). The journey can be a return home, like Odysseus' to Ithaca or the Israelites' to the Promised Land. It can be in search of a particular object—the Golden Fleece, the sacred Buddhist scriptures, the Grail, the White Whale. It can be a journey into refuge or sanctuary, like Sundiata's, whence he returns to defeat the evil King Soumaoru who has sought his death. It can be simply flight from bondage or from the pursuit of enemies or the law, as in *Martín Fierro*. It can be a voyage of self-discovery, like Dante's through the afterlife or Wordsworth's through revolutionary France. Or it can even be a road trip to a sort of sport fixture, an away game, as when in the *Popol Vuh*, the Hero Twins accept the challenge of the Lords of the Dead to play the ball game in the land of Xibalba, or as when Gawaine seeks out the green chapel for the return match of the beheading game, or Gunnar accepts the challenge to the horse-fight, or the Pandavas travel to the court of Duryodhana to play the dice-game. Often it is many of these things at once.

The common denominator, the journey, despite its many causes and goals, is never purely metaphorical. The absolute conservation in epic of the motif of physical change of place is a sign that it is ancient and fundamental to the genre, and that if the genre is, as I argue, the telling of the story of human evolution, then it agrees with the anthropologists that travel is not just something that humans do, but is in some sense constitutive of humanity.

Yet one could also argue, as we shall see when we examine the epic theme of founding and the city, that home, the basic and yearned for origin and abiding-place, is just as fundamental an element of epic. Thus the meaning of the quest, the journey, is not just travel in itself. To say that its motto is "the journey not the arrival matters" will not do. The arrival, and the departure-point, matter very much too. It is the meaningful relation between the journey and home, whether home is left or arrived at, begun from or found or returned to, that is the point. Home is defined by our departure from it, our discovery of it, our return to it. What is constitutive of humanity, to revise our previous aphorism, is the finding or recovery of home, a finding or recovery that is accomplished only through a journey. It is as if to say that a home that one simply remains in is not, paradoxically, a home at all. It is a home only if found or found again.

Obstacles and Enemies

Any story requires obstacles. The epic quest requires obstacles of a commensurate magnitude. It is almost as if great actions require some resistant medium, some hard ground to provide purchase, some viscous medium against which the argonaut's oar can pull, a burden that becomes the burden of the song and the burden of the sense. Obstacles are part of the given, the data, of the story—they are unwanted but valuable and useful gifts. They help define the value of the goal or prize of the quest.

One of the most recurrent initial obstacles of the hero is his or her kin. We will look at the problems of kinship later. Enemies of all kinds make the most common obstacles: members of opposing tribes or nations, envious peers, tyrannous rulers, rivals in love, or reputation or status or property or legal claims—all these and more are the human enemies. Often the enemy is a god or many gods, who must be propitiated or outwitted but who will not go away as dead humans often do—though ghosts of course can be formidable enemies, and proper burial is often very important. If a man is worth a hero's time killing, he is worth burying with due honor.

The point is that a hero is measured by the obstacles he or she overcomes, the enemies he or she defeats. Epic writers in even the most paranoid and xenophobic cultures, like crusader Europe, or the traumatized, conquered, and Arabized Persia of Ferdowsi, or the embattled Latvia of the epic poet Andrejs Pumpurs, find themselves building great heroes with rich psychological development and noble motivations on the opposing side. Those heroes are perilously liable to steal the show, as evidenced by Homer's Hector, Kakuichi's Kiyomori, Vyasa's Duryodhana, Virgil's Turnus, Shakespeare's Hotspur, Tasso's Argant, Lo Kuan-chung's Ts'ao Ts'ao, Milton's Satan, Pumpurs' Kalapuisis, and Michael Lind's unforgettable Santa Ana.

Monsters

The most obvious—and most dismissed—form of obstacle the hero faces is the monster. Despite Tolkien's spirited defense of epic monsters, they are still regarded, I believe, with embarrassment and even scorn by cultured readers; their presence consigns a work to the realm of children's literature, juvenile fiction, genre fantasy, or horror stories. At best monsters can be treated as camp or solemnly deconstructed as representing some kind of code for hegemonic marginalization of the Other. Yet we have all dreamed of monsters, really terrifying ones, and the popular imagination returns to them again and again. Science fiction, if it is intellectually substantial—and today it tends to be more so than "mainstream fiction"—can give us a respectable venue to encounter monsters, tamed by good scientific explanations, and this may be one reason why science fiction retains its imaginative vitality.

Why are monsters so important in epic? In terms of our earlier discussion of the way epic blazes a trail into the unknown, some of the answers are obvious. A monster is a confusion of categories, a challenge to the normal process by which we perceptually and cognitively identify something. A monster is in itself a statement that our world has limits and beyond them may be things that are not socially constructed or hegemonically controlled. A monster does not oppose you—it eats you, unless you kill it.[3] In other words, the threat of a monster is not defeat so much as annihilation, the reduction of one's meaning and purpose to being merely a meal for something else. Homer's Scylla and Charybdis, like the Laestrygones, are the ultimate brutal destroyers of all meaning, all narrative, all sense. The true horror of Beowulf's Grendel is that he simply grinds men up; attempts by John Gardner (in his novel *Grendel*) and Robert Zemeckis (in his recent movie *Beowulf*) to make Grendel into a moral agency, even an evil one, miss the mark. Zipacna, the monster subdued by the first pair of hero twins in the *Popol Vuh*, is clearly a phallic and sexual force, but one that has no moral meaning. He simply and literally eats the four hundred boys, a sort of shorthand for sheer empty appetite. The hero's battle with the monster is not a conflict between opposing principles or meanings, but between meaning and meaninglessness; it does not occur within the hermeneutic circle of socially constructed categories, but at its edge.

Ironically, the monster is really the perfect symbol for the sense of utter meaninglessness and social anomie that comes upon the existentialist hero in Sartre and Camus. The existentialist trope is always to suggest that all previous fears, threats, and dangers were within the cosy little essentialist world of meanings, of rewards and punishments, of transcendental signifieds that umpired and kept the grounds of the conflict—and that the truly enlightened one sees beyond all that into the basic indifference of it all. Not that I mean to suggest, as many do, that it is a gloomy credo; the gaiety of the true existentialist, knowing that it is down to him to make meaning of the world, is one of our finest recent cultural moves. But it is a move that has been made before, when Gilgamesh and Enkidu confront the utter strangeness and uncanniness of Humbaba, and when Odysseus decides to wait for Polyphemus' return instead of sensibly driving off the monster's flock and making a beeline for his ship. And in the great epics the hero does not simply accept the monstrosity of meaninglessness (as do the portraits of the painter Francis Bacon, for instance) and go off to make his own meaning elsewhere. The epic hero takes on the task of giving the monster itself a meaning—even using the occasion of the battle to articulate new categories, new semantic technologies for the benefit of the tribe.

Though the epic monster's basic challenge is to all meaning, epics take different approaches to the hero's (and epic poet's) task of wrestling the monster into some kind of linguistic or ideational cage. Grendel is identified with the descendants of Cain, and thus with the Fall. Humbaba is a nature spirit—or rather, becomes classified as a nature spirit as the hero friends fight him, dream, wake, and interpret their dreams, and fight him again. The many monsters, demons, and dragons of *The Journey to the West* are given ideational form as the desires and passions and sufferings that block the aspiring bodhisattva from enlightenment.

The dragons of the Volsungs and Nibelungs—and of *Beowulf* too—in their association with tainted gold seem to be nailed down by the meaning of avarice, the desire not to consume but to hold unused the accumulated social capital and value of the tribe. One of the oddities of the whole Nordic cycle of epic stories is that it hardly mentions the old Roman Empire at all, though it contains many historic figures such as Attila and Theodoric, who had much to do with Rome. Perhaps the dragon is the old Empire, the old legions that the epic writers' Gothic ancestors had been taught to fear, with their technology of Greek fire, their amazing treasure-chests of gold to pay the soldiers, and their military tactic of the *testudo* or tortoise, that must have looked to a victim city like a huge scaled many-legged beast. So the epic dragons are, in this interpretation, an act of linguistic control, getting to grips with the Empire's humiliating and irresistible power to reduce Germanic folkways and stories to ash. The Nordic hero gets his sword from the dragon, as the descendants of the gothic tribes got steel weapons from the Romans. Such rare Germanic victories as the defeat of Varus' legions in the Teutoburg Forest must have yielded huge troves of magically superior weapons and the contents of the bursars' and paymasters' treasuries, as well as establishing the Rhine as the permanent frontier of the Empire. But the Roman dragon's Rhinegold, when stolen from the oppressor, corrupts the old Germanic tribal and family structure, much as European weapons, trade goods, and currency corrupted the North American Plains Indian tribes.

Most often the monster is identified, in an act of heroic naming that is also a kind of magic spell, with Nature, especially human nature. Like Beowulf, Mwindo, the Bantu hero, kills a dragon as the last exploit of his adventures. But the dragon is a nature spirit, and Mwindo must do penance before he can return to his kingdom where he will rule peacefully enjoining harmony among humans and with nature. This topic deserves a chapter of its own—see "Natural Man and the Fall"—but one feature of it needs to be captured here. "This thing of darkness," says Prospero of Caliban, "I acknowledge mine." The monster could not terrify us as much if it did not dwell partly within us too. We recognize in the monster's inconsolable misery and vengeful woe our own deepest sense of utter abandonment and loneliness, our lust for something to fill our hunger for peace, our helpless rage at the arbitrary and unavoidable extinction of our existence. The monster's clawing hunger and emptiness is ours too. To be a hero is to kill that monster in ourselves—or rather, because it cannot be killed, to subjugate and bury it.

Not all traditional epics contain some kind of monster or demon that is slain by the hero. Two great exceptions are the *Heike* and *The Iliad*. But it is clear in the *Heike* that Kiyomori, the great Taira tyrant, turns in his old age into an authentic monster himself—not just a moral monster, but a physical one:

> His body was fiery hot; people could hardly bear to remain within twenty-five or thirty feet of the bed. His only words were, "Hot! Hot!" It seemed no ordinary ailment.
>
> The mansion's people filled a stone tub with water drawn from the Thousand-Armed Well on Mount Hiei, but the water boiled up and turned to steam as soon as Kiyomori got in to cool off. Desperate to bring him some relief, they directed a stream of water onto his body from a bamboo pipe, but the liquid spattered away without reaching him, as though from red-hot stone or iron. The few drops that struck him burst into flame, so that black smoke filled the hall and tongues of fire swirled toward the ceiling.[4]

In his wife's dream about his death, Kiyomori is met by terrible ox-faced and horse-faced figures, who carry him off to hell. Achilles, too, could well be said to become a monster in his *menis*, his demonic rage after the death of Patroclus. His treatment of the body of Hector is of the same kind as Polyphemus' treatment of Odysseus' men in the cave; the monster is that which reduces the human body to a mere thing, bereft of its sacramental meaning and ideational significance. Achilles' desecration of the corpse is not the same as ritual human sacrifice, which honors the victim; it is a truly monstrous action. The sacred act of Priam's journey to the Achilles' camp is among other things a shamanic exorcism of Achilles, a demonstering of him. Priam is the monster-slayer.

War epics like *The Iliad*, the *Heike*, and *The Song of Roland* do not seem to need literal monsters—war itself and the insane passion of war serve some of the same purposes. But already this analysis has begun to reduce the dreadful literalness, the physicality of the monster to moral and psychological categories. Epic composers in traditions that already possess canonical epics with monsters that have since been named and given a place in the linguistic universe must face a difficult decision—whether to include literal monsters or not. Virgil includes them, but his Aeneas prudently and sensibly avoids them when he can; the harpies, of which he was not forewarned, are a nuisance at the picnic compared to the full-blooded monsters of old. Virgil unleashes his bestiary in the land of the dead, however, and in the account Evander gives of Hercules' slaying of Cacus. In these contexts, the monsters' naïve and brutal literalism is softened by literary significance—the monsters are symbolic of sins or dangers that must be recognized and subjugated by the hero.

Virgil's allegorizing of the monsters is taken up and developed by Dante, Spenser, and Milton, all of whom knew imaginatively that there is no substitute for a good monster but must square this feeling with the danger of sounding childish or unintentionally comic to their sophisticated urban readers. But an allegorized monster has lost much of its power to terrify. This was the risk that Spenser and Milton ran in allegorizing the monster into Error and Sin; it is only their astonishing powers of sensory description, the disgusting and nightmarish details that save them. The comic and cartoon-like element of the monster is admitted, but subsumed into a kind of nightmarish grotesqueness. Perhaps the English writers learned this use of the graphic and gross from Dante, whose hellish demons are so very real, while also rather horribly funny.

William Blake's attempt to revive the monsters was largely ignored in his time. By the time we get to such epic writers as Wordsworth and

Eliot, the monsters have almost disappeared (though bats with baby faces make a brief appearance in *The Waste Land*). Herman Melville was evidently impatient with decadent old-world sophistication, and gives his American readers a very real and graphic monster of their own, one of the finest in any epic tradition—the White Whale. The problem of how to make the whale significant without reducing him to an emblematic label is brilliantly solved by giving him a wild excess of significances; his ghastly all-colored whiteness, since it means everything, also means nothing, and we are back to the ancient terror of not being able to specify or identify the monster. Future epics will perhaps find their own way back to the dragon's den; contemporary genres such as sword-and-sorcery fantasy fiction, Dungeons & Dragons, and science fiction attest to the continued imaginative validity of its inmates.

Magical Helpers, Weapons, Potions, and Talismans

Epic borrows from fairy tale many of the appurtenances of the heroic quest: magical helpers, magical weapons, tests or trials, potions and elixirs, and talismans.

Friendly magicians, divine mentors, gifted companions, hermit guides, faithful animal mounts, or familiars must be won to the hero's service by generosity, humility, mercy, or courage. These magical helpers seem to exemplify and externalize the mysterious and miraculous abilities and powers we inherited from our evolution, that we now regard as genius—the abilities that can make a person a great pianist or lover or aerodynamic engineer, though she or he may be genetically identical to a cro-magnon cave dweller. The shiftless and goofy young Aladdin finds in a cave the old lamp that contains a magical helper—as every young human (if you are lucky or even have a wicked uncle who wants to exploit your talents) finds his or her special gift some time in childhood or adolescence. Monkey is a magical helper who has become a novice hero in his own right. Helped by Mentor, Telemachus finds his own genius on his journey in search of his father. A hero must often find and saddle his miraculous horse—Sohrab's Raksh, Cuchulainn's Liath Macha, Roland's Veillantif, King Gesar's Kyang Go Karkar, Gawaine's Gringolet, Achilles' Xanthos, David of Sassoun's Dzelali, Prijezdra's Zhdral, El Cid's Babieca. Again, the idea is mastery over a free and donated power that might otherwise be dangerous if untrained.

Likewise, in epic stories fairy-tale-like potions and elixirs are consumed, sometimes conferring invulnerability or even immortality, as with Gilgamesh's herb of rejuvenation, Odysseus' moly, or Monkey's magic peaches in *The Journey to the West*. But sometimes too there are dreadful unintended results, like the destruction of Sigurd/Siegfried, Tristan, and the *Popol Vuh*'s four hundred boys after they are rendered helpless by intoxication. The "gift" is too often the German *Gift*, poison. The original elixir in the Judeo-Christian tradition is of course the forbidden fruit, "whose mortal taste/Brought Death into the world, and all our woe." Potions and magical foods are very important in stories of the Fall, which is a central element in epic, and which we will look at more closely in another chapter.

In epic as in fairy tales, swords must be plucked from stones, ancestral bows must be bent and claimed, shields must be forged by divine smiths for the hero's protection. Sundiata discovers his own powers when an iron bar is forged for him. Such weapons, like the helpers, also symbolize our amazing common human inheritance, but it is as if the hero re-enacts the evolutionary moment when our species was singled out as the recipient of these miraculous gifts—they are both shared with all humans and at the same time part of the hero's electness, like the strange circumstances of his birth.

One of the fundamental abilities that made us human is the hand with its opposable thumb. Once we can hold a stick—can turn our arm into a disposable probe, weapon, or manipulator—we can begin to deal with the world at a distance. At the same time, we transfer some of our own agency and will to a part of the physical world, but do it with impunity, leaving the spear in the tiger's jaws and beating a prudent retreat if necessary. The spear, the sword, the halberd, the bow, and the shepherd's crook are all extensions of this gift. Adding further significances we get the scepter, the thyrsis, the ceremonial mace, the ritual phallus, the crozier, and the crucifix. Add a sound-box and strings or an air-passage with stops or a drumhead, and we get the instruments of song and storytelling. As this process continues, staff into weapon into symbolic mediator, the talisman emerges, the object in which the hero's powers are vested.

The epic hero is usually equipped with some such implement. Many heroes have named swords: Durendal, Excalibur, Tizona, Caladbolg, Gram, Hrunting, Joyeuse, Kusanagi, Naegling. Monkey has his magic iron staff, as does Sundiata. Mwindo has his magic flyswatter, Arjuna his great bow Gandiva, Martín Fierro and Rostam their lariats, the

Kyrgyz Manas his handgun Kelte, King Gesar his whip, Hunahpu and Xbalanque their blowpipes, Karna his discus Sudarsana, and Ahab his lance. Among many epic talismans, the most important of all is the one that enables the hero to enter alive the realm of the dead and return unscathed: discussion of this talisman will also be saved for a later chapter, on the underworld journey. For now the point of indicating these many fairy-tale elements in the epic quest—magical helpers, magic weapons, potions, talismans, etc.—is that they have the characteristics of elements of a game, as Dungeons & Dragons game designers recognized at once.

Games, Rituals, and Trials

The epic quest often pivots around a game. In *The Cattle Raid of Cooley* it is the old Irish sport of Hurley, where Cuchulainn is first recognized. In the *Mahabharata*, the whole action stems from Yudhisthira's unwise game of dice with Duryodhana (who is playing with magic dice). So too the *Popol Vuh*, in which the central action concerns the ball games between the two sets of hero twins and the Lords of the Dead. In the *Shahnameh*, the last great era of Persian glory is the reign of Kesra Nushin-Ravan, epitomized by the invention by the wise sage Bozorjmehr of the game of Nard (thought to be an early version of Backgammon), and the successful mastering of the Indian game of chess, much to the discomfiture of the Indian Brahmins. Odysseus proves his worthiness of aid to the Phaiakians by his prowess at the discus during their ceremonial games. Aeneas' funeral games for Anchises preface and ritually permit the first entry of the Trojans into Italy, their future home. In Shakespeare's *Henry IV*, Part 1, the competitive role-playing game between Prince Hal and Falstaff in the Boar's head tavern summarizes, foretells, and explains the significance of the whole action of the epic tetralogy: what is going on is a symbolic revolution, a patricidal and regicidal sacrifice, in which Falstaff is substituted for the usurping Henry IV as the sacrificial victim. Sundiata, the Malinese hero, is a strong Oware player. Poetic games, in which the participants cap each other's verses with further allusions and images, are fundamental to the *Heike.* The Kyrgyz hero Manas first cements his youthful rebel army against the oppressive Uighurs by staging horse-games for them. The battle between the Bull of Heaven and the hero friends in *Gilgamesh* is very likely the mythic origin of the sport of bullfighting as it developed later in Crete and Spain. The horse-fight match in *Njal's Saga* is the start of the tragic

111

feud between Gunnar and his enemies that envelops also Njal and his sons. Examples could be further multiplied.

Why should this most serious of genres, epic, find itself drawn again and again to the very epitome of the unserious, the game? The answer to this question requires a further look at the grand theme of epic itself as we have seen it emerge from the comparative perspective. One immediate value to the storyteller of having the hero voluntarily participate in a game, especially a lethal one, is to illustrate the hero's insouciance, his carelessness of gain or loss, his insensitivity to risk, and his magnanimity of spirit. If even in a game his contentiousness and aspiration to excellence is untainted by considerations of prudence, we the hearers or readers of the story know that he will be unbroken by a more weighty struggle with higher stakes. The old Greek legend of the city that invented games during a siege, so that the citizens, addicted to game-playing, forgot their hunger and were able to hold out until the siege was lifted, may also aid our understanding. Our ability to play games, to invent other worlds of endeavor and alternate realities, enables us to rise above our existential wants and drives. *Homo sapiens* is *Homo ludens*, as Johan Huizinga argued so well.[5]

Ritual behavior is itself gamelike, in that its actions and motivations have separated themselves from any immediate existential drive or need, or rather, new virtual drives and needs have emerged from the dynamic structure of the ritual game itself. Our evolution as a species, featuring the astonishing hypertrophy of the cerebral cortex, is being explained by anthropologists as having been driven by the emergence of just such virtual realities.[6] The crucial point is that there is a peculiar overlap between the last phases of human biological evolution and the beginnings of human cultural evolution, an overlap of one to five million years, depending on how the terms are defined. In any case, there was a long period during which human culture could exert a powerful, indeed dominant, selective pressure upon the genetic material of the species and thus upon the final form it has taken (if ours is the final form).

For over a million years, the major genetic determinant in the environment of our genus was our own culture. A living organism that is living under cultural constraints is an organism that is undergoing an intensive process of domestication. Consider wheat, dogs, apple trees, pigeons: how swiftly and how dramatically they have been changed by human selective breeding! But we domesticated ourselves. There is a limestone cave near Zhoukoudian in northern China where human beings lived almost continuously for close to a quarter of a million years.[7] It is filled almost to the roof with eighteen feet of compacted human debris—ash, bedplaces, bones. At the bottom, the oldest layers contain great hamhanded hammerstones, cutting clubs with a shard knocked off for a blade, and the clumsy bones and skulls of *Homo erectus.* At the top, there are delicate leafshaped flint arrowheads, fine awls and augers, featherlike knives; and human jawbones made elegant by cookery, braincases made ample and capacious by ritual.

Imagine—and we hardly need to imagine this, for we have so many examples in our experience, if we could only see them as examples—a mating ritual, which directly affects the reproductive success of the individuals within a species. Those who are neurologically capable and adept at the complex nuances of the ritual would have a much better chance of getting a mate and leaving offspring. Now imagine that this ritual is being handed down from generation to generation not just by genetic inheritance, but also, increasingly, by cultural transmission: imitation, instruction, and eventually language (did it evolve in order to facilitate this transmission?).

If a behavior is handed down purely by genetic inheritance, any variations on it which result from individual differences and special environmental and social circumstances will be wiped out by the death of the individuals of a given generation and will not be transmitted to their offspring. Of course if over thousands of years those individual differences lead to improved rates of survival, and if those special circumstances persist, then there may be a selective advantage in the behavior as modified by the variation, and that variation will become frozen into the genes. But this is a very slow process: the learning is being done at the genetic level, not at the social or mental level.

But in the thought-experiment that we have commenced, changes in the ritual can be handed down very quickly, in only one generation; and so the faster system of transmission will tend to drive and direct the slower system of transmission. That is, cultural modifications in the ritual will tend to confer a decisive selective advantage upon those members of the species that are genetically endowed with greater neural complexity, a superior capacity for learning the inner principles of the ritual which remain the same when its surface changes, for following and extending the ritual's subtleties, and for recognizing and embodying the values that the ritual creates. Cultural evolution will drive biological evolution. This species, of course, is ourselves: perhaps what created us as human beings was an improved love song. In the beginning, indeed, was the word.

Once upon a time, then, there was a clever race of apes. Like many other species of higher animals, they possessed a sophisticated though instinctual system of vocal communication; they engaged in play activity when unoccupied; they possessed elaborate instinctual rituals, especially surrounding the functions of reproduction; their ranking system promoted wide variations in reproductive success; and they possessed a large stock of possible epigenetic variation (gene combinations now silent but capable of large systemic changes in the organism when activated by a master-gene). Like other higher primates they used rudimentary tools and passed their use down to the next generation by instruction as well as by genetic inheritance—and tool use can change environmental constraints quite quickly, requiring rapid adaptation.

It took only one individual to combine these capacities and environmental stimuli in such a way that the word became incarnate as a seed of culture and began to mold its host species into a suitable soil for it to flourish in. The competition for mates was intense, a competition which in other species had evolved structures as impractical as the antlers of the giant elk and the feathers of the peacock, and behaviors as contrary to survival as the mating dance of March hares or the courtship of the blue satin bowerbird. At the same time, the border between play behavior and mating behavior was paper-thin. Perhaps new sets of formerly silent genes were turned on. One individual, then, discovered that the desired mate responded favorably to playlike variation in the instinctual mating ritual.

This first pair was imitated by others, and those that did so achieved greater reproductive success. They were in turn imitated by their young, which had inherited a slightly improved capacity to alter their ritual inheritance by playlike variation on it. This contrast between inherited norm and playlike variation will be preserved later in the general information processing system of human beings, where a regular carrier wave is systematically distorted to carry meaning. We find it, for instance, where a regular poetic meter is tensed against the rhythm of the spoken sentence, or musical meter is stretched or compacted by rubato, or even where visual symmetry is partly broken by the pleasing proportions of the golden section.

Thus was born what we might call the Freedom and Dignity Game; as it became elaborated, it developed vocal forms that had at the time no referents: Honor, Soul, Purpose, Good, Love, the Future, Freedom, Dignity, the Gods, and so on. But those vocal forms were performative utterances, and so for the performative community of the tribe those mysterious entities actually came into existence, in the fashion that the knight's move in chess came into being by fiat. As if they were real all along, those abstract entities became independent sources of active determination, even though the medium of their being and of their continuity was no more than a communal convention. But after all, our bodily structures are maintained as realities not by themselves but by a mere arrangement of genes.

The ritual game indeed rapidly evolved. It developed cells of active reflexivity and self-criticism, such as rehearsal, schooling, debate, and satire. Each generation altered it competitively, introducing new complexities: kinship classification, decorative art, food taboos, hygiene, household conventions, law, storytelling, and all the rest. And in turn these complexities exerted irresistible selective pressure upon those wise apes. They developed an adolescence, with special hormones to promote rebellion against the traditional ritual. Infancy was protracted, to help develop and program the huge brain that was required to handle the complexities of the ritual, and lifespan was prolonged to accommodate the extra programming-time. A massive sexualization took place in the species, so that male and female were continuously in heat, females experienced orgasm like males, and they copulated face to face, thus transforming sex into a form of communication. The reward system of the brain was recalibrated to respond most powerfully to beauty, which is the quality that characterizes the ritual's dynamic relationship of stability and increasing coherent complexity. Body decoration and clothing banished body hair. The hands turned into expressive instruments. The otolaryngeal system was elaborated into an exquisitely sensitive medium of communication and expression. The two sides of the brain became specialized, one for recognizing and holding an existing context in place, the other for acting upon it and transforming it in time. The indeterminacy of the world was lumped together into a new concept, the Future, which was carried by the dissonance between right brain pattern and left brain sequence. The Present was born, as the realm of the Act. The epic quest is the narrative and symbolic form in which this process is reviewed and reenacted.

As in fairy tales, the epic hero must often endure a trial or series of trials—usually three. The whole of the *Popol Vuh* can be seen as the story of such a set of tests, since the initial premise of the work is the first gods' attempt to find out whether their various attempts to make a true human being with a real mind have been successful. Prince Hal must pass a series of tests, as must Parzifal, Odysseus, Dante, Rama, the Pandavas, not to speak of the heroes of the Pentateuch. Frequently, the trial is to test the worthiness of the hero to take his bride, that is, to become a father of his people; a mythological way of explaining what Darwin was later to call sexual selection in the evolution of the species.

Arjuna wins Draupadi by being the only suitor in an archery competition to pierce the eye of a rotating wooden fish by looking at its reflection in a tub of water. The anger of Duryodhana at having failed the test, and Karna at not being permitted to take it, is the beginning of the tragedy of the poem. Achilles wins Briseis in a kind of marriage-test, in which instead of satisfying the demands of the bride's father and brothers, he kills them, in the assault on Lymessus (as Lord William does in the mini-epic border ballad, "The Douglas Tragedy"). It is Agamemnon's confiscation of Achilles' prize that arouses the wrath of the hero and propels the action of the story. Odysseus, in an interesting retroactive reversal of the usual pattern that preserves its essential meaning, must prove on his return from the dead his worthiness to be Penelope's husband and Telemachus' father by proving himself to be himself in three tests. The first is that of the scar, the second—much like Arjuna's—is the archery contest, and the third is the riddle of the immovable marriage-bed that is a rooted olive-tree, itself a symbol of marriage, the family tree. In many epic stories (paradigmatically those of the Volsungs and Nibelungs), the marriage test implies a latent or overt tension with the hero's in-laws, so that the stuff of epic becomes a struggle between blood kin and affines, genetic insiders and outsiders. This struggle is well known to anthropologists, who observe ritualized abduction of the bride in many cultures, including our own; exogamy is one of the key social structures defining the human species, and the subject will require a chapter of its own.

One further reason for the presence of games in epic is the reminder that game-playing gives us that there might be a boundary to our own world-system, our own language, our own game-rules, beyond which might lie monsters or treasures. We might find the natural world we left when we joined the game; or the supernatural world of which we are one of its entertainments, like that of the gods of Olympus. If we recognize the absorption in an artificial world we feel when we play a game as analogous to the absorption we feel in ordinary life, the obvious conclusion is that ordinary life might also be a game—that we are living a play within a play. The epic quest, led by the epic hero, is to explore the borderlands of that reality, and even, like the Persian hero Bozorjmehr, to invent a new game (backgammon).

The Battle

The epic quest involves a great battle, which is either the climactic episode of the work or its entire substance. Every epic contains such a battle, even if, as in the Tamil *Silippathikaram*, the central figure is a woman and the intent of the poet is Jain nonviolence. Examples in the tradition could be multiplied—Troy, Roncesvalles, Kurukshetra, Kossovo, Sziget, Agincourt, the Alamo; the epic battles are part of world consciousness. The scenes of the indoor fights are no less deeply engraved in our cultural memory: the halls of Odysseus, of Attila, of Hrothgar, of Njal, the ballcourt of Xibalba.

Even modern epics, in which battles as such are usually avoided, have some major war in their background. Wordsworth's *The Prelude* contains the French Revolution and the Napoleonic wars. *The Waste Land* happens in the shadow of the First World War; Pound's *Cantos* cannot be detached from the Second. Walcott's *Omeros*, in addition to the fishermen's conflicts implicit in the names of his characters, Achille, Philoctete, Helen, and Hector, refers back to the battle of Les Saintes between Dutch and British naval forces that determined the colonial fate of St. Lucia. *Paterson*, William Carlos Williams' epic poem, centers upon the Paterson Silk Strike of 1913. *Davenport's Version*, John Gery's American Civil War epic, echoes the story of Troilus and Cressida from the siege of Troy; the sexual conquest of Bressie, his fickle Confederate heroine, by Davenport, a Federal officer, is paralleled with the breaking of the great boom across the Mississippi by the naval forces of Admiral Farragut.

The epic genre, then, recognizes war as a terrible human achievement as universal as tonal music or visual portraiture or cookery, as the tragedy that haunts all human social existence and at the same time shapes our genetic and cultural inheritance. Evolutionary scenarios that attempt to explain the origins of human cooperativeness are impossible without the postulate of war. Just as cooperative hunting—which is interspecies warfare—bred animals that could develop advanced forms of communication and form bonds of loyalty and friendship, so too the intraspecies violence of war breeds important human virtues.

Sociality, goodness itself, can only emerge as a possible behavior with emotional fuel if cooperative genes can survive and reproduce better within groups than non-cooperative genes can survive and reproduce within individuals. Only if group survival significantly trumps individual survival, if we pass more of our genes on to the future by loyally cooperating with our kin and friends than by defecting, and only if groups are in direct and existential competition with one another, can the virtues of altruism, self-sacrifice, and fidelity be selected for, inherited, and receive a genetic base. If we consider the endings of, for instance, *The Song of the Nibelungs*, *The Iliad*, the *Heike*, *Njal's Saga*, and the *Mahabharata*, one of epic's central tasks is to face and understand and finally defeat this beautiful and horrible engine of our transformation into *Homo sapiens*.

W. P. Ker's rather martial characterization of epic as necessarily including the defense of a narrow place against odds may itself be too narrow, but it is certainly an important feature of many epics. Last stands are among the most memorable epic moments—consider the Nibelungs besieged in Attila's hall, Gunnar and the sons of Njal defending their homes, Hector's defense of Troy, Odysseus facing the suitors in his hall in Ithaca, the besieged Trojan camp on the banks of the Tiber, the last stand of the warrior-monks at the great temple of Miidera whose burning precipitates the civil war in the *Heike*, the siege of Jerusalem, the embattled rearguard of Charlemagne's army at Roncesvalles, and the Quiché defense of their mountain fastness of Hacauitz against the combined tribes of their enemies.

The special significance of the "cornered rat" defense tale is revealed when we reflect that the human right of property is based upon the natural territoriality of our animal predecessors and relatives, the biologically universal rule that first possession confers and should confer a decisive advantage for any living organism. Without property, human life, which is irreducibly social, economic, and technological, is impossible. Game theory implies clearly that in cases where unnecessary conflict and loss can be avoided without cost by a simple rule (like driving on the right, for instance), such a rule will emerge in a breeding population. Since territory is most useful to the organism that has the longest experience of its potential, the rule of first possession is better than a rule ceding possession to the first newcomer, and much better than no rule at all, leading to endless destructive conflict. In advanced animals, a huge boost in hormonal and endocrine stimulation is available to any individual on its home territory, so a smaller and weaker animal can often drive a larger and stronger one away from its nesting-place. The special pathos of the "last stand," especially if it fails and the defenders are slain, is that some deep and ancient natural moral rule seems to be threatened or violated. The hero as either besieger or besieged again stands at the edge of the human world, where it abuts upon the realm of the animals, and where the most raw and terrible emotions are found.

The Hero's Death or Return

An "open form" in any art seems to imply freedom, but it can be a way of claiming territory, of appropriating content and relevance from other possible works of art. If an artwork has no clear edge, no place where it stops and something else can begin, it has preempted the cradle of new birth. If the old never finish their trajectory of life and die, the young languish forever in their shadow. The open forms of aesthetic revolution take the oxygen of new creation out of the space of its artform, as political revolution often claims for itself all significant change and frustrates or suppresses further evolution.

One of the generous features of epic is that it comes to decisive closure. It signs off, it passes the baton onwards. It is a closed form that opens up the world to its successors—and perhaps this is why epic seems to be such an enduring genre, returning again and again with infinite variations, limited only by the huge demands of genius required for its composition. This feature of epic is not just a formal or literary characteristic, but a basic and literal element of content and plot. Epics come to a decisive end. They have satisfying dénouements.

We have explored the way heroes venture to the edge of the human world, and with the help of their blaze, or *chinjikijilu*, pass beyond it. This journey does, in epic, come to an end, and that end is one of two kinds. Either the hero dies, or he returns alive, bearing the fitting gift for his culture and homeland. In either case, there is closure. If the hero dies—the tragic epic of Achilles, Siegfried, Cuchulainn, Enkidu, Roland, Noritsune, Zrini (of *The Peril of Sziget*), Duryodhana (for Duryodhana *is* a hero), Ahab, Beowulf, Njal—then there will always be someone to bring back the great story from the edge of the world to be a monument and final capstone, the epic itself. "And I only am escaped alone to tell thee," says Melville's Ishmael, quoting the Book of Job; words that are almost echoes of Sanjaya's to King Dhrita-Rashtra, telling of the defeat of his sons, or Odysseus' tale of the tragic siege of Troy, or Kari's, reporting the last moments of Skarpheddin in the burning house at Bergthorsknoll, or Wiglaf, telling the saga of Beowulf's fight with the dragon, or Gilgamesh, recounting his adventures with Enkidu to the boatman Urshanabi. If the hero survives—the comic epic of the messenger-heroes Odysseus, Gilgamesh, Kari, of Parzifal, Rama, Sundiata, Tripitaka, Aeneas, Henry V—they themselves carry back the precious secrets from the dark and the tale of how those secrets were found.

The quest *ends*. And this is perhaps the crucial element of the quest that makes it epic itself. In ending it points to the possibility of something new that comes next, but which is left up to another generation, equipped now with the knowledge gained on the last foray into the inarticulate.

Notes

1. L. L. Cavalli-Sforza, Paolo Menozzi, and Alberto Piazza, *The History and Geography of Human Genes* (Princeton, NJ: Princeton University Press, 1994).
2. E.g., Victor W. Turner, *Schism and Continuity in an African Society* (Oxford: Berg Publishers, 1996).
3. Paul Trout, in *Deadly Powers: Animal Predators and the Mythic Imagination* (Amherst, NY: Prometheus Books, 2011), makes the telling point that real predators were a major threat and terror to all members of our species through most of its evolutionary history, and is some places still are. "Sometimes," Freud is reputed to have said as he blew out the smoke, "a cigar is just a cigar." Sometimes a monstrous predator is not a symbol of social evil, but a monstrous predator.
4. McCullough, 209. Compare the almost identical hosing-down of the incandescent Cuchulainn, *The Cattle Raid of Cooley* (Charleston, SC: Forgotten Books, 2007), 66.
5. Johan Huizinga, *Homo ludens; a Study of the Play-Element in Culture* (Boston, MA: Beacon Press).
6. E.g., Gerhard Roth and Ursula Dicke, "Evolution and Intelligence," *Trends in Cognitive Sciences* 9, no. 5 (May 2005).
7. *Paleoanthropological Sites: Zhoukoudian, Blombos Cave, Koobi Fora, Sibudu Cave, Pestera Cu Oase, Atapuerca Mountains, Olduvai Gorge, Qesem Cave.* Books LLC..

5

Kinship Troubles

Kinship in Evolution

Anthropologists (notably Robin Fox[1]) are coming to recognize that the emergence of the human kinship system may be as responsible as any physiological mutation for the evolution of *Homo sapiens*. Or perhaps one should say that it is the *suite* of possible kinship systems generated by certain unique features in the timing of development and growth that drove the emergence of modern humans. In order to understand how a social feature of human life like a kinship system could be a cause, not just a result, of human physical nature, we must look more closely at human evolution itself and the very complex feedbacks that underlie it. We have already mentioned the overlap between cultural and biological evolution; to grasp the importance of kinship in epic we need to examine some of the implications of that overlap.

Many of the peculiar characteristics of the human body can be explained by a runaway feedback between human culture and human genetics: its upright stance, its long infancy, its developed vocal chords and otolaryngeal system, its extraordinary longevity (especially in the female), its relatively early menopause, its relative lack of specialized armaments—big teeth and claws, and so on—its opposable thumbs, its superbly refined and coordinated fine motor system, its continuous sexual readiness (most animals are in heat only for a few days in the year), its huge brain.

The upright stance reveals the full beauty of human primary and secondary sexual organs to each other; it enables hunters and gatherers to carry meat and vegetables home, and therefore to have to remember who gets which share; thus it also helps us to have a home to carry things home to, and thus a ritually charged place, and a kinship system that can serve as a set of rules for who gets which share; and it enables parents to carry babies in their arms who are helpless

121

because they require a much longer infancy period than the young of other species, a long infancy demanded by the need to program children in the complexities of the tribal ritual. The upright stance also changed the normal mating position from mounting to face-to-face, thus encouraging that extraordinary mutual gaze which is the delight of lovers and the fundamental warrant of the psychological equality of the sexes: an equality which was absolutely essential if the human traits of intelligence, communication, and imagination were to be preferred and thus reinforced.

Our ritual songs, improved every year, demanded complex voice-production systems that could also come in useful for communication in the hunt and other cooperative enterprises. Our long old age enabled the elders—especially the postmenopausal wise women—to pass on the ritual lore and wisdom. Our lack of bodily armament was compensated for by the development of weapons, which could be wielded by thumbed hands liberated by our upright stance and controlled by an advanced fine motor system—thumbed hands required to enact the ritual actions and paint on the ritual body-paint and carry the ritual objects and make the ritual clothing and gather the fruits and seeds and roots for our tribal kin. Sexuality was extended and intensified relatively to other animals, and was adapted from its original reproductive function into the raw material of an elaborate ritual drama that pervaded all aspects of society.

And the great cortex mushroomed out, transforming its substructures to the new uses and demands that were being placed on it, pushing out the skull, diminishing the jaws, wiring itself more and more finely into the face, hands, and speech organs, specializing particular areas of the right and left to handle new linguistic, musical, and pictorial-representational tasks, developing a huge frontal lobe to coordinate everything else and to reflect upon itself and its body and its death, and connecting that higher-level reflective consciousness by massive nerve bundles to the limbic emotional centers—thus creating a unity of function between the intellectual and the passionate that is close to the heart of our deepest shame and which has thus been denied by most of our philosophical systems. And as the skull expands and the jaws contract, cookery becomes necessary to soften the food that can no longer be ground by huge molars driven by powerful muscles and robust bones.

From this point of view, personal physical beauty takes on a new importance. Breeders of dogs and horses can tell by very subtle physical signs, in the carriage of the head, the set of the eye, the delicacy of proportion, whether the animal is likely to possess psychological characteristics such as intelligence, heart, and concentration. The intangible elements of human beauty—beyond those obviously related to reproductive and survival success, such as big breasts and hips, clear skin, broad shoulders, straight legs—are evidently such external bodily signs of internal neural sophistication. Those intangible elements that we refer to when we say that someone has beautiful eyes or a beautiful expression, or that we are captured by someone's way of moving—the things that make us watch a great film star—can be quite different from conventional beauty. They can quickly overwhelm any deficiency in the brute appeal of the hunk, the nice piece of ass, beefcake, or cheesecake. The lovely ambiguity in the word "grace"—divine favor, and excellence in physical coordination—nicely catches this other quality; though in the context of the darker price of human excellence it is significant that grace is also a purifying blessing (from Old English "blissian," to wound or make bleed) before meals. When we fall in love, and thus mate and have offspring, we do so often because we are captured by such qualities. Thus we look the way we look as a species, largely because that was the way our ancestors thought intelligent, strong, loving, and imaginative—ritual-ready—animals ought to look. We are the monument to our progenitors' taste.

Many of our creation myths show an intuitive grasp of the strange process by which the cultural tail came to wag the biological dog. The story of the clothing of Adam and Eve, where (the awareness of) nakedness is the result of shame, which is in turn the result of self-knowledge, expresses one aspect of it: we are hairless because we have clothes and clothed because our human stance presents our genitals to each other. Again in Genesis the punishment of Eve for her acquisition of knowledge, that she must suffer in childbirth, nicely expresses the fact that one of the parameters of a big-brained viviparous species like ourselves is the capacity of the female pelvis to allow the passage of a large skull. Hence also the beauty for the male of the female's wide hips and the motion they make when walking. The big (and to the male, attractive) breasts of the human female, and her dependency upon a protecting male during lactation—also referred to in Genesis—are likewise the sign of a nurturing power that can deal with a long infant dependency, and thus produce human beings of intelligence, wisdom, and esthetic subtlety. Babies without protecting fathers must enter adulthood earlier, and cannot be fully instructed in the tribal ritual; they thus need smaller brains, and smaller-hipped and -breasted mothers to bear them.

Our deep feelings of embarrassment and anger at these facts, the flush that rises to our faces when we think of our own biology, are the signs of that shame which we would deny but whose acceptance is the only gate to beauty. That beauty is summed up in the great pictorial genre of the Madonna and child. At present this tragic contradiction makes itself felt in our society by a conflict between female roles—of a nurturing that produces the best and noblest and most loving human intelligence, and of the very exercise of that intelligence. The means and the end of nurturance are thus perceived as opposed in our society. But we should not deceive ourselves that if this problem were solved, the solution itself would not produce its own contradictions even more tragic and shameful, and even more potentially beautiful.

If the human ritual, as we have envisaged it, was to have its original evolutionary function, it must have involved a dark and terrible element. For if some members of the tribe enjoyed greater reproductive success, others must have enjoyed less. If some were selected as preferred mates for their intelligence, wit, loving nature, prudence, magnanimity, honesty, courage, depth, sanguine disposition, foresight, empathy, physical health, beauty, grace, and strength; others—the dullards, whiners, liars, blowhards, hoarders, spendthrifts, thieves, cheats, and weaklings—must be rejected. The most brutal throwbacks—the rapists, those who grabbed the food and did not share it, those who could not follow the subtle turns of the ritual and internalize the values that it invented and implied—would be cast out from the tribal cave, into the outer darkness, where there is wailing and gnashing of teeth. Defective infants would be abandoned on the mountainside; adults polluted by impiety, crime, incest, madness, disease, or their own exercise of witchcraft would be led to the borders of the village lands and expelled. Oedipus, who was exposed though not defective at birth, is among other things a symbol of our guilt at such rejection: when he does return, as all buried shames must, he pollutes the city with his unconscious incest. The Old English monster Grendel, that wanderer of the borderlands, the descendant of Cain, is another type of such outcasts, and the image of the scapegoat.

But indeed, the fragile virtues of the human race would have been impossible without this terrible and most shameful selection process. If we consider how morally imperfect we are as it is, and how the best and most recent research shows that moral traits are to a considerable extent inherited, it may be a grim satisfaction to reflect how much worse we would be if we had not selected ourselves for love and goodness.[2] Abraham's willingness to sacrifice his son Isaac at the command of the Lord (whom we may take, for mythic purposes, to be the evolutionary imperative of the human species, the strange attractor drawing it into being) is necessary, paradoxically, to bring about a more just and loving humanity. We had better be worth the price.

Indeed our moral growth has, more recently, caused us to recoil in revulsion from those ancient practices; but that growth was partly their result. And the process has not ceased, and we had better face up to the fact. Every time a woman chooses a man to be her husband and the father of her children, for any good personal reason—for his gentleness, honesty and wit, his confident strength and his decent humility—she is selecting against some other man less noble in character, and either helping to condemn him to the nonentity of childlessness or to be the parent, with some less morally perceptive woman, of children who are likely to inherit their parents' disadvantages. It is horribly cruel and shameful, if we think about it, but I believe there is a strange and terrible beauty to the magnitude of the mating choice, that is at the root of the troubled exaltation we sometimes feel at a good wedding.

The basic foundations of human kinship can be divided into two types: those that we inherited from our primate, mammalian, vertebrate, animal ancestors, and those that are peculiar to the human lineage. The first can be summarized in J. B. S. Haldane's comment: "Would I lay down my life to save my brother? No, but I would to save two brothers or eight cousins." Genes, says Richard Dawkins, are "selfish" and "try" to perpetuate themselves. Being structures of matter rather than matter in themselves (a copy of a gene is the same gene), it does not matter to them what particular copies survive, as long as more survive in each generation than die. No motivations such as are implied by the metaphors "selfish" and "try" are actually involved at this level; the survivors are simply the ones that survived, and whatever caused them to survive in their own structure and behavior is preserved by their survival when other structures and behaviors are not.

This "selfishness" leads, of course, to astonishing altruism among animals. A multicellular organism can be seen as a group of animals or plants that are totally cooperative (except when cancerous) because genetically identical; colonial animals like polyps can exist either as individuals or as totally altruistic members of a group. Worker bees that slave for the queen die childless because their genes are multiplied by their queen; meerkat sentries risk their own lives in warning their kin-group of a predator's approach; almost any mammal mother recklessly sacrifices herself for her young. At the mammalian level emotions and motivations—and even what we might well call the primitive form of values and qualities—are indeed involved. But their microstructure is passionless genes that survive by specifying proteins that happen to generate hormones and neurotransmitters that drive the emotions and behaviors of the huge community of cells where the genes live. In the most advanced social animals, sophisticated sensors and action capacities are developed to recognize kinship, to signal it to others and bond with them so that the appropriate sacrifice is made, and the two "brothers" do not turn out in reality to be two cousins, containing only one-fourth of one's own genes, or two strangers. These behaviors, perceptual and cognitive abilities, motivations, and emotions are studied by biologists under the term "inclusive fitness."

This picture has been much complicated of late by the analysis of a wide range of types of cooperative behavior, resembling trading and markets, that do not rely on degrees of kinship and can happen between widely divergent species—symbiosis and commensality being the most obvious. Ecology is a whole science of its own, studying the cooperative preservation of ecological niches by their members, which can include not only animals but plants, fungi, bacteria, and viruses that have almost no genetic stake in each other. An ecosystem such as a wetland or forest is an extended form of inclusive fitness. More complications of the simple genes-determine-behavior model have arisen, often not recognized by hard-line genetic determinists. Development and maturation are now seen not so much as the enactment of a genetic blueprint, but as the selection by the individual on the basis of experience of a sequence of branches offered by a highly varied menu of choices, occasioned by environmental conditions and permitted by a genome replete with alternative behavioral strategies. Epigenetics, the science that studies the activation and deactivation of whole sets of genes by master-genes responsive to environmental contingencies, has shown how a pseudo-Lamarckian inheritance process can hugely accelerate changes in the bodies and behaviors of animals, thus thoroughly muddling any simple selectionist explanations of adaptation. The world of biology operates much more as a set of self-organizing mutually causing dynamical systems than as a mass of particles driven by simple causes. Emergent properties—the special structures and behaviors of a new species, to take the clearest example—explode onto the scene all the time. The likelihood that they will arise—whatever they are—though essentially unpredictable in detail and timing, is part of the collective genetic memory and expectations of the systems themselves. Genes are a record of past collective experience; and the sole survival function of that record is anticipation of future possibilities.

All these factors indeed complicate the selectionist story. But even if a deterministic evolutionary psychology is impossible, kinship is still an essential and foundational element in the motivation of behavior, as epic recognizes.

Out of this ancient base, we get some very familiar human characteristics. The most fundamental is that blood is thicker than water; we are clannish and tribal by instinct, and our loyalty to our group is one of our deepest motivations. No epic is without a rich consideration of this great driver of human survival. The epic battle often takes place in the service of kin loyalty—and the fiercest tragedy, as in the *Mahabharata* and the Icelandic sagas—happens when kin loyalty is divided. For even within the kin-group there are struggles that can constitute the narrative meat of epic.

Reproduction and kinship are controlled by a set of dynamic tensions:

The competition between sperm and egg over which shall have the greater share in the offspring's genes;

The competition between male and female as to which sex will be in the majority;

The competition between mother and father over the children;

The competition between male promiscuity (which promises a greater quantity of offspring) and male assistance in the care and feeding of the young (which promises greater quality of offspring and a better chance of grandchildren);

The competition between the female imperative to appropriate the best sperm for her offspring and her need for assistance to support them after they are born;

The competition between extended and nuclear family loyalties;

The competition between different kin-groups (feuds and war).

All these struggles ensure a system that is both highly flexible and responsive to environmental change, and at the same time robust and self-correcting. The related passions of sexual, parental, and familial love, of sexual jealousy, envy, revenge, acquisitiveness, grief at bereavement, and so on, all rich material for epic, are all shared more or less with other advanced social animals.

When the human line split off from the other primates, certain new elements emerged that are vital to our distinctive identity as a species. Many of them stem from the peculiarities of our developmental and maturational process—or rather were both the cause and the effect of those processes, for all is feedback here. Most important of all, as we have seen, is the long infancy of humans. We have also looked at the special neuropsychological and sociocultural implications of human adolescence. That adolescence is itself related to our long infancy; it is the final surge of that infancy as it makes the awkward transition to sexual adulthood. It is the harder for having been so long delayed; it is the more traumatic because so much rich but meaningless synaptic connection in the brain must be pruned away, in the wave of moral order that sweeps over the teenage cortex.

Almost as important as the extended infancy of humans is their extraordinary longevity. In order to look after newborns that are seldom and few, because of the huge resources both metabolic and economic that must go into the raising of each one—newborns do not reach maturity for many years—humans must live longer, in general, than other animals. Because more and more vital information is being transmitted from generation to generation by culture, learning, and instruction, individuals increase in value as culture-bearers and information archives as they get older, and selection encourages groups that contain aged sages and genes for longevity. Menopause, an apparently wasteful adaptation that cuts off the reproductive span, signals how important crones and old wives must have been to the survival and success of the species; the fact that women live longer than men is silently eloquent about the relative value of the sexes to the development of human culture.

Related to adolescence are exogamy—our practice of choosing a mate from an outside group—and the human incest taboo. We walked all over the earth, perhaps, in search of an exotic lover and to get away from our families. Robin Fox's fine book *The Red Lamp of Incest* documents the unique features of human kinship. Out of the combination of long infancy, requiring extended paternal cooperation in the nurture of the young, adolescent restlessness, increased intelligence, language, and the incest taboo come marriage, kinship classification systems, the Oedipus Complex, and all the rules of inheritance—matrilineality, patrilineality, primogeniture, and so on. Rules of residence also follow: patrilocality (the wife comes to live with the husband's parents), matrilocality (the husband lives with the wife's), and the social expectations in societies like ours that married couples create their own separate home. Do young men live apart from the rest? Do men live apart from women, like Malaysian Iban tribesmen or Victorian clubmen? Are women confined to the home, like ancient Athenian or modern Saudi ladies? Are children, or the aged, considered as a separate category of human being and segregated from others? When we add in the increasing importance of economic considerations—the material resources the male can bring to the rearing of children, the value to a family of its daughters' work, etc.—we get dowries, brideprice, and prenuptial contracts.

The very variety of possible combinations of such rules, and the epigenetic plasticity that accommodates and enacts them in the lives of individuals, lead to both innovation and struggle in the human way of life. In specific situations the "rules" can contradict each other, leading to the need to understand, explain, and revise them. New environmental challenges and opportunities—the availability of seasonal resources like fruit crops, floods, salmon runs, animal migrations, etc., climate that is colder or hotter, dryer or wetter, changing ecosystems as populations move about—can lead to changes in the kinship rules. Technologies emerge and are invented at the pressure points where these tensions demand them. Those technologies in turn change the environment and the ecological role of the tribe, creating new pressure points, new kinship tensions, and new myths and stories to explain them.

Further, kinship rules generated by the unique logic of the human species' emergence can be at stark variance with our more general but still deeply embedded mammalian and primate inheritance of emotions and drives. Hence we have adultery, young lovers tragically separated, sexual violence, suicide, inheritance fraud, intergenerational conflict, infanticide, patricide, oppression of women, sado-masochism, fetishism, sexual addiction, neurosis, bloodfeuds, and so on. The most important element that the human kinship system adds to the default higher-mammal system is a new competition—between blood relationships and affinal relationships—in other words, in-law problems, a subject of compelling interest to epic.

But epic, as should already be obvious, is acutely attentive to all of these factors in the story of how we became human. Some examples may show how anthropologically acute the genre is, and suggest the deep gist of epic as an artform.

Succession and Nepotism

In the *Ramayana*, Rama as the eldest of four sons is in line to inherit his father's kingdom. His stepmother Kaikeyi, however, wants to see her son Bharata, Rama's younger brother, become king. Remembering that the king had once promised to grant her any two wishes she desired, she demands that Rama be banished and Bharata be crowned. The king must keep his word and orders Rama's banishment. Rama obeys, and though justice eventually prevails and he returns in triumph to a crown, it is his saintly acquiescence that leads eventually to the defeat and purging of the great demons that render the land infertile.

Like the British Arthur, Feraydun, the future king of Persia in the *Shahnameh*, is raised in secret and learns of his royal ancestry only on the verge of manhood. He is provided with a magic weapon, his "Excalibur," the bull-headed mace, with which he defeats the black-magician usurper Zahhak. Like King Lear, Feraydun divides his kingdom in three among his three sons: Salm, Tur, and Iraj. Salm and Tur conspire to murder Iraj; Feraydun kills his two sons in battle and leaves his kingdom to his grandson Manuchehr, the son of the murdered Iraj.

In the *Popol Vuh*, Blood Moon, the mother of the hero twins Hunahpu and Xbalanque, goes pregnant with them to Xmucane, claiming that the father is Xmucane's sons One and Seven Hunahpu. She is skeptical, and even when she gets astrological proof of Blood Moon's claim she favors the sons of One Hunahpu by Egret Woman, One Monkey, and One Artisan, over their half-brothers. The half-brothers mistreat the hero twins, until Hunahpu and Xbalanque have had enough and by a clever ruse trap their tormentors, who lack imagination, in a tree where they reveal themselves as being only monkeys.

Sassouma, the first wife of King Naré Maghan in the *Sundiata*, resents his new marriage to Sogolon and becomes the bitter enemy of the young Sundiata, Sogolon's son by the King. She plots to ensure that her own son, Dankaran Touman, succeeds to the throne instead of Sundiata, despite the prophecies and divine decrees that Sundiate will be the king and savior of Mali. Eventually, like Kaikeyi in the *Ramayana*, she engineers the exile of her stepson, whence, with his mother Sogolon, he will return in victory to save his country.

In the *Henriad*, Shakespeare sets us a pretty problem: we are shown a king—Henry IV—who has the natural force and character to be king, as well as the genetic inheritance of kings, but who has violated the laws of succession by usurping the throne of the legitimate heir, Richard II, a man who, though genetically royal, is too weak and self-centered to be an effective monarch. What is Henry's son, Prince Hal, to do? He should succeed to his father's throne; he should hate and destroy the usurper of the throne, his father; he should be a loyal follower of his king in battle; he should love and honor his father; he should allow his own native animal strength and genius to flower into leadership and eliminate the opposition; he should honor the human traditions of the rule of law. All these "shoulds" contradict each other more or less.

The enormous importance of inheritance, and the struggle between human rules of succession and the pre-human biological imperative to promote one's genes, are clear in all these cases, and of course in many more epic stories. This conflict seems superficially to be an obstacle to human progress, a retreat from the rule of law and reason; but epic recognizes that it is actually constitutive of human progress, acting as a refining test of social rules and of the worthiness of the individual incumbents. Only the purchase given by our pre-human animal nature can support the pressure required to resolve the contradictions created by our human powers of choice.

This is why Rama must recruit an army of monkeys led by Hanuman, why Feraydun's mace has a bull's head, why the hero twins' half-brothers are monkeys, why Sundiata is the son of the buffalo-spirit woman, why Hal must recruit Falstaff, the "Manningtree ox," the "Bartholomew boar-pig," the "old pike," as a sacrificial animal stand-in for his father. And here we encounter again that essential epic theme, of the beast-man or natural man, which must be saved for a later chapter.

The role of women in the succession struggle is often important. In the Icelandic sagas the extraordinary violence of the men is egged on by the taunts of the women (Bergthora, Njal's wife, and Hildigunn, Flósi's niece, for instance) usually acting in favor of their blood kin, especially their children, and in resistance to male legal arrangements designed to overcome nepotism and clan conflict. Kaikeyi in the *Ramayana* and Sassouma in the *Sundiata* play the same role. On the other hand, in the *Mahabharata* Gandhara and Kunti, the respective mothers of the Kauravas and the Pandavas, are generally voices for peace and accommodation between the two sides; but Duryodhana gets his invulnerability from his mother. Kriemhild in the *Nibelungs* is torn between love of her murdered husband Siegfried and her loyalty to her blood kin. But these too are matters for a later section.

Adultery

The clearest case of a contradiction between a kinship system emerging from the peculiarly human life-pattern and the general vertebrate behavioral system is the practice of adultery. Certainly other animals practice monogamy but cheat on their mates—male sparrows will routinely peck out the sperm of their cuckolders from their mates' privates. But given the enormous stakes in the human world—the need for long and expensive male support for viable offspring, the need for males to be able to identify their offspring as theirs, the especially large metabolic cost of pregnancy and birth, the replacement of reliable biological markers of close kinship such as smell by cultural markers—a clear clash between evolutionarily older and newer motivations and emotions is inevitable.

The core institution of human kinship is of course marriage; but marriage is a great paradox, an attempt to create, so to speak, an artificial bond of blood kinship. To overcome our ancient natural tendency to bond only with those who share our genes, we are equipped also with a newer, humanly evolved instinct: the extraordinary neurochemistry of falling in love. Marriage is the human attempt to reconcile that capacity with the dynastic and child-rearing needs of the family. And it is not always successful. Tristan and Isolde, Siegfried and Brunnhild, Paris and Helen, Joseph and Potiphar's wife, Rudabeh and Zal in the *Shahnameh* all struggle with the duties and impulses generated by the paradoxes of human kinship. In the *Laxdala Saga* Hoskuld, Jorunn, Melkorka, Bolli, Kjartan, Gudrun, and Ingiborg are caught up in a net of adulterous betrayal, with tragic results, including the wrecking of the great "hero-twins" relationship between Kjartan and Bolli. But out of the disaster emerges the fully achieved character of Gudrun, one of the most remarkable female characters in all of literature, and her breakthrough at the end into a new mode of tragic Christian consciousness.

Youthful Rebellion and Oedipal Conflicts

In the *Mwindo* epic of West Africa the hero, having grown up in exile, pursues his murdering father to his birthplace and then into the underworld, where he must perform many great tasks and pass tests until the lightning-god of the underworld gives him back his father. With his father he returns to the land of the living, bringing back to life all those he slew in his battles against his father's supporters. Eventually father and son agree to share the kingdom. Here we see the epic response to the problem that Sophocles and Freud identified so clearly: how do we square the circle of human kinship rules and human nature? We are not far, clearly, from Shakespeare's resolution of the oedipal tension between Henry IV and Hal.

More tragically, Sohrab in the *Shahnameh*, raised apart from his father, rebels against the (rather unworthy) Persian king, Kavus, whom his father Rostam serves. Ignorant of each other's identity they meet on the field of battle; Sohrab overpowers his father but spares him, and the next day Rostam kills his son. Before Sohrab dies the truth is revealed, to the infinite grief of his father. The emotional importance of this episode to Ferdowsi, the author of the poem, is underlined by an unusually autobiographical interpolation later in the work: his lament for his own son, who died untimely and whom he accuses of having deserted him. Though obviously Ferdowsi did not cause his son's death, no father could avoid a sense of guilt at having outlived his son. Feraydun was compelled in justice to kill two of his sons: one central theme of the *Shahnameh* could be said to be the tragic conflict between generations.

In much the same fashion, Cuchulainn in ignorance kills his son Connla, who has come to Ireland in search of his father. I believe that the story is so similar to the Persian tragedy that they probably have a common origin in the Indo-European stock of legends. Thus they cannot be counted as independent confirmations of a human archetype; but the archetype perhaps shows itself still in the persistence of the tale in two branches of the same stock over many thousands of years of migration, when so many other tales died out or changed beyond recognition. Freud is illuminating here:

> It was then, perhaps, that some individual, in the exigency of his longing, may have been moved to free himself from the group and take over the father's part. He who did this was the first epic poet; and the advance was achieved in his imagination. This poet disguised the truth with lies in accordance with his longing. He invented the heroic myth. The hero was a man who by himself had slain the father—the father who still appeared in the myth as a totemic monster. Just as the father had been the boy's first ideal, so in the hero who aspires to the father's place the poet now created the first ego ideal. The transition to the hero was probably afforded by the youngest son, the mother's favourite, whom she had protected from paternal jealousy, and who, in the era of the primal horde, had been the father's successor. In the lying poetic fancies of prehistoric times, the woman, who had been the prize of battle and the temptation to murder,

was probably turned into the active seducer and instigator to the crime . . .[3]

In epic, oedipal conflict is rarely as overt as it is in the *Mwindo* epic and the *Shahnameh*. Often the great stories disguise the struggle, which is almost too painful to bear telling in a traditional society, but still find ways to face the basic problem of authority, love, self-actualization, piety, and reform. One of these ways is the strategy of the *Oresteia* and *Hamlet*; to have the younger brother commit the murder of the patriarch and usurp the patriarch's woman, position and authority, and have the son piously avenge him, thus separating the role of the revolutionary father-killer from the role of the young hero overthrowing oppressive and wicked authority. The issues are dealt with but at one remove, so that profound moral ambivalence and cognitive dissonance does not interfere with the narrative analysis of how to conduct true reform in the family and society at large.

So in epic the oppressive father is usually replaced by a more metaphorical kind of father-figure, or the rebellion is less drastic than parricide. In the *Heike*, the father-figure is the usurping Kiyomori. In *The Journey to the West* it is the Taoist and Confucian authorities whom Monkey bests on his way to Buddhist enlightenment. In *The Iliad*, the Old Man is Agamemnon. In the *Mahabharata*, it is the blind king Dhrita-Rashtra. In *Exodus*, it is the Pharaoh, Moses' foster-grandfather. In *The Secret History of the Mongols*, the hero Temüjin's father is murdered, and Temüjin must defeat first his Tartar murderers and then the authorities of his own tribe, including Toghrul, his father's blood-brother. Ganelon is Roland's stepfather. Njal is the father-figure in *Njal's Saga*, Alfonso in *Mio Cid*, Conchobar in *The Cattle Raid of Cooley*, Laban in the story of Jacob. Blood Gatherer, one of the Lords of Xibalba against whom the hero-twins must play the deadly ball game, is the maternal grandfather of the boys in the *Popol Vuh*. In the Tamil *Silappathikaram*, the young hero is Kannagi, a woman, and the oppressive father-figure is Neduncheliyan, the Pandaya king who murdered her husband and whom she overthrows.

These oedipal confrontations enable epic to get a grip on one of the fundamental themes of human evolution:

> But you must know, your father lost a father;
> That father lost, lost his, and the survivor bound
> In filial obligation for some term
> To do obsequious sorrow. But to persever

In obstinate condolement is a course
Of impious stubbornness; 'tis unmanly grief;
It shows a will most incorrect to heaven,
A heart unfortified, a mind impatient,
An understanding simple and unschool'd;
For what we know must be, and is as common
As any the most vulgar thing to sense,
Why should we, in our peevish opposition,
Take it to heart? Fie! 'tis a fault to heaven,
A fault against the dead, a fault to nature,
To reason most absurd, whose common theme
Is death of fathers, and who still hath cried,
From the first corse till he that died today,
This must be so.
(*Hamlet*, I.ii.89)

The "first corse" was Abel's, the victim of his brother Cain. Claudius, who says these words to Hamlet, is of course the murderer of Hamlet's father. But Hamlet in his own mind cannot escape the burden of guilt. If we do not kill our fathers, we betray them by outliving them and being who we are rather than who they were. But if we do not make a better world than they did, we have betrayed their own effort to improve on the world they got from their own fathers. And to make a better new world is inevitably in greater or lesser measure to discard the old. Humans are the species that not only evolve themselves by self-domestication, but are more or less conscious of doing so, and conscious of the tension between domestication itself—obeying the rules of one's masters—and the changing of the rules that hold back progress.

Absence of Incest

Given the enormous importance for epic of proper kinship relations (since as we have seen they are both result and cause of the emergence of the human race), one might expect incest to be a major epic theme. But it is not, not even in an oblique or sublimated form.[4] This is a case of Sherlock Holmes' famous dog that does not bark, and this absence is crucial forensic evidence. Why is it absent in epic? It is a frequent theme, overt or strongly suggested, in drama (*Oedipus, Hippolytus, 'Tis Pity She's a Whore, The Duchess of Malfi, Phèdre*, etc.) and in the novel (Fielding's *Tom Jones*, Emily Brontë's *Wuthering Heights*, Hardy's *Jude the Obscure*, James' *The Golden Bowl*, Faulkner's *The Sound and the Fury*, Nabokov's *Ada*, etc.). We have already seen that epic is not afraid of transgression, that it is committed to breaking new ground and exploring forbidden territory. Epic is also capable of tragedy of the starkest kind—it does not avoid the disasters of the human condition. Epic is indeed deeply imbued with tradition—but it is a tradition of transgression, of denial of limit. Why should not incest be a favorite realm of dark adventure for epic?

Is it that epic is interested in the disasters and struggles (as well as the triumphs and achievements) that flow from humankind's health, strength, and virtue—and not in those that flow from what it would regard as humankind's sickness, weakness, and corruption? That it wants to know what great obstacles and enemies and traps lie in wait for our noblest aspirations, rather than what consequences attend our handicaps and perversions? This explanation would suggest that the epic story is about us at our best even if ruined by the overplus of some peculiar human greatness, rather than what we do when we have broken the rules of our human nature and must, crippled, carry on anyway. No kind of progress, even at the tragic cost epic often demands, can be made if the human genome can be permitted to decay into impotence through inbreeding; epic is about human succession, human progress. The genre might indeed be concerned with the way that the human kinship rules contradict nature and each other, but it would not consider questioning the basic spirit of the rules, which is healthy human reproduction and succession. For the epic mind the two senses of the word "succession"—temporal order and blood inheritance—are one. Time itself, the essential medium of story, cannot be divided from the sequence of generations. Nature *is* natal order, as the word's etymology implies.

The importance of reproduction and orderly succession in epic is nicely illustrated by the story of Bhishma. The entire tragic action of the *Mahabharata* stems from Bhishma's fateful decision to take a vow of celibacy so as not have any children who would challenge the succession of his father's children by his new young wife. Bhishma gets in recompense for his selfless act the gift of endless life (unless he chooses to die); but if he had fathered children of his own and accepted the arbitrary mortality of humankind the apocalyptic battle of Kurukshetra would never have been fought. Epic is about peopling the world, and anything that threatens that process is taboo for the genre. Celibacy and immortality are acceptable for Brahmins, for monks, priests, mandarins, pilgrims, and hermits, but not for the central heroes of epic, the kshatriyas, the samurais, and the knights. The celibate Galahad achieves the grail, but his coming signals the destruction of the Round

Table. The only cells in the human body not programmed to die after a certain number of replications (by apoptosis, whose Greek root means "the falling of autumn leaves") are brain cells and cancer cells.

The whole premise of *The Odyssey*, as Homer carefully poses it by beginning the poem in Ithaca with the husbandless Penelope and the fatherless Telemachus, is the need for proper succession, which includes both reproduction and appropriate closure through death. The problem in Ithaca is that there is a gap in the succession—Odysseus is neither dead nor alive and present; is Telemachus to be king, and Penelope queen? The reason proper burial is so important in epic is that it certifies that the deceased is really dead and gone, we know where he is, and we can turn the wheel of succession to its next notch and let the ratchet click securely into place (or turn the hourglass, or light another candle, or refill the clepsydra). The clock of the days and seasons, the story of the family, can resume after the hour has struck. But there is no Odysseus to bury; and this is why he must return.

In my own epic, *Genesis*, the hero Tripitaka is born with AIDS and though healed of its symptoms still carries a resistant strain of the HIV virus. He takes a vow of celibacy so as not to infect others. But providentially he is seduced, and his daughter, born after his heroic death and transferred into another woman's womb, grows up to be the religious leader of the new republic of Mars.

If the hypothesis that reproductive succession is essential to epic is valid, why should adultery be an acceptable subject for epic, but not incest? Perhaps the implication is that incest threatens reproduction itself, whereas adultery per se does not threaten, and may even in some cases encourage healthy reproduction. For epic, adultery is like the foul in basketball, penalized but still part of the game and in its spirit; not like fouling in football or soccer, a damaging attack on the spirit of the game itself, whose analogy is incest. Tragic drama and the novel make us aware of the game we are in by showing us players breaking the spirit of the rules, committing football-fouls, so to speak; but the game is the worse for the fouls. Epic makes us aware of the game by showing us players who, like a point guard who, fully in the spirit of the game, routinely makes perfectly legal forty-foot fadeaway jump shots. Such a player-hero would expose the arbitrariness of the rules while paradoxically demonstrating their value as an arena for supreme human achievement—and would thereby force the commissioners of the game to change the rules or even create a new game. If the jump-shot expert is also a fine practitioner of the good clean hard foul under the basket, this characteristic might be a splendid episode in the story; but not if he is ejected for a technical foul. The hero can be an adulterer but not an incestuous lover. If Dido were Aeneas' sister, or worse, his mother, Rome could probably not be founded; but as an extramarital affair, the connection enriches his character with interesting shadows.

In my *Genesis*, though I did not know it at the time, the plot compelled me into a situation where the point about incest is starkly made. Wolf and his sister Irene, like Orestes and Electra, find themselves presented with an opportunity to avenge their beloved father Chance van Riebeck on their hated mother Gaea. They are suddenly aware that if they kill her, it would cause their relationship with each other to morph from passionate sibling intimacy into incest—they would be united by a polluted blood-bond that would substitute for the bond with the mother. They choose to spare her, however, and this choice leads on, as the story unfolds, into the successful establishment of the new republic of Mars: Irene is the woman who seduces Tripitaka and ensures his succession. The epic task can only be fulfilled—even though it is a profoundly transgressive one in itself—if incest is avoided.

But would pre-scientific societies be aware of the genetic dangers of incest? Perhaps not in a strictly causal sense, but every known human society votes with its feet against incest by kinship classifications that forbid marriage in cases of close consanguinity, and all human societies by definition practice some degree of exogamy, i.e., marriage outside the immediate family, clan, or tribe. This is a theme to which we will return.

Incest is an especially strong theme in two kinds of storytelling: in stories of the gods and in fiction of the European Romantic period. Many epics have in their background the scandalous stories of the gods that Plato so deplored in the *Republic*, but they do not dwell on them. In *The Odyssey*, Homer briefly mentions the incestuous marriage of the wind-god Aeolus's fifty sons and daughters. But his attitude to these deities verges on contempt—these winds don't get anywhere in particular, and indeed the whole episode of the winds simply returns Odysseus to the same place he started, and in a worse state.

Why is incest appropriate to the gods? Several reasons could be given. One is that since stories of the gods usually involve the creation and origins of everything, and since the original state of the world is one and the present state of the world is many, the gods must be not only the patrons of multiplication but also multiply themselves. As the basic model of multiplication for human beings is sexual reproduction, and if we begin with one divine being, matching the unitary state of the origin, the first births must be parthenogenetic, and the next generation of births must be incestuous. Even the Western Christian doctrine of the Trinity is in human terms incestuous—the Father gives birth to the Son, the Son and the Father together beget the Holy Spirit.

A second reason for the incestuousness of the gods is that the gods are by definition self-sufficient and perfect, and thus do not need to seek outside themselves for new blood, as humans do in their imperfection. The gods are complete, finished; their immortality does not require renewal. Epic deals precisely with the need for new story, new journeys, to recuperate the dynamic flaws of the old, and is not interested in stay-at-home incest.

A third reason for divine incest is that it is a marker of the pre-logical, pre-rational nature of the divine. The rational system of kinship is not the same thing as, and cannot pre-exist, the laying down of the axioms on which it is based. But the axioms, and their divine formulators, are not governed by the reproductive logic of mortal limited humankind.

A fourth reason for divine incest is that human kinship and reproductive rules are designed for beings that change and die and find their significance in succession and the leaving behind of a heritage. Even if doctrines of divine timelessness have not yet been concocted out of mathematical abstraction to describe Eternity, immortal gods do not experience time as we do and do not need incest taboos to ensure time's proper order.

The significance of these observations for epic is that when humanism arose in the Renaissance, it set in motion a process in which the divinity of human beings was increasingly emphasized, gathering force during the Romantic period, and reaching its apogee in the work of such figures as Nietzsche. If the gods are dead, humans step into their place. Existentialism demands that human beings are tasked with creating their own value de novo and ex nihilo—in other words, they must become gods of their own. As human lifetimes lengthened because of social and economic progress, death became much more remote, and a cult of extended youth—even the *puer aeternus*—took hold, thoughtfully epitomized in Oscar Wilde's "The Portrait of Dorian Gray." Naturally the rules that safeguard the meaning and order of mortal human life are relaxed, including those that forbid incest. Incest is important in Lamartine, Chateaubriand, Zola, Flaubert, Tieck,

Wagner, and Mann, among others. Brother–sister incest is a major theme in English Romantic and Victorian literature and on into early modernism. Unlike parent–child incest, usually regarded with horror, brother–sister incest is tolerated, even covertly admired, by many of the great romantics and their successors, some of whom had relationships with their siblings that were at least on the subconscious level incestuous. Wordsworth and Dorothy, Byron and Augusta Leigh, the Brontës and their brother Branwell clearly had bonds closer than that of siblings. Coleridge married the sister of his brother-poet's, Southey's, wife—another Sara, like Wordsworth's wife. Shelley wrote approvingly of some aspects of brother–sister incest. Their literary productions such as *The White Doe of Rylstone, Manfred, Cain, Wuthering Heights*, and *Laon and Cythna* are what happened when they composed narratives of epic scope under the spell of the incestuous imagination. Even Wordsworth's *Prelude* can be seen as the transition from a magical childhood world of intimacy with his sister, symbolized by the moon, into a more prosaic world of normal adult sexuality, symbolized by the sun of reason.

Wagner makes Sieglinde, Siegmund's wife and queen in the *Nibelungs*, into his long-lost sister. The symbolic meaning of this device is that Wotan wishes to create Siegfried, their son, a truly free human being, free of the gods' control, as part of his plot to regain Alberich's ring; and Siegfried now, as his own man, is equal to the gods. But as we can now see, this leap takes us beyond epic territory, back into divine incest myth and on into that of the novel or the drama.

So post-romantic writers attempting epic in the European tradition must somehow manage to recover epic's loyalty to fertile sexuality and healthy reproduction or find its moral equivalent, if the stakes for the human species are to attain epic magnitude.

Hero Twins and Male Bonding

The absence of overt homosexuality in epic (and its strong presence in drama and the novel), like the absence of incest, is another suggestion that epic is not interested in non-reproductive sex. For epic, physical homosexuality is paradoxically too safe a relationship—you know where you are with your own sex, you are not entering foreign territory. No squalling messy future is going to be birthed as a result of the physical biological connection.

This is not to say that male bonding, even the passionate friendships of Gilgamesh and Enkidu, Achilles and Patroclus, Nisus and Euryalus,

Martín and Cruz, Arjuna and Krishna, Roland and Oliver, Wordsworth and Coleridge, Ishmael and Queequeg, and so on are not true elements of epic: indeed they are central to epic. There is an emotional fecundity and originality in passionate same-sex friendship that contrasts with the biological sterility of homosexual physical union. Male bonding is for anthropologists one of the fundamental ingredients of the human evolutionary miracle: especially through its central importance in hunting it drove our talents of cooperation, communication, much of the immediately practical side of language, athletic physical grace and coordination, toolmaking, and probably much of our penchant for animal classification systems and natural knowledge. In *Gilgamesh*, the "hero twins" certainly prefer their friendship to the heterosexual snares of Ishtar; but Enkidu has sired many children in the wild and Gilgamesh countless more, no doubt, in his youthful sowing of wild oats through the exercise of the *ius primae noctis* in Uruk. The epic, though it is interested in the heroic friends' emotions about each other, is not interested in how they might be expressed in sexual terms.

So important is male bonding, however, that it is often literalized by various degrees of brotherhood, the most radical being twinship. Gilgamesh and Enkidu, Achilles and Patroclus, Roland and Oliver, Ishmael and Queequeg are not blood kin at all, though they achieve a brotherhood in bloodshed. Ferdiad and Cuchulainn are foster-brothers. Sigurd and Sinfljotli in the *Volsung Saga*, Bolli and Kjartan in the *Laxdala Saga*, Parzifal and Feirefiz in *Parzifal* are half-brothers. Gunnar and Kolskegg are full brothers ("Bare is back without brother behind it" is one memorable saying from *The Saga of Burnt Njal*). Hero twins include Hunahpu and Xbalanque, Castor and Polydeuces, Romulus and Remus, Nakula and Sahadeva the Pandava brothers, Lakshmana and Shatrughna in the *Ramayana*, and Kane and Kanaloa in the Polynesian proto-epic cycle.

The twinship theme focuses a more general issue that is an important part of the heroic identity: personal identity itself. One's friend is a sort of reflection of oneself; a brother or sister more so; a twin more so still, to the point of existential vertigo. The great Hungarian poet, Miklós Radnóti, who crafted for himself a heroic identity to sustain him as he entered the Holocaust, was an identical twin whose brother died in childbirth.[5] Miklós wove the myths of Castor and Polydeuces and Cain and Abel into his poetic self-identification; his strange question was whether his dead twin was the real Miklós and he himself, the dead brother, was the usurper of his living brother's identity. One of the most important things a hero must confront is himself, and he does it through his twin, brother, or friend. Self-awareness is one of the most crucial elements in the emergence of the truly human; in epic it comes often with the recognition of one's friend, especially in the encounter with one's friend's death. One first enters the underworld in pursuit of one's dead friend. This is the central theme of the first epic of all, *Gilgamesh*.

Twinship, though, is also sort of rebuff to the final importance of kinship; for twins are not the same as each other, however easy it may be to confuse them. Selfhood is not the same as physical identity; in the twin we must recognize a soul that transcends heredity.

The Dangerous Woman

Ishtar is only the first of epic's dangerous, troublesome, tricky, and transformative women. A partial list makes the point: Sogolon, Tiamat, Helen, Circe, Penelope, Draupadi, Kaikeyi, Rudabeh, Enkidu's sacred harlot Shamhat, Eve, Sarah, Rachel, Kannagi, Börte, Clytemnestra, Dido, Guinevere, Armida, Alcina, Angelica, Kriemhild, Brunnhild, Hallgerd, Bergthora, Gudrun—and the list could go on, with Blood Moon, Gery's Cressie, and my own Faith Raven, Ruth Quincy, Irene, and Gaea. The point is not just that these are major figures in epic, but that each of them, for good or ill and often both, changes the nature of the game, breaks open the old world and initiates a new. Eve is perhaps paradigmatic; in both the Bible and Milton she is the breaker of the status quo, the source of the knowledge of good and evil, and the cause of multiplicity, dissension, history, even in a sense time itself. When the dangerous women are good they exist at some fulcrum or point of greatest weakness in the human kinship scheme, and their goodness creates an attraction that cracks existing relationships and structures. When they are (more often) wicked or at least deceptively tricksy, their machinations drive humanity to create new institutions, languages, stories, media, cities, legal systems, moral perspectives, technologies, and economic relations.

Psychologists and child development experts tell us that girls are normally far ahead of boys of the same age in social awareness and social skills. Many anthropological evolutionists are increasingly of the opinion that if one single factor can be held responsible for the astonishing expansion of the human association cortex it is selection for political intelligence—that capacity to construct an internal model of the other's motives, set it in motion by a sort of dramatic or theatrical imagination, and thus predict and be able to alter the behavior of one's cohorts.[6] We can readily see that if those cohorts are simultaneously modeling the first modeler, and thus modeling the modeler's model of themselves, and the first modeler must therefore model the cohort's model of her model of them, and so on, there will be an exponentially increasing demand for computational complexity and a corresponding selection over the generations for social intelligence.

Some anthropologists have made the following kind of argument: Male physical strength and the objective demands of action in such activities as hunting, tool construction, and war would place limits and governors on the feedback process of political calculation. A capacity for practical communication and the formulation of rules and duties would certainly be selected for by the male role of protein-harvesting, and competition among males in such arenas would lead to greater reproductive success through larger shares in the products of the hunt and more to give their offspring. But the more subtle forms of one-upmanship, empathy, tact, popularity enhancement, dudgeon, emotional pressure, and suasion would not be called for and might well be a handicap in the heat of the hunt or battle, in the workshop, or in a storm at sea. Winners in the female competition for esteem and popularity would garner better mates and more resources for their offspring. Though males would of course benefit from inheriting their mothers' social subtlety, to the extent that such differences are sex-linked, males would be at a disadvantage in the very competition that drove the flowering of human intelligence.

Further, in the hunt or war or in the market (for it appears we were traders almost as far back as we were hunters, and this is a major distinction between us and the Neanderthals, who did not seem to trade much)—in these activities honesty, trust, reciprocity, and cooperation are essential and can be relatively easy to discern in others and sanction when in default. The kind of intelligence demanded of women, who are less able than men to physically enforce their wishes and police their rules, requires deeper virtues, greater secrecy, a richer conscience, and a finer sense of irony. More important still is self-knowledge: to know what others think of oneself, one must first know who and what one is and be able to compare the other's view with the inner reality. Such insight provides rich materials for deception if one chooses to use them. Much has been made of concealed ovulation in humans, unique among primates, and the opportunity for deceit and covert collusion among human females.[7] As Homer remarks, it is a wise man who knows his own father. The kind of cheating women can practice, and the kind of honesty that forbids one from doing it, are much less easily detectible than "mailing it in" in the hunt, fleeing in battle, or selling shoddy goods.

Even if we do not accept this gender typology, or believe that the differences in the sexes it suggests are the result of technological or social factors and thus rapidly disappearing, it certainly seems to fit epic storytelling well. To the male epic hero the greater subtlety of the female can be both a danger and the opportunity for transcendent growth and insight.

In *Paradise Lost*, Eve is looking at herself mirrored in the water when Adam finds her. More than potential vanity, this image suggests greater self-knowledge. She is in close contact with her dreams and her dream self, and Milton does not often tell us their content. She manipulates Adam into eating the apple, and though it is a fall, a fault, it is the beginning of human history and the material cause of the redemption and the fulfillment of the plan of God. Adam is, finally, blessed and enlightened by the pain and disruption Eve has led him into. In *Gilgamesh*, Enkidu on his deathbed first curses the harlot who caused him to fall from the immortal world of nature and opened his eyes to his mortal human condition: but on second thought he blesses her, for the seduction gave him a name, a culture, and a friend.

Even the lethal ladies of *Burnt Njal*, Bergthora and Hallgerd, who egg their males on to destruction, end up as the essential catalysts in the great game-change that made Iceland a nation, the creation of the Fifth Court. Without the female spur the men might have averted the crisis and settled the blood feud at the local level through male good sportsmanship. The nascent state required a further irritant to quicken.

Helen by her sin and her self-knowledge unites the Hellenes and gives them a name and political origin. Briseis initiates the fatal quarrel between Achilles and Agamemnon, which results in the slaying of Hector and the defeat of Troy. Penelope deceives and outplays the suitors, weaving and unweaving the shroud of Laertes as she weaves and unweaves the lining of her womb, and thus makes possible the healing of the Greek family system, so devastated by the concurrent events in Mycaenae, the terrible history of the house of Atreus, and the Trojan War itself. Blood Moon essentially betrays her ancestors, the Lords of Xibalba, by being impregnated by their old enemies the first hero twins, and giving birth to the second pair, who will defeat the realm of death itself and initiate the human race. Without Kaikeyi's nepotistic plotting against Rama in the *Ramayana*, the evil Ravana would never have been defeated. Tiamat foments a war in heaven but becomes the living world itself. Björte is both the bone of contention among the warring Mongolian clans and the catalyst for their uniting into a nation under Genghis Khan. Armida, Erminia, Sofronia, and Clorinda, Tasso's extraordinary shape-shifting women, drive the entire action of *The Liberation of Jerusalem*, as Angelica, Bradamante, and Alcina drive that of *Orlando Furioso*.

The status war between Brynhild and Gudrun in the *Volsungs* is at the core of the tragic epic itself. It brings about the end of the Volsungs themselves, and concludes the mysterious plan of Odin, which is what?—to demonstrate the perfection of human courage against overwhelming odds, to prove by destructive test the insane dignity and commitment of men? Perhaps the same basic pattern is found in the *Nibelungs*, where it is Kriemhild who will not accept the status quo, who stands between lineages and presses the conflict to its final conclusion.

Women, being human beings with all the human need for freedom and dignity, do not in epic accept their subordinate place meekly. But they use their greater social intelligence and psychological insight to make space for themselves in the world of men. Their political role can be either progressive or conservative in this project. In a society where male rules of status and property turn women into chattels to be exchanged and owned, women resist the tyranny by rule-breaking or magic, as do Sogolon, Ishtar, Rudabeh, Circe, Gudrun (in the *Laxdala Saga*), Dido, or Armida. In a society in which men are trying to forge larger political units like cities and nations (and by implication put the sacred female province of reproduction and family in the shade), they can stubbornly insist on the ancient bonds of blood kin, like Bergthora in *Njal*, Kaikeyi in the *Ramayana*, Sassouma in the *Sundiata*, or Antigone. In a society where the State trumps marriage, the epic woman can use her power of curse to bring down the monarch, as does Kannagi in the *Silappathikaram*. In a world of male justice she can conquer by mercy, like Beatrice in *The Divine Comedy*.

In-Law Troubles, Bad Gifts, and Bloody Feasts

One of the reasons why women can contain so much danger and so much promise in epic is that their traditional roles, as feminist scholarship has amply demonstrated, place them at the crucial axis where the reproductive imperative intersects with the most fraught and volatile channels of economic and social exchange. Until the nineteenth century, and then only in the developed world at best, the technology and the economic institutions available to human beings dictated a fairly strict division of labor between the sexes. Given the rates of infant mortality, death or injury in childbirth, violent conditions in general, male upper-body strength, and limited lifespans, together with the human mother's long pregnancy and infertile lactation period, our extended infancy and childhood, early menopause, the absence of birth control and hygienic baby-feeding technology, and the fact that multiple births are rare, any pre-industrial society in which most fertile women were not either pregnant or lactating would simply have died out for lack of natural increase. No pre-industrial society has ever permitted women and men to choose their occupations freely without social sanctions against role-change. Not enough babies would be born and survive to replace the population.

In such a condition, a nubile and fertile girl is a kin-group's dearest possession, but one which, because of the human genetic requirement for exogamy, cannot be deployed and used without risky and unpredictable contact with other kin-groups. Such contacts, and the formation of affinal (marriage-based) alliances, could lead to enriching trade, cultural exchange, larger and more powerful political groupings, and huge increases in knowledge about nature, history, medicine, and the human condition itself. But the divided loyalties they fostered also contained the seeds of betrayal, deceit, violent emotion, misplaced self-sacrifice, and extraordinary cruelty. Hildeburh in the embattled hall of Finnsburg, tragically torn between her husband Finn and her brother Hnaef, is the archetype of the tragedy that can result.

As the great French anthropologist Marcel Mauss pointed out,[8] human beings usually negotiate these difficulties through gift exchange or more formal means like dowry, brideprice, and entail. Festive gatherings prop up nascent or threatened bonds that do not come with blood kinship, yet can also be sources of discord—as any couple trying to decide which set of parents to spend Thanksgiving or Christmas with can attest. In-law jokes, so anthropologists insist, are culturally universal; the in-law relation is both essential and awkward for human beings, and our human sense of irony may itself have been nurtured by the cognitive dissonances and absurdities generated by the collision of different family eccentricities, expectations, customs, and histories.

Sometimes the situation gets beyond a joke. The archetypal joke is perhaps the bad gift—the gift that is valuable to the giver but valueless to the recipient, or, more subtly and perhaps worse, vice versa. The bad gift is used food—excrement. It has been enjoyed and discarded by the giver and has lost its spiritual meaning, like a diseased bride or a re-wrapped, unwanted present. It can even be a poisoned cup, like the one given to Temüjin's father by deceitful members of an enemy tribe while they are returning from Temüjin's betrothal to Björte. The German word *Gift*, cognate with the English word, means "poison." The words "host," "guest," and "hostile" are all from the same root.

In *The Saga of Burnt Njal* (Chapter 34) there is a wedding-feast scene that is a masterpiece of anthropological observation and can serve as a diagram that maps many of the profoundest kin-conflicts in epic. Gunnar and Hallgerd are getting married. The three tables are arranged like a pi sign: the high table, at which sit the bride and groom and most honored guests, is transverse at the head of the hall, the other two tables running down the length of the hall. What will end up as the two sides in a devastating blood-feud are seated on both sides of Gunnar. The family of Gunnar's bride Hallgerd, who will betray him, face Gunnar across the table. Nyal's wife Bergthora, who will quarrel fatally with Hallgerd, Gunnar's wife, serves the tables. An apparently unrelated quarrel breaks out in this charged space between Thrain Sigfusson and his wife, which ends an old bad marriage and begins a new one; but Thrain and his son Hoskuld, Njal's foster-son, will be slain by the Njalssons, triggering the burning of Njal at Bergthorsknoll. The cross-table, symbol of the marriage itself, cannot unite the two lengthwise tables; and at a return feast given by Njal, Hallgerd and Bergthora begin their long bloody war.

Similar in-law problems occur frequently in epic. The *Shahnameh* in its cycle of kings repeats again and again the theme of the foreign princess who becomes queen and the Persian prince who through a foreign marriage becomes king of another realm; often there are evil consequences as well as good ones. Persia, as Ferdowsi tells it, is the civilization of all civilizations that welcomes with eager curiosity the culture, wisdom, art, and knowledge of other cultures and so becomes the jewel of all cultures itself; but in so doing it opens itself up to external conflicts and promotes in itself internal divisions.

The feast that leads to quarrels is sometimes the upshot of such tensions. The holocaust in the feasting-hall of Etzel or Atli (Attila) in the *Nibelungs* and the *Volsungs* is of course the locus classicus. The feast at Finnsburg is another. The slaughter of the suitors in Odysseus' banqueting hall exemplifies what happens when the wrong sort of alliance by marriage is attempted. Likewise, the feast at the outset of the *Heike* in which the imperial Fujiwara courtiers plan to kill Tadamori, Kiyomori's foster-father, has all the flavor of in-law resentment. Kiyomori's policy of marrying Taira heirs into the imperial family, with the eventual intention of taking over the throne from the Fujiwaras and thus being in a position to crush the Genji, their hated rivals, is the root cause of the civil war.

The Burning House and Tragic Kin-Slaying

The most striking epic symbol of kin-strife, in general, is the burning house, often expanded to the burning city. The burning of Njal's house Bergthorsknoll, the burning of Attila's hall, the burning of Troy, the burnings of Miidera and Nara in the *Heike*, the burning of the Pandavas' "Blessed Home" in Varanavata, the burning of the city of Madurai in the *Silappathikaram*, the burning of the royal palace of the Lords of Xibalba in the *Popol Vuh*—this symbol seems appropriate to the epic composer for the theme. Why? Obviously "house" is often the metonym for the family. Fire can be easily started but not easily put out, as it starts to rage by itself and has a life of its own. Its heat is like the fever of vengeful hatred, fueled by the very promise of intimacy betrayed. The house or city is where we live—this fire does not just kill individuals, but destroys their very world, their habitat.

Heroes like Skarpheddin and Grim in Njal's burning house or Gunnar and Hogni (or Hagen) in Attila's burning hall, who refuse to escape and try to tread out the embers, embody the absurd grandeur of the human spirit that will not retreat from its chosen position when all is falling into ruin around them. When Njal and Bergthora take to their bed with their foster-son Thord the son of Kari between them, and Skarpheddin makes his little joke about their getting an early night's sleep, we are at the uttermost peak of tragic heroism. And it is a heroism that is occasioned and demanded by the constitutively human paradoxes of kinship, paradoxes that drove the evolution of the species.

Notes

1. Robin Fox, *The Red Lamp of Incest: An Enquiry into the Origins of Mind and Society* (Notre Dame, IN: University of Notre Dame Press, 1984).

2. Steven Pinker, *The Blank Slate: The Modern Denial of Human Nature* (New York: Penguin, 2003); Robert Wright, *The Moral Animal: Why We Are the Way We Are* (New York: Vintage, 1995).

3. Sigmund Freud, *Group Psychology and the Analysis of the Ego* (Eastford, CT: Martino Fine Books, 2010), 68.

4. The only exceptions I can recall are the story of Kullervo, in the *Kalevala*—and he of course comes to an unpleasant end—and the tale of Sigmund and Signy in the *Volsungs*. In the *Volsungs*, the story of their brother–sister incest belongs to the early mythological phase of the poem, before the epic story itself begins, and is thus within the category of "divine incest" that forms a background and contrast to the human story.

5. Zsuzsanna Ozsváth and Frederick Turner, trans. and eds. *Foamy Sky: The Major Poems of Miklós Radnóti* (Princeton, NJ: Princeton University Press, 1992). See also Zsuzsanna Ozsváth, *In the Footsteps of Orpheus* (Bloomington, IN: Indiana University Press, 2001).

6. E.g., Richard W. Byrne and Nadia Corp, "Neocortex Size Predicts Deception Rate in Primates," *The Royal Society* (2004), http://www.ncbi.nlm.nih.gov/pmc/articles/PMC1691785/.

7. E.g., Randy Thornhill, *The Evolutionary Biology of Human Female Sexuality* (Oxford: Oxford University Press, 2008).

8. Marcel Mauss, *The Gift: The Form and Reason for Exchange in Archaic Societies* (New York: W. W. Norton, 2000), First published 1950.

6

Natural Man and the Fall

The Beast-Man

The scandal that has accompanied current controversies about evolution—that human beings are, after all, just another animal—is not new. The beautiful animal paintings on the walls of the prehistoric caves at Lascaux and Altamira clearly show the artists' awareness that animals have consciousness and spirit, as we do. The deer-headed dancing shaman of the Dordogne, the lion-headed man of Hohlenstein-Stafel, are eloquent evidence of the artists' recognition that we are indeed animals, with the same kind of muscles and bone leverage and sex organs. Similar images in more recently discovered sites in South Africa and Australia are up to ten times the age of the European examples. One of the first questions we must have asked ourselves when we began to be conscious of ourselves in relation to the rest of the world was surely "What are we?" With that question come others: "What were we before we became what we are now? Are we another animal? Are we different from animals? How? How did we get to be different?"

Epic is both an example of that questioning and a complex sort of answer. It is an answer in the form of story, as we have already seen. The most direct and salient "deep allegory" of the answer is the persistent theme of the beast-man or natural man, and the story of how he is defeated by culture, falls into culture, or is seduced by culture, and looks back at his despoiled innocence with mixed feelings.

Immediately we see the advantages of epic's means of analysis: the story form virtually forces the storyteller to envisage the change from the natural to the cultural man as a complex and labyrinthine one—or else there's no story! Thus the condition of the natural man is not a single simple characteristic but a package of characteristics, and the condition of culture itself comes as a still more complicated package, with the good and evil elements of it inextricably mixed together.

Scientific method, excellent in many respects, is in some ways inferior to the storytelling system, as its reductive, deductive, and analytical procedure virtually dictates that a single cause with a single effect be identified as the answer. Thus from the nineteenth century onwards, we have had dozens of scientific hypotheses that have attributed our humanity and its origin to some single cause: bipedalism, increase in brain size, language, time concepts, awareness of death, hunting, the opposable thumb, social structure, concealed ovulation, fire, deception, politics, trade, art, toolmaking, longevity, temperature control, theory of mind, mirror neurons, ritual, extended infancy, etc. Not that any of these explanations are essentially wrong; we have already glanced at several of them and found them useful in understanding some part of an epic story. But the beauty of epic's account of our relationship with our natural precursor is that all these elements fit together and come as a package. One might argue that storytelling itself is the answer arrived at by epic—but this would be to fall into the monocausotaxophilia—my friend Ernst Pöppel's term for the love of single causes that explain everything—that is the temptation of science.

The beast-man is the essential mythical being in epic's great narrative thought experiment. He can vary hugely. Sometimes he is the brutish enemy—Grendel, Polyphemus, Humbaba. Sometimes he is the hero, like Parzifal, Zal, Cuchulainn, Sundiata the lion-buffalo, and even Wordsworth himself, who are raised in the wild like Mowgli or Tarzan, and must learn human ways when they come of age. Sometimes he is the hero's brave and loyal helper, like Enkidu, Benkei the vassal of Yoshitsune in the *Heike*, Hanuman/Monkey in the *Ramayana* and *The Journey to the West*, Queequeg in *Moby Dick*. In the *Popol Vuh*, the beast-man is represented individually by One Monkey and One Artisan and collectively by the various tribes who without fire, forethought, proper ritual piety, treachery, and other civilized traits, are enslaved or sacrificed by the Quiché. In his richest, most ambivalent form, he is the friend-enemy who must be sacrificed but who comes back from the dead—the Green Knight/Sir Bercilak in *Sir Gawaine and the Green Knight* and Falstaff (who was resurrected from the dead in *The Merry Wives of Windsor* by the decree, it is said, of Queen Elizabeth herself).

If a hero is raised in civilization, he must always undergo a return to nature—Rama and the Pandavas in the forest, Abraham in the wilderness, Odysseus in the caves of Polyphemus and Calypso, the Kyrghyz Manas as a shepherd, Hamlet at sea among the pirates, Prince

Hal in the Boar's Head. David of Sassoun, born a prince, is orphaned and becomes a poor shepherd, a wild man who must be tamed by his mentor Ohan. Young Temüjin must become a wild man too, learning his animal nature and the difference between himself and an animal before he can return to unite and liberate the Mongol tribes. Jumong, who will later become King Dongmyeong of Korea, is exiled from his homeland to the wild, but the forces of nature in the form of turtles and river-beings assist him, and he too returns, to unite the five tribes of Jolbon. It is as if separate tribes can only be unified by one who has gone back to the ancient natural crotch in our and the world's evolution when we all split off from the rest of nature; only such a hero can speak for and to all the tribes. Perhaps the storytellers themselves go even further back: Orpheus, Solomon, Vainamoinen, and Vyasa—like Mowgli and Tarzan—can speak the languages of birds and beasts, sometimes of plants, iron, and stone.

Sometimes the hero's bestial roots are concealed in embarrassment by later scholarly or priestly redactors, yet the essential signs of the beast-man hero cannot be removed. Moses is drawn forth from the Nile uncircumcised and though raised in the Pharaoh's palace he is wild enough to commit murder when he sees a Hebrew slave being mistreated. He is exiled to the wilderness of Midian, and encounters God in natural form as a burning bush. He must go through a strange traumatic fall, triggered by his marriage to the (gentile) Zipporah and symbolized by the terrible night when the Lord seeks to kill him. Zipporah saves him by circumcising their newborn son and smearing Moses' feet (often a priestly euphemism for the genitals) with his son's blood—as later the Hebrew firstborn are to be saved from the angel of death by sacrificial blood smeared on the lintels of their homes. Moses acquires a staff that can turn into a snake, reminiscent of the Mesopotamian snake-god Ningizzida (demonized by the Persians as Zahhak). In ancient Jewish folktale and imagery he is sometimes represented with horns.

What, then, characterizes the "wildness" or "naturalness" or naivety of the beast-man? What does he lack that civilized man possesses; what does he possess that the civilized man lacks? And if he falls, and becomes civilized, how does that happen?

The Fall

The full "package" of the Fall in epic seems to include the following: sexual imagination, drugs (especially alcohol), cooked food, clothes, manners, shame, awareness of death, awareness of time, disobedience, deceit, insight into the thoughts of others, planning for the future, moral knowledge, internal language, curiosity, self-consciousness, mobility, freedom, weakness, games, aesthetics, technology, domestication, and agriculture. By and large, the cultured or civilized human possesses these, the natural human does not.

Sex

Or perhaps one should say that the natural male does not possess these things. Epic seems to assume that women do not need to fall, or are born fallen. The Eve of both the Bible and Milton is already second-guessing her husband and her God and wondering what God's threat of death could mean, and Milton's Eve already likes to look at herself in the mirror. Blood Moon in the *Popol Vuh* has already sneaked away from her father Blood Gatherer, talking to herself in an internal dialogue, curious to taste the sweet fruit of the Calabash Tree, when she meets the skull of One Hunahpu and is impregnated by it and later cast out of Xibalba for her sin. It is hard to find in any epic a good candidate for an unfallen woman in this sense, one who falls and only then opens her eyes.

Perhaps this difference reflects the earlier sexual and social maturation of the human female. Or perhaps it is that unlike a man, a woman can be sure her baby is her own: thus she knows her physical life will go on after her personal death, and so the thought of death itself, the great catalyst for many other aspects of the Fall, is more bearable and familiar and arrives sooner. The Fall of Man is often in a sense a conversion of him by Woman to the fallen persuasion, a tutorial in human consciousness. It certainly is such in *Gilgamesh*, when the Harlot opens Enkidu's eyes. If Odysseus had been a woman, perhaps she would not have needed violence and technology to open Polyphemus' eye and make him do her bidding; and perhaps Polyphemus could, in an alternate myth, have fallen and grown a second eye.

In any case, sex difference and the emergence of that exciting, frightening, and energizing curiosity about the personal Other is a major factor in the Fall. The seduction of the horned wild man Rishyasringa by Santa in the *Mahabharata* is a classic example—in one of the most delightfully comic, erotic, and wickedly coy passages in all of literature, he naïvely describes the experience to his hermit father:

154

Father, a religious student came by today, as shining and gracious as a god. He was very beautiful, and he wore his dark hair very long, and it was fragrant and tied with golden strings. His smooth skin was fair as fine warm gold, and on his chest were two soft, round pillows. His clothes were wonderful, not at all like mine, and in his hair he wore a flower I have never seen and round his neck a sparkling ornament. His waist was slender, and he had musical rosaries on his wrists and ankles. His voice was happy and clear, like a bird's song in the morning, and over his eyes were beautiful black curves. He carries the large round fruit [a ball] that falls to the ground only to leap up again into the sky, and he held me, and caught my hair to pull down my mouth, and covered my mouth with his, and made a little murmuring sound. He gave me sweet fruit, without any skin, or any stone inside, and flavored holy water that made me very happy, and made the Earth seem to move under my feet.

Though this passage is a minor episode in the great poem, it can be seen also as a gloss upon the very important matter of Arjuna's transformation into a woman in the court of Virata. Arjuna is literally "converted"! The passage neatly encapsulates many of the great Fall themes: the recognition of sexual difference, the transformation from naïvety to knowledge, the dawning of aesthetic experience, the pleasure, shame, and titillation of clothing, the metallic products of technology, game-playing, sweetmeats, and alcoholic intoxication.

The seduction of Enkidu includes all these elements and more. The Harlot does a strip-tease for the wild man, who has come down to the drinking-hole with the antelopes to drink. He learns to speak by murmuring love-talk in her ear. He becomes physically weak and the animals now shun him: "Wisdom was in him, and the thoughts of a man were in his heart." He is clothed by the Harlot, who—significantly—divides her own clothes with him, and he is flattered by her that he has become like a god. He is given wine to drink instead of milk, which he is used to, and bread—the cooked product of agriculture. He is anointed with oil, an important industrial product, and given weapons to hunt with, the fruit of Mesopotamian technology. Finally he is introduced to politics, when the plight of the city of Uruk is explained to him, and forms a plan of political action.

Parzifal's fall into courtly manners has a similar course. When he meets his first lady, Jeschute, he does not know how to behave. He seizes her as she sleeps, takes her ring and brooch, and is distracted from her person by her offer of bread and wine. Her husband, Orilus ("Pride"), shames her—a shame that comes home to Parzifal when he later comes to understand proper manners. He does so by his own experience of shame when, because of his clownish appearance and behavior, another lady, Cunneware, laughs at him and is given a beating for it by Kay the seneschal. Parzifal's later avenging defeat of Kay in battle is the catalyst for his great quest of the grail.

The biblical Fall is likewise catalyzed by a woman, and it could be said that the whole of the Book of Genesis is a working-out of the nature and consequences of fall itself. Many of the elements are familiar in other epics; one, which is not in any of the others, could be predicted by contemporary evolutionary anthropology—Eve's special curse of painful and difficult childbirth. Milton adds to the Genesis account the detail that the forbidden fruit is intoxicating, thus collapsing the drug motif into the fruit and disobedience motifs. "Fruit" in this sense also means "consequence"—sequence itself, time, and the consciousness of time's passage. Milton also has his Adam and Eve immediately succumb to prurient sexual imagination, an episode absent in Genesis.

In the decree of partnership in enmity between Eve and the serpent, we can glimpse a mirrored hall of symbolic potentials. The serpent is both renewing life (because it rejuvenates itself by changing its skin, like the serpent that steals Gilgamesh's herb of immortality) and death (the serpent is venomous). The serpent's quick binocular intelligence paradoxically contrasts with its low habit of life; it is as much below the four-legged stance of other animals as they are beneath the two-legged hominid stance. The serpent is male in its form, but female in its cunning and sinuousness, and in its capacity for self-renewal; like a menstruating woman who changes her inner skin, the snake changes its outer. Eve is both bound to, and rejects, this ineluctable package; like Pandora, her box contains both the ills of human life and the great gift of hope.

As Genesis proceeds, more of the classic Fall implications emerge: agriculture in God's preferring of the farmer Abel to the herder Cain; technology in the inventive descendants of Cain and in the tower of Babel; mobility and freedom in the expulsion from Eden and diaspora (as Milton puts it, "The World was all before them, where to choose"); domestication in Jacob's skill in animal breeding; and all the psychological and moral elements of the Fall that arise in the stories of the Patriarchs: awareness of death, awareness of time, disobedience, deceit, insight into the thoughts of others, planning for the future, moral knowledge, internal language, curiosity, self-consciousness, and especially shame.

Clothes and Shame

We recognize in the fig-leaves of Genesis the clothing and shame motifs that we have seen elsewhere. Consider the human body, and its remarkable differences from the bodies of other mammals. One of the most obvious is our nakedness; we stand hairless but for odd tufts here and there, emphasizing such body parts as the head and face, and the genitals. All other land mammals of our size, and all of our relatives the primates, including all tropical primates, are covered with hair. Some much larger tropical species, like elephants and rhinoceroses, are, indeed, also hairless; the reason is that their greater size implies a higher ratio of body volume to body surface, and a larger and more stable thermal reservoir; and thus they do not need hair. Human beings, however, are pantropic in their habit—we live in all climates—and are much smaller; without clothing and/or shelter we would be at a massive disadvantage.

We, like the other animals, evolved; and it is a truism of evolutionary logic that if a given bodily structure (such as hair) is not necessary, and cannot be adapted to another purpose, those individuals that possess it will be at a disadvantage, if only because of the metabolic drain on their resources that the structure's production and upkeep requires. This disadvantage will tend statistically to result in fewer such individuals surviving to reproduce, a thinning out of the genes for that structure in the population, and a preferential rate of increase for genes not specifying that structure. The same applies in reverse; if a species would be better off with hair, say, to maintain a constant body temperature, hair will be selected for. As we see in the case of the peacock's tail and the elk's antlers, however, sexual ritual can contradict this biological law: body structures that actually hinder individual survival can be preserved and enlarged by sexual selection; structures that might be useful for survival will be selected against if they hinder the more powerful goal of reproduction.

The most plausible explanation for our nakedness, then, is that it is the result of sexual selection in ritual courtship, and that we developed clothing originally both for ritual body decoration and also to replace for thermal purposes the hair that we had lost. The invention of clothes, a by-product of our ritual, enabled us to survive even in cool temperate and arctic climates; and so as hair was no longer necessary for survival, it never came back. Our nakedness is a result of our early culture.

Thus the clothing motif in Fall stories is not a mere cosmetic detail but an essential insight. Our nakedness is both a reminder of our animal nature and a sign that we are not like other animals, which are decently and naturally clad in their own fur. The two-legged stance makes our sexuality harder to conceal, especially for the aroused male. The emotional correlate of this fact is shame—a feeling that is both painful and at the same time strongly associated with pleasurable arousal. Shame is at least partly a kind of cognitive dissonance, but one that is not just a detached puzzlement or mental discomfort but a full-blown emotional conflict. It is the living emotional fossil, so to speak, of our shameful emergence from the world of the other animals. It is also the beginning of human culture and technology; anthropological archeologists take body ornaments in an excavated site as a sure sign of *Homo sapiens*.

Clothing both expresses and conceals—in other words, it gives us control over who and what we seem to be, it is a sign of our own power and freedom to shape ourselves and become what we wish to be. "Unaccommodated man," says Lear to Poor Tom, "is no more but such a poor, bare, forked animal as thou art." When Odysseus must pluck up a branch of olive to shield his nakedness as he advances on pretty Nausicaa and her girls (who, like Santa in the story of Rishyasringa, have been charmingly playing catch with a ball), he is hiding not just the presence, but the state, of what he is hiding. The olive is a cultivated tree, we might note; and the episode, including Nausicaa's gift of clothes to the wild man, the games of the Phaeaceans, the description of Alcinous' gardens, and the civilized luxury and fine wine of his table, is a sure signal both that Odysseus' sojourn in the wild was effective in making him a wild man, and that it is over and he can come out of his cave.

Shame, as I have argued in an earlier book, *Beauty: The Value of Values*, is the necessary portal to beauty.

> If we look at the foundation myths of any culture we will find some deeply shameful act at the origin of the human world. Take, for instance, the Eskimo story of Sedna and her father Anguta. Sedna marries a dog against her father's wishes; the father kills her dog-husband; on the way back a storm rises and Anguta, to lighten the boat, throws his daughter overboard; she clings to the boat and he, to get rid of her, cuts off her fingers. Or the Shinto story of how the Sun-goddess Amaterasu was shamed by her bad brother Susa-no-wo, who threw a flayed horse through the roof of her

weaving-hall. Her subsequent retirement to a cave deprived the world of sunlight—as did the shamed rage of Ceres in the myth of Persephone. Or consider the shameful story of Cronus castrating his father Uranus with a sickle, and the generally incestuous provenance of the Greek gods; or the shameful murder of the corn god in Amerindian mythology; or the various shameful acts of tabu murder and incest in Australian aboriginal creation myths.

These myths express the essential knot of our human predicament. The threads of that knot include: the problematic coexistence of a reflective mind with a smelly, sexed, and partly autonomous body, the horror of death, the ambiguous relationship of human beings with the rest of nature, the incestuous paradoxes of kinship and parenthood, the capacity to lie given us by language, and the difficulty, obligation, and anxiety inherent in the socio-economic acts of gift-giving and dividing the fruits of the hunt. Our aboriginal human philosophy tended, with the natural economy of dualism, to divide the cultural from the natural. Today, in the light of evolutionary biology and cosmological science, we may be in a position to revise that ancient dichotomy. We recognize that to some extent other species share those reflexive paradoxes, and that our version of them is only an intensification—across certain crucial thresholds—of tensions inherent in the evolutionary process itself and belonging perhaps to the feedback nature of the universe as a whole. However, even if we do replace an absolute division between the human and the natural with a more continuous evolutionary gradient of increasing reflexivity, and even when we come to recognize nature as not just that which is given, but as the very process of accelerating evolution that transforms the given, we must still deal with a world in which greater and lesser levels of self-reference, feedback, intention, and freedom must somehow coexist.

And this coexistence is essentially shameful. We are ashamed about our sexuality, about how we came into the world, about how we did not at one time exist, either as a species or individually. We are thus ashamed of our parents, especially when adolescence forces on us a constant attention to the process of reproduction that originated us; and the reflexive appetite of the mind makes us at the same time seek out the nakedness of father Noah, the nakedness of mother Jocasta. We are ashamed at our bodies, which display an impure and inextricable mixture, a mutual *adulteration*, of the intentional and the instinctive. We are ashamed about eating, because, whatever we eat, we are assuming, upon the confessedly untrustworthy warrant of our own biased judgment that we must be more valuable than what we destroy with our teeth and digestive juices. Hence we naturally find the end-products of eating to be objects of disgust. We are at the top of the food chain and feel an anguished and unrepayable obligation to those beings which gave up their lives for us.

We are ashamed about our economic system, whereby we define ourselves as members in good standing of our community, and thus as human beings; we are never quite sure whether we have given the right gift, or given a gift when we should not have, or not given a gift when we should; and we are shamefully anxious about whether we have been given the right gift. We are ashamed at what we have made, whether because of uncertainty about its worthiness or because of the obligation we incurred to those parts of the world we destroyed to make our new contribution to it. The institution of money, by which we extend through time and space the reckoning-up of the balance of obligation for past gifts and so transcend the limitations of memory, is a basically shameful object of contemplation; we call lucre filthy and are always seeking ways to delegitimize our own economy, at least as it applies to ourselves. We are, finally, ashamed at our own feelings of shame, our own reflexiveness, our awareness of our awareness.

However, as James Hans points out, it is precisely in this whole area of experience—the reflective interaction at the deepest level with nature, with our origins, with our means of life, with our closest kin, with our community as an object of obligation, and with our very self-consciousness itself—that we encounter the beautiful. Thus in ways that are bearable to us because their story-nature insulates us from their direct personal application without denaturing their meaning, our myths conduct us into the realms of shame where the hot blush of consciousness—the "Blank misgivings of a creature/Moving about in worlds not realized," as Wordsworth put it—can be transformed into the delicious shiver of beauty. The severed fingers of Sedna become the beautiful warm-blooded marine mammals by which the Eskimos survive; the sun-goddess Amaterasu is lured forth from her cave by the newly-invented mysteries of dance, comedy, and the mirror of self-awareness; Adam and Eve get knowledge as well as death, and give birth to history and to human redemption; the genitals of Cronus arise from the sea-foam as the beautiful goddess of love; the corn god's golden hair waves in the wind as the silk of the ripening maize; and the pratfalls and transgressive gaucheries of the aboriginal tricksters are the source of all human arts and graces.

Shame and beauty, then, share a common root. The work of such myths is both to show us how to experience the beauty we have paid for with our shame, and to remind us that if we attempt to avoid or repress the shame, we will find ourselves as cut off from beauty as the world was from sunlight in the myths of Amaterasu and Persephone. Why beauty and shame should be so closely connected is a matter of considerable interest . . . both involve the emergent and aroused reflexivity, self-reference, and feedback of nature, both within and beyond the sphere of human culture.[1]

We have already looked at the role that shame plays as the portal to spiritual experience in *Parzifal*. The central pivot of Eschenbach's poem--where the Round Table is founded, Parzifal begins his redemption after the initial failure at Munsalvaesche, the two stories of Gawan the courteous and Parzifal the grail-achiever diverge, and the hero is captivated by the snow-and-blood image of his wife's beautiful body--is also the point where he recognizes the shame of his earlier deeds, avenges the shame of Kay's beating of Cunneware, and begins his own humiliation at the hands of Cundrie and Trevrizent.

There is an old anecdote about King Edward III that catches something of the medieval insight about shame. The English king was dancing with the Countess of Salisbury. Her garter slipped down to her ankle, and bystanders (like Cunneware in *Parzifal*) sniggered at her humiliation. In an act of chivalry Edward placed the garter around his own leg, saying "Honi soit qui mal y pense"—"May he be ashamed who thinks ill of it." The Order of the Garter is still England's noblest honor. The motto of the Garter, as of the British royal coat of arms, is thus *Honi soit qui mal y pense*, where honor and shame are combined in the French word *honi*. It still survives on the British passport.

The mini-epic *Sir Gawaine and the Green Knight* can be seen as a sort of myth expanding the meaning of the order of the Garter (the motto is inscribed at the end of the poem). Here the garter is a woman's green girdle, a gift to Gawaine from the wife of Sir Bercilak that Gawaine honorably accepts in lieu of her offer of her own body. But he shamefully refrains from giving it to Bercilak in exchange for the gift of game from Bercilak's hunting, an exchange previously agreed upon as a sort of wager or game. He does so because next day he must, according to another game-contract, meet the giant Green Knight, the immortal Natural Man of the poem, and allow him a deadly return blow in exchange for his own a year since; and the lady has told him that the girdle can protect his life. Since a vegetation god's head can grow back again, like a plant, while a mortal's can not, the contract is an unfair one. But of course the Green Knight's other identity is Sir Bercilak himself, who could have been cuckolded by Gawaine but was not; and the delicate scales of honor give Gawaine the benefit of the exchange. The green girdle, green for nature, green for growth, green like the fig-leaves of Eden, now ratified by the red thread of blood that is left by the glancing blow of Bercilak's axe, becomes the sign of English honor thereafter. Honor, which is beauty of human behavior, is bound up with shame, and together they make up the state of grace, the grace of the honorific "your Grace," as well as the grace of divine humility.

Similar complexities attend the Persian story of the refusal of Zal, himself a postlapsarian Natural Man, to dishonorably accept the advances of Rudabeh; so too the Biblical tale of Joseph's denial of Potiphar's wife, Enkidu's refusal of Ishtar, the naked sword that lies between the lovers in the stories of Tristram and Iseult and Siegfried and Brunnhild. All these stories hint at the same ambivalences, the strange beauty that results from the shame of the dropped garter, the hero's secret garment from the body of a woman, the woman left holding the cloak of the naked man, the warrior's weapon in the bed of love. All are reminders of the shame and thrilling election of our promotion from the animals and the special human beauty that emerges from the paradox.

Human beings re-experience the Fall, the emergence of the human from the holy beast, every time we experience shame. Epic is the way we tell that story.

Drugs

The fall of natural man and loss of innocence is often associated with the taste of a drug, especially alcohol. The essential element in Odysseus' defeat of Polyphemus, and the beginning of his own delivery from the cave of lost identity, is the potent and delicious fortified wine that the hero has providently brought with him. Like Caliban on Shakespeare's magic island, the Cyclops can be tricked into the service of weaker but two-eyed thinking beings by the power of alcohol. (Caliban says that the liquor is "not earthly."[2]) In the selective process by which Odysseus' crew is gradually reduced and eventually eliminated, drugs play a central part. Consider the lotoses of the lotos-eaters that make them forget, the drugged wine of Circe that turns men to beasts. A superficial reading would take these drugs as a symbol of our reduction to animals by physical pleasure.

But what is Odysseus doing carrying and valuing the wine in the first place? The drug is not an enemy, but a friend. It is an essential test of our civilized cultural identity as human beings. It sorts out the truly human from the merely bestial. It gives us a way to make a controlled and reversible descent—if we are mentally strong enough—into the world of nature, and return. Dionysus the god of wine is a great god, a friend to culture, if a dangerous one. He can be a psychopomp between the land of conscious life and the land of nature—of the dead and the ever-living, as he was for Ariadne on Naxos. Odysseus needs the capacity to become beastlike—he must counterfeit a ram to escape Polyphemus' cave.

Gilgamesh can help us further with this paradox. The wine that the harlot gives Enkidu is part of his blessed/cursed fall, his acculturation. To have been drunk and then sober up is an experience that forces upon us an awareness of the nature of consciousness, and an uncomfortable *self*-consciousness as we look back ashamed at the foolish things we did under the influence. We develop, so to speak, a second eye—or because, tipsy, we see double, we become aware that we have a second eye, that the world we see is not necessarily the world as it is, but how it is seen. This gives us an advantage over the teetotaler. The one-eyed man when he runs up against the two-eyed will soon be blinded, no king in the country of the blind. When Gilgamesh sets out on his great journey to the land of the dead-and-everliving he must encounter Siduri, the divine bartender, and entertain her temptation to merriment and forgetfulness, as Odysseus does with Circe (Aeneas with Dido, Rinaldo with Alcina, and so on). It is through this encounter that he is able to complete his quest, however disappointing its outcome.

Perhaps we could say this: that a culture is no better—no deeper, no stronger, no more interesting, no more beautiful—than the drugs it must compete against. Drugs are the necessary spur to culture. A society that is not willing or able to propose to its young people cultural ideals, glories, challenges, high achievements, beautiful risks, entrancing puzzles, and transcendent experiences of peace and acceptance, that overmatch the pleasures of the strongest drug present, must die—and it deserves to. No drug can induce an experience that is not already available to the undrugged mind—a drug only works because it mimics the chemistry of one or more of the brain's own neuropeptides or neurotransmitters, designed to reward or transport us under the appropriate real circumstances. Societies that attempt to ban drugs are ipso facto admitting their own insufficiency to provide those circumstances—and if they do not, what is the justification of their existence? Joy and the journey into other states of consciousness—the psychedelic and the psychotropic—are going to draw us in any event. We will find either the real thing in our social world, and thus work to maintain that world, or prefer the counterfeit and let our society die. Drugs are the bar that society must leap, and if it does not need to leap, it will not. We can almost gauge the achievements and progress of human cultures by their drugs—alcohol, tobacco, peyote, opiates, khat, kava, cocaine, tea, cocoa, coffee, ephedrines, and our present pharmacopia.

Accordingly the epic is profoundly interested in drugs. The Four Hundred Boys in the *Popol Vuh*, believing they have bested the huge phallic monster Zipacna, celebrate with wine, and in their drunken stupor they are crushed in their hut by the monster. Unlike the Four Hundred Boys, and unlike the first pair of hero twins, Hunahpu and Xbalanque are able to refrain from smoking the cigars that they are given by the Lords of the Dead as a test of their humanity. Both the *Mahabharata* and the *Ramayana* have injunctions against drunkenness, especially in the voice of the wise Vidura, but the heroes do not refrain; they can both take and hold their liquor. In the feast on the Raivatak Hill Arjuna and Krishna himself, the avatar of Vishnu, get distinctly tipsy. Monkey, the beast-man in *The Journey to the West*, is a great drinker; his pilgrimage is to find a spiritual enlightenment that overmatches (and is implicitly tested by) the power of the drug.

Noah and Lot are famously drunk in the Book of Genesis, which can be seen in toto as an extended account of the Fall; both episodes have profound consequences in human social history. The future destiny of all the world's peoples is decided by Ham's spying on his father's nakedness; and the descendants of Lot, whose daughters seduce him while in his drunken stupor, become the Moabites, the old enemies of the chosen people. Beowulf, unlike Unferth, the scoffer in Hrothgar's hall, can hold his liquor. Egil, the hero of *Egil's Saga*, is a famous drinker, as are Cuchulainn, Sigmund, and Atli. Falstaff, the beast-man of the *Henriad*, is the poet of sherris-sack, and Prince Hal must learn from him how to drink. Milton's Eve and Adam get drunk on the fruit of the forbidden tree. Ahab in Moby Dick welds his crew together with neat rum drunk from the hollow shaft of their harpoons.

The power that a drug gives us to change our own brain-state epitomizes the mixed blessings of the human condition. Used wisely it enables us to explore a universe of different modes of being; but it is always liable to create a feedback spiral in which the changes we create in ourselves cannot be undone and may lead to further, possibly catastrophic, metamorphoses. Thus the "chinjikijilu" or blaze of the master-explorer, the shaman, is needed by the epic hero to enable him to return. The moly-root that Hermes gives Odysseus is one version of that blaze. The golden bough of Aeneas is another, and so, perhaps, is the presence of the poet Virgil to Dante. But this track may be explored more appropriately when we examine the underworld journey.

Technology

Sigmund, son of Volsung, and Arthur, son of Uther, both get their mission—and the proof of their heroic identity—by drawing a sword forth from a natural trap when no other man can do so. This moment can itself be seen as a sort of blessed fall from the naivety of nature.

Sigmund gets his sword from the tree Barnstock—"bairn-stock," the root that keeps producing offspring, the family tree, the tree of human nature. Siggeir, jealous of Sigmund for his being so chosen, kills Sigmund's father Volsung, and this in turn initiates Sigmund's return to nature, his sojourn in the forest as a werewolf, his return and revenge on Siggeir, and his reclamation of his cultural patrimony. In this, Sigmund is like Odysseus, who is identified by his ability to draw his bow when others cannot, and who must take on the guise of an animal and go through the cave of the wild man to become the true king. Later Sigurd, Sigmund's son, will ask Regin, his foster-father, to forge a sword for him, the great blade Gram. The forging takes two unsuccessful tries before the blade is perfect, and splits the anvil rather than breaking upon it. With Gram, Sigurd avenges his own father's death. Regin also teaches Sigurd the arts of civilization—sports, chess, runes, and languages.

In the language of epic story, it is clear that some kind of relationship is being proposed between technology—specifically, that of smelting and tempering—and the boundary between nature and culture, the fall from natural innocence into human forethought and guile. That fall is also paradoxically ratified by the human ability to *pretend* to be an animal when necessary. The sword of techne is inherent in nature, but it must be won with difficulty from a resistant medium and only a special kind of person—one who can take on the guise of an animal—can do it. Regin drinks the dragon's blood, and Sigurd eats the dragon's heart. Were the first shamans, with their animal heads, also the knappers of flint weapons and, later, the smiths?

Copper, tin, and iron are literally extracted from the rock; Arthur's achievement, as the naïf who has grown up in rustic obscurity as a natural man, is to extract the iron from the stone. The passage from one-eyedness to two-eyedness, so to speak, the dawn of the age of reason either historically or psychologically, comes with the difficult

165

birth of technology. Arthur proves his royal ancestry by his feat. We extract the sword from the wood of our own natural family tree or by our natural talent from the rock of the physical world. As Roland is dying he attempts to break his sword Durendal on the rocks of the Pyrenees; the great natural gap, *La Brèche de Roland*, is said to be the result. But the human sword, once won from the stone, cannot be returned to it; the human sword can split the anvil on which it was made.

Over-interpretation might be a danger here, were it not that the same pattern emerges again and again in epic, with variations. When Enkidu, fresh from his fall into human culture, accompanies Gilgamesh to battle with the forest-monster Humbaba, he is armed by Gilgamesh's smiths with a massive sword and axe. Sundiata, the buffalo/lion king, emerges from his infantile state when a great iron staff is forged for him by the soothsayer/griot/smith Farakourou, a staff too heavy to be carried by any single man. Sundiata, who until this moment has been unable to stand like a man and has gone on all fours like an animal for his first six years, kneels and picks up the staff without effort. As he rises to his feet with its help, it turns into a bow, the bow with which he will later become a great hunter and later still defeat the forces of Soumaoro, the usurper of his kingdom.

Parzifal falls from his natural state when he sees the knight Karnah-karnanz and marvels at the golden bells of his harness, the rings of his chain-mail, and his sword. The shaming episode with Cunneware is sparked by the dispute over whether the unarmored Parzifal is entitled to the armor of the knight Ither, whom he will later slay with his rustic javelin (rather as David the shepherd brings down Goliath the warrior with a slingshot). Parzifal dons the armor but has put it on wrongly, causing much ridicule. He must be taught by Iwanet and Gurnemanz, his Regin/Farakourou figures, how to dress properly, and this is where he completes the loss of his innocence.

In the *Popol Vuh*, the first pair of hero twins, One and Seven Hunahpu, invent soothsaying, the flute, singing, writing, carving, jade-working, and metalwork. They teach these skills to One Hunahpu's sons by the Egret Woman, the beast-men One Monkey and One Artisan; but the latter lack the cunning and reflectiveness nurtured by the ball-game, at which their half-brothers Hunahpu and Xbalanque are experts, and so are defeated by them and become monkeys. In like fashion the Quiché people establish their dominance over the other tribes by means of the gift of fire; in return for giving the gift to the others they demand human sacrifices and so establish the ritual piety of the Maya world.

The *Shahnameh* likewise recognizes the huge role of technology in our transition from animal to human. The reigns of the early kings Hushang, Tahmures, and Jamshid are a virtual catalog of fundamental human technology. The mighty blacksmith Kaveh forges the ram-headed mace of Feraydun, with which he defeats the evil brain-eating wizard king Zahhak. But, on the other hand, the hero must not lose touch with nature. Rostam needs the powers of nature to defeat the various natural opponents he meets during his trials. The taming of his horse Raksh is the key; Raksh defeats the lion that attacks them while Rostam himself is sleeping. Rostam learns from a ram how to find water, is alerted by Raksh to the threat of the dragon, is nearly ensnared by a witch when Raksh is unsaddled, and he uses a lariat, the cowboy's tool, to defeat other enemies.

In this light, Melville's pervading and minute concern with the technology of whaling takes on a deeper significance. The boat-captains and harpooneers are characterized as knights and squires; the harpooneers are all civilized savages of one kind or another. The war with nature that Ahab undertakes is intimately bound up with the nuances of technology; Ahab keeps the more primitive tools and weapons, but one by one discards or remakes to his own purposes the more sophisticated technological controls of our own nature. The quadrant is discarded, the compass remade, the log-line lost. He has the smith forge him a harpoon out of horseshoes and temper it in the blood of pagans; and he himself, as critics have often pointed out, is a prosthetic man, a cyborg.

Melville sees, as many other epic poets do too, that technology is double-edged and can wound its bearer. After all, it is Sigmund's sword that causes all the trouble, the envy, and the feud. In *Njal*, Gunnar's famous magic halberd is both his glory and the weapon with which he makes so many enemies; his bowstring once cut cannot be mended, because the resentful Hallgerd will not give him a lock of her hair. Beowulf's sword Hrunting is given to him by the envious Unferth and fails him in his battle with Grendel's mother; only a sword made by giants can kill her. Naegling, Beowulf's second sword, breaks on the dragon in the last battle. Wiglaf's sword, which does bite on the dragon, was made by giants. Here the implication is that a purely man-made sword will not work against the great forces of nature; nature itself must supply the weapon. Ahab's harpoon is useless against Moby

Dick; Odysseus cannot escape the cave by his own strength, but must use that of Polyphemus himself.

Technology can be seen as either the gift of gods to humans with special qualities or a human cultural victory over nature. Perhaps this is merely a matter of emphasis—what raises humans culturally above the rest of nature is the divine spark. Depending on the relative valences of nature, culture, and the divine, the role of technology in the Fall can vary. If natural innocence is valorized, technology can be one of the punishments of the gods—Adam must get his bread by the sweat of his brow and can no longer live on fruit plucked from the bounteous tree; Cain's descendants invent metalworking and build the ill-fated tower of Babel. Wordsworth must be driven forth from his arcadian lakeland home and, getting and spending in the city, lay waste his powers. If cultural self-knowledge, courage, and control are valorized, technology can be a divine reward for our courage in breaking the shackles of nature, as it seems to have been for the Norse and the Persians. But technology can also be the Promethean weapon by which we defy both nature and the gods—as is the case in Odysseus' defiance of Polyphemus and Poseidon, the hero twins' revolution against the lords of Xibalba, or Ahab's harpoon-strike through the mask. On the other hand, if the gods and the divine in humankind are given the highest value, both nature and the culturally created technology that enables us to control it must be sacrificed in pursuit of divine favor or mystical transcendence, as in the Chosen People's renunciation of the fleshpots of Egypt and their grudging acceptance of the asceticism of the desert—or in the princess Kenreimon's final rustic retirement in the *Heike*.

But in any case, the Fall always involves the birth of technology, whether as an evil or a good. In fact, epic usually mixes the evil with the good; even when the overt meaning of the Fall is one of the above alternatives, it contains an implicit hint of the others.

Mobility

To fall is to lose one's original home. But it is also to be freed from one's home. No human tribe lives today where its most distant human ancestors lived; even the Kalahari San people, the most indigenous of all of us, live thousands of miles from Ethiopia, where we humans are thought by anthropologists to have originated. How odd, one might note, that this location corresponds to the location of the Garden of Eden in the Old Testament. Could traditional folklore preserve such a memory of origin for over a hundred thousand years? Certainly Ethiopia was once a lush, well-watered, and temperate land, during the period known as the Abbassia Pluvial, before the desertification of Africa in the late Pleistocene era.[3]

As we have already noted, humans are one of the most efficient long-distance walkers in the animal kingdom. Our unique upright bipedal stance, singled out by no less than Sophocles and Plato[4] as a defining characteristic, is one reason for our mobility; our nakedness, a handicap when we are sedentary, becomes an advantage when we are running, because of our improved ability to sweat and so control our temperature. (Wolves and dogs, by contrast, do not sweat and must cool themselves by panting.) The exodus from Africa evidently began as soon as we achieved the full upright stance, lost our fur, and had to wear clothes.[5]

Fall is in epic followed by hegira or diaspora. We have already looked at the theme of journey in epic; we can now identify its cause as the Fall. Whether this restless journeying is collective, in the migrations of peoples, or individual, in the human adolescent's urge to leave home and find a mate, epic almost always evokes it in its exilic wanderings, its quests, and its nostalgic yearning for home. The Trojans, the Quiché, the Israelites, the Heike, the Pandavas, the crusaders, the martian colonists, the Icelanders, the Pequoders, Sundiata, Odysseus, Siegfried, Tripitaka, Dante, Gilgamesh, Martín Fierro, Wordsworth, Parzifal, Vasco da Gama, the Cid, Cuchulainn—all are driven by the same wanderlust, the same aching nostalgia.

The great question is: can we go home? And the answer is almost always: no, or if not no, then home when we return to it is another strange island. So the second question is: can we—how do we—make a new home? And this question is, according to epic, the most important practical question for the human race. This issue may be the basis of a key distinction between the epic and the novel; the novel is about being at home—however difficult that may be—but the epic is about finding and making a home.

Human Weakness

In epic, human beings gain many strengths from the Fall, including some physical bodily ones like the long-distance endurance mobility we have recognized. The mental strengths are obvious: foresight, self-criticism, insight into other minds, linguistic ability, a flair for lies and fictions, abstraction and generalization, planned tool-making and tool-use, game-invention and game-playing, conscious decision, irony, humor, courtesy, a "binocular" ability to resolve different points of view into a rounded depth-perception, and so forth.

We also gain physical dexterity and grace, and the ability to train ourselves for very delicate tasks; the stringing and use of Odysseus' bow requires a fine grasp of leverage and targeting as well as physical power (we have seen him train these abilities in the cave of Polyphemus). The Mayan hero twins are experts in the ball game, Cuchulainn is a master of Hurley, and so forth. Gilgamesh and Enkidu defeat the Bull of Heaven by their bullfighting skills—the Western evolution of bullfighting from its Mesopotamian origins through the Minoan and Hispanic civilizations into Latin America is a sign of its ancient and continuing appeal as a graphic symbol of the Fall's great trade-off.

But with these strengths come radical weaknesses. Enkidu can no longer run with the animals (though he can walk hundreds of leagues carrying hundreds of pounds of armor and weapons). Odysseus is not strong enough to roll the stone away from Polyphemus' cave, an easy task for the beast-man. (When Superman falls for Lois Lane and falls into mortality, he loses his strength.) In epic the hero seems to be betwixt-and-between as regards physical strength; relative to other men, he has the bestial strength of natural man, but relative to the beast, he has human weakness and must use cunning, leverage, tools, and devices. This general pattern, though, is sometimes reversed and questioned in epic. Beowulf, for instance, is strongest against his monstrous opponents when he is unarmed. Perhaps the superhuman frenzy of the berserker, as distant from the fallen human as from the brute, trumps the brute's own strength. The Fall weakens humans, but also lays them open to the entry of divine power, possession by the war-god, help by powerful spirits.

Again, the epic accurately reflects in its deep allegorical mode the actual history of human evolution. Our nearest animal relatives, the chimpanzees, have as much as eight times our physical strength. The relatively tiny proportion of genes that had to change to separate our lineage from that of our common ancestor (1.5 percent to 3.7 percent depending on how it is measured) included a mutation in a gene for myosin, or muscle fiber, that radically enfeebled us. Dexterity and endurance—the ability to manipulate the environment in ways that give us leverage and enable us to use nature's own strength against it, and the ability to maintain an action over time and thus master a segment of the future—are the recompense that we seem to have received for the loss. Tools and travel (and trade) more than compensate for our fallen weakness, or so epic implies.

At the same time it is known that human beings are capable of calling up superhuman hysterical strength in conditions of great emotional stress, an ability not normally under conscious control. Mothers have been known to lift heavy vehicles from their trapped children. An Inuk woman in Quebec fought off an eight-hundred-pound polar bear that was threatening her seven-year-old son.[6] The physical achievements of yogis, zen martial arts masters, and even Christian ascetics show that we can to some extent master these powers through spiritual discipline. So the epic is right in recognizing that the weakness caused by the Fall can be supplemented at supreme moments of *chairos* by a sort of divine frenzy.

Domestication

The victory of Gilgamesh and Enkidu over the Bull of Heaven takes to another level the skills of the Trapper who originally domesticates Enkidu. Thanks to the Fall, we can not only entrap other animals, but trick them or lever them into serving us. The staff or wand of Jacob, like Moses' staff, is a branch from the Tree of Life and is also the shepherd's crook, with which the wise stockbreeder hooks and controls his animals so that the strongest breed with the strongest, the tamest with the tamest, so turning nature's creation into humankind's.[7] (We will look more closely at the staff of Moses and Jacob, and its relation to the Greco-Roman karykeion or caduceus, when we focus on the great talismans by which the hero moves safely through the land of the dead.)

The art of husbandry, the skill of Abel, is one of the gifts of the Fall. Husbandry is a rich term, including laying by resources for the future, taking care of the land, putting the right husband to the right mate, and binding to a home. Thus Rostam must tame his wild horse Raksh, Odysseus is first recognized on his return by his dog Argos, the tragic war that animates *The Cattle Raid of Cooley* is fought over the Brown Bull of Cooley, Martín Fierro is a cowboy, and falconry is important in *Gilgamesh*, the *Shahnameh*, the *Mahabharata*, Shakespeare's *Henriad*, *The Aeneid*, *The Odyssey*, and many other epics. Kriemhild dreams of a hawk, which is identified as her future husband Siegfried. Mwindo, in one version of his tale, is at the depth of his misfortunes left with only his magic flyswatter and his two faithful dogs. The heroic epithet of Kraljevi'c Marko, the hero of the *Kossovo Epic*, is the grey falcon; he is dressed in green, like a falconer, and can speak to his falcon and his horse.

Agriculture

One of the tools that Polyphemus emphatically does not possess is the plow. Odysseus notes with a keen and rapacious colonist's eye the fine plowland of Cyclops-land that is not under cultivation. Enkidu's first human meal is of bread, the fire-made product of cultivated (and as we now know mutated, domesticated, and "genetically engineered") wheat. The very word "culture" itself, with its Latin root *colere*, to plough or till, and its cognates including cultivate, cult, coulter, skill, school, scalpel, cutlass, and sculpture, is etymologically suggestive— even perhaps a palimpsest or abstract of west Eurasian thinking on the subject. If Adam's curse is to get his bread by the sweat of his brow, that bread comes from the plow.

To till a field is to turn back again and again, like a shuttle on the loom, upon the edge of the already-plowed ground, and turn a one-dimensional furrow into a two-dimensional field. It is the turning back, the feedback we use and need to make progress in our fertilizing, that is the special quality of culture, which remembers its past, and cult, which habituates us by repetition to worship and commitment. We turn the soil itself over upon itself. The *arua Lauinia* of Virgil (*Aeneid*, IV.236), the plowlands of Lavinia the heiress of Italy, are also her womb that is to be cultivated by Aeneas to seed a line of emperors. The coulter is the organ of intromission. Achilles, when Odysseus encounters him in the underworld, would rather be tilling his fields than lording it over the dead. Odysseus is alive because he used the cunning arts of culture; Achilles is dead because he could not withdraw from his divine and berserk plunge back into the state of natural man.

Epic, then, remembers in its storytelling mode the Neolithic agricultural revolution.[8] The four primal gods of the Quiché, in their attempt to make true human beings, try mud and wood as their raw materials; these prototypes fail, and the final successful material is corn-meal. We are made of maize! Blood Moon, the mother of the second pair of hero twins, is impregnated by a calabash, another cultivated plant; the calabash is the skull of the one of the first pair of heroes. We are inheritors of the cultivation of our ancestors, fertilized by their sacrifice. Blood Moon proves her human worthiness by making the corn multiply, and employing animals to carry the produce. Like her, Mwindo raises a crop of bananas in one day.

In *Njal*, the key moment that sets the tragic events in motion is the episode where Gunnar decides to defy the Allthing's edict of exile. He is already leaving, but his horse stumbles and he looks back at his farm, Hlidarendi. "Lovely is the hillside—" he says, "never has it seemed as lovely to me as it does now, with its pale fields and mown meadows, and I will ride back home and not leave" (Chapter 75). What follows is a terrible string of deaths and revenges.

The cultivating way of life binds us to a place that we will defend at all costs; like all consequences of the Fall, it is two-edged. Anthropologists note that though the early farmers were able to multiply enormously because of the huge increase in preservable food that resulted from agriculture and domestication, the food was starch, and the skeletons of peasants are smaller and less finely formed than those of the hunter-gatherers they replaced (and sometimes exterminated). Cain, the farmer, is the first murderer as well as the ancestor of literate city-dwellers. Epic, clear-eyed, sees this connection and digests it.

Notes

1. *Beauty: The Value of Values* (Charlottesville, VA: University Press of Virginia, 1991).
2. II.ii.130.
3. See: William J. Burroughs, ed., *Climate: Into the 21st Century* (Cambridge: Cambridge University Press, 2003); Spencer Wells, (*The Journey of Man* (Princeton, NJ: Princeton University Press, 2002). R. C. L. Wilson, S. A. Drury, and J. L. Chapman, *The Great Ice Age: Climate Change and Life* (London: Routledge, 2000).
4. "What goes on four legs in the morning, two legs at noon, and three legs in the evening?"—the Sphinx's riddle, in *Oedipus*; "a featherless biped"—*The Statesman*, ch. 4.
5. L. L. Cavalli-Sforza and Francesco Cavalli-Sforza. *The Great Human Diasporas: The History of Diversity and Evolution* (New York: Addison-Wesley, 1995).
6. http://www.goodnewsblog.com/2006/02/10/mother-fights-off-polar-bear-to-save-children.
7. I owe this insight, together with others, to my gifted student Johnathan MacEachern.
8. Epics can be produced by herding cultures like the Oghurs, Mongols, and Hebrews and by horticulturalists like the Malinese and the Nyanga, and the creation symbolism reflects the difference. The key factor seems to be whether the ecology and the technology of the culture support a critical mass of people and accessible tradition. But in all cases the enhanced control of nature is seen as part of the nexus of the (un)fortunate fall.

7

The Descent into the Underworld

The Dead Companion and the Need for Funeral

The greatest challenge to any human being is the fact of death. And the realization that we are going to die may be one of the most significant features of the human species, setting it off from all others. Essentially, for a hero to be a *human* hero he or she must fully experience death; and to be a human *hero* he or she must be able to return and tell the tale, or at least pass a record of the death experience to the storyteller.

Many epic heroes actually die and are resurrected; often Death plays a trick on the hero, but the hero turns the trick back on Death, killing Death, and making a fool of him. The death-god Nyamurairi gives Mwindo a magic cowrie-shell belt (perhaps partly symbolic of money attachments: cowries were a form of currency in central Africa[1]). The belt squeezes him to death. But he is resurrected by his magic flyswatter, his hero-weapon, and throws the belt at the deathgod, who is strangled to death in turn.[2] "Death, thou shalt die," as Donne says in his sonnet. In compassion for Death's daughter, however, Mwindo brings the Nyamurairi to life again with his swatter. There is an uncanny parallel between this story and that of the Mayan hero twins, who likewise hoist the deathgods on their own petard. Osiris resurrects as Horus; Dionysus hoodwinks Death; and we find similar feigning-death, lying-doggo, and hoodwinking-death stories in *The Odyssey*, *The Aeneid*, the *Mahabharata*, and elsewhere, including the feigned death of Falstaff in *Henry IV*, Part 1. The whole of the *Divine Comedy* could be said to be a prophylactic death on the part of the author, who, following Jesus, dies to defeat death.

For many of us, the first awakening to the reality of death comes when we lose a friend of our own generation, and the fact that death could happen to us too becomes apparent. The personal identity of our friend seems so real that it is hard to accept that it could disappear. In order to get our imagination around the loss of our friend we are forced to look at our own personal identity and step back from it, as it were, to try to grasp the idea of its not being there. We recognize that we are certainly still there when we are asleep, so our being there is not solely a matter of the continuity of consciousness. If we brood on the matter further, we recognize that we are not the same body that we were seven or fourteen years ago; not even, in exact detail, the same body as we were when we last fell asleep. And yet somehow our personal identity has leapt over the slight or large difference in its embodiment, and over changes of mood, attention, feeling, memory, abilities, opinion, and intention. We expect someone to keep promises he made when his body was made of an entirely different collection of matter. In all languages we come up with words denoting soul or spirit—often defined in highly different ways—to be able to refer to whatever it is that survives bodily change. It is but a short step to imagine that it could survive death too. But then we must ask, Where has it gone, then? And how is it there embodied?

Gilgamesh will not let his friend's body go until the worm seizes on it; and then he sets out on a great journey to find out where he has gone. Most of us do not know how to even start to do so, and we content ourselves with burying the dead and giving them a proper funeral farewell. At least we may thus be able to put away or put down the spirit of our friend, if we cannot restore it to us; better it be gone than that it hang around invisible, insatiable of a life that is irrecoverable, angry at being forgotten and left out. Perhaps we can give it rest, consign it to the sleep in which we have our own experience of unconscious being, severed from bodily awareness.

For Gilgamesh, funeral is not enough. There is no description in the poem of a burial or a funeral pyre—instead it is the Annunaki, the dreadful lords of the dead, that drag Enkidu's body from his arms and down into the earth. Gilgamesh does not accept the death. He causes to be made a great statue of his friend in gold and lapis lazuli, with offerings of honey and butter, and sets off to find him—a journey that turns soon into a search for everlasting life.

In some epics, funeral is enough, though—there is true finality in the funerals of Hector in *The Iliad* and Anchises in *The Aeneid*, accompanied by the games that remind us of our capacity to live a second virtual game-life, defying the necessities of real life. But what if the body is unburied? The unburied body is perhaps the deepest nightmare of epic, especially terrible in the case of death by water. Here the hero's task is not only to go down into the underworld and confirm that the friend is still there after all, but also to find out where the body is, return to the upper world, locate the corpse, and give it burial, so giving rest to the unhappy ghost. It was an unburied body—that of Milton's friend Edward King, and Milton's determination not to let him "welter to the parching wind/Without the meed of some melodious tear"[3]—that was the first inspiration of *Paradise Lost*. At least we could speculate that without that body, perhaps, Milton would not have changed his mind about the epic he wanted to write, from a Spenserian heroic allegory to a descent into and redemption from the underworld.

How to lay the ghost of the unburied body? The *Heike* is a wilderness of unburied and unburned bodies, the most terrible being the ones drowned and self-drowned in the final sea-battles around Kyushu and Shikoku. The Japanese imagination sees the faces of the dead on the shells of sea-creatures, a conception closely akin to Milton's dreadful image of the corpse visiting "the bottom of the monstrous world" in "Lycidas." The *Heike* as a whole, begun and ended with the great temple-bell of Buddhist transcendence, full of splendid cryptic epitaphs for the dead warriors, could be said to be Japan's funerary ritual for its dead, a symbolic solemn burial.

The Odyssey is itself about an unburied body—Odysseus' own. For Ithaca and his nearest and dearest he is dead and gone, but there is no corpse to bury. Penelope, like Gilgamesh, refuses to accept his death; Telemachus, also like Gilgamesh, sets out on a great unsuccessful journey to find him. Odysseus, hero as he is, has his moly-plant, his talisman, and can return from the land of the dead, and this is what makes *The Odyssey* so rousing a claim for Western optimism, Western belief in human agency, Western discontent. Seen in this light, Odysseus' "laying to rest" at the end of the epic is also a repudiation of various other afterlives that have been proposed or dreamed of for the human soul and that are sketched in the course of Odysseus' travels. The only afterlife that obviously suits Homer is one in which the deathbed becomes the marriage-bed, and there is still another journey to be made. As Florizel says to Perdita in *The Winter's Tale*, if he is to be buried he would rather be "quick, and in thine arms."[4]

Again and again the hero trails a dead friend or kinsperson into the underworld. Mwindo pursues his tyrant father into the lower dark. The dead shipmates, Elpenor and Palinurus, call the Greek and Roman heroes to them. The ghost of Gunnar sings from his barrow, like an oak from the forest of battle, and calls to Skarpheddin, who will follow him by and by. Arjuna enters the land of the dead and sees there Duryodhana, his old enemy, as Aeneas sees Achilles. Hunahpu and Xbalanque go down into Xibalba for a return match of the ball-game, to settle the score of their dead fathers.

Anthropologists normally regard any sign of funeral behavior in an archeological site as a sure marker of *Homo sapiens*. In doing so they are agreeing with the composers of epic, for whom the imagination of the continued being of the dead marks us off from the beasts and is both a sign of the Fall and an opening into another virtual world of the divine. Elephants, chimpanzees, and other advanced animals have been reported to display grieving and even mourning behavior at the death of close kin and even a temporary denial of its factuality. But what makes us human—and that is epic's subject—is the further step of constructing or positing a sort of physical embodiment of the dead person's spirit, whether as a verbal index of his or her location in the form of a story, or as a mummy, a shrine, a statue, a monument, or an institution.

Funeral Games

The role of games in the construction of an embodiment of the deceased is often highly important. We have already looked at games in epic as an important symbol of the rule-boundedness of cultures and value-systems, as an explanation of the bizarre arbitrariness of the axiomatic game-rules as opposed to the rationality of logical play itself, as an example of the heroic capacity to create performative truths and thus alternative or virtual worlds, as a way in which we rise above natural animal instincts, even as a way in which speciation can happen through sexual selection. The most poignant function of games, which brings all the others together, is in funeral. Computer game addicts have been known to die of starvation at the joystick; this capacity to step off the world into another and kick the old one away is a pathological version of our most characteristic glory as human beings.

Games may be important in yet another sense, that of game theory. Computers can now model huge numbers of iterated game-encounters among different real or virtual players with alternative strategies in a wide range of games with different payoff matrices. Trading, breeding, or competing behavior among animals and even other organisms all the way down to bacteria can be modeled in game form and thus brought to light, with useful scientific, technological, economic, and ecological implications. Perhaps conscious reflectiveness is needed for the most sophisticated and multileveled games, but many animal species have socially adapted brains, and even blood chemistry and genetic lineages can act as calculators for optimum minimax choices in game-type situations where more than one player must compete or cooperate. Cultural models of coalition creation, contracts, moral values, and political expectations are brilliantly illuminated by cross-cultural studies of the results of controlled experiments in game behavior among human subjects. The records of actual multiplayer games like Warcraft can be data-mined as a huge sample of human competitive/cooperative action. Game strategy is the inscape of much natural and cultural behavior, a second layer of action beyond mere happening.

Game theory, with its new set of scientific and practical applications, is, however, not new. Narrative plot is the ancient and traditional human way of analyzing the world in terms of games theory. Any story-plot implicitly sets up a matrix of risks and payoffs for all the players, a branchy flow-chart of mutual responses, and a set of incentives. These incentives can be for alliance, aggression, cooperation, theft, signaling, the recognition of signals, labeling, disguise, deceit, betrayal, the policing of honesty and compliance, the sanctioning of defection, the definition and reward of good behavior, trading, contracts, the beginnings of governmental institutions, and the refinement of institutional ethics. The popular reality-game show *Survivor* is a fascinating example of the spontaneous emergence of such elements, and its much-deplored popularity over Hollywood's fictional stories with their expectable story arcs and simple-minded conventions is a tribute to the vitality of living games. That vitality is recaptured again and again in epic, however, because epic as a genre must encounter its own limits and premises, and include that encounter in its story.

It is precisely this boundary-transcending and emergent property of games, their opening to a newly emergent future, that makes them so attractive a ritual practice for funeral. It may be that the twentieth century's existentialist rejection of the concept of the afterlife has something to do with the rationalizing of funerary ritual in main-stream religion, the loss of the mad and playful spirit of the wake. The reduction of death to a separation between two detachable entities, body and soul, perhaps rendered sterile the possibility that nature and flesh themselves are capable of transcending themselves in playful and gamelike activity with emergent properties. Traditional religions all recognize the existence of the spirit, and even its transferability between different embodiments. But the idea that the spirit could exist by itself, instead of as the emergent property of a wildly entangled physical process, is an Enlightenment abstraction.

Existentialism, which denied the dualism of body and spirit, is an understandable and even admirable response to Enlightenment theology and the antiseptic demise of funeral charivari. But Existentialism never really seemed to recover the embodied spirit of the wake. Existentialist funerals are rather grim. By contrast the most satisfactory funeral I personally ever attended was that of my father, Victor W. Turner. For this occasion his friends, many of them anthropologists and theater people, combined to replicate an Ndembu funeral for a chief in the big basement of my parents' home in Charlottesville, Virginia—complete with custom-made ritual masks, drums, and music, competitive symbolic dancing that allegorically depicted the triumph and defeat of death itself, and much drinking, anecdote, ribaldry, and hilarity. It is this spirit that we find in different ways in the Mayan ball game in Xibalba, Bercilak's wager with Gawaine, and Anchises' funeral.

The Hero, the Shaman, and the Animal Spirit Guide

Shamanism may be the most universal feature of human religion, perhaps of human society itself. Shamanic rituals have been studied on every inhabited continent, and traces of practices and artifacts that have all the hallmarks of such rituals show up in archeological remains deep in the Paleolithic era. As with any religious practice, however, there is a fierce human tendency to claim that one's own version is unique; thus, the definition of shamanism has become politicized. Shamanic cultures sometimes resent being classed with strangers and savages, or despise "Western" "appropriators" of shamanic practices. The Abrahamic religions, blind to their own classic shamanic rituals and myths, disclaim the term "shamanic" and even dismiss religions no more shamanic than their own as pagan, primitive, or diabolic.

But there is an astonishing unanimity of local religious practice throughout the world and through human history and prehistory. Mircea Eliade, the great scholar of shamanism,[5] has been attacked for lumping all such practices together. But the basic elements of shamanic practice are found everywhere—the vocation of shaman, the shaman's call, the suffering or illness of the initiate, the use of drugs from alcohol to psychedelics, the shamanic musical instrument, rhythmic chanting or drumming, rites of passage including ritual death, the trance, the spirit guide (animal, human, or divine), the healing function (both individual and ecological), the shamanic journey (usually both through the air and under the ground), the conversation with the dead ancestors, the shaman's power over and acquaintance with natural spirits, the use of a talisman, the shaman's social role as diviner, seer, moral judge, storyteller, and myth archive, and the shaman's subjective experience of flight, ecstasy, and sparagmos, or fragmentation.

Ironically, both Abrahamic and traditional folk religions have colluded in distinguishing themselves from each other. Indigenous shamanists protest against "New Age" claims to shaman status, trying to keep shamanic authenticity to themselves. Mainline "Western" believers have until recently wanted to distance themselves from primitive superstition. But churches, synagogues, and mosques have always had priests, mystics, religious poets, rabbis, ministers, mullahs, or imams who go through a difficult initiation and psychological struggle, who use incense, chanting, music, alcohol, physical stressors, repetition, dance, fasting, and so on to achieve trance states, who heal the body and restore the soul to the body, who tell stories and myths, who divine the individual and collective future, who help their people communicate with the dead, and who go on spiritual journeys and pilgrimages.

Though the Abrahamic shamans, often urbanized, are less immediately connected to natural and animal forces, much of the imagery of their religious practice and storytelling still involves doves and eagles, winged men, lambs and sheep, lions, bulls, fish, snakes, and so on. The European epics—even relatively recent Christian ones—have shamanic episodes that are as graphic and richly detailed as those from any other part of the world. Modern Western theology may not be shamanic, but modern Western religious and poetic practice remains so. Even dissenting Protestantism, despite its Reformation origins in the cleansing of old shamanic practices, has reverted to them in the form of faith-healing, snake-handling, rhythmic call-and-response preaching, Gospel music, ritual near-drowning, trance, and so on when ordinary people get hold of it.

It is on the underworld journey that the relationship between the shaman and the hero becomes most salient. Sometimes the hero and shaman are two different people, and the shaman becomes the hero's guide; sometimes the hero is or becomes a shaman in the course of the journey. Gilgamesh is both hero and shaman, though he gets shamanic guidance from Urshanabi the ferryman and Utnapishtim's compassionate wife. Odysseus' shaman is Circe, but once he has got directions from her it is he that becomes the sacrificer, the master of spirits, and the interrogator of the dead, with his usual seamanlike competence. The frenzied Cumaean Sibyl is Virgil's masterpiece in the shamanic mode.[6] Dante's guides are Virgil and Beatrice, with double roles as shamans and spirit guides.

One feature of this continuous West Asian/European epic tradition is that though the hero/shaman encounters a shamanic animal at the gateway to the underworld, it is not a friend. Gilgamesh kills the lions at the mountain portal to the land of the ever-living. Odysseus and Aeneas must placate and buy off Cerberus with a drugged sop. Dante has to evade the leopard, the lion, and the she-wolf, not to speak of the other chimeric animal gatekeepers that threaten the poets in their descent. One might argue that this is a sign that the "Western" tradition has diverged from traditional shamanism in refusing the potential help of naturalistic animal guides. Other epic traditions do feature them. Mwindo is led to the underworld by a hawk, but his chief helper there is the god Lightning. Hunahpu and Xbalanque are summoned to the realm of death by a louse that has been eaten by a toad that has been eaten by a snake that has been eaten by a falcon. The hero twins are later helped by a mosquito to identify the Lords of the Dead.

But I believe it more likely that the reversal of the role of animals in the "Western" epics is a device indicating the distinction between the hero and the shaman, the step that the epic hero takes beyond the shaman, the same step that epic takes beyond myth. The shaman plays, so to speak, the ordinary role of psychopomp as conductor of the soul from life to death; the hero's work is to take a violent short cut to the land of the dead and moreover to return, in unnatural violation of the rules.

> facilis descensus Averno;
> noctes atque dies patet atri ianua Ditis;
> sed revocare gradum superasque evadere ad auras,
> hoc opus, hic labor est.[7]

In Dryden's elegant translation:

> The gates of hell are open night and day;
> Smooth the descent, and easy is the way:

But to return, and view the cheerful skies,
In this the task and mighty labor lies.[8]

In *The Journey to the West* the normal role of the shaman is turned upside down in a different fashion. The hero, Monkey, *is* the animal helper, and the priest Tripitaka does not play the shaman's role of guide in the great journey through the valley of the shadow of death; instead, he is the one who is guided. In the *Mahabharata*, the hero Yudhisthira on his own journey to the land of the dead refuses to abandon his devoted dog: but the dog turns out to be the god Dharma in disguise—Dharma, duty, righteousness.

The Lords of Death

One of the curious features of world epic is that the place where the dead go is always ordered, and the order is always personalized. If epic is the human story, we do not seem to be able to imagine an anarchic realm of death, and certainly cannot conceive that nobody will take charge of us. Of course we may very well not want to meet our captors, despite the fact that some of them are our own ancestors. The daemons or gods that rule there have great authority, are usually hostile or at least very severe toward their human charges, and are terrifying to look at—even the ones that turn out to be terrorizing us for our own good. Ereshkigal and the Annunaki of *Gilgamesh*, Yama and his demons in the Indian epics, Minos and Rhadamanthos in the Greco-Roman epics, Hel in the Nordic epics, Satan and his devils in the Christian epics, Kanaloa in the Hawaiian Pelé cycle, Tuoni in the *Kalevala*, the various dragon/demon/wizards of *The Journey to the West*, the Nyanga deathgod in *Mwindo*, and the lords of Xibalba are all depicted and characterized in much the same way.

They are all fearsome, callous, magically powerful, capricious, and fond of their authority. They enjoy terrorizing their victims. They are often tricksters, with a nasty sense of humor. They frequently have an elaborate bureaucracy, and keep huge records. They like games and wagers, in which they usually win by cheating. They are to some extent corruptible, and have been known to take bribes. They have a certain aesthetic sense that makes them vulnerable to a beautiful gift or especially to a fine poetic or musical performance. They are very wealthy; indeed, they may double as gods of wealth.

But the lords of death have an oddly ambiguous mission and always seem to have higher authorities, that are not themselves underworld dwellers, to whom they are responsible. The deathgods are jailers who must live in the jail they control and suffer its pains. As subordinates to higher authorities they resent their subjugation and take their resentment out on their inmates. They can be mastered, too, if the hero is equipped with the right talisman or musical instrument that acts as a certificate of free passage back to the world of light. They can also give great gifts—of magic tools or weapons, of useful knowledge or poetic ability. They can permit the hero access to his dead ancestors and friends.

Their trickiness is often a test—whether of their own design or their superiors'—that is also an ordeal whose successful passage is the gateway to an enormous enlightenment, a metamorphosis of the soul. The horrors of Hell are sometimes illusions, as they are explicitly in the *Mahabharata* and implicitly in many other epics. Like the angel in William Blake's *Marriage of Heaven and Hell* (where it is Blake himself who plays the devil), the victim sometimes undergoes a radical change of perception in which the inferno turns into Elysium.

Why this strange unanimity, and on a subject—what it is like to be dead—on which nobody alive has any experience? Epic's close agreement everywhere on subjects like agriculture, animals, storytelling, weapons, kin, and maturation can be understood to some extent as based on common experience (though the response of the experiencers is also uncannily similar). But the agreement on the death regime is much stranger.

In Arthur Clarke's novel *Childhood's End*[9] the overlords, technologically advanced aliens, arrive on Earth and set human society to rights, ushering in an era of peace and plenty. But they keep themselves physically hidden, and eventually the reason comes out. They are horned, hoofed giants, black in color, with long tails—the conventional image of devils. The novel suggests that the human race has an emerging collective consciousness that transcends time and space, and its prospective race memory contains an image of their liberators. Why is that image the essence of what is terrifying, the enemy of the human race? Because, as it turns out, the Overlords have a purpose beyond helping the human race to achieve comfort and prosperity. They are the ushers of the final transformation of the human species into an enormous group mind, an oversoul—childhood's end. Naturally we would fear the coming of those who would take our children from us and put an end to humanity as we knew it.

What if—we might speculate in this science-fiction vein—epic's unanimity on the lords of death is a similar collective intuition? A dream of our future resurrection by some unimaginably advanced human or alien civilization perhaps? Such a society could have discovered the art of piecing back together the immortal information that constitutes us (and that flies off from us every second of our lives at the speed of light and in all directions) and reconstituting our bodies—DNA, brain connections, and all. The therapists, judges, teachers, and guides we would encounter when we awaken might well strike us as frightening, capricious, wealthy, powerful, authoritarian, sadistic, persuadable, under the command of others—even as potential midwives of enlightenment. Their technology would be to us indistinguishable from magic. In dealing with the huge volume of the past dead they would require elaborate record-keeping and rigid institutional rules to ensure our orderly passage into future society and satisfaction of outstanding debts, crimes, and obligations. They would be deeply interested in our aesthetic abilities, as representing artistic resources long lost to history, and good new music or poetry or art from ancient genius would have economic value and even justify the huge cost of the undertaking. They would use advanced psychological techniques—perhaps even temporarily traumatic ones—to facilitate our enlightening passage into the state of free, active, creative peacefulness that would be our civil right as new immigrant citizens.

The Protecting Talisman

We have already looked at the staffs, swords, lariats, discuses and other magical tools, and talismans that embody the spirit and power of the epic hero. A very special kind of talisman is sometimes required to allow the hero entry into the land of the dead, to protect him there, and, most important, to allow him to leave. The form of this talisman, and its relation to other epic elements, is quite protean.

Hermes gives Odysseus the moly plant to protect him from the spiritual death of being turned (back) into an animal by Circe. But the plant has a further significance; it is ambiguous whether its protective effects are provided by its simple presence and possession, its smell, or its taste, as a potion. In addition, it is clearly related to the herb of immortality that Gilgamesh acquires and loses on his journey to the land of the dead (and everliving), the herb that confers renewal of youth and immortality on its consumer. Using the moly, Odysseus subdues Circe, who is the shamaness who can give him access to Hades. Is its operation medicinal as a prophylactic, or more in the nature of a wand? In either case, it is needed not just to ward off bestialization, but to achieve the higher goal of entry, with impunity, into the land of the dead.

Virgil is clearly following Homer in providing Aeneas with the golden bough, though this time the shamaness, the Cumaean Sibyl, helps him obtain it rather than standing as the obstacle that he needs its aid to overcome. Here the bough is more in the nature of a wand—it is broken from a tree in the same way that the angel Metatron breaks off the branch from the Tree of Life that will become the staff of Jacob and Moses in Hebrew folklore. Its yielding only to the true hero is also reminiscent of the sword in the stone and the sword in the oak that certify Arthur and Sigmund. Mwindo, on the other hand, is born with the magic flyswatter/scepter by which he subdues the dangers and achieves the tasks presented by the realm of death. King Gesar has a magic whip as part of his birthright as the incarnation of a god, which enables him to conquer the forces of death. Dante's talisman could be said to be the book of Virgil.

In *Parzifal*, the whole story becomes the search for the Grail, which is the talisman of the Arthurian cycle, in general, and that can only be found in the waste land itself, that is, the land of death. Here the talisman is not so much the way in and out of the underworld, but the symbolic goal of the journey itself. What makes Parzifal able to obtain the grail is precisely his humble admission of his unworthiness of it, that he comes to under the tutelage of Cundrie and Trevrizent after his initial moral failure to qualify for it, his polite inability, so to speak, to pluck the sword from the stone. Eschenbach makes the achievement of the grail the moment of meeting between the two separated half-brothers, Parzifal and Feirefiz, a reconciliation of Christian and Islamic wisdom, the beginning of a new form of society, and instruction for a new world. Parzifal is released from his quest (and from the waste land itself, which is no longer a place of death) by the achievement of the grail, and is able to return to his wife—a sort of mirror-opposite of the Orpheus story.

It may be worth following up in detail one particular group of talismans, as a way of thinking about the mythic roots of epic: the caduceus or metatron, the snake-staff of Hermes, Mercury, Aesculapius, Jacob, and Moses. Here the reader will, I hope, forgive me for quoting at length some passages from an earlier book of mine, *Natural Religion* (Transaction Publishers, 2006).

The symbol was already ancient when it appears in the mythology of the Hebrews, Greeks, and Romans. Snakes twine about the terracotta arms of tiny Minoan goddesses. The Sumerian court physicians of circa 2000 B.C.E. carried a staff entwined with two serpents as a sign of their office. The mediator-god Ningizzida, whose symbol is the snake-entwined staff, is depicted in bas-reliefs from the Mesopotamian city of Lagash conducting the king, Gudea, into the presence of the supreme god Enki. (John Armstrong: *The Paradise Myth*, Oxford University Press, 1969—a most useful book for this study.) The iconography of the Edenic serpent, coiled around the Tree of Knowledge, may be older still, and the story of the serpent in *Gilgamesh*, which, clearly in the same tradition, steals the herb of immortality that the hero has obtained, may be as much as 7,000 years old. The twined-snakes visual motif can also be found in ancient Hindu diagrams of the *chakras*, or energy centers, in the human body. Where the snakes intersect—at the caste point between the eyes, the heart, the navel, the genitals, and so on—the chakras are found. It may even be implied by the yin-yang symbol of East Asia. In Norse mythology, the roots of the world-tree Yggdrasil are gnawed by the world-serpent Nidhoggr.

The snaky rod is called the karykeion, or messenger's staff, by the Greeks, and the caduceus by the Romans. In its earliest Greek form it appears as a forked stick, the branches knotted to form a loop, but later the staff is twined about by two serpents in a helical embrace, the heads facing each other. This is the form it takes in Roman iconography. The visual motif of the snake-encircled tree is a pervasive motif in Roman funerary statuary, where a hero, almost always accompanied by a horse and a dog, pours a libation with his consort to the psychopomp, Mercury. It is also familiar in the story of Hercules, who must contend with a serpent coiled around the tree when he goes to fetch the golden apples of the Hesperides. The myth scholar Jane Harrison believes that the combination represents Life, and she is clearly right as far as she goes. But the equally strong death associations—the snake/tree seems to grow at hell-mouths, between life and death—should make us question further.

There are various Greco-Roman myths of the origin of the caduceus. One is that Hermes came across two snakes fighting each other, and found a way to turn their war into love. He took a staff, given him by Aesculapius, and threw it between the snakes, whereupon they twined around it in the familiar double helix. At once they ceased their conflict; war turned to love, hostility to copulation.

It will be immediately evident that this myth is closely related to the story of Tiresias, who, seeing two snakes mating, killed the female, whereupon he turned into a woman. Seven years later he again saw two copulating snakes, and this time killed the male, upon which he reverted to being a man. Zeus and Hera, who had been arguing about whether men or women derived more pleasure from sex—Zeus maintaining that women did, Hera that men did—took the opportunity to ask Tiresias, who had experienced sex as both a man and a woman. He replied that women derived ten times more pleasure from sex than men. Hera, angered by this response, blinded Tiresias. A different version of the tale of Tiresias' blinding also casts light on its meaning—that Tiresias was punished by Athena, the goddess of wisdom, as Actaeon was by Artemis/Diana, for watching her bathe naked. In any case, as compensation for Tiresias' blindness, Zeus conferred on him the gifts of prophecy and longevity.

What are we to make of this rich mess of tales? The copulating snakes stories clearly establish the meaning of the caduceus as, generally, life itself; more specifically, life as reproduction, and more specifically still, life as sexual reproduction. By an amazing coincidence, the fundamental life-symbol of the ancient world happens to be a pretty exact diagram of the DNA molecule, in which two strands of bases or nucleotides, strung along a chain of phosphate groups, coil in a double helix around a central sequence of weak hydrogen bonds. I argue that this correspondence is more than a coincidence.

Some versions of the copulating snakes myth seem to indicate that the sexual harmony of opposites is achieved against a background of sexual strife—a strife which is itself acknowledged in myth terms to be necessary and beneficial. There is an echo in the story of Tiresias' punishment of the more dreadful fate—foretold by Tiresias in Euripides' play—of King Pentheus, who likewise gazed upon forbidden female sexual mysteries. The "moral" of that tale, as of the related story of the dismemberment of Orpheus by the Bacchantes, is that there must be a complementary balance between the warring powers of Apollo and Dionysus. Tiresias' attempts, before he has acquired this wisdom, to restore peace by removing one side or the other in the battle results in a compensatory and catastrophic metamorphosis of his own sexuality; and the strife of Zeus and Hera is the cause of Tiresias' distinguishing gifts of prophecy and long life. In some sense, then, the gift of knowledge is related to the tension between sexual hostility and sexual amity, and to the sense of shame experienced by all three characters (and by Athena in the observed bathing myth). The parallel with the Biblical story of Eden is obvious.

The central element of the myth is a snake wrapped around a tree—the supreme symbol of the disruption of order and protean transformation, embracing the supreme symbol of stability, order, and continuity. The snake, whose venom can both poison and, in the hands of a physician, heal—which dies but is reborn when it sheds its skin—is linguistic slippage personified. But it is reconciled symbolically in the caduceus with the staff or tree, whose ancient significance is suggested by the fact that the word "tree" itself is derived from the Indo-European root *deru*, which also gave us the words true, trust, and troth—the keeping of promises and the continuity of meaning.

The speculations of contemporary evolutionary biology on the origins of sexual reproduction show interesting resemblances to the meditations of these ancient mediterranean mythmakers. Geneticists suggest that sex arose out of conflicts on the micromolecular level between viral invaders and the host DNA, and between the need for genetic stability and the need for genetic variation. Ethologists and sociobiologists attribute the elaborate ritual behaviors and ardent pair-bonding of sexually reproducing species to conflicts between territorial/aggressive drives and simple copulatory drives, some—for instance, Konrad Lorenz—even suggesting that the pressure-cooker of sociosexual selection and competition drove the emergence of higher cognitive faculties and self-awareness, and the concomitant extension of lifespan required by species that must learn the complexities of social sexuality. Tiresias the shaman, the ritual adept, acquires his expertise in the future and his longevity, just as the human species apparently did, through an elaboration of a sexual dialectic; a dialectic found, in an even more economical form, in the Hebrew identification of sexual with mental "knowing."

The other major branch of Greek and Roman myths that deal with the caduceus involves its exchange for the lyre, the contract between Apollo and Hermes. What does the trade mean? To answer this question we must come to a deep understanding of the meaning of the lyre and the meaning of the god Apollo. In yet another story, the caduceus came into the possession of Hermes/Mercury by means of an exchange. Mercury had already invented the lyre, using forked sticks and the shell of a turtle. He traded the lyre to Apollo, who gave him in exchange the caduceus, which was originally in his possession. Apollo then gave the lyre to his son Orpheus, who later used it as the essential talisman to pass as a living man through the gates of the underworld in his quest for Eurydice, and return unharmed. The lyre was, of course, the instrument by which Greek poets marked the metrical divisions of their oral poetry—the ancestor of the instrument by which modern Serbian and Bosnian *guslers*, or oral poets, punctuate their epic verses on the battle of Kosovo. In myths and folktales trading usually indicates symbolic equivalence, or at least a further, leaked-over, meaning for each of the objects traded.

The tradition in which Apollo, not Hermes, was the original possessor of the caduceus, is also supported by the fact that

Aesculapius, the god of medicine, is another possessor of the caduceus (now the symbol of the *pharmakon*) having got it, presumably, from his father Apollo. Apollo was originally not a very "Apolline" god at all, being associated with plagues and arrow-wounds, and nicknamed "Smintheus," the mouse-god. In ceding the caduceus to Hermes and taking on the lyre instead, he is being cleansed of his more earthy and organic Dionysian connections, and prepared for his role as the sun-god of reason and order. Likewise, he slays the serpent Python and takes over the Delphic cult from the old chthonian goddesses who governed it before; but the ancient associations cannot be dispelled. The oracle is a woman, not a man, and she uses the laurel leaf, from the tree of the nymph Daphne who rejected Apollo's advances, as her psychotropic agent to achieve the oracular trance.

The best and most succinct gloss I know on the subject of Apollo's lyre is Rilke's third sonnet to Orpheus (first series), which I quote in A. J. Poulin's translation:

A god can do it. But tell me, will you, how
a man can trail him through the narrow lyre?
His mind is forked. Where two heart's arteries
intersect, there stands no temple for Apollo.

Singing, as you teach us, isn't desiring,
nor luring something conquered in the end.
Singing is Being. For a god, it's almost nothing.
But when do we exist? And when does he spend

the earth and stars on our being? Young man,
your loving isn't it, even if your mouth
is pried open by your voice—learn

to forget your impulsive song. Soon it will end.
True singing is a different kind of breath.
A breath about nothing. A gust in the god. A wind.

Rilke remembers that the lyre, like the caduceus, began as a branched stick. The journey of the poet is the shamanic one: to pass down the branches of the mind's—not the body's—arterial tree into the underworld. Shamans need certain specific skills, that are symbolized in the old underworld stories by the golden bough, the lyre, the clue, the magic flute, the shamanic drum or bagpipe, the spirit-doctor's rattle, or the mask of the angakoq. These talismans refer to the ancient techniques of the arts—melodic structure, poetic meter, dramatic mimesis, the picturing power and pattern design of the visual artist, storytelling, and so on. New research is showing that these artistic forms have a double nature, a twofold loop structure like the figure eight or the infinity sign, with one feedback loop inside, within the neuroanatomy of the human brain, and one feedback loop outside in the cultural tradition. Poetic meter, for instance, is culturally universal on all continents and in all societies from the most technologically simple and isolated to the most advanced and cosmopolitan, with one interesting exception—the Western free verse of the last eighty years.

The human poetic line, with this one exception, is always about three seconds long, rhythmically shaped by regular patterns of long and short, heavy and light, or tone-changing and tone-unchanging syllables, and by such devices as rhyme and alliteration. The three second line is tuned to the three second information processing cycle in the brain, which preserves three seconds of short-term memory before storing its essentials as long-term memory and forgetting the rest. If this internal cycle is driven by the external rhythmic stimulus of poetic meter, significant changes in brain activity and brain chemistry occur, as studies of the effects of ritual chanting have shown. The right brain becomes just as active as the left, the limbic system is awoken, and a cocktail of neurotransmitters is released, whose known properties combine alertness, relaxation, pleasure, and challenge. Listening to poetry literally makes us smarter—just as listening to Mozart has been shown to do by recent research.

The Orphic poet uses his lyre as Theseus used his ball of twine, to enter the labyrinth of the human racial past and to return. As Rilke says in sonnet 17:

> Deep down, the oldest
> tangled root of all that's grown,
> the secret source
> they've never seen.
>
> Helmet and horn of hunters,
> old men's truths,
> wrath of brothers,
> women like lutes . . .
>
> Branch pushing branch,
> not one of them free . . .
> One! oh, climb higher . . . higher . . .
>
> Yet they still break.
> But this one finally
> bends into a lyre.

In a few brief lines Rilke here recapitulates the entire Darwinian evolutionary tree of humankind, with glimpses of the growth of primitive hunting technology, the rituals and social structures of kinship, the Venus of Willendorf, the first arts. Through tragic waste and amputated branches the process refines itself into freedom and spirit. The lyre actually grows out of Darwin's tree of evolutionary descent, as its flower (and perhaps as the seed of a future tree).

Thus the lyre itself, in the sense of poetic meter and the other traditional artistic techniques, was both a product of the evolutionary process and, as it articulated itself, the guide of evolution. The human species is, technically, a domesticated species: the domesticators being ourselves and the method being artistic ritual leading to differential reproductive success. Like the human race itself, which eventually renounced its ancient eugenics and called upon its ritual adepts and priests to be celibate, Rilke too rejects the merely sexual compulsions that were human evolution's first fuel—"learn to forget your impulsive song." No temple to Apollo stands at the blood's meetings of three ways; the temple is raised at another crossroads, where the mind's Oedipal questionings lead us to forbidden knowledge of our own origins. But the mental branching grows out of the biological; the tree of knowledge is a branch of the tree of life.

Thus one meaning of the trade of caduceus for lyre is that the caduceus, the mechanism of life, can develop into the lyre, the art of poetry, or that poetry is at bottom the further workings of the mysterious language of living organism. The myth is thus a myth of the origin of language. In modern terms we might say that the trade recognizes the deep parallelism between the discrete combinatorial generative system of DNA and those of human grammar and human poetic meter, and celebrates the latter as an outgrowth of the former. Poetry is fast evolution. Biological evolution is slow poetry.

Turning to the Hebrew tradition, my earlier book went on:

> The significances I have adduced here for the caduceus might arguably seem tenuous or at least idiosyncratic to the Greco-Roman tradition. But a similar constellation of meanings emerges when we turn our attention to the mythology and commentary of the Jewish tradition. Here my scholarship is even more incomplete, but the material is so rich that even a superficial treatment reveals highly suggestive parallels.
>
> The Hebrews' version of the caduceus is a staff—Moses' rod—which can metamorphose by magic into a snake, and can by the power of Jahweh turn back into a staff. The distinction between the two transformations is emphasized by the story of Moses' contest with the Egyptian magicians in *Exodus*, in which the Egyptians, like Moses, are able to turn their staffs into snakes and bring plagues upon the lands, but Moses' staff-snake eats up the snakes of the magicians. The *Zohar*, a remarkable Kabbalistic work from mediaeval Spain, expatiates: the Egyptians cannot turn their snakes back into

staffs or dispel the plagues, whereas Moses can reverse the process. The Egyptians are good deconstructionists, but only Moses can manage the necessary reconstruction.

I believe the *Zohar* is right in discerning a symbolic correspondence among the many rods, wands, or staffs by which the power of Jahweh is exercised in the Hebrew Bible. Moses' rod is usually associated with the mediator-angel Metatron in Jewish folktale and mysticism; the legend is that the rod or staff was originally a branch of the Edenic Tree of Life, and was plucked from the tree by the angel. (Angelo S. Rappoport's *Ancient Israel: Myths and Legends*, Bonanza Books, New York 1987, is a useful source.) Metatron is evidently related to the Mesopotamian god Ningizzida, who is like Metatron a messenger, a mediator between the divine and the human, and a psychopomp. Ningizzida is sometimes depicted with the two snakes emerging from his shoulders.

Moses first obtains the rod during his exile in Midian, when he is commissioned by the Lord of the Burning Bush to lead the chosen people into freedom, and his lips are circumcised by the fiery coal of Jahweh. When Moses raises the rod, the Israelites are victorious in battle. He uses it to part the waters of the Red Sea, and to strike the rock and create a spring of life-giving water during the sojourn in the desert of Sinai. More mysterious still is the role played by the staff when the chosen people begin to doubt the promises of God, and they are bitten by snakes and fall sick. Moses, taking the role of Aesculapius, then constructs a caduceus—a bronze snake upon a staff—and raises it up before the people. Whoever merely looks upon the serpent is cured. Recalling this ancient episode near the beginning of the Gospel of John, Jesus likens himself, as healer, to this serpent fastened to the tree; and thus we may see the icon of the crucifix as itself a version of the caduceus, with the cross as staff and the savior as snake.

In much Western iconography, the snake is symbolically equivalent to the newborn child, especially the foundling child or the child born outside the normal limits of society. Moses' name is the Egyptian term for "son of," a constant reminder of his strange foundling status, his origin among the bullrushes of the great snake of the Nile, and his adoption by the Uraeus-wearing daughter of the Pharaoh. Milton, in the Nativity Ode, likens Christ to the infant Hercules, who strangled snakes in his cradle. I have seen Celtic crosses in Galicia, the Celtic region of Spain, which on one side carry the crucified Christ, but which on the other carry, also crucified as it were, the Virgin mother, in exile, with her baby child.

In the Jewish Bible the rod reappears again and again. Of particular interest is its role in the story of Jacob and Laban. In the story, Jacob serves as the ranch manager for his uncle and father-in-law

Laban, who is a hard man who reaps where he does not sow. Jacob is so expert and creative in his work that he makes Laban rich, and despite the fact that Laban keeps changing the rules of his employment, Jacob ends up with both of Laban's daughters and huge flocks and herds of his own. He serves seven years for Laban's elder daughter Leah, seven years for the younger daughter Rachel, and six years for his share of Laban's flocks and herds. Jacob's peculiar expertise seems to be in animal breeding: he mates the most vigorous stock in his uncle's herds and improves the breeds. His knowledge of stockbreeding is symbolized by the rather mysterious procedure of setting up a peeled branch before the herds when they come to drink; this peeled branch is interpreted in the Kabbala as being related to the Metatron-rod of Moses. Like Moses' healing bronze snake/staff, the peeled branch is efficacious simply by virtue of being held up and seen. As we have already noted, the caduceus is an exact diagram of the double-helix DNA molecule. Jacob is evidently an ancient expert in recombinant DNA. Simply to know how snake and staff can be reconciled is sufficient to produce healing and fertility. Jacob's genetic expertise, the story insists, is taught to him by God, who also promises to bless Jacob himself with a multitude of descendants.

. . . In modern Egypt snake charmers have a special trick; by winding a cobra around a stick they can induce in the animal a kind of rigid paralysis or trance state. The snaky rod can then be handled with safety as a single object. But the moment the stick is flung to the ground, the trance is broken and the snake begins to move again. Evidently this ancient practice is at the core of the Moses staff story. Moses' difference from the priestly snake charmers is that he can reverse the process. What the story is getting at, then, is the art of taming or domesticating animals. Moses not only can do it, as the priests can, but he can understand it and thus do it backwards. Likewise, in the Jacob story, there are otherwise inexplicable details that science can illuminate . . . Jacob has agreed with Laban that he can keep for his own all the piebald or parti-colored animals that are produced by the flock. Under the guidance of God he sets up his peeled staff in front of the ewes when they give birth, whereupon they produce piebald offspring. What is going on? New studies of Russian fur-foxes and of animal domestication in general give us an answer. If animals are bred specifically for tameness—that is, tractability and fearlessness with respect to human beings—the tamest offspring of wild parents being bred with each other, the tamest of those matings bred in turn, and so on, many wild species can swiftly be domesticated. But with the trait of tameness comes a group of other characteristics: a tendency to curly and shortened tails, floppy ears, curly hair, neotenic or infantile behavior, a neotenic tendency in the shape and relative size of head and body, and above all, piebaldness or multicoloredness in the coat or skin. Thus the story of Jacob is a story about selective breeding for domestication; and perhaps even more remarkably, it is a story about how we humans selectively domesticated ourselves, and then became conscious of that process itself and were able to assist it. For after all, the whole point of the story is who is going to be the ancestor of the tribe.

The rod of Jacob and Moses is connected in the *Zohar* with the institution of circumcision, the process by which a Hebrew male was enabled to give birth to himself a second time and be reborn in the spirit. In the *Zohar*, as the anthropologist Harriet Lyons interprets it in a brilliant unpublished Oxford B.Litt thesis, the peeled branch of Jacob is a willow-sapling whose bark has been removed to reveal a part white and part red inner body. This wand, which combines the red of transgression with the white of purity, is associated with various mediating figures: Metatron, the mediating angel; Jacob himself, who mediates between the gentleness of Abraham and the severity of Isaac; the Sabbath, the time that mediates between ordinary human time and the time of God; the Shekinah, the mystical female spirit of the chosen people, who as the bride of Jahweh mediates between individual Jews and God; and the male and female principles in general. Circumcision in this view symbolically provides a man with an orifice like a woman's through which he can give birth to himself a second time. Moses, significantly enough, as a foster-Egyptian, was not circumcised. During his return from the land of Midian to Egypt the angel of God, angry at his impurity, takes the form of a great serpent one night and swallows him down to his feet—almost returning him to the animal womb. Moses' wife Zipporah rescues him by circumcising their baby son and smearing the blood upon Moses' feet. In so doing, she transgressively takes the role of the male moyl or mohelet who performs the briss (Berit Mila) or circumcision ceremony. Furthermore, this is a symbolic circumcision of Moses himself, as she explains when she says to him: "truly now thou art a bridegroom of blood unto me." Jacob's rod, then, is part of a symbol-complex which includes both biological life and the cultural or spiritual transcendence of life.

Thus among other things the Jacob story is about what one might call traditional evolutionary theory. Success is defined as reproductive success; Jacob is the fittest in these terms. He himself sires twelve sons by various women. He prospers by acting as a selective force on his herds, accelerating their evolution by what in modern terms we would call genetic engineering. What the story says about God is that God is the spirit of evolution and the true guide for what will survive into the future. But God, like Laban, reaps where He does not sow: a rentier, so to speak, an owner of the means of production who gives employment to his workers. God, like Laban, is a kind of friendly adversary whose demands for repayment create the economic discipline and stimulate the technical ingenuity that ensure prosperity, and whose arbitrary tests warrant the survivor as the rightful heir to the future. The Bible story hammers this point home by having Jacob wrestle all night with a man (usually interpreted as an angel) who actually turns out to have been God Himself. Jacob suffers a torn sinew in his thigh from this battle, but gets in recompense a divine blessing, and a new name: Israel, that is, the position of ancestor to the whole nation. Jacob, the great saver, is saved.

. . . We can, therefore, summarize the meaning of this ancient symbol in terms of a cascade of transcendences. The snake-encircled tree is certainly a symbol of life; but it is also a symbol of the transcendence of mere life by means of a dialectic which includes death itself. The snake venom can kill or cure. The tree merely grows—though it branches, and thus opens up a future richer than the past. But the snake renews itself, changing its skin in a symbolic death and rebirth, unpeeling itself from itself. The snake breaks the rules. In biological terms, we see imaged here the moment of evolutionary transition from asexual reproduction to sexual reproduction—an innovation which, in evolutionary history, carried with it a complementary invention, genetically programmed death by aging. Sex and death are one process; programmed death clears out each older generation to make room for the next generation, created as true unique individuals by the genetic reshuffling of sex. After billions of years of glacially slow asexual evolution by mutation and selection unassisted by sexual recombination, sex made possible the acceleration of evolutionary change in the last few hundred million years that came with sexual selection and social behavior. Success in territorial and mating ritual, a criterion meaningful only at the level of social interaction, could begin to act as a powerful selective pressure of its own on the genome not only of other species but its own, reversing the traditional causal flow from genotype to phenotype. Species could domesticate themselves to their own social requirements. In one case at least, the human, the sociocultural tail came to wag the genetic dog; the innovation represented by the snake became coupled to the biological conservatism of the tree of descent. Thus in a further sense, the caduceus symbolizes also the coevolution of biology and culture.

. . . The final step in this cascade of meanings is suggested on the Greek side of the Mediterranean by the morphing of tree into lyre, the exchange of caduceus for lyre. On the Hebrew side, it is symbolized by the rite of circumcision—the caduceizing of the male Jew that qualifies him for the poetic hermeneutics of Torah study. The pun on hermeneutics is intentional; Moses has long been associated with Hermes Trismegistus, the mythical Egyptian sage from whom we derive the term "hermetic." The creation and interpretation of poetry is the final significance of the caduceus/metatron. Genetic evolution is slow poetry; poetry is fast genetics.[10]

Hermes and Moses are among those who can travel safely between the land of the living and the land of the dead. They are psychopomps and hermeneutical interpreters. It is no coincidence that each of them is equipped with a magic snake-staff that contains the rich significances suggested above. We should read the epic journey to the land of the dead not just as the hero's encounter with death but as a bringing to bear of our whole amazing evolutionary history upon the problem of our mortality.

The Conversation with the Dead

Perhaps the most uniquely potent human gift is being able to talk with the ancestors—as stories, poetry, monuments, artworks, writing, and cultural institutions enable us to do. What marks us off most effectually from other highly intelligent animals is that we are able to hand down from one generation to another by cultural transmission a body of information that significantly dominates the body of information handed down in the form of genes. The astonishing ingenuity of the DNA genetic code, refined over the four billion years or so of biological evolution, can pack about eight hundred megabytes of information (equal to about four hundred thousand pages of text) into the human genome, in the form of forty-six chains of atoms (chromosomes) so small as to be invisible, and pass that information along to a newborn baby. But at a certain point—when a human culture had amassed the equivalent of two thousand books—as much information could be bequeathed through culture as by the biological inheritance of a human baby. My computer has a disk drive capable of containing as much as that, the great library of Alexandria contained about 250 times more, and the Library of Congress about fourteen thousand times more. A present-day Cray computer can hold about four hundred terabytes of memory, about seventy Libraries of Congress.

The epic journey to the land of the dead essentially has one goal: the opening of lines of communication to the ancestors, and the acquisition from them of the information necessary to survive as a society and as a species. The journey expands the evolutionary process, so that information can be passed not just collectively through the biological fate of each generation, but individually, by name, from the dead to the living; evolution is no longer just a line of succession, so to speak, but a plane of intercommunication. Evolution becomes "meta": we take control of it to some degree, our skill at evolving evolves. The conversation in the underworld symbolizes the crucial human ability to consult the dead, to extend the senses through time and through a group mind rather than a group flesh, and to achieve some degree of immortality thereby. In the *Popol Vuh*, as soon as the lords of Xibalba are defeated, the hero twins reconstruct their father Seven Hunahpu and speak with him. At that moment, the dawn of the light that reveals the universe takes place, and the human race begins.

In like fashion, Mwindo's meeting with and reconciliation with his father in the underworld starts a process of learning for Mwindo under the tutelage of the god Lightning that will make him a wise and peaceful king. Odysseus learns from the dead much practically useful strategic information about post-Trojan War politics that he will use when he returns to Ithaca. Aeneas learns from his dead father Anchises the great mission of Rome. Dante gets a summary of medieval theology, inherited from Aquinas before him and opened up by him imaginatively to become the core of Catholic thought for seven hundred years. In the *Bhagavadgita* episode of the *Mahabharata*—itself a sort of death-journey for Arjuna, who sees Vishnu as only the dead may do—the hero learns of the prior incarnations of his friend Krishna and brings back from the conversation the most perfect summary and critique of Vedic spiritual wisdom, still foundational for perhaps a billion people. Moses' conversation with the Ancient of Days on Mount Sinai, his climb another death-journey, gave the world the Ten Commandments.

The epic is itself, of course, one of the most ancient and important ways in which information is passed from the dead to the living; to hear or read an epic is to make a journey to the underworld and speak with the dead. For Dante and Milton to *write* an epic is to walk with the dead in the land of shades. For us to read them is to walk with them, as T. S. Eliot does in "Little Gidding." Before writing was invented, the human memory and capacity for memorization was, apart from visual images, the most potent and effective form of information storage over long periods. Epics range in length from a few thousand lines to over a million. An enormous amount of information can be stored and retrieved in such a device. This information, the source code for a community's customs, mores, natural science, and linguistic unity, was the most precious possession of any human group.

The innately given and culturally enhanced forms of storytelling and poetry could pack in still more than could a mere manual or treatise of the same length. Consider such techniques for condensing information as multileveled symbolism and allegory, characterization (so that we know, for instance, how a character would behave in many situations not specified in the story itself), plot (whose whole dynamic and source of suspense is the proposition of alternate timelines, so that many different chains of implication can be condensed into one episode), imagery (so that one significant detail can, when played out on a human listener, evoke a whole scene), debate (in which the hearer can flesh out the arguments of the disputants), and so on. It is commonsense that these human abilities were picked up and used by epic composers; but there is a further implication, compelled by the ineluctable nonlinearity of human biological and cultural coevolution, that epic helped to bring these human skills into being. If epic or proto-epic paraphernalia—musical instruments, cave-paintings, idols, ritual fictions—are, as indeed they are, the signatures of human presence up to at least one hundred thousand years ago, it is evident that epic performance could have been a major determinant of the direction of human evolution, one of the ways humans domesticated themselves. So essential to human survival was communal storytelling, the logic runs, that the neural basis of skills such as symbolism, dramatic mimesis and identification, the recognition of narrative point, visualization from verbal cues, and logic was strongly selected for in every human group, and the unskilled, too dull to get a mate, left no genes behind.

Oral epic is, moreover, as Albert Lord and Milman Parry have shown, exquisitely adapted to the human memory storage and retrieval system. The information in it is redundantly mapped onto several powerful human memory modules: our capacity to remember and hold a tune and its rhythm; our good memory for stories (gossip is a powerful survival trait for any human community, and was selected for in our evolution); our excellent spatial memory, so powerful that Renaissance orators used an imaginary memory theater to place their topics in order without missing any. In the case of the *Popol Vuh*, Tedlock makes a persuasive case that graphic cartoon-like illustrations were a central part of Mayan epic performance, almost like a slide-show or multimedia powerpoint presentation. The performance space itself, the gusler's coffee-house, the shining planking and cushions of the biwa hoshi's dojo, the griot's teahouse, the mead-hall, or the Globe Theater, was a mnemonic of its own. As soon as writing appeared, the epic was carefully transcribed—and as we shall see later, the moment of transcription from one medium of memory to another was itself the occasion for a new epic flowering.

So the hero's conversation with the dead in epic is a sort of "meta" device, sometimes more than one ply deep, as when the dead ancestor in turn tells an epic story. The reminder of the meaning of the conversation is an invitation to the audience to consider itself as in the same relation to the dead as the hero. The audience is not just learning about the process by which we became human; it is participating in it. In remembering the epic it is re-membering the dead.

The Prophecy

The information that a hero receives in the underworld is not just of antiquarian value. Often it is of immediate practical use, both tactical and strategic. Always, by the very nature of the encounter, it outlines the big picture, the meaning of the cosmos in terms of our place in it: the very possibility that we can talk with the dead immediately changes time from a meaningless succession of events to a multidimensional manifold with complex links among all events. Certainly epic is not backward-looking only; indeed, it could be said that epic argues persuasively that the only way out of the present and into the future is via the huge freedom offered to us by the past, both as the store of examples of what can be done and as the informational tools to do it.

The most radical form of information is the epic prophecy, as we find it most explicitly in the dead Anchises' words to Aeneas, throughout the Jewish and Christian Bibles, and everywhere in Dante's journey through the afterlife. "The Ballad of True Thomas" and the myth of Orpheus, though not epics as such, are marvelously economical digests of the underworld journey, and in both the poet-heroes receive the gift of soothsaying, become prophets themselves.

But the prophetic mise-en-scène need not be very explicit: once we are aware of the archetypal theme of the underworld journey as informational guide to the future, we can interpret even brief encounters with ghosts, dreams, and visions as abbreviated versions of the underworld journey. We may see it for instance in the series of dreams, visions, and symbolic riddling predictions that accompany the battle of Clontarf in *Njal's Saga*, where the Christian future of Northern Europe is foreshadowed in the wake of the apocalyptic collapse of the old pagan world. Sometimes the underworld sojourn is itself an implicit prophecy. The hero twins' adventures in Xibalba explicitly map in advance the vicissitudes and triumphs of the Quiché people. *The Liberation of Jerusalem* is full of prophecies, each of them with some degree of the hadean in their atmosphere and setting. Tripitaka's success in the passage of the Himalayas foretells the path of Buddhism across China to Japan and Korea and to the world at large. Mwindo's novitiate under the lightning god foreshadows a visionary realm of good consensual government; Parzifal's under Trevrizent the leavening future presence of the secret Templars of the Grail.

The peculiar form of the epic prophecy needs to be noted. Epics are (with the exception of modern and contemporary science-fiction epic) set in the more or less distant past, and the epic prophecy can validate itself very conveniently by the fact that the events it predicted have indeed happened since. The prophecy of the sorceress to Bradamant in *Orlando Furioso*, after Bradamant has of course fallen into a deep abyss in the ground and entered a dark cave, is a classic example. The sorceress has learned her knowledge from the dead Merlin, whose tomb is in the cave; the prophecy itself is a fairly accurate account of the Este family in the light of Italian history, in general, since the era of Roland. Ariosto is on safe ground and not likely to be falsified. Nevertheless, the curious tense-structure of the prophecy contains in itself the epic perspective: Ariosto is telling a story in the past in which a sorceress is relaying a message she received in an earlier past, spoken at that time in the present by a ghost who presumably gained the knowledge of the content of the message during his own past life as a soothsayer; the message is about his and Bradamant's future, most of it in the past but part of it in the present of Ariosto's Ferrara audience, though all of it is in the past of Ariosto's anticipated future audience.

But epic prophecy goes beyond twenty–twenty hindsight. Anchises does not stop his account of future history with the advent of Augustus. He also prefigures the historical role of Rome after him as lawgiver and as the prime example for the world as a whole of an ecumene of different ethnic communities—a prediction that has since proved largely accurate. The sayings of the Hebrew prophets still structure the future for billions of people. The words of the Chorus in Shakespeare's *Henriad* explicitly remind us that within the cave of the theater we are hearing the words of dead English ancestors; they do not just direct us to the future events that will bring about the reign of the Tudors, but also point more universally to the role of England as a new kind of regime in which the work of the king is to give his power back to the people as they gradually learn how to handle it.[11] All Christian epic is predicated on the uncanny way that the life of Jesus did, with such comprehensive elegance and depth, fulfill the words of the prophets. In other words, the very idea that past prophecies did come true, *even if the past prophecies are fictional*, is a prophecy in itself of a kind of temporal consistency or even solidarity that is constitutive of the human world.

It is this larger meaning that accounts for the caution that epic often shows with regard to prophecy. Often we should not know the events of the future, especially if our curiosity has selfish motives, of the order of buying a stock we know will rise or betting on a winner in a future horse race. Saul's discomfiture when (having got no prognostications from Adonai or the angels) he asks the Witch of Endor to summon the ghost of the prophet Samuel to tell him the result of the morrow's battle with the Philistines, is a good example.[12] Saul's very application for future knowledge results in his being punished by losing the battle. Similar paradoxes are explored in the story of Oedipus, in Shakespeare's *Macbeth*, and in much contemporary science fiction.

Basically, prophecy is only good for us when it comes under the sign of a higher apprehension of the harmonic relationship and mutually modifying feedback of all events past and present: what is called the mandate of heaven, or providence (or in Robert Wright's awkward but insightful term "nonzerosumness").[13] Aeneas' and Bradamant's (and, one hopes, Rinaldo's and Dante's) virtuous piety is such that prophecy will not harm them. Our freedom lies in the branchiness of time, the possibility that many lines of action and event are genuinely open to us. If our desire to know the future is to amputate all but the one branch we want, we are trying to destroy the autonomy of the world and end up destroying our own in the process. Only those prophetic visions that represent the great consensus of actual and possible events, a consensus we can trust because it has already given us this beautiful universe with all its vital and self-expressive free agents, its compellingly suspenseful story, can truly help the hero. The only kind of prophecy that does not harm us is the kind that frees us and everybody else.

This is one of the central issues of my own *Genesis: An Epic Poem*. The narrator relays his narrative backwards in time to its redactor, the querulous scholar of the twentieth century. But it is clear that this is not the sort of prophecy that, with ingenious and inescapable logic, leads us to try to avoid the prophecy and so brings us to the fatal three-way fork in the road from Delphi where our fate is sealed. Instead, it is the future prophet that is sacrificed, not we, the recipients of the prophecy. In fact, knowing one of the branches our time could take, we are in a better position to make a free choice than if we continued to blunder on in the course we are already taking. And if we do take a different branch, our friend from whom we got the message must disappear together with the future that begot him, and we are back with a straightforward science-fiction tale that requires no creepy time travel, and fate is in our own hands. The best way of traveling into the future is free action, and we can do it as quickly as we like, with no fear that time will not keep pace with us.

The Commission

Thus the information that the hero gets in the underworld, if it is not the ruinous kind that destroys Macbeth, Oedipus, and Saul, is a call to action, an assignment of a task or duty. In fact, we might say that the whole story of the journey to the underworld is a sort of close analysis in narrative terms of the correct process of decision-making. Read allegorically, it might be paraphrased thus:

We can only take a real decision in the context of death. Since one will not be around to enact one's decision if it is oneself that dies, the death has to be of someone close, a friend, kinsperson, or spouse in whom one's own identity is bound up enough so that part of oneself dies with one's friend. Failing that, imminent danger of death oneself, or deep contemplation of one's future death however distant, may be enough for the decision to carry real weight. In other words, a true decision takes place where we butt up against the irreducible indeterminacies of life; it is not enough for us to be simply taking one of various ordinary paths or, worse, taking the known path of least resistance. What comes after death is the most radical of all such indeterminacies: it is the undiscovered country from which no traveler returns.

But substantive decision resulting in action cannot be free or responsible if we have no knowledge of the possible outcomes. Here we take the classic human finesse; by using our cultural ability to consult the past and speak with the dead, we can at least find out how earlier decisions panned out. We see into the future by seeing how the past stepped forward into its own future. We bind ourselves in solidarity with all crossers of the great boundary, we jump into the grave of Ophelia, so to speak. By agreeing to share our encounter with death with others before us, we give ourselves at least company on the ferry across the dark river. And company is, after all, one of the main reasons, perhaps the main reason, why we would want to be alive in the first place. Furthermore, company only becomes company when one is *doing* something with one's companions; and since it is life, not death, that is the place where things are done, matter the expressive medium of action, the consultation with the dead must lead us back to life. And it leads *them* back to life as well, in that our actions then become theirs, we are their executors and agents in the land of the living, and they live again in us.

The chief complaint of the dead is frustration; armless, bodiless, they can do nothing. They cry out to us that their civil and human rights have been violated by their death, they no longer have a vote in the constitution of reality, and after all what happened to them is a contingent, not necessarily constitutive aspect of their being. Their death was not a just punishment but an accident or an arbitrary imposition. Our job, if one is a hero, is to give them peace; and this is the true meaning of the burial that the unburied dead demand. It is not that they want to sleep, but that they want to be freed from the great corpse that, headless, wallows by the seashore.[14] Burial frees them from the corpse, and frees us from their haunting of us; but it frees them in that they are now embodied in us, we must carry their identity and moral concern with us.

Thus the dead free us by giving us a glimpse of the future paths that branch out before each of us and all of us together; and in turn we free them by taking them into ourselves and letting them exercise their agency in our own work. Thus one is conceding to them in this process a certain amount of one's own purely individual agency, the kind of agency that is one's unearned privilege in being alive, but that is also subject to the arbitrary limit of mortality. In return, however, one acquires a much greater mass and gravity of presence; in making my "I" theirs, I am making their "we" mine. Carrying this inheritance, we also have something substantial to pass on when we do reach the mortal limit; we may even by that time have transferred our allegiance and identification from the chattering self of our mortality to the large soul-shape that our individuality has formed out of the rich material of our inheritance.

So the commission, the assignment of the quest or task or duty, is also a sort of definition of freedom itself, in all its limits and also in all its great power. It is a profoundly conservative concept, since it accepts, like the old corrupt electoral district of Chicago's Cook County, the vote of the silent majority of the dead. As Chesterton put it:

> Tradition means giving votes to the most obscure of all classes, our ancestors. It is the democracy of the dead. Tradition refuses to submit to the small and arrogant oligarchy of those who merely happen to be walking about. All democrats object to men being disqualified by the accident of birth; tradition objects to their being disqualified by the accident of death.[15]

But the commission is also a radically liberal concept. It frees us from current fashion, from the conformism of conventional wisdom; dangerously so, even. For most revolutions, good or bad, have been predicated on some call from the dead, the restoration of ancient freedoms or virtues or covenant, the lost promise of some past imagined future, the fundamentals from which the trivial or tyrannical present has torn us away.

The Return: Time Anomalies

The return to the land of the living is often handled with an odd swiftness in epic. It is really a resurrection, but it is handled with surprising casualness. Odysseus sees that his time is up when Persephone, her gorgon, and a horde of shades are about to descend on him, and beats a hasty retreat. Aeneas and the Sibyl simply glide through the gate of ivory, despite the earlier warning that the ascent is an "opus" and a "labor." Dante and Virgil emerge from Hell on the far side of the world in a few lines. The emergence of Hunahpu and Xbalanque is handled with similar abruptness. The moment they have spoken with their dead father, it is over:

> And then the two boys ascended this way, here into the middle of the light, and they ascended straight on into the sky, and the sun belongs to one and the moon to the other. (141)

In William Buck's translation of the *Mahabharata*, Yudhishthira's return from the underworld is uncannily similar to the words of the *Popol Vuh*:

> Then in his dream all was confusion—the darkness was hit by lightning that remained still where it cut, and night fell away in pieces from under his feet. Yudishthira fell into the sun. He fell into the arms of Dharma, whose long golden hair was blinding bright. (369)

Gilgamesh and Urshanabi similarly make the long trek back to Uruk in a few words, and Moses' successful emergence from the encounter with the angel of death is taken as a matter of course once Zipporah has performed her shamanic rite of circumcision.

What is the meaning of this apparent off-handedness in handling a subject of supreme importance and interest? Is it simply the great artistry of the literary geniuses that coined these stories—recognizing that once the point has been made, there is no need to labor it?—or that the completion of the task of obtaining the vital information is what is important, and the mere miracle-working of resurrection would be a distraction? Or are each of these epic composers finding the same hidden image for the ascent, that is, the sudden emergence of the dreamer from the dream when the dream-work is done, and the desperately swift dissolution of the dream and its atmosphere, as waking consciousness returns?

Is Virgil offering us a clue with his much-debated choice of the gate of ivory—conventionally, of false dreams—as the portal through which Aeneas and the Sibyl emerge? Is Virgil thus apologizing for the fact that his account of Aeneas' journey is a false dream, a mere fiction—obviously one, since Virgil's Roman readers would know perfectly well that the accuracy of Anchises' prophecies is not miraculous at all, but Virgil's hindsight? Jorge Luis Borges argues with typical ingenuity and insight that the message may be the other way around: perhaps it is the "waking" side of the portal that is the false side. Perhaps Elysium is the true side, and the upper world, to which Aeneas and the Sibyl return through the appropriate gate, the false. Has Yudishthira really visited hell and heaven, or was it just a dream? Is Chuang Tzu dreaming he is a butterfly, or the butterfly dreaming he is Chuang Tzu? "Do I wake or sleep?"[16]

The necessarily questioning mode into which we have fallen marks the transition from the underworld to the upperworld. It is also perhaps linked to another oddity that we sometimes find when the hero returns, a sort of Rip van Winkle effect. When True Thomas emerges from Elfland he finds that seven years have passed. When Odysseus gets back from the land of shades the plot of the poem, which up to that point has carried us and the hero further and further into the mysterious darkness of unknown and lands and fantastic supernatural landscapes, abruptly changes direction, and Odysseus begins his return to the historical land known to the Greeks.

First he returns to Aeaea, the land of Circe. Next he encounters the Sirens, whose threat corresponds to that of the Laestrygonians, whom he encountered just before coming to Aeaea. Next he arrives at the island of Helios, god of the sun, corresponding to the encounter with Aeolus, god of the winds, the adventure preceding the Laestrygonians. Then come Scylla and Charybdis, corresponding to the land of the Cyclops. He is wrecked, then, on Ogygia, which in its temptation to forget mortal cares corresponds to the land of the Lotus Eaters. Lastly he comes to the human city of Phaeacea, corresponding to the last human city he encountered before his plunge into the magic lands: Ismarus. His return to Ithaca matches his departure from Troy. The whole descent and return through these concentric rings of enchantment (as if Dante has to turn back when he reaches the center of the earth and return through the concentric rings of Hell) takes eight years. The episode of the land of the dead is its centerpiece and epitome; and again there is an implicit time-dilation, for what should be a few days' voyage has turned into an era, a place of historical change in which Greek myth has turned into Greek history.

The shape of this descent and return closely resembles the form of those life-crisis rituals that Arnold van Gennep[17] and Victor Turner[18] identified as culturally universal, with their three-phase chiastic or concentric structure. That structure comprises the rite of separation from ordinary social time, the sojourn in a betwixt-and-between state that Van Gennep dubbed the "liminal" phase, and the rite of reaggregation into regular time and society. The participants return but with the new social roles the ritual has prepared them for: if a funeral, the heir is now the master or mistress; if a marriage, the couple has become man and wife; if a birth, a fetus has become a person and a woman a mother; if an initiation, boy or girl has become man or woman.

The peculiar subjective time-distortion that attends these epic episodes strikes one almost as if the great storytellers had anticipated the great science theme of relative time dilation/time contraction, where the near-lightspeed space travelers return after a voyage of a few years to find that hundreds of years have passed on Earth. (Indeed, our astronauts are a few microseconds younger than they would have been if they had stayed behind.) But perhaps the intuition is a common, if sophisticated one: to journey in space is to journey in time—it may be thirty miles to town, or it may be an hour. But this very fact is a dim suggestion that time may not be as irreversible as our terrors persuade us; space is not irreversible, and time and space are not separate.

When Hunahpu and Xbalanque return from the underworld a still larger and stranger temporal apocalypse occurs. For their adventures correspond exactly to the experimental struggles of the four aboriginal gods to create the world and a fit human dweller in it, to the future history of the Quiché, and also to the placing of the heavenly bodies and their "winding up," so to speak, so that they will tell the time thenceforth. The twins' campaign against the lords of death is a sort of time-loop at the very moment of creation that determines the way things will play out thereafter. Thus when they return from Xibalba the world clock begins to tick, both astrologically and historically.

We may now read other chiastic plot structures in epic as more generally representing the descent to and return from the underworld: the exiles of Manas, David of Sassoun, Temüjin, Sundiata, Rama and the Pandavas, Beowulf's sojourn in the waters and caves of the monsters, Tripitaka's ordeal in the Himalayas, Martín Fierro's captivity by the Indians, da Gama's whole voyage, Hamlet's sea journey and visit to the graveyard, Parzifal's quest, Gawaine's midwinter tryst, Wordsworth's fall from and return to innocence, Milton's Fall and redemption of humankind, the voyage of the Pequod (mapped against the chiastic history of Queequeg's coffin), and so on. In Julia Budenz's *The Gardens of Flora Baum*, Flora/Julia's visit with the ghost of Torquato Tasso fuses the mortal writer with the immortal protagonist, and the writer steps aboard her pluritemporal tale, leaving mortality behind. My *Genesis: An Epic Poem* ends with a return from the 2070 AD narrative to the 2151 world of the frame tale. As it does so it makes explicit the time-paradox that the story itself may abort the future world it depicts, and initiate another future in the 1988 world of the publication of the poem. It is not just that the Martian clocks and calendars are different from Earth's, but that the temporality of one future differs from the temporality of the other, and the story marks the interface of the two.

In each case of epic return from the dead a historical era passes and a new one is born, and there is a space between them when the clocks and calendars of neither era are applicable, and new—and at the same time globally valid—things can happen. Sometimes the descent and return is identified with the Fall; sometimes it is seen as a return to nature; but perhaps it is always a transforming encounter with death that changes our view of time.[19]

Notes

1. The gods of death are often associated with money. Hades is a deathgod, but also a plutocrat. The Hindu god Puchan, like Mercury, leads souls both into wealth and into the underworld. The lords of Xibalba are associated with the Mayan monetary currency, cacao beans, and their roasting to make the sacred cacao liquor, drunk from a skull or gourd at sacrifice rituals. See Michael J. Grofe, *The Recipe for Rebirth: Cacao as Fish in the Mythology and Symbolism of the Ancient Maya*, www.famsi.org/research/grofe/GrofeRecipeForRebirth.pdf. Why this odd connection? One answer may be obvious: all our inherited wealth comes, by definition, from the dead, and our own deaths are the repayment of the debt. In Shakespeare's fourth sonnet:

> Then how, when nature calls thee to be gone,
> What acceptable audit canst thou leave?
> Thy unused beauty must be tomb'd with thee,
> Which, used, lives th' executor to be.

   The sin of Shemwindo, Mwindo's father, is that he does not wish to pass his possessions on to his offspring; thus, like Kronos and Herod, he kills them as they are born, all except for Mwindo, who is born, by a trick, from his mother's navel and who escapes drowning, like Moses and Tripitaka, by means of a makeshift raft.

2. After the funeral of my father Victor W. Turner, the anthropologist, I took part in a wake based on the funeral of an Ndembu chief, with ritual dances performed by friends who were ethnodrama experts from both the anthropology community and the theater community. The Ndembu are a Bantu people of Zambia, related to the Nyanga people of Zaire, from which the Mwindo epic comes. In the funeral dance, a terrifying but comic masked dancer, personating Vic's death, threatens the bystanders, but they cannot help laughing at his antics, and his brandishing of a silly crooked gourd rattle. If they laugh, they must pay a money fine to the Master of Ceremonies, who is also costumed comically as a sort of sad clown. The fine is destined for the widow who presides over the ceremony. The death figure at this wake was played by the distinguished anthropologist Roy Wagner.

3. "Lycidas", l. 13.

4. IV.iv.132.

5. Mircea Eliade, *Shamanism: Archaic Techniques of Ecstasy* (Princeton, NJ: Princeton University Press, 2004).

6. Virgil's villa was only half a day's walk from the cave of the Sibyl, and it is still a place to inspire strange dreams and visions.

7. http://www.thelatinlibrary.com/verg.html, VI.126–9.

8. John Dryden, trans. *Virgil's Aeneid* (New York: Penguin Classics, 1997).

9. Arthur Clarke, *Childhood's End* (New York: Ballantine Books, 1953).

10. *Natural Religion* (New Brunswick, NJ: Transaction Publishers, 2006), 51–69.

11. The poor condemned English,
    Like sacrifices, by their watchful fires
    Sit patiently and inly ruminate
    The morning's danger; and their gesture sad

Investing lank-lean cheeks and war-worn coats
Presenteth them unto the gazing moon
So many horrid ghosts. O, now, who will behold
The royal captain of this ruin'd band
Walking from watch to watch, from tent to tent,
Let him cry 'Praise and glory on his head!'
For forth he goes and visits all his host;
Bids them good morrow with a modest smile,
And calls them brothers, friends, and countrymen.
Upon his royal face there is no note
How dread an army hath enrounded him;
Nor doth he dedicate one jot of colour
Unto the weary and all-watched night;
But freshly looks, and over-bears attaint
With cheerful semblance and sweet majesty;
That every wretch, pining and pale before,
Beholding him, plucks comfort from his looks;
A largess universal, like the sun,
His liberal eye doth give to every one,
Thawing cold fear, that mean and gentle all
Behold, as may unworthiness define,
A little touch of Harry in the night.
Henry V, Act IV Prologue ll. 22–47

12.   1 Samuel 7–16.

13.   Robert Wright, *Nonzero: The Logic of Human Destiny* (New York: Pantheon Books, 2000).

14.   In his description of the unburied body of Priam, is Virgil thinking of Pompey, beheaded in his exile by the Egyptians?

15.   G. K. Chesterton, *Orthodoxy* (1908), http://www.leaderu.com/cyber/books/orthodoxy/orthodoxy.html.

16.   John Keats: "Ode to a Nightingale."

17.   Arnold Van Gennep, *The Rites of Passage, 1909* (Chicago , IL: University of Chicago Press, 1960).

18.   Victor W. Turner, *The Ritual Process: Structure and Anti-Structure* (New York: Aldine, 1995).

19.   The distinguished science fiction writer Vernor Vinge tells me that even as a child he only wanted to read stories in which the world itself was a different place at the end of the story from what it was at the beginning. Here, perhaps, is as neat a definition as there could be between the "mainstream novel" and epic. In the mainstream novel, the waters of the social consensus close over the heads of the protagonists at the end—"human voices wake us, and we drown" as Eliot puts it in "Prufrock." Not so in the epic: Ishmael bobs to the surface on a coffin, and America has been redefined forever.

8

The Founding of the City

The Idea of Home

The human species exists at the cusp of a profound geographical and behavioral paradox. The nurture of our helpless and immobile young, the need for a center where regular local trade and manufacture can be successfully pursued, the vulnerability of the human individual when alone and unsheltered, our dependence upon a shared local language, our inherently social and political nervous system, the value of shared and inherited experience of the same local conditions—all these dictate that we are at our best when we stay in one place. At the same time, an equally powerful array of forces demand that we move about: an incest taboo that demands that we find mates outside our kin group, our rebellious adolescence, the use of our intelligence and cooperative skills to exhaust the resources of game and produce locally available, our excellent long-distance walking and running abilities, our insatiable curiosity and restless susceptibility to boredom, the advantages of long-distance trade, a volatile glacial and postglacial world climate that can require migration or nomadism, and the need to decamp in response to the threat of war with other stronger groups.

Thus, psychologically we are caught between an anguished nostalgia for a real or mythical former home and an anxious and excited questing for a new and promising future home. Every epic without exception evokes, mourns, and celebrates this condition. Odysseus standing at the end of Calypso's island weeping for Ithaca, Aeneas grieving for Troy and striving for Rome, the Israelites yearning for the promised land, Tripitaka questing for India, the long hegira of the Quiché, the Heike in exile from Kyoto, the Pandavas banished from Hastinapur, Gunnar stopping to gaze at Lithend, Sundiata exiled from Mali, Gilgamesh and Enkidu in the forest shivering with the strangeness and the glamour of the place, Vasco da Gama sailing for the Indies, Sekandar's journeys of discovery in Asia—all evoke the same pit-of-the-stomach homesickness, the same reckless desire to see what is over the next ridge, what

211

new island lies beyond the horizon. Sometimes the homesickness is uppermost, sometimes the adventurousness, but the ambivalence is always there, whatever the proportions of the mixture.

How does epic resolve this paradox? Essentially, by making a home of its own. To do so it must somehow satisfy or reroute the demands that make us want to wander. The city must be big enough to have room for many kin-groups, for true strangers, so that one can find an exotic mate within its walls. It must therefore have schemes to translate the tribal languages into each other, to de-Babelize, so to speak, the human world. Epic is the main way to do that. The city must be able to boost its productive capacity, both by expanding the territory it controls and by extending through agriculture or horticulture the temporal endurance of the land's foison and plenty, so as to support a large and varied population over time. The city must develop political relations with other cities to enable trade and the transfer of technology, relations that include war and the development of a warrior caste. It must make a common currency. It must control the climate by dams, causeways, bridges, aqueducts, durable fired tile roofing and bricking, heating and cooling systems. It must develop laws to ensure property rights, and protect the individuals, families, demes, factions, castes, congregations, and boroughs from each other, and build walls and gates to control entry and exit of persons and property. It must, above all, create excitements and puzzles equivalent to those of exploration and adventure. If we cannot have a jungle, we will make an urban jungle, and the most immediate way of doing that is to fictionalize the long trials of the founding itself, in epic.

All epic is about the founding of a city, or a refounding that is also a founding. Sometimes, as with the two tragic epics of Greece and Japan, *The Iliad* and the *Heike*, it is about the unfounding of a city, but its first founding is retold in the details of its fall. Here we may find another way of outlining epic and distinguishing it from other genres. Where epic differs from myth per se is that epic has gathered the scattered myths, legends, and fairy tales into a coherent architectonics and connected them with real history and a real place. Those nations that were conquered, absorbed, or obliterated before they could grow themselves a Jerusalem, an Uruk, a Quiché, or a Rome can often leave us a proto-epic cycle of tales, but it takes a city or its equivalent to make an epic. Much is lost in that making: for to make a city the clans and tribes must be united and made to speak a common language, and much of their deeply local and idiosyncratic symbolism—the wonderful world of Lévi-Strauss—must be rationalized or buried to ensure collective comprehension.

Walls and Gates

Like all living organisms, a human body needs a skin, a boundary between self and other that is permeable under the control of the organism. A skin can admit chosen beneficial matter, energy, and information, can expel alien lifeforms, toxins, and waste, and can discharge messages, information, and gifts to allies and kin. To make control of these movements possible, part of the skin must be impermeable, other parts permeable and attended by central control. The body must have walls to prevent movement between the outer and inner, and gates to permit it. This description may immediately suggest the image of the body as a nine-gated city, as it is found in the *Ramayana*, the *Bhagavadgita*, and throughout the Vedic canon. The trope of wooing as siege is standard in Europe. The seven gates of Thebes, named for the offspring of Amphion, carried a similar suggestion, and the five senses are also imaged as gates of a city in traditional European medicine and theology.[1]

The establishment of a skin for the city—walls and gates—is an essential function of epic. A city, to meet its paradoxical need to be both a home and an adventure, must possess the organic wholeness that a skin defines, must resemble a living body, which is both a thing and a process, both a place and an act. A city is also a community of reciprocators, traders who need markets; and markets require to be protected from liars and thieves who are not reciprocators or cooperators. In game theory, the only advantage that cooperators have over defectors is that cooperators can form groups, whereas there is no honor among thieves. Contracts must be enforced, and contract breakers expelled from the gates. People built walls around their markets to keep cooperators safe and keep defectors out.

The earliest of all known epics, *Gilgamesh*, begins and ends with an evocation of Uruk's city walls, and its hero is famous chiefly for having built them. The first adventure of the two hero friends is the despoliation of the nature-god's forest for the timber of Uruk's gates. However, the actual building of walls and gates is not a major element in epics thereafter. In several other epics, the walls and gates of the city are indeed important—consider Homer's Troy, Virgil's Rome, Kakuichi's Kyoto, Tasso's Jerusalem, Dante's Hell, Vyasa's Hastinapur, and the *Popol Vuh's* Quiché. Of the *Pequod's* hull Ahab cries: "Its wood could only be American!" But of course the walls of Troy, Dante's Hell, Tasso's Jerusalem, and Vyasa's Hastinapur are held by the enemy; Virgil's future Rome is yet unbuilt, the Japanese emperor Antoku is to be expelled from the imperial capital; the *Pequod* will sink; and the Mayans built walls more to play the ball game than for defense. It is the metaphorical walls of a civilization that are of the deepest interest to epic composers.

How are the city-dwellers themselves mentally and morally walled and gated? A walled city in the possession of barbarians or strangers who did not know its holy places would not be a city. Epic defines those inner walls and gates, creates the narrative that identifies their makers, owners, and heirs, and establishes the rituals, tests, marks, renunciations, and duties that constitute heirship. Perhaps the fundamental marker of the inner walls is the initiatory sacrifice.

Sacrifice and Commutation of Sacrifice

Every founding requires a sacrifice. The founding of a great city demands human sacrifice or its equivalent, the ante for the civic game. The bodies of the heroes and builders are figuratively (and often literally) buried under the walls, and their ghosts defend the ramparts. Sacrifice creates a bond that identifies the citizens with each other and with their leaders. If the walls and gates of the city are figurative, the internalized principles of the citizen—the Fifth Court of Iceland's Allthing, for instance, or the laws of Rome or the Covenant of Jerusalem or the Persian royal *farr* or the imperial Japanese mandate of Heaven—the sacrifice must itself be metaphorized. In the process, an abstract language can be created, a language of values and concepts that shape the self and its relations. If that language loses touch with its literal sacrificial roots, it needs to be reminded of them, and epic serves this function among others. The need for sacrifice is one reason why epics are so frequently bloody. For the citizen, the bond paradoxically constitutes his or her freedom—the open trust that enables us to leave our compatriots to their own devices and to be left unharassed ourselves, a trust based on the investment or bond of sacrifice offered by each citizen and subsidized by the huge deposit left by the originary heroes and martyrs. But the thirsty roots of that freedom should not be forgotten. The tree of liberty, in Jefferson's words, must be refreshed from time to time with the blood of patriots and tyrants.

How does the metaphorization of the sacrificial bond take place? Here we can draw on insights from René Girard's thoughtful book

Violence and the Sacred and combine them with recent work in the sociobiology of signaling, the semiotics of metaphor, and the theology of what I shall call commutation.

Perhaps a good starting point would be to look at the emergence of meaningful action among animals and early humans. In mating rituals and ranking contests in animal species, we find symbolic gestures and behaviors that express the intention and the qualifications to mate or enter into a contest (sometimes both, resolved in symbolic displays like the triumph ceremony of graylag geese[2]). Trading and trusting coalitions also require such signals. In order for these signals to be believable, they must be what ethologists call "costly." Though they may not cost as much as rape or overt battle to the death or risky robbery of resources, they are still expensive—they are sacrifices, paid in terms of scarce metabolic energy, the development of bodily pigment, antlers, decorative feathers, and nervous tissue to control the song or dance of the animal. Animals, and we humans, communicate by sacrifice, and we trade for what we want by being prepared to give up something we already have. The things that are traded—the proffered food of the male for reproductive access to the female, the pack leader's status for the follower's membership of the pack, the sentinel meerkat's safety for the preservation of her genes among her kin—are thus equivalents for each other, and they make up a relationship of worth or value.

When evolutionary anthropologists try to date the emergence of language among our ancient ancestors, they look for signs of artificial sacrificial behavior. It seems that human conscious self-awareness, the recognition and performance of sacrificial behavior as such and its transformation from a hardwired signaling device into a culturally rehearsed and agreed upon ritual, and the origins of language, are all intertwined. As humans, we no longer trade just with each other but with the gods or God—i.e., with whatever out there gave us what we have and are, and perhaps can give us what we want. The great old religious myths of the creation—and of the awakening of human beings to what they are—root the origin of the word in the rituals of sacrifice.

Among humans, sacrifice has a peculiar element, which we might call "commutation": every sacrifice is an act that in other circumstances would be a crime of violence, waste, imprudence, or impurity, but which is excused on the grounds that it commemorates and expiates a previous sacrifice, in which some much more bloody violence or costly loss was required.[3] Each new sacrifice is a little ascent on the Maslovian pyramid of valued goals,[4] its purpose a little more intangible, intellectually demanding, ambiguous in form, rich in significance, inclusive in sympathy. We sacrifice first for survival, then for sustenance, then for power, then for status, then for love, and then for spiritual transcendence. And as we do so, the actual demands of the deity to whom we sacrifice are tempered and gentled. The capital punishment for the disobedience of Adam and Eve is commuted to pain in childbirth (presumably because of the enlarged braincase of the newly human infant) and the need to work for a living (presumably because humans can and must take thought for the morrow). The punishment for Cain's sacrifice of his brother Abel to God is commuted to a sign of his eternal homelessness, the human fate. Abraham is allowed to sacrifice a ram instead of his son, who was due to the Lord. Instead of a whole firstborn son, only a shred of flesh from the foreskin need be given. Later the prophets tell us that God prefers the benevolent moral sacrifice of philanthropy over the meticulousness of ritual, and the generativeness of mercy over the strictness of justice, and so human blood sacrifice is gradually tamped down physically and amped up morally until it becomes love for one's neighbor.

Likewise, because of the sacrifice of Prometheus ("forethought"), the Greeks no longer need to sacrifice the whole bull, but can burn its fat and bones and hide to the gods, and eat the flesh themselves. The blood sacrifice demanded by the Furies is commuted to the civic service required by the Eumenides. In the *Upanishads*, the *Bhagavadgita*, and the sermons of the Buddha, animal sacrifice, asceticism, and costly ritual are trumped by moral duty, which is in turn trumped by spiritual submission and compassion.

When the process has been going for a long time, the sacrificed object can become apparently rather trivial. Cucumbers are sacrificed in some African tribal societies; Catholics and Buddhists burn candles; almost all Christians break bread, simultaneously commemorating, re-evoking, and symbolically atoning for the bloody sacrifice of the Cross—an act of ritual cannibalism that excuses our real cannibalism. Thus every sacrifice is an act of impurity or violence or waste that pays for a prior act of greater impurity, but pays for it at an advantage, that is, without its participants having to suffer the full consequences incurred by its predecessor. The punishment is commuted in a process that can be seen as the original dictionary by which we learned higher meanings.

For the process of commutation has much in common with the processes of metaphorization, symbolization, even reference or meaning itself. The Christian eucharistic sacrifice of bread not only *stands in* for the sacrifice of Christ (which in turn stands in for the death of the whole human race); it also *means*, and in sacramental theology *is*, the death of Christ. The Greek tragic drama both referred to, and was a portion of, the sacrificial rites of Dionysus—both a use and a mention, as the logicians say, or both a metaphor and a synecdoche, in the language of the rhetorician. The word "commutation," which I have used here in the legal sense of the substitute of a lesser penalty for the greater one demanded by strict justice, nicely combines these senses: in general use, it means any substitution or exchange, as when money in one currency is changed into another, or into small change, or when payment in one form is permitted to be made in another; in alchemy, it can be almost synonymous with transmutation, as of one metal into another; in electrical engineering, it is the reversal of a current or its transformation between direct and alternating current; in mathematical logic, it refers to the equivalency of a given operation, such as A multiplied by B, to its reverse, B multiplied by A.

Thus sacrifice is the meaning of meaning. What this implies is that the death of sacrifice is the death of meaning. The crisis in modern philosophy over the meaning of the word "reference," for instance,[5] perhaps has its roots in the denial of commutativeness; for reference and meaning to come to life, some deep sacrifice is required. Without it we are left only with *différance*,[6] trapped in the circular ruins[7] of the dictionary. Fact is bonded to theory in science by the costly and sacrificial work of experiment. Price is bonded to utility in economics by the hard knocks of the marketplace. Good intentions are welded to actions by the sacrificial submission of the donor to the real needs and wants of the recipient. Lofty artistic conceptions are realized as beauty in paint or words or stone or sound by the exacting and even agonizing ordeal of learning and exercising the craft. When the pain of the commutative process is denied, the bond is broken.

And when the bond breaks, it leads usually to some catastrophic bubble or inflationary explosion either in the realm of the signifier, or of the signified, or both. Science goes wrong when theory and data get separated—what follows is a proliferation of meaningless data-gathering or an arms race of empty theorizing, or both. When morality goes wrong, we get either brutal expediency (unprincipled action) or hypocrisy (principles not being matched by actions). When law goes wrong, we get excuses for bad behavior or cruel legalism. When religion goes wrong, we get idolatry or puritanical iconoclasm: too many things chasing too few ideas, or too many ideas chasing too few things. When philosophy goes wrong, we get know-nothingism or sophism. When our economy goes wrong, we get hedonistic materialism or the fantastical escalation and inflation of utterly immaterial derivatives and complex but bloodless financial instruments. When art goes wrong, we get a philistine welter of empty prettiness or an arid desert of conceptualism. Or both, in each of these cases—is this familiar?

The place where a sacrifice takes place is an altar. For a social animal, the altar is its home territory. For a human, the altar is the hearth or the dining table, the place one carves the sacrificial turkey at Christmas or the Tikka Masala at Diwali—by extension one's city and nation. The choice of and commitment to one's homeplace is, extended and abstracted, the choice of an identity, a set of promises constitutive of who one is. It is what we are prepared to defend to the death. The altar is where the idea and the fact, the signified and signifier, the thing and the label match each other. The city is the place of the public lares and penates, the public altar. In America, we are familiar with that place as the Washington Mall, with its memorials and commemorations of sacrifice, its costly dedication of treasure to a nonutilitarian purpose, its axial relation to the Arlington Cemetery where the heroic dead are buried.

Ritual Origins

From the originating sacrifices that morally funded and accredited the city come the basic rituals of its citizens. The self-sacrifice and death-god sacrifice of Hunahpu and Xbalanque define the form of the sacrifices that the mythical Qiché tribe exacted upon their subject peoples and in turn the historical sacrifice cult of the Maya and the literary form of the *Popol Vuh*, itself an imaginary journey up the pyramid steps. The smearing of sacrificial lambs' blood on the lintels of the Israelites and the death of the firstborn of Egypt specify both the form of the briss, the circumcision, and the liturgy of the Passover (and in turn the meaning of the crucifixion and the choreography of the Mass). The *Bhagavadgita* spells out the ritual implications of the battle of Kurukshetra with its bitter and tragic sacrifices of friends and kin, and shows the way in which kshatriya dharma can be turned into brahmanic ritual and then into mystical self-abnegation in communion with the divine. The journey of Tripitaka and Monkey, with its successive renunciatory sacrifices, is the template of the spiritual journey of the Chinese Buddhist. The death of Njal symbolically establishes the Christian rite in Iceland; the deaths of Iphigenia, Agamemnon, and Clytemnestra establish the ritual of the Athenian jury system. Epic is the conduit by which the blood of the originary sacrifice flows on into the public rituals and feast-days of the city and the private observances of persons and families by which human life is given larger meaning.

The rituals that proceed from the primal sacrifice have the essential function of marking the citizen as a citizen, giving him the keys to the city, the freedom of the city. Indeed, the ancient meaning of freedom is precisely in this sense, that is, that one is as free to come and go and use what is at hand as one is at home, where one is accepted and known as *one of us*. The rituals also mark the citizen off from other communions, tribes, and polities.[8]

Often the mark is quite literal: circumcision is only the most obvious example. Tattoos, caste-marks, piercings, body-paint, cranial deformations, dental modification, keloid scarring, shaving practices, and so on almost always identify the bearer as a member of a tribe or totemic group, whose origins are told in a heroic myth, wherein the hero first acquired the mark in his adventures. Sometimes the hero's sufferings are recreated in a scarring practice, as when Shiite Muslims commemorate the suffering of the martyr Hussein ibn Ali or Christian flagellants reenact the scourging of the savior. Ellen Dissanayake and others, like Irenaeus Eibl-Eibesfeldt and Kathryn Coe,[9] describe such body-markings as creating an artificial kin-group whose members are immediately recognizable to each other, as are members of one's real family. These marks, they claim, convey to the individual the subliminal message that the fellow-wearer contains many of one's own genes and thus that self-sacrifice for his or her sake would be a prudent genetic investment. Odysseus is, after all, identified to his kin by his scar, Cain by his mark, Ahab by the white line of the lightning-bolt; and Henry V's warriors at Agincourt, his "band of brothers," will, he promises, one day strip their arms to show the marks of battle. And of course every male Jew bears on the most intimate part of his body the memory of the emergency circumcision of Moses' son Gershom. Significantly, Gershom's name means "stranger" or "exile," in commemoration of the epic journeys of the people of Israel, and their separation from all other nations.

The observance of food laws and customs can also identify the citizen and serve as a demonstration that he has paid his ante for admission to the community. Few epics have as explicit an account of the connection between the great story and the food laws as Leviticus and Deuteronomy. Here—and with further elaborations in the Zohar and the Midrash, in general—the connections between food practices and the original acts of sacrifice, covenant, commutation, communion, and separation from strangers are spelled out in terms of which animals, plants, foods, and food combinations are taboo, and for whom and at what times. The stories of the plant and animal sacrifices of Cain and Abel and of the pottage-making and stock-rearing wizardry of Jacob are interpreted explicitly as the founding justification of Jewish food-raising and food preparation practices. The anthropologist Mary Douglas has shown in Leviticus the exact mapping of permissible and impermissible organ meats and butchery methods onto the stages of Moses' ascent and return from Mount Sinai.[10]

But even when the mapping of epic gest onto food choice and preparation is not so exact and explicit, it is very often profoundly important in epic, especially as regards the usually sacramental meaning of staple foods. Consider the importance of rice, even specific rice dishes, in the *Heike*, and the identification of rice with the imperial house. Rice planting and harvest festivals mark the points in the story when some kind of defense against the rising chaos of the times is mounted (and usually defeated), where the connection with ancient mythic times is asserted and broken. Here the central ideology of the great Japanese epic becomes clear: the need to return to a state of Buddhist/Shintoist harmony that was tragically shattered by the civil war, a refounding that includes both the restoration of the institution of the emperor and the proper cultivation and preparation of the staple food.

Corn (maize) plays an exactly analogous role in the *Popol Vuh*. Indeed, the story of the beheading, death, and resurrection of the two sets of hero twins can be read allegorically as a manual for the harvesting and sowing of the maize plant, and even, perhaps, of the selective breeding methods by which the strain was improved. After all, not all descendants of the ur-parents survive to reproduce, and the differential rate of reproductive success is directly dependent on the fitness and virtues of the survivors. The mother of the second set of hero twins, Blood Moon, proves her worthiness by her corn skills, as do her sons. Other important food plants and animals are also woven closely into the story, and their use demonstrated in the history of the Quiché people.

Christian epics all dwell explicitly or implicitly on the connection between the eating of the forbidden fruit and the sacrifice of Christ. Milton sings "Of Man's first disobedience and the fruit/ Of that forbidden Tree." More important still in most Christian epic is the link between Christ's crucifixion at Passover and the rite of Holy Communion. Again the staple food of the West, wheat corn, is central, though other foods such as lamb (especially important in Greece), wine, and fish, are also prominently featured. The Mystical Body of Christ, the new Jerusalem, is conceived as a feast in which the ordinary transubstantiation of animal and plant protein and carbohydrate into human brain, mind, and heart is given its true significance as the miracle it is; and participation in the feast qualifies the guests at the table as members one of another. Even today Catholics avoid meat on Good Friday and fast before Mass.

A different kind of sacrificial equation appears in Shakespeare's *Henriad*, where the sacrificial beast is Falstaff, persistently compared with the central victim in the old English autumn festivals in which fat beasts were slaughtered and eaten or salted for the winter. Falstaff's habitat is the Boar's Head tavern, he is imaged as a "roasted Manningtree ox with the pudding in his belly," Pharaoh's fat kine, a "Bartholomew boar-pig," an "old pike"; he "sweats to death/ And lards the lean earth as he runs along."[11] Here the connection between sacrifice and the fundamental fertility of the nation's soil is explicit; King Henry V will sacrifice Falstaff, together with his own unruly youth, to restore the peace, unity, and fecundity of his kingdom. In the act of ritual cannibalism that is at the heart of Shakespeare's national epic, Falstaff is the fat beast, the jolly old man, that England raises and consumes to make itself England. He is John Bull, the merry knight Sir Bercilak in *Sir Gawaine and the Green Knight* (who, like Hunahpu, can be beheaded and grow his head back again), he is Chaucer's Miller, Dickens' Pickwick, Benny Hill.

The founding of the city, with its initiating gest and sacrifice, also establishes sexual and reproductive practices, and codifies kinship rules. The themes of kin violence that we have already examined set up the problems that city founding must solve. Uruk cannot make its name as a city until its king is restrained from indiscriminate sexual domination; if anyone could have been sired by Gilgamesh, there is no guarantee against incest, no secure genealogy, no reliable system of kin obligation and generational succession. Ithaca, missing the essential link between Laertes and Telemachus and the essential separator between Telemachus and his mother, is paralyzed until Odysseus returns and reclaims the nuptial bed. The theme of possible incest between Penelope and her son is touched with shocking suggestiveness in the moment when Telemachus considers for a moment whether he might try to string his father's bow (the test for worthiness of Penelope's hand), but draws back from it. The ways in which sex and love are managed in the relations of Parzifal and Condwiramurs, Siegfried and Brunnhild, Cuchulainn and Emer, Aeneas and Dido, Rama and Sita become exemplary or cautionary for all members of the city, defining their difference from those of other nations.

The exclusiveness that comes with the sacrificial separation of the citizens from all others can have tragic consequences. It is partly the exceptionalism of the Chosen People in the Jewish Bible that gets them into the terrible trouble, the repeated exiles and persecutions in Biblical history. The difference between inclusive and exclusive cultures seems to be measured by the extent of their exogamy, i.e., their choice of foreign spouses. For generations the Patriarchs send back to the homeland in Ur for a spouse for their sons, that is, a spouse who is a blood relation; Jacob marries two of his cousins. This insistence on preserving the ancestral gene-pool gives the Israelites their identity. When they need a savior, they must turn to a man who was raised by a foreign princess, uncircumcised, and who marries a Midianite—Moses. But he is of Hebrew blood. Similarly, the Mayan Moses twins in the *Popol Vuh* are apparently strangers, but were sired miraculously by the first Hunahpus: it is perhaps the exceptionalism of the Quiché people that renders them unable in the end to unite with other Mayan tribes against the Spanish.

When, as in the Roman, Persian, and American epics, the nation is defined inclusively, other problems and opportunities emerge. Aeneas loses his native Trojan wife, Creusa, in the fall of Troy, and must seek a foreign spouse. His two foreign entanglements, with Dido and Lavinia, create untold trouble both in the time of the story itself—the wars with the Rutulians and Italians—and in the future, since Dido is the ancestress of the Romans' Carthaginian enemy. But the inclusive policy itself results eventually in the possibility of a multiethnic society, the Roman Empire itself, united by a common law. Persia's inclusiveness in the *Shahnameh* is even more ambivalent in its results. Constantly Persian royalty marries outside the race, often gaining huge territorial inheritances thereby and always enhancing Persia's reputation as the acme of civilization and the nerve center of trade, art, technology, and diplomacy. But the practice of inclusiveness also leads to great schisms and civil conflicts, and Persia eventually falls prey to the Arabs, whose much narrower culture gives them a cohesiveness lacking in their victims.

A different sort of ambiguity attends Melville's America in *Moby Dick*, where the *Pequod* gathers the talents and vision of every race of human beings in its little republic. But here the universality of Ahab's claim to allegiance paradoxically gives the ship a much greater consensus than would be provided by mere local kinship. In Melville's *Battle Pieces*, his great and much underappreciated collection of poems on the Civil War, the poet forebodingly evokes the image of the iron dome—the battle-armor erected by Lincoln over the Washington Capitol building against the rebel artillery—as a symbol of a potentially imperial presidency with a similarly tall, dark, lean, ugly, charismatic, biblical, and visionary leader. Melville saw that if humans from all over the world could be united into one overwhelming "Babelonian" tribe under a godlike Nimrod, it might then challenge Nature, even God himself, to its own undoing. But though the meaning of the city-welding may be different from that of the old epics, the method is the same: blood sacrifice and communal meal. The whole crew drinks the rum from the socket of Ahab's harpoon.

Genealogies of Humans and Gods

In the careful genealogies compiled by the epic composers can already be found the rudiments of an evolutionary theory of the origins of the human race and even of the cosmos as a whole. Even now Iceland's Ministry of Health uses the meticulous genealogies found in the Sagas as the database for an extraordinary genetic survey of its 275,000 pure-bred inhabitants. This survey has already revealed important knowledge about our own evolution and that of some of our guest symbiotes and parasites. Many families in Japan today can trace their ancestry to the dramatis personae of the *Heike*, as English genealogy buffs trace theirs to the characters in Shakespeare's Wars of the Roses. The biogenetic researches of Luca Cavalli-Sforza and others, conversely, cast strong light on the great conquests, migrations, ethnic mergings, and geographical origins of the peoples celebrated in epic.[12]

Rather embarrassingly, the old aristocratic theory of blood inheritance and family seems to receive some confirmation from

223

contemporary genetics (though its conclusions about individual natural superiority and inferiority, and its confidence in the persistence over generations of specific acquired traits, have been thoroughly exploded). An epic composer, faced with the task of explaining how the city came to be, who its inhabitants are, and how they emerged in the first place, must pay close attention to genealogy. The audience of an epic expects to hear about its ancestors; the more curious among them want to know how we are different from the animals, if we are, and if we are related to them—as our shared characteristics seem to suggest—then how. Some might even want to know how we are related to other natural forces that seem to have agency as we do—wind, sun, sea, plants, the passions—and how we can engage with the spirits of places and of human tribes themselves.

These questions, though ancient and fully interwoven with shamanic lore and practice, are basically evolutionary ones. Indeed, the oddity of the history of evolutionary research is not that it suddenly appeared in the nineteenth century but that the radical dualism and essentialism of the Enlightenment could have so thoroughly dismissed such questions that they could be felt as new when Darwin and Wallace revived them.

Most heroes descend from natural forces, sometimes from animals, just as evolutionary theory says we all do. There is an element of the totemic in all the ancient stories. Some epics go to some lengths to give us separate independent origins from those of other animals—the Biblical account of creation is one. But most see an unbroken genealogical line back from current humans to the natural world—and to the divine world too. Did we emerge from this world, or were we planted upon it? Even Genesis, in one of its versions of creation, has God create humans out of clay. The *Popol Vuh* seems to have it both ways: humans are a separate creation of the gods, they are both begotten and created by them. If there is an element of transcendence over nature in the Mayan view of the creation of humans, it is what one might call a natural transcendence, not a supernatural one. The gods themselves include the natural force of the hurricane and the natural process of childbirth, and the material humans are made of is corn. Humans can, like One Monkey and One Artisan, degenerate into animals, and heroes can temporarily become animals if they please, as the hero twins do when they become fish. The northern European epics often associated their heroes with totemic animals, as witness Beowulf's very name; Sigurd and Sinfljotli are werewolves. The West

African hero Sundiata is descended from both the lion and the buffalo. In the *Mahabharata* the relatedness of humans and animals—as of humans and gods—is taken for granted, as one might expect within a reincarnational worldview.

Though Genesis and Exodus deny our descent from other animals, they are perhaps the most thoroughgoing epic attempts to trace the genealogical lineage of their readers directly all the way back to the beginning. They explain why, in the branching process of reproductive descent, some nations have the favor of God and some do not, some possess the conscience that makes them prosper and others must be destroyed. In the earlier parts of the Bible, the old Hebrew genealogies and their explanations are a perfect example of Herbert Spencer's survival-of-the-fittest social Darwinism.[13] Later, with the moral calculus of the prophets, who seem to have intuitively "gamed" the superiority of group selection and the need for altruism and cooperation within the group, evolution begins to favor justice over canny self-interest, and then mercy over justice. In the second Isaiah especially (Isaiah, chapters 40-55), the glimmerings of a multinational altruism begin to emerge. Jahweh is, in this sense, evolution itself: for even when his commandments inflect toward love of neighbor, his promise and covenant is that his chosen shall have descendants as numberless as the sand grains upon the shore.

Epics without some kind of genealogical record are quite rare, though the genealogies get sketchier in later times. As the city gives way to the nation-state and the world market order, ethnically open trading nations like renaissance Italy and England, chimeric new nations like the United States, or colonial empires like nineteenth-century Britain tend to lose the coherence of perceived kinship. Too many families contest the limelight; mixed race marriage becomes normal; so epic must find other means to establish the solidarity of the multiethnic community it addresses. It can, as in Dante's poem, assert the common destiny of us all in the last judgment, or as in Milton's, assert our common origin in the creation of the world. It can create an international mini-nation, as in *Moby Dick*, or appeal to our common experience of childhood, as in *The Prelude*, where, as Wordsworth says, "The child is father to the man." Science fiction epic derives our solidarity from our common future. But even with such examples it is hard to make sense of an epic without a good grasp of the genealogical skeleton of the city it defines. In my own epics, family trees are very important, making possible such ironic dialectical relationships as are implied by

225

the schisms of the Quincy and van Riebeck families, and the strange birth of the Sibyl after having been transferred from the womb of Irene the warrior to that of Beatrice the gardener.

Genealogies of the gods serve the city in a somewhat different role. Though they are often part of the ur-genealogy of the hero and his people, they are also a way of establishing the city's fundamental metaphysics and therefore the spirit of its laws. God-genealogies work by a sort of generative logic, in which fatherhood and motherhood indicate presupposition, begetting indicates inference, marriage or mating indicate the relationship between major premise and minor premise in a syllogism, and descent in general stands for the noncommutative direction of the primal logic. In Hesiod, for instance, the logical structure of the basic Greek concepts is explicitly spelled out, to be both used and argued with in later ages by the Greek philosophers. The fact that Chaos, the primal deity, gives birth to the parents of the Fates shows that the Greeks felt necessity to be secondary to the self-organization of a chaotic realm, that deterministic order is emergent, not primary. In Homer, the allegory is darker but still there: the quarrels of the gods over the fate of Troy and the return of Odysseus spell out, for instance, the necessary subordination of Aphrodite (sexual love) to her stepmother Hera (marriage), and the need to outfox or appease Poseidon (who wrecks ships but also constitutes the communicative medium of Greek civilization) with help from his niece Athena (wisdom).

The same kind of calculus can be seen in the family tree of the gods of Uruk, with Anu, Enlil, Nanna, Shamash, Ishtar, Ea, and Ereshkigal representing primal concepts of the Mesopotamian world that Gilgamesh must understand and negotiate with. Likewise the family tree of the Mayan Gods—Tzacol, B'itol, Xpiyacoc, Xmucane, Hurricane, Seven Macaw, the lords of Xibalba and the others—constitute a basic abstract vocabulary for the city of the Quiché. One of the functions of epic itself may have been to formalize for the city the various local tribal gods into a coherent philosophical structure, and connect it with the kinship line of the city's people, thus making the city's demes into a map of the city's basic ideas. Even when monotheism has largely pruned the divine family tree, epic poets find ways to use the old "genealogic." Milton, for instance, clearly depicts the quarrel in heaven in terms of a family rift, and in his account of the births of Messiah, Eve, Satan, Sin, and Death the old implications of logical priority and inference are in play.

Establishing a Civic Language

We have already seen how the human instinct of reciprocity becomes sacrifice in our relationship with the gods. We have seen how the implied equivalence between the goods of existence and the sacrificial gift could mark the beginning of a process of symbolization. And we have looked at the phenomenon of commutation, how the imputed mercy of the gods could, by substituting a lesser debt for a greater, lead to the formation of increasingly abstract and conventional meanings. We have also noted that whereas ordinary language must obey the rules of language, the half-mute mythic utterances by which meanings are defined in the first place must, almost by necessity, be bizarre and counterintuitive, if they are to serve as markers of the radical emergence of language out of physical reality.

When in epic the city is founded, whether literally or allegorically, the originary myths and sacrifices belonging to the tribes or clans must now be tamed to the use of a super-tribal *polis*, and it is out of this taming that the city's language is created. The taming can take place in various ways. One tribe, such as the Mayan Quiché, can claim a special favor with the gods, a special insight into the divine that gives it dominance. Other tribes must accept the role of sacrificial victims. The Quiché tribe is no longer content with having one cult out of many, but raises its cult to a level of universality and abstraction, powered by a history of sacrificial commutation, that subsumes and governs any purely local myth. It can do this by means of a powerful story, whose logic, more gripping and suspenseful because less bizarre and arbitrary than the old myths, carries a compulsive conviction. This is the task of epic especially. Epic uses meanings created by myth and sacrifice to rise above the very cults that created the myth and sacrifice.

Obviously the most thoroughgoing versions of the epic that dominates all other tribal cults are the biblical epics. In the Tower of Babel story there is an explicit parable of God's rejection of another city's hegemonic attempt to create a super-language. The great tower is thrown down, the people's language separates into mutually incomprehensible dialects or jargons, its sacrificial tradition forgotten. The story serves both as a triumphal rejection of any other attempt at radical unity, and as a warning to Israel that it must not forget its own blood debt to Jahweh. Likewise, the Egyptian attempt at linguistic and cultic hegemony is defeated in the Book of Exodus.

Another way that the city can tame the idiosyncratic meanings first generated by myth and sacrifice is to include, rather than dominate, the various cults around it. Here cult meanings are tamed not by being transcended but by being contextualized as a genuine magic among other genuine magics. The *Mahabharata* depicts many different societies with their own religious stories, miracles, and rites, and weaves them all together. The pattern that results accepts multiplicity as a defining feature of divinity rather than denying multiplicity in pursuit of radical unity. When Arjuna sees Krishna in his divine form, the terrifying change is not from multiplicity to unity but from relative unity to bewildering multiplicity. Instead of his "normal" four arms and one mouth, Krishna now, as Vishnu, has a thousand, a million arms and mouths. Civilizational language-creation now becomes a matter of threading together all the varieties of culture and story into a coherent narrative.

Much the same could be said of Wu Cheng-en's *Journey to the West*, which explicitly embraces three religions and accepts revelation from an alien culture, India, without embarrassment. Here again, like the *Mahabharata*, a vast rambling plot is held together by a single quest: the regaining of the kingdom, the acquisition of the sacred texts. Epics of this kind tend to have a variety of tones and moods, often dominated by a kind of playfulness or irony. *Moby Dick* is of the same mould, inclusive, rambling, sustained by a single quest.

There are also epics that combine the exclusive and inclusive strategies. *The Aeneid* and *Paradise Lost* are examples. In Virgil's poem, Rome will dominate legally but concede many kinds of cultural superiority to other cultures. The language of the poem, with its copious and varied vocabulary and free borrowings from the many peoples of the Mediterranean, especially Greece and the Italic tribes—yet held together by the strong and flexible rule of the meter—reflects Rome's ambition to be the city of humanity. Milton, perhaps the most internationally learned person of his time, includes perhaps a score of languages in his poem, if we count the place-names and personal names. The poem is culturally open, but theologically closed. Milton borrows its grammar from Rome, as Virgil borrows his meter from Greece.

Yet another way mythic language is tamed and forged into the civilized instrument of the city is in the refining fire of tragedy. Here the great examples are *The Iliad* and the *Heike*. In *The Iliad*, the great rituals of piety—from which come the basic concepts of ethics and value—are violated again and again: the abduction of Helen and the confiscation of Briseis, the theft of the Palladium, the wounding of a goddess by a mortal, the barbaric dragging of Hector's corpse around the walls of Troy. It is in their violation, and in the terrible consequences—the deaths of many heroes, the eventual death of the city—that the fundamental ritual sources of meaning are analyzed and reasserted. The funeral of Hector, which ends the poem, constitutes that reassertion; but it cannot stave off the catastrophe in the immediate context of the Trojan War. Whether it will be effective for Greek civilization itself Homer leaves up to the Greeks themselves. But in any case the tropes that are required to describe the violation of the old codes then become the enduring vocabulary of Greek moral philosophy, to be refined by dramatists and philosophers in succeeding generations.

The *Heike*, with its tragic and horrific climax in the extermination of the Taira clan followed by the gentle and meditative conclusion tracing the last days of the princess Kenreimon-in, follows much the same path. Desecration follows desecration, sacrelige follows sacrelige; the ritually purified bureaucracy of the capital is perverted to private ends and then yielded up to destruction as *realpolitik* dominates all. But in the very process of their destruction, the old unifying sources of value and meaning are enshrined in the Japanese heart with an unbearable pathos and nostalgia. The high points of that process of enshrinement are of course epitomized in the poems extemporized by the central figures in their extremity: poems that fix in place forever in the Japanese language the basic connections between natural objects, emotional feeling, and moral and philosophical principle. The language of Nippon is thus built up and deepened by its tragic epic.

Orientation in Space and Time

But it is not only in the area of abstract concepts and moral vocabulary that epics build the city's language. One of the great functions of epic is to name places both within and outside the city, and thus map the city and set it in a geographical context that is also a linguistic and symbolic one. We have already looked briefly at place-names in the context of the Australian song-lines, and mentioned Mount Moriah, Misenum, and Thorgeir's Ford as examples of the way that a story can memorialize a place by making it operational in human action and fixing it in relation to other places.

To these we could add hundreds of other examples—consider the way in which Virgil's Rome is defined in relation to Troy and Carthage, Heorot is placed between the seacoast and the wasteland of Grendel, the Allthing with its booths and courts defines Icelandic law and politics, or Kyoto is centered among its satrapies and dependencies in the *Heike*. The section of the *Popol Vuh* dealing with the history of the Quiché is virtually a map of the Mayan world. Milton's world is so elaborately named that it governed Coleridge's imagination two hundred years later in "Kubla Khan." *The Odyssey* sets the actual Ithaca in the center of a series of concentric circles of places—the historical Argos, Pylos, Troy, Ismaros, Egypt, and so on, the semilegendary Phaeacea, the legendary lands of the Lotus Eaters, the Cyclopes, and the Laestrygonians, the divine worlds of Helios' island, Aeaea, and Ogygia, and at the uttermost periphery, the Land of Shades. The city of Uzgen in Kyrgyzstan is still renowned as the place where the epic hero Manas is buried. Karakorum gets its ideological identity from *The Secret History of the Mongols*. Perhaps the most elaborate and unforgettable map of all is Dante's in the *Divine Comedy*, which is not just a world geography but also a city map, or rather a compendium of three city maps.

The Israel of the Pentateuch is a diagram of the adventures of the Patriarchs, elaborated further in the exact specification of the Temple and its precinct, and developed on the grand scale in the later historical epic of the conquest of Palestine. Of special interest in the Biblical epics is the way in which named boundary markers are established, separating the Promised Land from all others, defining the exact limits and legal provenance of God's real-estate grant in the Covenant. This feature, rarer in other epics, is the product of a combination of characteristics in ancient Hebrew culture: its strong sense of justice and legality, predating the creation of its city; its exceptionalism and sense of election; and the peculiar geography of the Middle East, settled—and over-settled, perhaps—very early in human history, with very choice fertile areas alternating with desert, and much competition for arable land, wells, and pasture. Long disputes over borders are not new in the region.

Though the biblical sense of legal land tenure is an outlier in the epic traditions of humankind, it is not unique. It can certainly be found in the *Heike*, in the *Popol Vuh, Sundiata, The Three Kingdoms, King Dongmyeong of Goguryeo*, and *Njal*, among others. Shakespeare gently satirizes this feature of the epic in the episode where Henry V unearths a legal justification for his invasion of France. Palestine, Japan, Central America, the fertile southern margin of the Sahara, China, Korea, Iceland, and Britain are all parts of the world where scarce real estate is contested, whether because of long and early settlement, scarce agricultural land, or the geographical limits of islands, isthmuses, or peninsulas.

Epics do not only specify the location of their city, its spatial relationship to its surroundings, and the boundaries of its writ. They also set up an internal chart or charter of their city, which results in the establishment of architectural terms defined by their function and demonstrated by their role in the story. We have already looked at the function and meaning of gates and walls; to these we must add the temple, the palace, the hall, the audience chamber, the citadel, the marketplace, the dungeon, and so on. Imperial Kyoto in the *Heike* is itself a chart of the imperial bureaucracy, with certain parts forbidden to lower orders, the very streets organized as an institutional grid. We get glimpses of the physical arrangement of the epic city in such social roles as the temple prostitute in *Gilgamesh*, the Keeper of the Mat in the *Popol Vuh*, the Left Gate Guards Novice in the *Heike*, and the Griot in *Sundiata*.

What epics do, then, when they come to the building of the city, is create what Frances Yates calls a "memory theater." A memory theater is a mnemonic system for mapping our narrative memory talent onto our spatial memory talent, and using the mutually correcting result as a grid to remember the logical relations of an argument and the correct rhetorical sequence by which that argument can be used to convince. The best place-name evokes the story of its role in an epic and the moral and political meaning of that story.

Besides providing landmarks, storied names, a basic architectural vocabulary, and a spatial mnemonic system, city founders and city healers must offer a fundamental set of directions to orient the city-dweller with respect to the cosmos. One set of directions is already given at once to all human beings by the condition of being a land-dwelling animal on the flat surface of a world between earth and air, and being subject to gravitation: up and down. Upon this basic distinction a vast superstructure of rational, moral, and metaphysical meaning can be reliably erected, and epic, with its architectonic plotting and strong moral and spiritual impetus, always does so. *Per ardua ad astra*. An epic is a city of words, with foundations, rooms, sanctuaries, and towers.

It is on the two-dimensional plane, the face of the earth, that the citizen needs cosmological directions not given immediately to experience. Of course terrain can help: a city on a coast is given a binary orientation, *mauka* (mountainward) and *makai* (seaward), as the Hawaiians say. A river can usefully bound or divide a city. These directions in turn lend themselves to the construction of meaning—the fertile relation of liquid process and solid being, for instance. Feng shui, the Chinese believe, is necessary to mental and physical health; otherwise the psyche and cosmos are cut off from each other, and the basic institutions—family, justice—have no context and guide. So the founders' choice of site is of first importance; and a city that has lost the meaning of its site requires either an epic story or a great architect, or both, to restore it.

In its destruction Troy reveals the physical principles, the feng shui, of the Greek city: overlooked by Mount Ida, it lies at the meeting-point of the Dardanelles, the Troad, the Simois, and the Scamander. Likewise, imperial Kyoto lies at the meeting of the Katsura and the Oi Rivers, between Lake Ogura-no-Ike and Mount Hiei (with its great monastery of Enriyakuji where all the trouble began). Rome, with its Tiber, its relation to Ostia and the sea, and its seven hills is again iconic in its feng shui. Even a moving city—the *Pequod*—with its fore-and-aft class distinctions, its three masts, and its elaborately described layout, has its own system of psyche-cosmos orientation.

Note that the orientation system is always basically binary. Up and down, *mauka* and *makai*, *rive gauche* and *rive droite*, split up the world in multiples of two, not three or five. Rome's seven hills make sense only in terms of the binary distinction given by the Tiber. Twoness, though, can give us only linear directions: twoness must be multiplied by itself to give us the planar world we inhabit. So in the absence of other physical constraints the four cardinal points of the compass constitute the usual guide to a city's orientation. The American grid system is not new: it recapitulates the layout of Kyoto and the Forbidden City. Two implications immediately follow from the fundamental orthogonality of the city: fourness and the axial center.

Fourness, as Emily Lyle and the scholars of the Traditional Cosmology field[14] have shown, is a central principle in almost all social classification systems. When fully developed, as in the *Mahabharata*, it becomes the four castes, the Brahmins, Kshatriyas, Vaisyas, and Sudras. The clearest example of the caste system is an old story told by low-caste sudras to the researcher Clyde B. Stuntz in the 1920s.

There was once a great and powerful man who ruled over all the land. He had four sons, all of whom were intelligent and gifted. When the man died he left his undivided property to all four sons. For a time they lived contentedly together, sharing the work and the wealth.

Then the second son went off, with other warriors, to seek adventure and further riches. He asked his youngest brother to take care of his share of responsibilities for the property while he was gone and to see to whatever his family needed done, promising to re-assume these burdens when he returned. The youngest brother generously agreed.

After a time the oldest brother decided to go to a hermitage and seek spiritual fulfillment. He, too, asked his youngest brother to take over his chores and family cares. The third brother was very clever in business and became so pre-occupied in trading ventures that he also left to his younger brother the everyday burdens of property and family.

So the youngest brother rendered service to the older three for some years. At last the older three brothers returned, each success-ful in his own endeavors. And they no longer wished to reassume the burdens which their youngest brother had carried for them in their absence. They preferred to continue to pursue their own interests unhampered. And so, instead of showing their youngest brother gratitude and honor for all he had done for them, the older three banded together and burdened him permanently with all those tasks that were distasteful to them, requiring him to be their servant. From then on, all the descendants of the youngest brother were named Sudras and were required to be the servants of the descendants of the three older brothers.[15]

Despite the obvious and probably justified resentment implied by this mythic version of the origins of caste, the story conveys a certain truth about the divisions of society. Even today we can still identify four basic ethical systems among our fellow-citizens: the ethos of priests, teachers, lawyers, literati; the ethos of warriors, rulers, commanders, organizers; the ethos of traders, merchants, artisans, industrialists; and the ethos of farmers, ranchers, gardeners, and all practitioners of husbandry. Cities were once—and still are in many parts of the world—literally divided into "quarters," with guild associations and streets devoted to some particular craft or profession. The indiscriminate modern city may be disorienting by comparison (though supermar-kets are beginning to take on a recognizable "guild" shape, driven by market necessity). The four castes, as the major divisions of the city, can plainly be found in many epics: the *Shahnameh*, *The Cattle Raid of Cooley*, the *Mahabharata*, *The Odyssey*, and the *Henriad* stand out particularly. Epic is mainly concerned with the exploits of Kshatriyas and, secondarily, Brahmins; but the other castes usually appear, fully characterized as such, among the minor characters. Tripitaka, Monkey, Pigsy, and Sandy in *The Journey to the West* are themselves, I believe, representative of the castes, respectively: the priest, warrior, artisan, and farmer.

Of course the four cardinal points of the compass are our immediate connection with the cosmos as a whole. North, south, east, and west are a value-system in themselves; in the Northern Hemisphere they stand for temperature differences (boreal cold and austral heat), beginnings and endings (eastern dawn and western dusk), and all the derivative moods of spring, summer, autumn, and winter. We understand the movements of the stars and planets only in terms of the four cardinal points, and we navigate by the North Star and the plane of the ecliptic, anchored upon the pole.

Thus the building of a city involves not only spatial orientation with natural geography and the constants of the heavens, but also temporal orientation, i.e., the calendar. North, south, east, and west both imply and presuppose morning, noon, and evening, the lunar month, the solar year, the houses of the zodiac, the planetary orbits. Not all epics pay as much close attention to the celestial calendar as do the *Divine Comedy*, the *Popol Vuh*, *Paradise Lost*, the *Shahnameh*, *The Gardens of Flora Baum*, and the *Heike*. But the central epic feature of genealogy itself, with its implied measurement of time by the very variable human lifecycle, needs to be calibrated and synchronized by regular units of cosmological time. Telemachus needs the sixteen years of Odysseus' absence to grow up and be ready to assist his father. The daily weaving and unweaving of Laertes' shroud symbolizes the monthly flow of Penelope's unviolated chastity, as well as the weary yearly waiting for her husband's return to take up the role of his father's successor and his son's father. Any epic composer—I know this by experience!—must make time-charts to make sure that a character does not have a twelve-year-old grandmother, or that a baby conceived in spring does not get born in summer.

Hunter-gatherers and nomadic pastoralists have created sophisticated calendrical tricks as specific applications for purposes of predicting the abundance and locality of game, the maturing of fruits and tubers, and the availability of forage. But cities need much more universal general-purpose calendars to coordinate their multifarious activities of manufacture, trade, and hydraulic control. As we have seen in many other areas—the transformation of myth into epic, the consolidation of local vocabularies into a civic language, the welding of tribes into nations—epic depicts the process by which the various idiosyncratic cycles of natural, biological, and local human time are fitted together into a system that also expresses civil ideals and national history. It is in the Book of Exodus that the first main features of the Jewish lunar calendar are sketched out,[16] to be elaborated in Judges, Kings, and Chronicles as the city of Jerusalem takes on its full identity and the Israelites change from pastoralists into city-dwellers. Hastinapura, Ctesiphon, Rome, Jerusalem are in a sense calendars and time-charts as well as landmarks.

Orthogonality, "fourness," implies an axial center where the two sets of opposite directions cross and mark out the quarters of the city. The earliest geometry appears to have been for real-estate property and architectural purposes. It was essential to ascertain the right angle, 90°, probably by using "compass strokes" marked by stick tied to a string centered upon first one and then the other end of a line, joining the two points where the two sets of strokes intersect, so bisecting the original line at right angles—or by the proto-pythagorean trick of constructing a triangle with sides of three, four, and five units. The city starts at a crossroads where trade is most convenient: it is a center and has a center. As it takes on more and more ideological and cosmological significance, it acquires a zero-mile-marker or omphalos, a navel marking its origin and from which all distances inside and outside of the realm are measured. The city center is also the zero-point of the number system; in normal times the still axis of all the movement around it, the still point of the turning wheel. It is also, so to speak, the present moment, the fertile absence in which action can happen, neither already occupied by event as in the past, nor impossible to occupy, like the future. It is in the palace or the temple or the citadel at the center that all events and actions are ratified into history. Normal times are when the center is not moved. If outward events and actions do not move that center, epic-scale change cannot happen.

The center is, moreover, where the other set of directions originates—the one given to us immediately and intuitively, where we are never at a loss to decide which way is which—up and down. In the ancient shamanic practices—that city epic rationalizes and generalizes—the shaman's tent or hut establishes (more or less temporarily) the four cardinal points of the compass; Navajo sand-paintings with their axial world-division and implied totemic and social classification system beautifully present this mode of orientation. But the shaman traffics not only with the plane of the earth's source but with what is above and below it. A third axis ascends and descends from the central point—it is the central tent-pole, the central peak of the roof, open to let out the smoke of the fire and let in the influences of the stars and the gods. When the shaman, with the aid of his or her animal familiar, takes flight or descends into the earth to speak with the spirits and the ancestors, it is along that third axis. It is the world-tree Yggdrasil, Asvattam the great banyan tree of Chapter 15 of the *Bhagavadgita*, the Ceiba tree of the *Popol Vuh* that joins the thirteen realms of heaven with the nine underworld realms of Xibalba.

Transformed into city terms, that axial relation with the upper and lower worlds, with Asgard and Niflheim, becomes expressed in the central altar or dais, or magnified into the pyramid. It is the holy grail at the center of the castle of Munsalvaesch, the sword in the oak Barnstokk, the Holy of Holies, the chamber of the Cumaean Sibyl where three caves meet. It is the intersection, not so much as Eliot says, of the timeless with time, but of time, and all of time's creative potential, with space, or perhaps of sacred time with secular space-time. Since it is the passage both to the upper worlds of the divine and the lower worlds of the infernal, it is the place of moral judgment, and thus the place where human responsibility confirms human freedom.

The Code of Laws

All epics are concerned in one way or another with the creation, violation, reinstatement, or change of the laws. The tragic epics, especially the *Heike*, *The Iliad*, and *The Song of the Nibelungs*, depict the consequences of the breakdown of law. In the *Heike*, it begins with an apparently minor infraction, the singing by disgruntled imperial courtiers of satirical versions of the ceremonial songs at the Gosechi festival when newcomers deemed unworthy performed their expected dances. A tiny point of punctilio, perhaps, but the poet comments: "Who could tell what might happen in these latter days of the law?" One victim of this prank, Tadamori, has brought what appears to be a dagger to the party, to guard himself from jealous court rivals, but weapons are forbidden in the palace. The dagger is actually a wooden dagger, wrapped in foil, so he has not technically violated the law. But Tadamori is the father of Kiyomori, who will ruthlessly rise to such a position of power that he will have the hubris to attempt to kidnap the imperial house that had insulted his father. He does so by means of a series of strategic marriages, thus precipitating the catastrophe.

In *The Iliad*, the violations of law also begin on a fairly small scale, with the dispute between Agamemnon and Achilles over the spoils of battle, namely, the princess Briseis. Of course, that dispute echoes the grand violation, the abduction of Helen, that began the war in the first place. But in the poem, Agamemnon's relatively minor injustice, the taking by the commander of the rewards of victory from the warrior who achieved it, is surely very common in the annals of war, and if Achilles had been anyone but Achilles he would have put up with it. This breaking of the law cascades into a series of greater and greater violations (including offences directly against the gods), destroys a city, and causes appalling slaughter and waste.

In the *Song of the Nibelungs*, the tragic process is set in motion by another violation of law: Gunther gets the credit for the victory over Brünhild, and wins her as his bride, when it is actually Siegfried's strength that has defeated her under cover of his cloak of invisibility. Step by step the breach in justice widens, creating further cracks and fissures, until kin murders kin and friend murders friend in the final holocaust. In all three of these tragic epics, law is asserted by the consequences of its breaking: the story implicitly turns over to the audience the task of mending the law; there is a need for a re-founding, a re-enactment of the original sacrifices that created the law in the beginning.

Other epics, like *The Cattle Raid of Cooley* and *Martín Fierro*, also define the law in terms of its destruction. But most are more concerned with the establishment of law than with its violation and reinstatement. Perhaps the most explicit and exhaustive example is the Book of Exodus, where the events and actions of the Passover, the deliverance from Egypt, and the ascent of Mount Sinai are directly translated into the system of Jewish governance, ritual protocol, and jurisprudence, culminating in the gift of the tablets of the commandments. But the spelling out of the laws of Karma and Dharma in the *Mahabharata*, the justification of divine law in *Paradise Lost*, the specification of the Quiché bureaucratic system in the *Popol Vuh*, and the enactment of the new legal basis of the English monarchy in the *Henriad* are scarcely less obvious. Though *The Aeneid* does not go into the specifics of the *lex Romanum*, it is just as vehement in its praise of the laws of Rome.

Njal's Saga ends with the establishment of the Fifth Court of Iceland. *Parzifal* ends with the founding of the Templars, the spiritual version of Arthur's great institution, the Round Table, itself a founding legal concept. *Mwindo* ends with a new rule of harmony for the Nyanga people. In the *Silappathikaram*, the heroine Kannagi's final act was to establish a new law of cooperation among the Muthuvans. Epic does not usually apply and vindicate the existing law, like a detective story: it marks and celebrates the origin of law, or the significant emergence of new law, or at least a transformation, reform, or new interpretation of the old law.

Notes

1. E.g., Bartolomeo del Bene's *Civitas Veri Sive Morum* (1609), http://kostisvelonis.blogspot.com/2010/07/civitas-veri.html.
2. Konrad Lorenz, *On Aggression* (New York: Bantam, 1967), ch. 11.
3. I am deeply indebted in this discussion of sacrifice to René Girard's *Violence and the Sacred*, translated by Patrick Gregory (Baltimore, MD: Johns Hopkins University Press, 1977).
4. A. H. Maslow, "A Theory of Human Motivation," *Psychological Review* 50, no. 4 (1943): 370–96.
5. E.g., Ludwig Wittgenstein, *Tractatus Logico-Philosophicus*, trans. C. K. Ogden (New York: Cosimo Classics, 2007); Willard V. O. Quine, *Word and Object* (Cambridge, MA: MIT Press, 1960).
6. Jacques Derrida, *Writing and Difference*, trans. A. Bass (London and New York: Routledge, 1978).
7. Jorge Luis Borges, *Ficciones* (New York: Grove Press, 1994).
8. See Kathryn Coe, "Art: The Replicable Unit," in *Biopoetics: Evolutionary Explorations in the Arts*, eds.Brett Cooke and Frederick Turner (Lexington, KY: ICUS Books, 1999), 263.
9. Ellen Dissanayake, *What Is Art For?* (Seattle, WA: University of Washington Press, 1990). See note 8. Irenaeus Eibl-Eibesfeldt, *Human Ethology* (New Brunswick, NJ: Aldine Transaction, 2007).
10. Mary Douglas, *Leviticus as Literature* (Oxford: Oxford University Press, 2001).
11. 1 *Henry IV*, II.iv.452, 473; 2 *Henry IV*, II.iv.231, III. ii.330; 1 *Henry IV*, II.ii.108.
12. L. L. Cavalli-Sforza, Paolo Menozzi, and Alberto Piazza, *The History and Geography of Human Genes* (Princeton, NJ: Princeton University Press, 1994).
13. Herbert Spencer, *Spencer: Political Writings* (New York: Cambridge University Press, 1993).
14. See Emily Lyle, *Sacred Architecture: In the Traditions of India, China, Judaism and Islam* (Edinburgh: Edinburgh University Press, 1992). Also *Cosmos: The Journal of the Traditional Cosmology* Society (published by Edinburgh University Press). Lyle and others in the field generally follow Dumézil in identifying a *triad* of castes as being important in the imagery and stories of traditional societies; but the triad implies a fourth group—all others

within the society, those who "don't count" in the mythical apportionment of divine responsibility, the unimportant ones, the helots, sudras, villeins, and serfs.

15.   Hyla S. Converse, and Arvind Sharma, "An Ancient Sudra Account of the Origin of Castes," *The Journal of the American Oriental Society* 114 (1994).

16.   Exodus 12:1, 34:22.

9

The History of the People

From Myth to History

One of the chief differences between epic and myth (though epic certainly contains, enshrines, and celebrates a plurality of myths) is that epic plays out the myths in historical action, and extends the ritual of which myth is the script into real military, legal, political, economic, and social events. The explicitly fictional merges into the putatively factual. Epic also organizes and adjusts the often contradictory myths of the various clans and tribes it unites or subsumes, so that they are in relative harmony or at least creative tension with respect to each other. Epic does not just *contain* the transition from myth/ritual into philosophy/action; it *is* the transition, so to speak. It performs the act of incarnation by which primal symbolic equations, at first not much more than collective dreams, are embodied in action and institutions, in the logic of a plotline, in the individuality and moral character of epic's dramatis personae. It collates, implicitly criticizes, and rationalizes its many inherited mythic versions of how we became human.

Thus all epics have a historical dimension, some more than others; and one of the persistent puzzles for the epic composer is how to combine the individual and temporally brief exploits of the epic hero with the collective and centuries-long story of a nation's emergence and destiny. Various strategies suggest themselves. One, which we have already considered in *The Aeneid, Orlando Furioso*, and *Paradise Lost*, is the epic prophecy, in which the hero gets a quick overview of the future history of his people. Another is to concentrate into the lifetime, character and actions of the hero the defining features of the nation, or to make the hero's adventures allegorically or symbolically foreshadow the future vicissitudes of his society. Achilles can be usefully read as such a hero; Aeneas' encounter with Dido foreshadows Rome's with Carthage and Octavius' with Cleopatra. Roland epitomizes France; the Cid defines the Spanish character;

241

Cuchulainn is the quintessential Irishman; Martín is the archetypal gaucho; Ahab is the dark side of Uncle Sam and Abe Lincoln. Moses' struggle to liberate the Hebrews from Egypt foreshadows the Babylonian captivity and the return to Jerusalem. The exploits of Hunahpu and Xbalanque are directly mapped onto the history of the Quiché.

Another method is for the epic storyteller to take time off from the account of the hero, come to the edge of the stage like the Chorus in *Henry V*, and simply tell us the history, as the griot does in *Sundiata* and as Camoens does in the *Lusiads*. Or, of course, the epic composer can settle for a succession of heroes or central figures, unified by a central theme: sin and forgiveness in Genesis, the loss and recovery of the royal *farr* or mana in the *Shahnameh*, overreaching heroic and dynastic ambition in the *Heike*, and national division and reunification in the epic of the *Three Kingdoms*.

In any case, epic's task is partly to trace the articulation of the originary myths of the clan or band into the wider and wider realms of the tribe, the multi-tribal city, the multi-city nation or empire, even into a world where the world of the national epic encounters other epic worlds, and foreign policy and global concerns come into play. Certainly epics are founded on the fierce passions of solidarity, group loyalty and rooting for one's own side, passions shared by both the epic subjects and the epic audience, ancient or modern. Without that in-group loyalty, group selection could not have worked, and the higher virtues of altruism and self-sacrifice could never have been selected for. But the very presence of potential nonzero-sum games such as trading and the exchange of knowledge and technology opened up the way to the formation of larger and larger cooperating groups, even in the teeth of our inherited clannishness and xenophobia. A large part of the drama of epic is this very struggle.

At the end of *The Iliad*, in the meeting between Priam and Achilles, an ethic that transcends the differences between cities and nations can be glimpsed. The catatrophic end of the *Song of the Nibelungs* suggests a perspective that goes beyond the tribal loyalty of the Nibelungs, the patriotism of the Burgundians and the Huns. *Parsifal* ends with a suggestion of a Templar secret society transcending nationality itself. The Jewish Bible evolves from being the story of Israel's revelation *against* all other nations to being a story of Israel's revelation being *for* all other nations—where someone like Cyrus can sometimes better exemplify the ethic of that revelation than can the chosen ones themselves. Shakespeare's *Henriad* does not end with victory in battle but with a bilingual wooing and marriage.

So epic's story of the evolution of humankind cannot be confined to the emergence and definition of the city or nation. Epic's view of history is inexorably one in which the process of sacrificial commutation finally generates abstractions so universal that they are sharable across epistemes and hermeneutic systems, no longer confined to the idiosyncrasies of their early mythic and ritual context. Epic's work is to make those abstractions so fully embodied in passionate action and humanly shared physical detail that they perform not just the logical function of unification but the moral function of empathy. Epic is a discovery of higher universals that command our moral reason, but it is also a rediscovery of the shared passions, instincts and drives that began the process of discovery itself.

War

We have already looked briefly at the role of war in epic in the context of the hero's great battle. The emergence of the city and of recorded history itself can scarcely be imagined without the phenomenon of war. As we have seen, epic's view of history necessarily involves the establishment of super-tribal world, as the tribal world involves a transcendence of the clan and family. In this process, some of the most violent passions that humans are capable of are inevitably aroused. Antigone will bury her brother, despite the civic laws of Thebes, even at the cost of chaos, catastrophe, and death.

We evolved as viviparous nurturers of our young and our kin. The emotions of solidarity and altruism we required for this life-habit were further amplified by our specialization for wider cooperation and reciprocity. Artificial kingroups are created by shared ordeals, food rules, stories, scars, and so on, and by the emergence of sophisticated signaling systems and languages, "theory of mind," "mirror-neurons," deceit detectors, vengeful sentiments against free-riders and defectors, and selfless devotion to comrades. Trust, love, and comradeship are now known to be associated with high levels of oxytocin in the blood. But the "dark side" of oxytocin is that it also increases the tendency to punish perceived betrayers or enemies of the group—and even punish perceived non-punishers of defectors. The paradox is this: the smaller the group, the more intense the attachments and the enmities, but the larger the group, the more chance that the interests of the individual—survival, reproduction, comfort, fulfillment—may be served by collective cooperation.

When those innate human capacities and motivations, so well adapted to a band of about 120 people (roughly the size of a military company) are challenged by the demands of a city or a nation, and when nations themselves, having achieved internal cohesion, find their interests at odds with each other, war is almost inevitable. There is perhaps no way of creating those larger organizations of humans that make possible the huge benefits and freedoms of civilization, without running the risk and usually the actuality of war. The only alternative to war is trade, and trade is a delicate and complex plant that is very vulnerable in its infancy.

This analysis provides us with a classification of the kinds of wars to be found in epics. The scale runs from those human groups that are bound most strongly, the family and clan, through those that, not much weaker, rely on shared tribal and ethnic bonds and those that, weaker, unite the citizens of a *polis*, to those, weaker yet, of the artificial tribe of nationhood and those, weaker still (and tending toward personal economic interest) that tie together an empire. At the micro end of the scale lies the kind of family or clan feud so meticulously examined in the Icelandic sagas. Under certain feudal circumstances such feuds can amplify themselves up to the point where they can determine the fates of nations, as we see in all their appalling glory in the *Heike*. The collective interest can sometimes be no match for the absolute personal attachments and shared enmities of kin.

On a larger scale we find intertribal wars, as in *The Saga of the Volsungs*, *The Secret History of the Mongols*, and the *Popol Vuh*. When a tribe that is part of an emergent nation, or feels itself about to become such a part, resists its absorption into the whole, another sort of war results, pitting fierce ethnic loyalties against the might of the imperial or colonial regime. This type of war dominates the Book of Exodus and *The Three Kingdoms* and is a vital factor in *The Aeneid* and the *Shahnameh*. Not easy to distinguish from such wars are those that pit a nation against a hegemonic empire, as in *The Peril of Sziget*, *David of Sassoun*, *The Kossovo Epic*, *King Gesar*, or my own *Genesis: An Epic Poem*. Whole confederations of nations, united by religion, inspired leadership, kinship, or ideology, confront each other in another kind of war in *The Iliad*, the *Ramayana*, *The Song of Roland*, *Jerusalem Liberated*, and my *The New World*. As we go up the scale we find more and more subplots involving the more personal and intimate loyalties of clan rivalry, ethnic loyalty, sexual contests, and kin-strife, as narrative leaven for the more abstract and impersonal strategies of large-scale war.

Two odd observations might be drawn from this list of conflict types in epic. One is that one never finds one city fighting it out against another, one-on-one, though in the historical record there have been many such conflicts, in Mesopotamia, Greece, Mesoamerica, and Renaissance Italy, for instance. Perhaps this sort of symmetrical warfare, in which ideally two irreconcilable ecumenes confront each other and there is no higher court of appeal, is a subject that defies the fundamental program of epic itself, which is always looking for the evolutionary finesse by which conflicts are transcended and made productive for the future. The idea of closed and incommensurable hermeneutic circles, of untranslatable regimes of power and knowledge, is attractive to poststructuralist foes of "progress" precisely because there can be no fertile and reconciling exit from such a struggle. A deconstructivist epic, if such could be written, might well take as its subject the mutual destruction of two cities locked in an unreconciled, implacable, and untranscended conflict. It would be the dark side, so to speak, of the postcolonialist claim that no culture can subsume another.

The other observation that we might draw from our war-list is the absence of straightforward commercial wars. Indeed it seems odd at first glance that trade, which in the historical record has been the only long-term alternative to war or piracy in the relations of human groups, is largely absent in the main plot-lines of epic. But this impression is only partially correct. True, in the grand actions of the heroes and heroines, tawdry considerations of profit, payment, and haggling do not apply. The dragon's gold is not earned or traded for by Beowulf, the Volsungs, or the Nibelungs, but stolen; when it is treated as money, as something to buy or sell with, it corrupts its possessors. The wild bulls of Cooley and Connacht are not bought or sold but won and lost by battle.

But epic is not uncognizant of what is being set aside in the heroic actions of the founders. Trade and markets and wages enter epic *sous rature*, as deconstructionists put it. In one of Odysseus' fictions about himself he is a trader: the fiction is designed to demote himself from epic status, a disguise (like his beggar outfit) to conceal his threat. The Pandava brothers enter the trading and employment world in a similar fashion, as a disguise in the land of Matsya (Arjuna even changes sex). In the *Shahnameh*, tradesmen and artisans such as the heroic smith Kaveh sometimes appear, as they do in the *Heike* (mostly in the form of their exquisitely crafted handiwork). Though the central story of *Silappathikaram* concerns a theft, or attributed theft, not a purchase, the heroine Kannagi is the wife of a merchant's son. In the Icelandic sagas, the heroes sometimes get rich not just by raiding—the preferred method—but also by trade. Though Ahab explicitly rejects the purely commercial and industrial purpose of the *Pequod*, Melville meticulously describes the mechanics and economics of the process itself.

How are we to account for this oddity in epic, if epic, as I have argued in this book, is about human emergence and progress, if progress is at least partly the formation of larger human communities, and trade is the way that such communities are bound together? Why is war, not trade, the dominant theme? To reply that the epic is the story of kshatriyas, samurais, knights (with some Brahmins, monks, and priests thrown in) is to beg the question.

I believe that epic is about founding. Gilgamesh and Enkidu go to the forest and fight Humbaba to steal timber for the city gates; the city gates are how the marketplace is regulated and protected. The wealth of Ferdowsi's Persia is of course the work of its merchants and artisans, but such people cannot exist without the coercive force to create, coordinate, and preserve the laws of the city. Paradoxically, the rules that govern the founding of markets are different from the rules that govern markets—just as the logic of the myths by which language is created and defined is different from the logic of how language is used.

Perhaps the best explanation of this paradox is in Shakespeare's *Henriad*, where the heroic prince uncharacteristically (for epic) descends into the world of the marketplace, explores the price of sack, capons, hobnails, and maidenheads, and shows how civil war damages the market. "You may buy land now as cheap as stinking mackerel," says Falstaff. The wars against the insurgent clans of the Percies and the Douglases are to make the world safe for honest markets, where the Chief Justice is not mocked for seeking the repayment of debts, where government service does not mean fraud and rent-seeking (of which Falstaff's recruiting scam is a classic example), and contracts are defended. The war with France, which is to create a fertile union of the two economies, is successful partly because the old rule of plunder is overturned, and Hal's old friend Bardolph is hanged for theft.

Prince Hal is not a buyer or seller in the literal sense—a prince is above such things. He is a thief, as are all warriors: but he steals from thieves, and returns the stolen goods to their owners. He "steals" the (stolen) crown from his unwilling father, since he cannot legitimately inherit it as the receiver of stolen goods. He "never promiseth but he means to pay." His role as king is to return the stolen sovereignty to the people of England, which he does symbolically with the glove-full of British gold crowns that he gives to Williams after the battle of Agincourt. Note that Williams is a Welshman, one of the tribal minorities united under the British crown; and the name itself refers to the playwright, a subject of the Queen who can ply his trade of theater in peace, defended by her arms. The play appeared just after Essex's unsuccessful rebellion against Elizabeth—his attempt to steal the crown—had been put down.

Epic heroes are magnanimous in both senses—great-souled and generous. They do not buy or sell. Instead, when they are not simply taking what they want, heroes give and receive *gifts*; they do so in every epic in this study. But heroic gift exchange is the precursor and reminder of the regime of reciprocity that the hero's military conquests initiate and enable. One might argue in a strict game-theory sense that *someone* has to start the reciprocal process of social cooperation that constitutes a market, and show by a gift, or an "ante," that he is a trustworthy player. The first player in a series of nonzero-sum "prisoner's dilemma" type games to start with an act of trust (and an implicit invitation to respond in kind) is a hero. The first "purchase" is not a purchase but a gift until someone freely reciprocates and pays for it.

Gift-giving does not expect a return (though it sometimes gets one, of a thousand times the value). But in epic the gift-giving and plunder-taking initiate a state of things in which contracts must be kept and return can be expected. War in epic would be theft, if there were a law to make it such; but it is a theft that establishes law, that retroactively legitimates itself by its fruits. Until that moment epic characters are in a "state of nature" with respect to one another—altruistic and coopera-tive in small groups, xenophobic and untrustworthy in large ones. Even if there is—as there is—a natural territorial law of property, the epic hero is permitted to flout it because he has, by his great free gifts to others, exempted himself from the charge of self-seeking, and because the city he founds will defend the property rights of its inhabitants and be the haven for a productive marketplace.

Singled Out by the God(s)

The epic people or nation is always the subject of special attention on the part of the gods, or God. Here we must clearly understand what is meant by terms like "god," "divine," and so on. In the twenty-first century, these terms are loaded with millennia of theology, poetic imagery, and symbolic narrative that have hardened into dogma, defensive philosophical definitions, and so on. The tendency is for the faithful to explain the world and its events by appeal to God, as if what God is, is already given in the word; and for unbelievers to reject the term altogether as an unnecessary hypothesis or a meaningless fiction. To understand the epic world, we must recover a state of mind in which the burden of proof truly lay upon any non-divine hypothesis to adequately characterize the world. What our ancestors saw, and what habituation and fatigue causes us to take for granted and to ignore, is the sheer miracle of the universe. Science is not at fault for this dulling of our sight; if anything, the scientist's wonder and insatiable curiosity is a recovery of that old sense of the marvelous.

The point is that the world, its history, and especially the emergence into consciousness of speaking human beings, are very wonderful. For the ancients "god" was a word for that marvelousness, that specialness, oddness, idiosyncrasy, individuality—the imperative demand of the world that its amazing gift be noticed and acknowledged. The myths, stories, rituals, sacrifices, philosophical and scientific speculations, and moral codes that came out of that acknowledgement are extremely various, even within a single culture, let alone among many. But it was not that God explained the world, but that the world seemed to be explaining, or trying to describe, God—God conceived of as whatever could or would give so astonishing a gift as the world and our perception of it. Theology began as an inductive science, a bottom-up, even reductive, attempt to make sense of the given but inexplicably intricate and beautiful order of the universe.

What was especially striking about the universe—and why, for instance, the same word served the Anglo-Saxons for "god" and "good"—is the remarkable "non-zerosumness" of the world, as the thoroughly non-theist Robert Wright puts it.[1] We experience this non-zerosumness immediately as the way the world strangely produces a new moment every moment—it does not just stop. For the epic composers, that continuous gift of new time was divine, or rather divinity was that gift-giving of new time. For us, perhaps, an odder way of putting it, which harnesses our scientific understandings, may help recover the sense of epic wonder. Let us try.

The world explores as much of the available information-space as it can for any of its dynamical situations. That is, entropy increases over time, and every permutation of the energy-budget that is more economical than the present state of a system (and even some that are momentarily less economical) can be randomly touched on in a system's trajectory toward its lowest energy-state. At the same time, energy systems can support or compete with each other, and only some of them can survive. There is nothing worse than nonsurvival; there is no such thing as negative survival. Thus if the random exploratory process can only go in one direction, that is, positively from zero, the world has a ratchet that ensures that more and more positive—that is cooperative and internally coherent—systems will emerge over time.

The nineteenth-century understanding of—and profound pessimism about—the increase of entropy, characterized as the increase of disorder, may have been totally mistaken. It is precisely the "disorder" in which DNA explores its possible recombinations through mutation, bacterial gene transfer, and sexual reproduction that makes possible the branching-out of new species, genera, and families, that generates new unique individuals in the living world. Together with the equally entropic process of natural selection, this random—or better, exploratory—process results over time in more and more complex, sensitive, intelligent, and social organisms, even as it preserves many very primitive ones too.

A narrative plot works in much the same way. A storyteller is at liberty to add any event or action he pleases to the story up to that point: the alternatives branch out before him, limited only by the fact that they are being *added* to an existing state of affairs and must survive—that is, be narratively plausible—in the existing ecology of characters, past actions, and mise-en-scène. A good story is one in which the adding is called for imperatively by the situation as it stands: the grail must be found, the battle must be fought, the word must be got back, the lovers reunited, the obscure deserving one recognized. The degree of that gradient, that steep slope toward the next episode in the story that commands our suspense and keeps the audience listening, is the birthplace of morals and values; we the audience know what *should* happen, and wonder if it will. We know we have a contract with the storyteller, even if she is dead, and we will be patient up to a point about how she will fulfill it. Maybe what should happen will not happen, but the teller has something even better up her sleeve.[2] A moral relationship has sprung up, the beginnings of a community. So just in the constrained but open exploration of a narrative space a non-zerosum game—an evolutionary process—has sprung up, divinely it seems, out of nowhere.

Thus to say that in epic the hero's nation is singled out by the god or gods, is to say in one sense simply that it has survived and prospered enough to generate an epic, that it has reciprocated to the process of emergence that brought it forth by observing the process and telling it in a story. The "godness" or goodness of the story is what makes it a story at all, it is the *life* of the story, the non-zerosumness of its plotting, the way the characters mutually shape each other, and the events and actions both reflect and generate their experiences and performers.

The unanimity of epics all over the world on the special relationship between the epic people and their god or gods is thus no coincidence. Epic merely expresses the basic principles of all living organisms, and one of those principles is the efficacy of certain teleological assumptions. Those teleological assumptions need not be consciously held, and need not even be the property of individuals, but they are always the property of reproducing species. Life assumes the conditions for its perpetuation; the basic character of life as an *emergent* phenomenon is another way of stating the same principle.

The apparently plodding research of the great universities, in such fields as embryology, development, horticulture, ecology, and animal reproductive ritual, has been examining the mechanism of how the mess of amino acids specified by the genes can self-organize into proteins, embryonic cell types, organs, individuals, and communities. Once the individual or an ecosystem has emerged, its structure is so complex and the way it got there so iterative and tangled that the initiating conditions are largely lost in the integrity of the whole, as the brushstrokes of a Rembrandt or a Michelangelo are lost in the commanding image that organizes them. In an almost Aristotelian way, the Final Cause of the adult individual seems to pull the fetal developmental process toward its goal; and in an almost Platonic way, the strange attractor of the process itself, fractally deep and inexhaustible in its elegant articulations, seems to hang above or reside within the mere matter of the organism. Evolution itself is the archetypal iterative nonlinear dynamical feedback system. One could interpret the same facts that the neo-Darwinists describe in terms of genes "trying" to survive through their expression in individual organisms, as archetypal species-forms "sorting" through the huge random catalog of genetic recombination for a "good enough" mess of protein-makers to embody their development.

Such considerations expose how metaphysical is the doctrine of dialectical materialism as it is now found in the genetic reductionists. After all, the key idea in evolution is survival; yet living organisms by definition are dying all the time; they live by dying, which is metabolism. Biological "survival" is a grand, breathtaking, and accurate metaphor, but only a metaphor. Nothing of a gene is surviving in material reality when it reproduces; what "survives" is a piece of abstract information, the sequence of nucleotides on the DNA chain. My liver dies and resurrects itself every forty-eight hours or so. It is no more "surviving" than a flame. A chunk of granite that has survived in good hard fact for a billion years would, if it could, both laugh and shudder at the lunatic claims of a living organism to be surviving by hatching its eggs, or even by eating and excreting. Yet life is very effective—there is as much limestone around as granite, and limestone is the corpses of living organisms. A mere phantom—a pattern of information—can move mountains; for the crustal plates of the Earth and the eruptions of volcanoes are now driven by the boiling and fizzing of life-created rocks as they are subducted into the mantle. And if so abstract, so spiritual a thing as that pattern can masterfully determine the structure of large chunks of matter and the whole surface of our planet, why should not the even more abstract and metaphysical entities of goodness, freedom, spirit, soul, divinity, and beauty? And has not the success of the epic-composing societies borne out this strange fact in the realm of human history?

I have argued that the missing category in both the social and the biological reductionisms is beauty.[3] Only with an aesthetic eye can we come to really understand what is going on in nature, because the aesthetic eye is the organ nature has evolved in us for seeing the inner form of complex interactions. Our genes determine our bodies and brains, and our bodies and brains determine how we think and feel and behave. True. But our feelings and thoughts determine our behavior, which determines how our brains and bodies grow (which determines which genes get turned on), and whom we choose as a mate (which determines how future genes will be distributed in the species). Only the aesthetic vision can turn the dizzying circularity

251

of these propositions into the loveliness and intellectual clarity of a Madonna and Child or a great epic poem—or the striking cognitive beauty of such theories of dissipative systems or evolution through sexual selection and reproduction as have been produced by epic-creating cultures.

Even the assumption that there will be a future at all is already teleological and metaphysical; even the possession of some kind of memory by all living species is a bet that there will be a future that will resemble or be caused by the past (an assumption that Hume showed was logically unjustified, but works in practice[4]). The structural arrangement of something is already something immaterial. What is the codon sequence of a bacterium but the soul of the bacterium?—it's certainly immaterial. In theory, one could put that sequence into a computer in the form of a pattern of zeros and ones, and then use them as the blueprint to stack the necessary chemical atoms together into a living organism.[5] Here, spirit—the abstract form of the genes—would be governing matter. It is not the ink that determines the pattern of the sonnet, but the sonnet that determines the pattern of the ink. The sonnet is real, but it is "only" an arrangement.

Suppose that beauty, value, meaning, freedom, planning for the future, teleology, soul, etc., were complete nonsense, a mere arbitrary arrangement of matter, but for a species to operate *as if* they were real—by giving birth to young and nurturing them, self-sacrifice, ritual, cooperation, sanctions against noncooperation, and the like—such a species would be at a competitive advantage with others. In order to keep up, those others would in turn be forced to develop teleological behavior, and thus adopt its core value assumptions as a guide to preserve consistency. To predict the behavior of another organism, which is essential for the survival tasks of foraging, defense, and reproduction, one would have to model that organism's (counterfactual) belief in the future, its belief in eating (which prepares for future energy needs), in reproduction (which implies the replacement of the parent by future offspring), and in the need for defense (which implies planning on the part of one's assailant). If that (counterfactual) model is usually the best way to survive, it would save a lot of neural hardware to adopt it oneself and not have to maintain two different basic models. Eventually every part of the world would be filled with organisms and structures that acted *as if* the universe were meaningful, valuable, possessed of an alterable future, and full of intentional design.

The most hardened biological reductionist cannot resist the language of function and even purpose when actually describing biological structures and behaviors. Even "structure" and "behavior" are words that imply design, and when biologists use those words, even if they deny that there is any design, they implicitly concede the point that organisms at least act *as if* they were designed, which is the point here. Concede still that design and all of those other abstractions are still complete nonsense. But if all the organisms one studies share that fallacy, and cannot be understood without imagining that one shares it oneself, that concession is now a purely metaphysical one, with no practical or scientific relevance. Those abstractions—value, meaning, freedom, intention, etc.—will have become laws of nature. A belief in the meaninglessness and valuelessness and directionless of the universe would then be an act of purely religious faith, maintained in the face of the cold hard facts of meaning, design, love, progress, and beauty. The austere and faithful dialectical materialist, in his sackcloth and ashes, could then say with the mystic "Credo quia absurdum est"—I believe because it is absurd.

Epic assumes that meaning, value, purpose, design, love, progress, and beauty are real. The shorthand for that collective reality is "god." To be the people of the god is to have made the bet that there will be a future that is desirable, and that can be chosen and acted toward in preference to other less desirable futures. The future can only partially be predictable, though, so choosing and acting imply also adapting oneself to radically new things—we must have adventures.

So being singled out by the gods is a mixed blessing. There are three basic versions of this blessing: the comic, the tragic, and the moral. By "comic" I do not necessarily mean funny, though many epics, like *The Journey to the West* and *Don Quixote* are immediately funny, and others, like the *Popol Vuh*, the *Mahabharata*, and *Martín Fierro* are funny once one catches their idiom. The comic epic is one in which the people's history directly and immanently demonstrates the reward of the "goodward" or "godward" way of life of the hero as representative of the people or as sacrificial gift of the people. *The Odyssey*, the *Ramayana*, *The Aeneid*, *Sundiata*, *Mwindo*, *The Song of Roland*, and many others exemplify this basic epic gesture; it is the most frequent in the record. Here the existence of the people, their chosenness by the god, the virtue of the hero, and the shape of the epic itself are uncomplicatedly at one.

More complex and difficult is the tragic epic—*The Iliad*, the *Heike*, *Gilgamesh*, *The Saga of the Volsungs*, *The Song of the Nibelungs*, *The Cattle Raid of Cooley*, and *Moby Dick* are the clearest examples. Here the hero and the people are indeed chosen by the god or gods, but chosen to extend the boundary of the teleological regime, to kick the epic dialogue upwards into another realm of possibility, through terrible waste and loss, through the implacable opposition of irreconcilable values, through the affirmation of the beauty of something that cannot survive or be efficacious. The hero is flawed, but flawed in a way that perversely increases our allegiance to him. Humans often defy the gods in such stories, and we find ourselves both rooting for the humans and recognizing the need for gods to push us into higher forms of experience and suffering. Diomedes wounds Ares: War itself is wounded, its moral ascendancy is questioned. The gods cannot achieve this emergence without the help of their mortal collaborators/victims/ rebels. The hero and people are losers, but losers within a meaningful context in which even to have been seeking after purpose, design, love, beauty, spirit, glory, and so on, *and to have failed* is better than not to have done so at all. Perhaps all those things are counterfactuals, but they make a more bewitching game than any commonsense.

This perspective proves its value especially when we try to understand *The Saga of the Volsungs*, where all of Odin's mysterious interventions seem to result not in the success of the Volsungs but in their utter and appalling destruction. It is almost as if he spurs them on to their ordeal. But their singling-out by the god results in actions (including an attack on the god himself) that exemplify supernatural passion, courage, and insouciance in the face of misfortune. They are singled out in the sense that they are individuated, they achieve their distinct existence and worthiness to occupy the epic story and be part of the memory of a people.

If the divine singling-out of the epic nation combines both the comic and the tragic sense of the term, another element is necessary so that the work does not collapse into incoherence. I have called this element, rather inadequately, the moral. Here the tragic events serve a divine purpose, but it is not to initiate a new regime of values beyond even what the god or gods could achieve on their own: rather the catastrophes push the people into their next approximation of the divine ethics. The tragic events are a warning, a punishment, a lesson, a harsh step in the progress of the chosen people. If the people prosper, it is because they heed the god and his prophets; if they suffer, it is because they disobey and can only learn a higher morality by that disobedience and its punishment.

Of course the most obvious and overwhelmingly influential examples of this kind of singling-out are the Biblical epics. Here it is the passionate moral and personal relationship between the god and his heroes (and his people) that seizes our narrative interest, substituting for the intoxication we feel at the magnificent impieties of Gilgamesh, Kiyomori, Achilles, Sigurd, and Kriemhild. Jacob wrestles with God, and gets his blessing. Jacob is injured, wounded, in his loin, like Bran the Blessed, Adonis, and the Fisher King; but the wound symbolizes the moral advance that is being made in the ethics of the chosen people, from the mere struggle over birthright to the making of a commonwealth. From the demand God makes on Abraham to sacrifice his son, through the night attack of God's angel upon his chosen prophet Moses, to the Egyptian and Babylonian exiles, being singled out by God is not a comfortable thing; but the suffering opens more and more of God's mysterious goodness to the people.

There are several other epics in which it could be said that the singling-out of the people by the gods is primarily moral rather than tragic or comic. They might include *The Three Kingdoms*, in which the Chinese people learn through bitter experience that the higher unity of the empire, of the moral writ of the Chinese ideographic language, must supersede local loyalties, or harmony will never flourish. Another would be *The Peril of Sziget*, in which a whole tradition of Hungarian self-reproach for its faults and exhortation to reform its ethics find their central text. Ferenc Kölcsey's national hymn to God (1823) finely captures the spirit of that epic:

> Ah, but wrath upon our faults
> In your bosom blazing,
> Lashed the clouds with lightning bolts,
> Thunderstrokes amazing;
> Now the ravening Mongol's shaft
> You let howl upon us,
> Now, yoked like a beast of draft,
> Turkish masters own us.
>
> Oft indeed upon the tongue
> Of the Osman heathens
> Clanged their harsh victory-song
> O'er our bone-heaped legions!
> Worse, O country, 'gainst your breast

Rose your own sons often,
You, by your seed's rebel quest,
Turned your own seed's coffin. . . .

Pity Magyar souls, O Lord,
Racked to dissolution,
Stretch your arm, of love and guard
O'er their pain's dark ocean.
Bring a year of joy at last
To your wounded nation,
That for future, as for past,
Has done expiation![6]

Dante's *Divine Comedy* also falls, despite its title, into the category I have designated as the moral epic. The sufferings of Italy and of Dante are an essential part of the progress of the human race toward redemption and transcendence; but it is a transcendence that will find God waiting for us in the end with a disposition of things that will perfectly reflect divine justice. It is the humans that experience transcendence, not the god. By contrast, the Greek pagan view, when it is tragic, suggests that the present pantheon will one day be transcended, when Athena, Zeus' brain-child, will replace him; and the gods will be aided in their own ethical development by the suffering and defiance of men. But possibly the contrast is too easily drawn: Dante's is an infinitely complex and dialectical mind, and perhaps the three great ladies of heaven who help the poet are themselves, if not a potential replacement like Athena, a new supplement to the pure math of the Trinity. Certainly the *Shahnameh* can be seen as a moral epic, in which the royal *farr*, like the Mandate of Heaven in *The Three Kingdoms*, can be lost through folly and sin and regained through virtue.

As with any classification of literary works, much escapes this crude trichotomy. *Njal's Saga*, for instance, definitely begins in the tragic mode but ends in the moral mode, and the implicit struggle between transcendent human valorous passion and transcendent divine compassion and peace remains in play at its conclusion. Part of us wants Kari to smite Flosi at the end, despite our knowledge that Flosi is a good man and that the future peace of Iceland depends upon the reconciliation. The value of classification, as we have seen often in this study, is that when employed with an eye to counter-examples, it opens up, rather than closing down the complexity and richness of the text. Epic composers are, I believe, aware of the other directions they could have taken when they choose the comic, the tragic, or the moral mode for their major theme. One of the advantages of the comparative and cross-cultural view of the genre is that we become aware of the potentialities the epic composer has left implicit, half-silenced, in his text.

Faults and Flaws of Epic Nations: Epic Hero versus Epic Ruler

Epic is sometimes regarded, by those in the literary academy who do not read it, as propaganda for the particular national hegemony in power and as a buttress for the authorities in charge. There are indeed epics that praise the national virtues and celebrate the exploits of a king; such kings include Gilgamesh, Aeneas, Gesar of Tibet, David of Sassoun, Manas of the Kyrghyz, Temüjin of the Mongols, and Dong-myeong of Korea. But the role of hero and the role of king are much more often separated, and this separation inevitably implies a critique both of the nation and of its leadership.

Even in the case of those epics that do depict a combined hero-king, they often show him in a state of ambivalence between his two roles. Gilgamesh must be tamed from dominating hero into responsible leader by his great rebel and then friend Enkidu. Aeneas is torn between his humanity and his role, most signally when he must leave Dido and when he should spare Turnus. The Armenian David begins as a delinquent, with many of the wild and disorderly characteristics of the berserker hero; Dongmyeong is an exile. Often the hero-name is different from the king-name; Abram becomes Abraham, Jumong becomes Dongmyeong, Temüjin becomes Genghiz, Don-grub becomes Gesar (and "Gesar" is probably derived from "Kesar," the Mongolian word for Caesar, so he has morphed from a person into a role). Moses is so uncomfortable with the dual role of prophet/hero and political leader that he asks God for, and gets, a king figure in the form of Aaron.

When the king and hero are literally separated, they are almost always at odds in one way or another. Most famously, Achilles confronts Agamemnon. Rostam must serve an unworthy master, Kay Kavus, and if there is a single dominant theme in the role of hero in the *Shahnameh* it is that the hero is tragically better fitted to lead than the monarch. Cuchulainn and his king Conchobar are almost enemies. Roland, seeking greater glory, refuses to blow his horn to get help from Char-lemagne. Siegfried's faithful service to his lord Gunther is ill-fated and leads to his death. The friendship between the hero Gunnar and the lawgiver Njal is strained almost to the breaking point by their women, and the strains themselves lead on to tragedy for both. In a significant reversal of the usual pattern, it is the hero Kiyomori, in the *Heike*, who betrays his proper role, deposing the rightful emperor and replacing him with his grandson Tokuhito. Godfrey, Tasso's leader, disciplines Rinaldo the troublesome hero. The hero Prince Hal must deliberately distance himself from his father and king in order finally to unite the roles of hero and king at Agincourt; and to do so he must also sacrifice the King of the May, Falstaff. In *Moby Dick* Starbuck, who would be the hero of any ordinary tale, unsuccessfully resists Ahab's assumption of both roles, hero and king; to be a hero, Ahab must be a bad king and lead his ship to destruction. In my own *Genesis* Tripitaka, whose role as hero is to serve his "king," Chance van Riebeck, is persuaded by Ruhollah to assassinate his leader instead, and must then in penance sacrifice himself for the emergent republic of Mars. The Quiché lords are not reincarnations of the Mayan hero twins, but rather guardians of their legacy and subject to their judgment from beyond the grave.

Thus the tension between king and hero can be said to be fundamentally constitutive of epic. Comparison between the two cannot narratively be avoided. One or the other must be relatively at fault dramatically speaking, and the fault redounds either to the discredit of the nation as represented by its king or its chosen hero, or to the discredit of the leadership of the nation, or to all of them. Sometimes the nation should be ashamed that it does not value its heroes, because of the envy of its ruler, as with *The Iliad*, the *Shahnameh*, or *The Cattle Raid of Cooley*. Sometimes the nation should be ashamed at its proclivity for producing heroes who tear the nation apart, like those of the *Three Kingdoms, Njal's Saga*, the *Mahabharata,* or the *Heike*. Sometimes the flaws of the hero are the nation's writ large; sometimes the flaws of the king are those of a nation ungrateful to heroes who call it to transcend itself.

This essential feature of epic tends to preserve its poets from the pressure to flatter the nation and its past worthies and in so doing flatter the current ruler and get his favor. Even the patriotic Virgil and Shakespeare cannot help noting by implication the bloodiness of Aeneas' imperialism and the ruthlessness of Henry V. Homer knows the manipulativeness and over-reaching of his Greeks and gives those traits to Odysseus. And so from epic to epic we get a compendium of the characteristic faults and flaws of the epic nations; we might list some of them, thus:

Persians: Over-generosity and desire to be admired and loved, misplaced trust, prodigality

French: Insane covetousness of *la gloire*

Romans: Sheepish piety

Italians: Distracting sentiment, especially in love

Greece: Hubris, pride in its "polypragmosyne" or cleverness, Machiavellianism, overweening confidence that its skills will prevail

Hebrews: Stiffneckedness, ingratitude, obstinate refusal to have faith in the Lord, legalism, over-reaching

Spanish: Machismo, cupidity, less than fastidious choice of allies

Chinese: Eternal backsliding into materialism, literalism, expediency; inconsiderate and addled energy, conformity to formulae

Hindus: Kshatriya arrogance, lack of a sense of proportion, refusal to yield the point, unbendingness

Mayans: Over-impulsiveness, recklessness

English: Political manipulativeness, cynical pragmatical empiricism, self-interest, egotism

Icelanders: Excess of masculinity, combined with female envy, manipulation, and ambition

Irish: Lunatic obsessiveness, rivalry

Nordics: Grudges, betrayal, vengefulness

Feudal Europeans: Fatuous over-faithfulness to the chivalric code in war, morals, love

Americans: Idolatry of the individual conscience, fanaticism, autodidacticism

Argentinians: Lawlessness, levity

Mesopotamians: Imprudence, impiety, lack of self-restraint

Malinese: Misuse of magical powers, witchcraft

Nyanga (*Mwindo*): Kin betrayal, envy

—And so on. Of course these vices are seen as accompanied by the great virtues of the nations the epic composers celebrate, and often the epic composer has a definite soft spot for his homeland's flaws, especially if they are those of heroic excess. But epic is neither propaganda nor apologia at bottom; True Thomas speaks truth to power, even if he is as tactful as he can manage; and he speaks truth also to the coxcomb or schemer side of his hero and his hero's people. The very form of epic ensures its integrity: king and hero do not entirely mix.

National Destiny

Obviously the word *national* is a "contested site" in this context. Political theorists might well argue that the term has real meaning only in the context of the modern emergence of the nation state and the ideology of nationalism.[7] Etymologists would point out that the root of the word, *nat*, implies common racial descent, implying that the word "nation" is really just a polite way of saying "tribe." But many epics, even from premodern and very ancient times, do indeed require and even define something close to the term "nation," and make clear how a nation is more than a tribe. One way of putting this is to say that a nation is an artificial tribe, in which ethnic, cultural, and shared historical characteristics, when united by leaders of sufficient charisma, substitute for the perceived sense of kinship enjoyed by a primordial band. Epic often documents in its own story terms the formation and legitimation of that substitution.

When Gilgamesh is made to desist from impregnating every bride in the city (thereby ensuring blood kinship!), the transformation has already begun. The *Oresteia* chronicles the transfer of sacred authority from the family to the city, from Furies into Eumenides, from sacred custom to law, from clan to nation. Temüjin must unite the Mongol tribes to make a nation; Moses must weld twelve tribes into one holy people; the Han must unite China into the Middle Kingdom (and in so doing, give up its own tribal claim to special loyalty). Henry V enlists the men of England, Ireland, Scotland, and Wales in his great victory. Virgil's Rome became the model, still being worked out today, of a super-tribal Europa.

Certainly the nation as envisaged by the epic poets is not the nation-state of the last couple of centuries, with its institutions of government, constitution, lawcourts, bureaucracy, currency control, and nationalist state propaganda. On the other hand, we can surely see the embryos of some of these institutions, the emergence of councils and representation in Exodus, Iceland's Fifth Court, the specification of court roles in the *Popol Vuh*, the very subtle and perceptive understanding of coinage and sovereignty in the *Henriad*, the elaborate bureaucracy of the *Heike*.

But more is needed to draw together a nation against the centrifugal claims of family and clan than efficient rule of law and protection of markets. The moral authority of an Antigone, who clings to the tribal piety of the past, cannot be directly denied. Nations exist, according to many epics, because they have a destiny, a promised role, the custodianship of a great hope, even a universal mission to the whole human race.

In other words, this most traditional of literary forms is oriented essentially toward the future. Each of the nations whose origins it celebrates finds its final justification in a promise, an explicit or implicit covenant. From the epic story's trajectory or arc we find out in what direction the consummation or fulfillment is likely to lie. It differs from nation to nation, obviously; it can be as simple as the free open-endedness of the gaucho life in *Martín Fierro*, as heavily freighted as the Christian eschatology of *Paradise Lost*, as Darwinian as God's promise to Abraham of numberless progeny, as sober as Anchises' assurance to Aeneas that Rome will make good laws for the world.

In the *Popol Vuh* the implicit promise that the Maya will rise again was enough to spark the Caste War for independence in 1845 and the Chiapas uprising of 1995. Even though the *Shahnameh* ends with defeat at the hands of the Arabs, it is a testament to the special gift of high international civilization that was Persia's pride and destiny, and again an implied prophecy of Persia's resurgence. The Latvian *Lacplesis* foreshadows the independence of the Baltic nations from Teutonic and now Soviet domination. The *Kossovo Epic* predicts the liberation of the Christian Balkans from Muslim rule. In the epics of Homer, the Greeks' huge contribution to the intellectual, imaginative, and scientific future of humankind is already prefigured: to be civilized is to have heard of the Trojan War and thus to know the meaning of human excellence. In *Moby Dick*, America is to be the first nation composed of all nations, a further echo of the promise of Yahweh that Jerusalem would be a light unto the nations. Wordsworth's *Prelude* foresees a time when all humans can experience the freedom and self-development that the poet has been blessed with. My own epics poems, set in the future, simply literalize the element of destiny in the epic genre itself; *The New World*, composed in the early 1980s when many expected the human world to end in nuclear apocalypse, explicitly sets itself to envisage a future in which the apocalypse had been evaded and a new, strange but familiar order of human politics had taken its place.

Epic is by its very nature not a reactionary genre. As this book has argued throughout, it is an evolutionary genre. When its nation has been crushed by tyranny internal or external, when no opportunity is offered to transcend the nationalistic impulse and speak to and for the human race as a whole, and when its very existence has ensured the survival of its culture even under alien domination, epic can indeed be a revolutionary medium. But the kind of revolution epic implies is one that takes into account the whole of the human past, the evolutionary struggles of our ancestors, and the requirements of beauty—our ancient instinct for what is fitting yet productive. Epic cannot easily be subverted into the pitiless, blinkered, and schematic utopianism with which we have become all too familiar, the arrogant dismissal of all that is, in Yeats' words, "accustomed, ceremonious":

> For arrogance and hatred are the wares
> Peddled in the thoroughfares.
> How but in custom and in ceremony
> Are innocence and beauty born?
> Ceremony's a name for the rich horn,
> And custom for the spreading laurel tree.[8]

Notes

1. Robert Wright, *Nonzero: The Logic of Human Destiny* (New York: Pantheon Books, 2000).

2. As George Eliot does in *Middlemarch* (Oxford: Oxford University Press, 2008); Dorothea does not end up with Lydgate.

3. *Beauty: The Value of Values* (Charlottesville, VA: University Press of Virginia, 1992).

4. In Hume's words:

   > If we would satisfy ourselves, therefore, concerning the nature of that evidence, which assures us of matters of fact, we must enquire how we arrive at the knowledge of cause and effect.

   > I shall venture to affirm, as a general proposition, which admits of no exception, that the knowledge of this relation is not, in any instance, attained by reasonings a priori, but arises entirely from experience, when we find that any particular objects are constantly conjoined with each other. Let an object be presented to a man of ever so strong natural reason and abilities; if that object be entirely new to him, he will not be able, by the most accurate examination of its sensible qualities, to discover any of its causes or effects. Adam, though his rational faculties be supposed, at the very first, entirely perfect, could not have inferred from the fluidity and transparency of water that it would suffocate him, or from the light and warmth of fire that it would consume him. No object ever discovers, by the qualities which appear to the senses, either from the causes which produced it, or the effects which will arise from it; nor can our reason, unassisted by experience, ever draw any inference concerning real existence and matter of fact. (David Hume, *An Enquiry Concerning Human Understanding* [1772]. Hackett Publ Co. 1993; Chapter on Cause and Effect.)

5. Something very similar to this operation has already been achieved at the J. Craig Venter Institute. The synthetic genome functioned as a new bacterium. E. Pennisi, "Synthetic Genome Brings New Life to Bacterium," *Science* 330 (December 17, 2010): 1605.

6.   Zsuzsanna Ozsváth and Frederick Turner *Light within the Shade: Hungarian Poetry Over Eight Hundred Years.* Unpublished manuscript; our translation.

7.   For an excellent critique of the conventional "Whig history" of the nation, see Steven Grosby, *Biblical Ideas of Nationality: Ancient and Modern* (Winona Lake, IN: Eisenbrauns, 2002).

8.   W. B. Yeats: "A Prayer for My Daughter," in *Selected Poems and Two Plays of William Butler Yeats*, ed. M. L. Rosenthal (London: Macmillan, 1962), 92.

10

Setting an Example

Building a Value Language

We have already examined the commutative process by which (in the view of the epic composers) iterated sacrifices can generate abstract and conceptual meanings out of existential facts, events, and feelings. We have also seen how narrative can be a way of conducting a fairly sophisticated argument by way of a natural and polyvalent allegory. We have understood epic to concern itself with the problems of making a city and nation, of how to generate shared meanings and values that can unite different clan mythologies and vocabularies. And we have seen how the concept of the divine can act as the necessary "skyhook" to organize and thematize the nonzerosumness of productive interaction.

The methods and constraints under which linguistic meanings emerge impose common boundaries and themes upon their products. The poststructuralist turn, in which different "culture worlds" or "epistemes" are thought of as being radically incommensurable and arbitrary, confined within their respective dictionaries, is now itself under question—and rightly so, in the light of the insight of the epic composers. Epic, one might say, inherits a human world in which different families, clans, and tribes speak incommensurable and untranslatable languages; but through the transgressiveness and sacrifice of the hero a common measure and a Rosetta Stone of significant action are established—the unmeasurable is measured, the untranslatable translated. The idea of humanity becomes inclusive rather than exclusive. Epic reverses the diaspora of languages imaged in the story of the Tower of Babel. It creates a pantheon or a deity or a divine milieu out of the babble of local spirits.

Thus the feature that emerges from the close study of epics from all over the world is overwhelmingly how deeply similar they are under all their differences. It is almost as if epic is a rediscovery, a recovery, a second emergence, of our common human biological nature. The common human language of sacrifice, story, and larger community-building is dredged up from the chaotic layers of idiosyncratic myth laid down by the cranky genius-shamans of the primordial bands. The city of epic is not just a step forward into civilization but a clear backward look at our own nature.

Epic's attempt to recover the essential unity of the human experience requires the construction of a vocabulary of value; let us look at a few of the many value distinctions that epic lays down upon the cleared and ancient human foundations.

Good and Bad

The most basic value terms cannot be defined in the manner of dictionary or a philosophical argument. That is not to say that they cannot be explained at all: but the way it is done is by storytelling, and it consists of arranging characters, actions, and events in a temporal sequence and then pointing to the underlying distinctions that make that sequence make sense and give an aesthetically satisfying closure. To do this of course is the *forte* of epic. Good and bad for the great stories are not labels whose meaning is already known, that can be pasted onto persons or acts, as they might be in the later narratives of lawcourts, political cartoons, press reports, or sermons. An epic *constructs* good and bad.

But it does so using the more primitive scaffolding of our mammal and primate tropisms toward security, pleasure, reproduction, social standing in the group, and sympathy, and our hardwired aversions to danger, discomfort, loss of kin, shunning, and the dislike of others. It creates a narrative that engages our feelings on behalf of the protagonists and then refines and ennobles them until they have become partly free from local prejudice and blinkered self-interest. It could also be said to be *rescuing* our natural moral sentiments from earlier cultural embodiments that trap them within closed local hermeneutic circles. Epic's constructions are reconstructions: the implication is not that social rules and structures are arbitrary, but that their deep commonalities must be discovered through exact and accurate storytelling. Epic teases out the logic of the species (which, though impulsive and dangerous, is often altruistic and beautiful) from the logic of rational self-interest, and in so doing enables a critique of both.

In the biblical epics, the human race and the chosen people do not start with a set of rules defining good and bad behavior. Adam and

Eve are allowed to do anything at all, except eat of the forbidden fruit; they are given two commands, to increase and multiply, and to name the world, both of which they want to do anyway. The whole of the rest of the moral law must be inferred from the outcomes of actions and events and our feelings about them. In terms of Kantian morality, which evaluates ethical behavior on the basis of compliance with a maxim, what Cain does to Abel is not culpable, and God is right to not punish him: there is no maxim yet to comply with. Cain has to find out that killing your brother is bad by losing his home (since home is where your kin live); and characters such as Lot, Abraham, and Jacob construct/discover the law by various potential or actual infractions of it. The actual Ten Commandments come late in the story, and are almost a grudging concession by God to the people's legalistic desire for mindless and automatic rules, for a substitute to replace the slower but deeper process of finding out by experience what is good and bad.

Similarly in *The Odyssey* the natural human proclivity to take other people's stuff, epitomized in the hero's soubriquet, "raider of cities," is gradually refined through Odysseus' (and, vicariously, our) experience of getting into trouble for taking other people's stuff, of losing all his own stuff, of being given stuff by people to whom he is polite, and defending his own stuff from others. The *Mahabharata* begins with the joyous, heartless immensities of the natural/divine universe, takes up the code of Kshatriya honor (itself a local and confining version of our drive to survive and reproduce), and then refines it by storytelling until its essential ethical meaning is revealed in passionate action, tragedy, and mystical transcendence. At its peak, in the *Bhagavadgita*, the language is scarcely distinguishable from the sayings of the Judeo-Christian mystics, the Sufis, Laotze, and the Native American shamans. But the language is earned and validated by the stories of Drona, Karna, Duryodhana, and the Pandavas. Far from deviating away from each other, great civilizations converge through their deeper narrative understanding of human nature and human history.

Right and Wrong

Laws seem, as many philosophers have opined, to be based on one of two foundations: what is good and what is right.[1] The distinction, even more generally, is between what is commanded of us by the gods or God (or, in later ages, by Humanity, by Nature, by Reason, or by Popular Will) on one hand, and what is required of us in the honest fulfillment of a contract, on the other. The former sees law as a way to enforce the good—the good as a transcendent endowment of human society that we can partly intuit, especially if we are talented, trained, learned, and morally upright. The latter sees laws as the way to make sure the humble contracts that human beings make with each other have the support they need over and above the natural sanctions built into our families, our markets, and our practical agreed systems of mutual trust. The first emphasizes the good, the second, the right.

Epic loves to play with the difference: sometimes pointing out where what is right is not good, sometimes the reverse. The good transcends any means of ascertaining it; it is not bound to the veridical. Significantly, we can use "right" and "wrong" just as easily about the answer to a math or logic problem or a statement of fact as we can about the moral content of an action. The right is by definition what is arrived at by due process, by the exact performance of a truth-finding operation like a theorem or a legal case. In this, the distinction differs from true and false; the right answer, in the sense that its reasoning carries out the procedure correctly, may be untrue.

Epic heroism always involves decisions in which the good trumps the right, in the sense of the prudent, the law-abiding, the normative. But even if he hero breaks the rules, the epic's purpose in founding a civilization is to make the right, which does not require heroic visionary inspiration to ascertain, sufficiently close to the true and the good that its citizens, obeying the new rules, doing the right thing, allow the city to flourish. Epic heroes do the wrong things, and good comes of it; but this is no law for a city.

Elevated and Base

How does epic develop and contextualize important value distinctions and distinguish their axes from each other? The normal method is to establish a pair of terms or even of unnamed but obviously opposing characteristics, set them into a narrative context in which we "root" for one of the pair and execrate the other, and then to execute a twist that partially rehabilitates the despised term, questions the preferred term, and sets both into opposition with other pairs of value terms. In *The Journey to the West*, for instance, we are given at the beginning two major characters, Monkey and Tripitaka, one of whom is clearly base and the other clearly elevated. Base is bad and elevated is good. Monkey's baseness gets its punishment when he is imprisoned. But the twist is that Tripitaka's noble and elevation mission does not stand a chance without the baseness of Monkey (and his companions Pigsy and Sandy). Base can be good, then; and elevated—if it is too refined, fastidious, and timid to be effective—can be bad.

It is the crafty baseness of the Mayan hero twins that enables them to defeat the lords of death, the baseness of Odysseus that is partly responsible for getting him home when his elevated hubris has got him into trouble, the baseness of Falstaff that redeems the elevatedness of feuding feudal England. Parzifal fails the test of the Grail because his initial baseness has been replaced by an elevated sense of courtesy. Yet "elevated," though its limits are revealed by its narrative vicissitudes, is also ennobled and sharpened in definition by its being detached from more practical virtues and set up as admirable and beautiful in itself.

Admirable and Despicable

But the narratives we have been citing have already led us into further value distinctions, "admirable–despicable" being one. Again, at first glimpse in an epic the distinction appears exactly parallel to the "good–bad" one. But when we have characters like cross-dressing Arjuna, beggar Odysseus, delinquent Prince Hal, David of Sassoun the near-brigand, Sundiata the crippled and obese child, and Gilgamesh the rapist himself at the beginning of his story, who take on the roles of the despised, we are forced to recognize the social nature of this distinction. It depends upon admirers and despisers for its bite and moral purchase, and the social consensus may be wrong or premature. When Yudhisthira sees Duryodhana in heaven and his own friends in hell, it becomes clear that there can be a despicable elevatedness and an admirable baseness. The admired can be bad, the despised good; and out of this insight comes a whole critique of society, a critique of old provided most comprehensively by those epics so dismissed in modern times as upholders of the regime. It is not a cheap paradox: usually the despicable is bad, the admirable good, and it requires judgment to recognize where the crucial exceptions create new openings for moral and civilizational advance. Epic trains that judgment.

Similarly, though the elevated usually correlates with the admirable and the base with the despicable, important reversals can occur. Homer's Agamemnon, Milton's Satan, Dante's Ulysses, Kakuichi's Kiyomori are elevated in style and passion but despicable; even more confusingly, they are both admirable and despicable at the same time. Dante's Ser Brunetto Latini is bad by definition, being in Hell; but he is both admirable and elevated. Paolo and Francesca are another example in the *Divine Comedy*; indeed the work as a whole is a searching test and education of our value judgments. The *Heike*'s Yoshinaka is base in his manners but admirable in his military might and courage. The Japanese term *hougan-biiki*, meaning sympathy for a tragic hero, based on one of the names of Yoshinaka's cousin Yoshitsune, nicely catches the mixed feelings of the epic audience: he is admirable, elevated, and bad in many of his actions. Meanwhile, base figures like Parzifal's Cundrie, Sancho Panza, the common soldiers in *Henry V*, Martín Fierro, Sundiata's mother Sogolon, and my own Maury Edsel in *The New World* can be oddly admirable. The work we must do in sorting out these feelings enlarges our ethical vocabulary, makes us better able to live productively in a city.

Firstness and Secondness

Our term "second nature" implies that there is a "first nature." The temptation is to take "first nature" to be the only authentic nature, and then to look for first nature and try to get back to it. One of our most pervasive moral solecisms is to identify the original, the first, with the best, the truest, the most essential; epic questions this view. It is Plato's mistake in the myth of the cave—to value the abstract logical and mathematical laws that govern physics (and that current cosmologists believe created the universe) over the feelings, opinions, and changing wills that make up the human world. The philosopher, fresh from the cave, values the hydrogen bomb of the sun more than the cave-dwellers and poetic puppeteers of the human world. If, as we now know, the universe evolved, from a condition that can only be described mathematically, into the worlds of physics, chemistry, biology, and anthropology, should we reverse the universe's evolution? Is the universe "falling" from its most authentic reality, or seeking out its own truest reality in its free exploration of the future? Is it, in thermodynamic terms, running down or gearing up?[2]

Much epic plays with the relative valuation of firstness and secondness, in various senses: the primitive versus the advanced, the naïve versus the sophisticated, the original versus the perfected, and so on. Do we judge something by its sources and roots, or by its destiny and its fruits? Beside posing interesting and revealing cases of naïvety that is elevated, sophistication that is base, perfectness that is bad, admirable actions that are naïve, and so on, epic has a special problem with this dualism. By its nature epic deals with origins, archetypes, foundings—and must give them high value. But at the same time, as we have seen, epic also celebrates liberation from existing conditions, transformation, emergence, hope for a different future, even the Fall. So one task of epic is to show what kinds of actions and characters manage to affirm both, to honor origins by their outcomes, to return to firstness through a full exploration of secondness, to discover the archetype in the promethean advance. Parzifal's civilized secondness betrays him in the grail castle when naïvety is called for; but his failure results in a great journey of moral and sentimental education and a greater achievement than the callow youth could have attained. Milton's Adam could not have composed *Paradise Lost*.

Meso and Meta

English, uncharacteristically, does not have commonly accepted current words for this distinction, which is very important in epic. I am using "meso" here as a sort of coinage to correspond with, and be the opposite of, "meta." To be "meso" is to be in the middle of things, not taking the larger comparative view: it can be stance of the honest follower of the rules, or the state of the hero in Nietzsche who gathers his horizon about him, takes no thought for other points of view, and endorses his own limitations—and thus is capable of original action in the face of death and fate that expresses and constitutes his being.

To be "meta" is to meditate the rules of the game as one plays it, to worry about how to prove what one knows, to acknowledge the ethical necessity of empathy for other worldviews. "Meta" is beginning to be accepted in the academy as a term to indicate the relationship of "aboutness," the position we assume when we use quotation marks in writing or brackets in mathematics. When I use the word "use" in this sentence, the first use of it, without quotes, is a use, and the second use of it, in quotes, is a *mention* of it; I have assumed a "meta" position in relation to it. Of course this sentence as a whole is about itself, and is thus both a use and a mention of its constituent words. Linguists use the word "recursion" to refer to the syntactical constructions that make such expressions possible; philosophers use the word "intentionality" to refer, among other things, to the corresponding human capacity to know something as opposed to simply experience it. In the words of Daniel Dennett and John Haugeland: "A belief can be about icebergs, but an iceberg is not about anything; an idea can be about the number 7, but the number 7 is not about anything."[3]

"Meso" in Greek means "middle." By "meso" I mean the iceberg rather than the belief, the number rather than the idea about it.

Polyphemus is defeated by Odysseus because he is completely "meso," in the middle, like the single eye in the middle of his face. He cannot step back from the word "Noman" that Odysseus has given as his name so as to know it as an object rather than just use it. Of course the whole of *The Odyssey* is multiply self-referential; storytellers tell stories of storytellers that turn out to be the storyteller himself. The *Mahabharata* goes even further. As we saw at the beginning of this study, epic thematizes its own narrativity, its "aboutness," its "meta" quality, and thus pushes us to imagine the natural man who can *not* thematize it.

Like the other value-distinctions, this one is not reducible to any of the others. Is the "meso" primary—does it have the character of "firstness"? Or is it secondary—does there need to be a primary context of "aboutness," of meta, in which meso emerges as an object? Can meta evolve from meso? This quibble itself encapsulates millennia of theological disputation. Descartes initiated the most recent bout of it, "I think" being prior to "I am," an argument between ontology and epistemology that is still raging among Heideggerians.[4] In epic, most of the creation myths portray the origin of the world as an emergence from the intentional "meta" acts of the gods into the unthinking immediacy of "meso" matter and dumb animals. The goddess Tiamat and the god Ymir must be killed and dismembered to make the world. So "meta" precedes "meso." But Adam, Enkidu, Parzifal, and Wordsworth before their Falls are "meso" and fall into "meta"; so "meso" comes first.

If meta is good and meso is bad, then essence precedes existence in value, and a life of Augustinian asceticism is the only ethical way of life. Epic lovers or berserkers like Rinaldo, Cuchulainn, Aeneas (before his warning by Mercury), Paolo and Francesca, Gunnar, Siegfried, and the first two Hunahpus have sinfully given up their "meta" objectivity in pursuit of pure experience. But it is precisely the gift of throwing caution and forethought and "aboutness" to the winds that makes heroes heroes. The "meta" Tripitaka, whose very role is to carry the Buddhist meta-knowledge from India to China, is utterly helpless without the very "meso" Monkey; and Monkey's power of immediate experience and innocent action only needs a little tinkering to become a very high form of enlightenment. The Pandavas must be plunged into the "meso" world of the forest to discover the "meta" quality of their souls.

If meso is good, meta bad—the unlived life is not worth examining—then Nietzsche and the existentialists are right. But if so, to be perfectly consistent, it is wrong for existentialists to use quotation marks and refer to the form and content of their own sentences, indeed wrong to be philosophers who do these things, and wrong to be human language-users who cannot help getting an unjust advantage over the objects of their words by making them objects. We are in bad faith to read them at all. But concede the point: the unlived life is not worth examining. So Odysseus becomes the villain, and Polyphemus the hero, and we are in the midst of a contemporary argument about the post-colonial condition. Epic has already anticipated, often by thousands of years, the "theory" we are so proud of; and has done it in a way so much more subtle than the crude bivalent vocabulary of academic rhetoric, has set the ideas in play in narrative action, and has pushed us into deeper and more tragic distinctions.

Pure and Impure

One of the most important functions of sacrifice is purification. We sacrifice to rid ourselves of pollution, shame, and obligations that would otherwise hang on us, festering, unrequited. With other humans one can always attempt in good faith to repay our debts and be in good standing with our fellows; but with God or the gods to attempt to do so literally is a kind of hubris. So, as we have seen, we assume that the god will commute part of our debt and sentence. But the sacrifice itself, necessary as at least an earnest of our intent and good faith, is a further pollution, a further impiety. If the altar is a table for the meal of a god, we flood it with hot uncooked blood. If nature itself is the god's gift to us, what else but nature supplies us the gifts we try to give to the god, and is it not insulting or cheating, in a way, to give back a gift to one who gave us the gift in the first place? If the waters of the world are already fouled by the blood of past sacrifices, do we not cleanse ourselves in our ritual ablutions with the fluids of past corruptions?

What epic does is show by story that these paradoxes are, in Dame Julian's word, "behovely." The drama that is played out makes the returned gift acceptable: we are shown how to "pay it forward," to accept the same covenant that we make with our parents, to give to our children and successors what in strict logic we owe to our progenitors and ancestors. Thus epic's story often begins with a deep impurity, a *foedus*, a polluting crime, an awe-inspiring putrefaction; Virgil is well aware of the terrible crimes and impure mixtures that brought about the Roman Empire, but he turns them mysteriously into mechanisms of ritual purification.[5] When Krishna tells Arjuna that he must drench himself in his kinsmen's and mentors' blood on the field of Kurukshetra, the assumption of the task is itself the purifying sacrifice. The only way such crimes can be expiated is by further rectificatory crimes, and true purity comes only after fully "taking aboard" the corruptions of the grave.

Foedera of this kind abound in epic literature. In *The Three Kingdoms*, a great hunter who has no meat to give to his future Emperor kills his wife and cooks her flesh for his lord. Gudrun feeds her two sons to their father Atli at a feast. The atrocity of the death of the eight-year-old Fukusho, one of the last of the Taira heirs in the *Heike*, is a similar *foedus*. The whole story of the biblical Passover is rich with the dark, supernatural stink of the *foedus*, from the Nile turning to blood, to plagues of locusts and frogs, to the deaths of the firstborn, to the counter-impurity of smearing the blood of an innocent animal on the lintels of the Hebrews and the emerging ritual of circumcision. Rotting human heads become game balls in the *Popol Vuh*. One of the things that bring home to us the *mysterium tremendum et fascinans* is the smell of putrefying flesh; epic sometimes rubs our noses in it. But it is a prophylactic, an imaginative inoculation so that when we do walk in the valley of the shadow of death we will fear no evil. We learn purity of soul through the pollution of the body.

Out of the corrupted past comes a new innocent generation; out of bloody force comes the purity of law and justice. The "ceremony of innocence"[6] derives from "the frogspawn of a blind man's ditch."[7] This is not to argue that in epic purity and impurity are the same thing, that the value-axis the terms represent is not valid. Purity is real, and it is good. Rather, the distinction between the pure and the impure is real but dynamic, embedded in the action of a story in which impurity is made to serve purity. If dirt, in Mary Douglas' words,[8] is matter out of place, purity is matter in its proper place. Purity is the purer if it has moved from its first proper place to a second proper place, and knows what a proper place is like in general. The goodness of an untried purity—a "fugitive and cloistered virtue, unexercised and unbreathed," as Milton put it,[9] is not as good as a purity that has "walked among the lowest of the dead"[10] with Tiresias and Dante.

Playful and Serious

In the *Mahabharata*, the troubles really begin when Yudishthira plays at dice against Duryodhana, who is dishonorably playing with magicked dice. Yudishthira ends up staking and losing everything, including his kingdom and his wife, a very serious outcome of an explicitly playful activity. We have already looked at the role of games in epic (funeral games in Homer, the ball game in the *Popol Vuh*, and so on); of course they play a very important part in the playful/serious axis of value. Epic certainly distinguishes playfulness from seriousness by including games and contrasting them with other activities. But, as with the other antinomies, it gives life to the axis itself by dwelling on our peculiar human proclivity to turn play into real action, to make fictions into fact, dreams into reality.[11] In a sense we are a fictional species, the result of so many past lovers pursuing their imagined sweethearts, so many struggles over goals and prizes that are of no more practical value than Monopoly money or checkmate or home runs, but whose achievement leads to more numerous progeny. Epic notes that we can get into trouble playing games, but promises that it is better to have played and lost than never to have played at all. And after all epic is a storytelling game itself, and the best way to get one's name and kin remembered.

Every real act, as we have already noted, is also an "act" in the theatrical sense of play. In the moment of performance many paths to the future open themselves up; to be truly playful we must not pretend that there is a single right path. But once a path is chosen, we cannot pretend that it was not chosen or that it does not now constrain us; and this is the true meaning of seriousness. The play realm is where there is a "save and reboot" option, and we have as human civilizations hugely expanded that realm. But there are still many situations where there is no saving and rebooting, and this is serious. Epic deals both with the serious constraints of the past and the playful opportunities of the future.

Natural and Artificial

Epic almost always postulates a tripartite reality of nature, culture, and the divine. By telling the human grand narrative, epic is essentially building a conceptual bridge between the natural and the artificial, and invoking the divine as the builder and regulator of the bridge. Epic tells how human beings became makers, how the emergence from "first nature" of *Homo sapiens* was also the emergence of *Homo faber*, man the maker; how experience can give us a second nature if we persist at it, open ourselves up to it, and act on it. The culture that epic envisions, either in its triumph or its tragic defeat, is a second nature.

Wise and Foolish

One good way of defining the purpose of epic is that it is to imbue wisdom. It is a wisdom that comes from an intuitive and symbolic knowledge of how we became human in the first place. With that knowledge—acquired in the bones, so to speak, by our unconscious inner mimicry of the actions of the characters—we learn how to avoid the twin traps of being hoisted back up into our animality and leaving behind our animality altogether. We learn of the unavoidable stresses and breaks that come along with the human kinship system, with the formation of communities larger than the troop of kin, with the making of cities, with the encounter with divine forces, with the opening up of the future that happens when action is attempted. And we reflect, consciously or unconsciously, on the immortality that attends the participation in a good story.

Not that epic is merely didactic; indeed, epic's method, the grand narrative, is a splendid invention, since without actually teaching us it persuades us to teach ourselves. Being told the mere facts is tiresome, and being told how we should morally behave is offensive. The acquisition of wisdom by following a story is actually pleasurable, where there is no explicit reflection upon ourselves, the disasters that result from unwisdom are fictional, and we can in the privacy of our own minds recognize the attractions of good behavior. Of course we should not be knocked on the head with "good examples"—it is important that the hero encounter the same flaws and weaknesses in himself, and make the same mistakes, that we do (though of course on a much larger scale). But the trick of epic is not just to instruct by delighting, as Philip Sidney had it, but to delight by instructing.

It may seem that this definition of the purpose of epic begs the question, what is wisdom? The point here is that wisdom is what epic imbues. Our earliest conceptions of wisdom derive from narratives; it is no coincidence that Greek philosophers, Plato especially, referred to Homer when trying to explain some virtue or concept, that Vedic wisdom literature illustrates its ideas by means of the *Mahabharata*,[12] that Biblical wisdom theory emerges from the epic stories of Genesis and Exodus. It is a little beside the point to try to define the precise mixture of cognitive, moral, emotional, psychological, and experiential elements in wisdom, since those concepts themselves came along after the story-based category of wisdom itself, and partly sprang from it.

Folly, though, like the other darker value terms that epic constructs, has its own virtues in the right circumstances. Folly can be magnificent, witness Roland at Roncesvalles. It can be the path to wisdom, witness the education of Parzifal. It can be a necessary place of experience, witness the pranks of Prince Hal with Falstaff. It can be the very making of a hero's name, witness Odysseus' bragging out his real name to Polyphemus, son of Poseidon, upon whose ocean Odysseus must sail. Monkey's folly is also the energy and vitality that makes him the best guardian of the holy pilgrim in *The Journey to the West*. It is the wisest of the Pandavas, Yudhisthira, who foolishly gambles away the kingdom of Hastinapura. Wisdom itself includes some recognition of the impossibility of avoiding folly and of folly's uses when, as human beings, we fall into it yet again.

Sacred and Profane

Epic is very careful to establish and contextualize the experience of sacred space and time, together with their appropriate virtue of holiness, and to provide them with names, ritual symbolism, and a demonstration in action. Epic does so because it is only the sacred, the holy, that can check us in the full kshatriya or samurai pride of animal impulse or spiritual power, that can raise our aspirations beyond those of the mundane given social world, and that can legitimate a city with all its cruel toll upon nature. The city must have temples; the temples must be set apart from quotidian motives; and there must be sacred times, as during a funeral or a sacrifice, when the temple, not the palace, rules.

Epic cultivates the special precincts of sacred space and holy behavior also, paradoxically, to make room for the profane as not necessarily wicked and unholy. In *The Liberation of Jerusalem*, Godfrey of Bouillon is holy partly so that Rinaldo can be profane; in *The Journey to the West*, Tripitaka is holy so that Monkey can be profane; in the *Mahabharata*, the Vedic meditative practice is sacred so that Vyasa's full-blooded stories can be profane. Falstaff's profaneness, and his satire on the holy language of virtue, are necessary when bishops are no less voraciously ambitious than dukes and earls, and prelates are willing tools of state policy. Sacred time's boundaries define profane time's permissible freedoms; profane time's admission of its own profaneness (the word literally means "outside the temple") allows for a place where the whole, the holy, can be contemplated and served.

Sacredness is attained not only by abstention from mundane action that would pollute it, but also by violent action, by pollution itself if it is of the most extreme kind, a *foedus*. The sacred is where meanings come from, where myths are formed, and it is not bound by the rules and grammars of the mundane. Sometimes the only way of breaking the habit of the mundane is through blatant and terrifying violation of the rules. When the Hero Twins of the *Popol Vuh* challenge the Lords of Death to play the ball game, they are violently reenacting the way in which a popular Mayan sport became a dreadful and exhilarating ritual of bloody sacrifice, where the profane was cracked and riven by what would otherwise be a terrible crime into a portal leading to the sacred.[13]

Venerable and Ridiculous

Contrary to its reputation among those who have not read it—and the notions of decorum imposed on it by Augustan neoclassicists!—epic is of all genres the one boldest in its juxtaposition of the venerable and the ridiculous. The mainstream novel is usually too knowing to set up the truly venerable without ironies that deflate and denature it, so the full force and shock of the ridiculous is blunted in the relative absence of its true opposite. In *The Iliad*, Thersites shocks us with his impiety, the grating inappropriateness of his cynical ridicule. Hera's efforts to outflank her husband's plans are ridiculous in a more comic way, as are the amorous antics of Ares, Aphrodite, and Hephaestus in *The Odyssey*. The ways in which both sets of hero twins in the *Popol Vuh* outwit their dim-witted opponents are quite frankly slapstick and practical joking, in the vein of Br'er Rabbit. So too Monkey's tricks and ruses. Cundrie in *Parzifal* is in herself the perfect juxtaposition of the venerable and the ridiculous. The *Mahabharata*'s Vyasa is himself a trickster, again reminiscent of Br'er Rabbit and Coyote in his ingenious narrative jokes: the railroad tunnel the Roadrunner paints on the cliff wall emits a real train to flatten Wiley. Jacob cheats his father with a bit of hairy hide on his arm, Laban plays the bed-trick on Jacob, Rachel ingeniously hides the household ikons she has stolen from Laban.

Epic is so at home in the larger world it inhabits that it has no fear of breaking the solemn illusion, because it is not an illusion. The world of the venerable is venerable because it has included and subsumed the ridiculous. But it does not confuse them with each other either. When Achilles meets Hector, when Jacob wrestles with the angel, when the grail is found, when Arjuna has his great conversation with Krishna, veneration overwhelms us precisely *because* we have been inoculated against barren mockery already, and our sense of the ridiculous has been reschooled into something fertile.

Tragic and Comic

When anthropologists, archeologists, and mythologists study the most fundamental and universal ritual narratives of our species, what they find does not offer a clear distinction between the comic and the tragic. The basic transactions between the human and the natural, the human and the divine, are conducted, as we have seen, in the language and currency of sacrifice, and sacrifice is always both tragic and comic. It is tragic in the need for real bitter loss and waste, certainly. But it is also comic in the huge advantage that the sacrificial commutation allows us, whether through the indulgence of the gods or through our clever human way of dictating the terms and tilting the ballfield when we negotiate with nature in the hunt or the harvest. The deal has a brutal cost, but we come out of it ahead of the game.

By the time works of fiction whose purpose is explicitly to entertain are produced by a civilization, they have already started to separate into genres, the better to advertise to their audience or readers what they can expect. Tragedy and comedy (and satire, eclogue, lyric, history, the ode, the romance, the novel, and so on) have more or less sorted themselves out. Epic, however, if we accept the account of it that our survey suggests, comes somewhere in between the originary myth and the entertaining fiction. Although some epics—the *Heike*, the *Nibelungs*, *The Iliad*, etc.—are more deeply tragic in overall tone, and others—*The Journey to the West, Orlando Furioso, Don Quixote*—more comic, epic encompasses both the comic and the tragic, and could be said to be the place where they are defined and differentiated, to be used as such in later fictions. Epic, then, would be the place where the tragic and the comic are still joined, but have shown their differences and their potential to branch.

Shakespeare knew well that the tragic vision and the comic vision are at the root the same, and that they are strongest when together. Just as in *Hamlet* the comic graveyard scene is the true turning point of the play, and in *Lear* the bitter comedy of the Fool and the grotesque black comedy of the encounter with Poor Tom are the catalysts of enlightenment, so in his Henriad, with its generally comic trajectory, it is the tragic deaths of Hotspur, Falstaff, and Bardolph that drive the moral meaning of the story.

We have already looked at the difference between the heroic fate that cuts its blaze at the edge of the world, ventures beyond, and returns with the spoils, and the destiny that in its heroic insouciance breaks out beyond any possibility of return and is lost. These fates—often associated with the right and wrong choice of woman as mate—are respectively comic and tragic. Life wins, or death does. But in epic each is implicit in the other. In the *Popol Vuh* the hero twins do not escape death—they defeat it by undergoing it. In *The Liberation of Jerusalem*, Argant and Clorinda tragically die but Rinaldo and Godfrey triumph. In the *Song of the Nibelungs* Siegfried is tragically slain, but he has had his heroic glory and his love; Roland falls, but Charlemagne avenges him. Kurukshetra is a victory for one set of heroes, defeat for another. Beowulf dies; Wiglaf survives to tell the tale. Odysseus wins, but at what cost; Patroclus and Hector die, and so will Achilles, but the Greeks win in the end. Aeneas founds his new city, but never ceases to be haunted by the old one.

As in so many things, epic is originary, then—it *is* the origin of the tragic and the comic.

Honesty and Trickery

As the narrative genre *par excellence* epic cannot escape the issue of fiction and truth: in what sense is fiction true, given that the term "fiction" can serve as an antonym for "truth"? Even if epic's fictions are true in some deep sense, the truth it tells is conditioned by craft and imaginative contrivance. Some epics, notably the *Mahabharata*, seize the bull by the horns and openly declare their fictionality. The *Mahabharata* still preserves its authority and life-and-death seriousness, however, because its theology itself asserts that we and the whole world are fictions, dreams in the mind of Vishnu: the fiction *is* the truth, and the contrivances and craft of fiction are of no other substance than the laws of physical reality. If it's all a virtual world, the virtual is the real, one virtual being is genuinely real for another, and owes the other the moral concern we owe to a real being.

The Iliad and *The Odyssey* are not quite so explicit in their acknowledgement of their fictionality, but here again the Trojan War is, when it comes down to it, an entertainment fomented by the gods, and the heroes strive and die to be remembered in song, their lost words reimagined and reinvented by bards, their deeds revised for effect and ornamented with literary meaning.

So when epic settles to its exemplary purpose, to define the basic value-terms of its city's language, it cannot simply declare honesty good and trickery bad. After all, the singer of the tale is using trickery to get us to listen, surreptitiously counting syllables and planning the narrative surprises, manipulating our sympathies and, sometimes, suggesting a contribution to the collection-plate. In the *Three Kingdoms* the teller of the tale, Lo Kuan-Chung, is of the same type of magically insightful scholar as the virtuous and all-wise Imperial adviser, Chuko Liang; both consciously adopt the stance of the Confucian sage who seeks to be the guide of the prince. Often the specious rhetoric of Lo's scholar-emissaries can hardly be distinguished from his own explanations of the political motives of Liu Pei, his anointed First Ruler. And Chuko Liang (like Odysseus, Hunahpu, Temüjin, Sundiata, Jacob, Njal, and so on) is nothing if not tricky.

With our fall into humanity, as epic seems to explain, came theory of mind, the ability to model internally the mental state of another. With that came the ability to model one's own mental state, and to model a mental state not one's own, i.e., to play the actor. Our whole advantage over other animals—and the advantage human survivors have needed to have over their human competitors—was that we were better predictors of the future; and since the future is contingent, to be better creators of plausible alternative scenarios for the future. When language came too, and with it the ability to say *the thing which is not*,[14] the implicit power of fiction became the explicit power to lie and mislead. Further, we could say that the future does truly offer alternative paths, action truly is free, moral responsibility therefore truly becomes real, only to the extent that beings exist that can model alternative futures, alternative realities, and alternative worlds.

It is in this context, of the human need for trickery, that the great honest innocents of epic also get their fair due. Again, the paradox: as Niels Bohr said, the opposite of a correct statement is a false statement. But the opposite of a profound truth may well be another profound truth. To be a hero is not only to be able to represent alternative realities (and thus to be able to lie), but also in a world of lies to see what is true, to step with heroic innocence into the dangerous den of deception. Odysseus lies to get out of Polyphemus' cave, but he naively entered it in the first place, frankly addresses his monstrous host, and naively boasts of his true identity afterwards. Parzifal can only achieve the Grail when he recovers the honest frankness of his humble forest childhood. Cuchulainn, Achilles, and Arjuna are always magnanimous innocents at heart.

The very fact that epic is, with music, the greatest art of time, dictates that both honesty and trickery are necessary (as are in music harmony and counterpoint). Time itself is a paradox: the past is fixed and inescapable, and only an honest and innocent recognition of it can bear fruit; but the future—which will, strangely, become the past—is open and multibranched, and only an inventive, anticipatory, and by definition duplicitous mind can be free to explore its contingencies and outflank rival predictors if necessary.

Beauty and Ugliness

Unlike other pairs of value terms that epic implicitly or explicitly defines in action, epic does unambiguously prefer one side of the antinomy. No epic has much good to say about ugliness, at least ugliness defined in the epic's own terms. Even badness—as witness such figures as Milton's Satan, Dante's Farinata, Kouyaté's Soumaoru, Kakuichi's Kiyomori, and Lo Kuan-Chung's Ts'ao Ts'ao—can have its dark grandeur.

Perhaps this oddity is because in human terms goodness is not self-sufficient: a good person is someone who serves or symbolizes a greater good, or a loved being, or the people, or the defenseless, or God—but something other than itself. Beauty, however, at its highest, is a goodness that is self-sufficient: in Dante's terms, God is good in himself, is the supreme beauty, and need perform no act of generous creation to prove it; his beauty is enough. Beauty is a kind of goodness that need have no other point than itself—that need not represent or serve something other. The buck of value stops here. Certainly the self-centered kind of beauty is less loved by epic than the kind that is also good and self-giving, but it can be beautiful nonetheless, as Shakespeare understood:

> They that have power to hurt, and will do none,
> That do not do the thing they most do show,
> Who, moving others, are themselves as stone,
> Unmoved, cold, and to temptation slow;
> They rightly do inherit heaven's graces,
> And husband nature's riches from expense;
> They are the lords and owners of their faces,

Others, but stewards of their excellence.
The summer's flower is to the summer sweet,
Though to itself, it only live and die . . .[15]

Thus although all epics admire goodness as defined in their own local terms, they serve a higher master. Even an evil beauty must be acknowledged. Beauty in this sense can be defined as that richness of coherence and internal relations that enables anything to have an identity, to be (though always inadequately) namable, to play a part in the free continuous creation of the future, to be open to further unpredictable emergence.

None of this need imply that epic does not have any use for ugliness. Epic is full of examples of grotesque cruelty, loathsome objects and environments, scenes of unrelieved horror—the massacres of the *Heike*, the brutalities of *The Three Kingdoms'* Ts'ao Ts'ao, the tusks of Cundrie, the dusty feather-choked hell of Ereshkigal, the human head used as a ball in the Mayan ball game, the spectacle of Milton's Sin and Death. But the ugliness is in service to an overarching beauty. The beauty is the greater for the ugliness it has surmounted and subsumed; and it is the beauty of human life itself. Epic is not impious, but it does weld us loyally to life, to this world, and it insists that mortal physical action is significant, valuable, and at its root good. If the divine world is to be desired, it must be because of, not despite, the beauty of this world of time. That beauty will not tolerate a merely ascetic or quietist renunciation of life. Yeats, who was a true scholar of epic, put it well as usual in the self's retort to the soul:

The consecrated blade upon my knees
Is Sato's ancient blade, still as it was,
Still razor-keen, still like a looking-glass
Unspotted by the centuries;
That flowering, silken, old embroidery, torn
From some court-lady's dress and round
The wooden scabbard bound and wound
Can, tattered, still protect, faded adorn.[16]

Contradictions and Choices among Values

Epic, then, creates a multidimensional value space that the hero and we, the readers or audience, must negotiate in our journey through the story. The given geography and history, the facts of the place and culture, do not allow for all positive values to be chosen at once, and

283

to achieve one value must often be to slight some and even violate others. Eschenbach's Gawan can achieve his destiny of love and social acceptance through courtesy, but Parzifal's higher calling to love and holiness requires the sacrifice of court manners. Odysseus must be deceitful to serve a lower but indispensable goal of survival and a higher goal of wisdom. Adam must choose impurity over purity, folly over wisdom, secondness over firstness, if the human race is to acquire the need and destiny of redemption. Tripitaka needs the natural, playful and in some ways despicable Monkey to achieve the sacred, the serious, and the good. Prince Hal must go through the way of the ridiculous, the comic and the profane on his way to the palace of wisdom and the kingly elevation. By so setting these values in play epic instructs us as to what those values are and how they can shape action and give it plan and efficacy.

Notes

1. E.g., W. D. Ross, *The Right and the Good* (Oxford: Oxford University Press, 2002), first published in 1930.
2. See J. T. Fraser's important essay "Out of Plato's Cave: The Natural History of Time," *Kenyon Review* (Winter 1980) and reprinted in various other venues.
3. R. L. Gregory, ed. *The Oxford Companion to the Mind* (Oxford: Oxford University Press, 1978), 383.
4. E.g., Parvis Emad, *On the Way to Heidegger's Contributions to Philosophy*, (Madison, WI: University of Wisconsin Press, 2007), 36.
5. See: "*Foedera*": *A Study in Roman Poetics and Society* by Gladhill, Charles William, PhD, dissertation, Stanford University, 2008.
6. W. B. Yeats: "A Prayer for my Daughter."
7. W. B. Yeats: "A Dialogue of Self and Soul."
8. *Purity and Danger: An Analysis of the Concepts of Pollution and Taboo* (London: Routledge Classics, 2002).
9. *Areopagitica. A Speech for the Liberty of Unlicensed Printing to the Parliament of England.* Merritt Y. Hughes, ed. *John Milton: Complete Poems and Major Prose* (New York: Odyssey, 1957), 716–49.
10. T. S. Eliot: *The Wasteland*, part 3, "The Burial of the Dead." *Selected Poems* (New York: Harbrace, 1964).
11. Victor W. Turner, *From Ritual to Theater: The Human Seriousness of Play* (New York: PAJ Publications, 2001).
12. "Veda" is itself a Sanskrit cognate of wit, wise, wizard, wisdom. "History" and "story" come from a Greek cognate, "histor," from the same root, "weid" in Indo-European. A "histor" is a wise man who is both a historian and a prophet. The whole set of words based on "vid," "vision" also comes from the same root; the wise man is a seer, a visionary, a prophet. See the *American Heritage Dictionary*.

13. New archeological research has turned up many modest local ballcourts throughout the Mayan cultural world, dating to as far back as 2,900 years ago, before the rise of the great metropolitan centers of elite religious ritual. The ball game most likely began as a commoners' pastime, a "profane" activity. At some point it must have been adopted by the priest-aristocrats as a sacred and sacrificial activity. See Andrew Lawler: "Playing Politics or Just a Game" 30 April 2010 Vol. 328 *SCIENCE* www.sciencemag.org.

14. The Houyhnhnms' term for a lie in Book IV of Jonathan Swift's *Gulliver's Travels* (New York: Penguin, 2003).

15. Sonnet 94.

16. "A Dialogue of Self and Soul". W. B. Yeats and M. L. Rosenthal, ed., *Selected Poems and Two Plays of William Butler Yeats* (London: Macmillan, 1962), 130.

11

A New Medium of Communication

From Mute to Spoken

Epic seems to be evoked especially when a new system of recording and retrieving information has just emerged in or been adopted in a culture, or when its implications have suddenly crossed a threshold of crisis.

We have already considered the way in which epic includes and subsumes myth. We have seen how epic does two apparently contradictory things: it steps out into a "meta" position to look back and tell the story of how myths themselves originated, and it excavates into myth to find the elements that, because they truly represent our common human evolutionary history, can gain the assent of the different phyla within a city.

Epic consciously bestrides the boundary between prehistory and history, situating itself imaginatively where we as a species first began to speak; epic is a theory of the origins of language, so to speak. All of those epics that include a creation myth and trace the hero's relationship with or descent from that myth must explicitly encounter the profound problem of naming and even indicating, so lucidly explicated by C. S. Peirce and linguistic philosophers like Wittgenstein and Quine.[1] How can we establish what "refer" means without using reference? How does one point at the pointing activity in order to single it out to name it and give a definition of its meaning? We know that babies and even dogs pick up the use of names without much difficulty, but how?

Epic's answer, in narrative terms, is story itself: action and its consequences, and the internal modeling of action and its consequences, as superimposed onto the motivational landscape of our biologically inherited moral sentiments. We develop the act and concept of naming by action in a field of feeling. Peirce's pragmatic argument for the emergence of icon, index, and symbol is not so different, and Wittgenstein's practical context-framed language games are not so different either. "The meaning of a word is its use in the language," said Wittgenstein; in other words, if you want to know what a word *really* means, don't look for its definition but for its use. The most signal action is sacrifice, which thematizes the cost of any assertion of initiative in a world that both resists us and gives us purchase. Sacrifice itself, and the profit gained by it, is enough, as we have seen, to constitute a powerful engine for the production of meaning and the emergence of the conventional out of the ad hoc—the arbitrary (and hence potentially free) out of the necessity of the moment. Epic is deeply interested in the originating sacrifices. Certainly by the time epic becomes possible—as I will argue, when written records emerge—the earlier moment when myths sprang into being, together with human language itself, was long past. Epic must reconstruct it through the very stories and oral traditions that mythic/sacrificial action originated.

Even when epic does not explicitly contain and integrate a creation myth, it finds a way to recover the awesome and terrifying atrocity of origins, the *foedus*, by other means. One of the reasons war is so large a topic of epic, especially of those epics that do not include a creation myth, is that war is literally the place where we return, as Hobbes put it, to a "state of nature," where the originary conditions are reproduced. War is a time machine that can transport us back to the origins of language, myth, and sacrifice even if the oral history of creation is lost, theologically tamper-proof, or too cumbersome for the narrative flow of the hero's story. The ghastly barbarism of parts of the *Three Kingdoms, El Cid*, the *Heike*, and even the *Henriad* reenacts the need for mediating ritual, games that play violence rather than actually do it, meanings that relieve the posttraumatic disorder, rule-making and wall-building that moderate or at least justify the carnage.

Thus epic recovers imaginatively the first great "media revolution" of our species: the moment when myth itself emerged as the first form of human language, that is, language not emulated by the communications of other animals. Epic paints the course of the hunt on the cave wall and so transforms it into a virtual reality. Epic celebrates the birth of the collective intelligence of a human language.

New Age dreamers postulate the imminent coming of the Singularity—the point where the Moore's Law exponential increase of the human world's stock of information and information processing capacity goes vertical vis-à-vis the specious present of the system, where the Internet becomes aware of itself as a collective sentient brain and starts to reprogram itself into greater intelligence and self-knowledge, and human beings upload their minds into this vast virtual reality. It could be argued that the Singularity has in fact already happened, perhaps as much as 190,000 years ago. It happened when humans first began to speak; language was the engine of the super-intelligence's computations, each human being a self-programming neuron, each human linguistic connection a differentially weightable synapse, each conversation a neuronal discharge.

At that point the abstract world of meanings began, the game of story-hypotheses and predictive scenarios; the language began to think and reprogram itself by means of grammatical, metaphorical, phonological, and etymological innovations; the self-organizing forms and attractors that emerged in this massive nonlinear system of exchanges were named as persons, spirits, and gods. The physical world of nature was uploaded into the virtuality of the language (which of course included images, music, dance, stories, etc.) by means of trade and advancing technology; the individual persons that emerged from the process were in turn uploaded into the immortal game by ritual enactment of funeral and invocation, by physical monuments, and by commemorative stories.

Though epic imaginatively harkens back to the emergence of language itself, it actually begins to be produced, as we have seen, when a culture has achieved and maintained a city or its equivalent in terms of a critical mass of continuous communication among persons. A tradition of oral poetry emerges, relying on the mnemonic devices described by Albert Lord, Milman Parry, and other researchers,[2] and professional bards trained by long apprenticeship under their elders begin inventively to link the legends, stories, and myths together into coherent wholes. Like Homer, Kakuichi, and Vyasa, such professionals are often peripatetic, and travel from one venue to another to tell their tales. In so doing they are both limited by the extent of the linguistic community they serve and, surely, among the factors that expanded and preserved that community against linguistic drift. They could create a "virtual city" even where settlements were spread out over a wide area—Greece *was* where people had heard of the siege of Troy, Iceland *was* the family stories of the great lineages. The first wave of epics can be associated with this media revolution.

From Oral to Written

The "city-equivalent" critical mass eventually demands and usually gets some form of writing, whether that of the divinatory "oracle-bones" and tortoise shell inscriptions of the Chinese, the calendrical and astronomical signs of the Mesoamericans, the Qipu knottings of the Incas, the burnt clay cuneiform of the Mesopotamians, the heiro-glyphics and narrative wall-paintings of the Egyptians, or the alphabets of the Hittites, Phoenicians, and many other cultures.

The oral stories start to be written down. Although the medium is not the message, it can make a big difference. Epic goes from being almost totally a temporal art—a string of spoken or chanted words, gestures, musical notes in time—to being a significantly spatial art—a set of tablets or scrolls, a manuscript book. Epic also becomes a partly timeless art, in the sense that when it is not being performed it exists as an unchanging record and a text that can be revised at leisure without loss of the original. It stands still for analysis and improvement; the parts of it can be compared side by side. Subtleties of proportion, parallelism, repetition, and architectonics can be built in that might be beyond the oral storyteller, who may alter the performance every time for reasons of length, context, mood, and memory. Perfection can be aimed at, the ideal and archetypal version of the story (that can still be cut or revised ad hoc for performance): we see that perfection in the works of Homer especially.

Epics composed and published in manuscript form (as opposed to composed and performed orally, or written to be published in print) include such works as Genesis and Exodus (c. 950–850 BC), the *Shahnameh* (1010 AD), and many other Asian epics; *The Aeneid* (19 BC), *The Song of Roland* (c. 1155), *Parzifal* (c. 1210), *Njal's Saga* (c. 1300), and *The Divine Comedy* (c. 1330).

The advantages of the manuscript text are still not much affected by its potential disadvantages. Performance is still oral; the infinite subtleties of the live human voice have not been sacrificed. Most people in such a society still cannot read, since manuscripts would be rare and expensive. The text would be at most a reminder for an off-book performance, not the work of art itself. Perhaps, as Plato suspected, the powers of memory might be blunted by ease and laziness; but we know today of oral narrative poetry traditions coexisting vigorously, with high levels of expertise, side by side with plentiful texts, as in Balkan folk poetry and American "Country and Western" and "Mountain" music. In *Gilgamesh*, the oldest epic of all, the storyteller is already explicitly referring his audience to the written record that is inscribed on the stone or brick. The *Popol Vuh*, as Tedlock has pointed out, likewise refers its hearers to pictorial representations that incorporate, from early times, glyphs and ideograms.

Indeed, as far as the evidence goes, we do not need to assume that epic ever emerged in a culture before the invention of some kind of medium of literacy, at least among the elites. The "tipping point" for the transition from orality to literacy is not discernibly later than the "tipping point" from myths, tales, and other disconnected stories to organized and extended epic. The curious way in which the *Gilgamesh* poet communicates with us may usefully illuminate the relationship between oral memory and written text. The narrator assumes the role of a docent, orally explaining by memory assisted by verse the mythic history of the wall of Uruk and its builder to a live audience, but referring for authority to the stone on which Gilgamesh himself is said to have inscribed the story. So what we got when we unearthed the tablets on which the poem was written, was the written (dictated) version of the storyteller's oral expatiation on the city walls using as a source the original inscription by its hero. Gilgamesh, presumably hundreds of years before, had taken the same docent role in showing off the walls of Uruk to Urshanabi the ferryman, who had accompanied the hero back to his home city. Presumably it is Gilgamesh's oral account to Urshanabi that is inscribed on the stone. So what we read is the docent/translator's written version of the narrator's oral version of the written version of Gilgamesh's oral explanation to the Ferryman of his adventures, including versions of the Flood story, for instance, that Gilgamesh knows from older oral or written versions of it.

When Tedlock got his contemporary Mayan informant Andrés Xiloj to explain the *Popol Vuh* to him, the same complex scene was being acted out.[3] Xiloj is acting as docent to Tedlock; Tedlock and Xiloj reenact the scribe–oral docent relationship between Francisco Ximénez and his own Mayan informant, who are in turn echoing the form in which the original version was passed down from the Quiché lords to their successors.

The Nyanga oral poet Rureke enters into a similar dialogue with Daniel Biebuyck, his anthropologist scribe, in Biebuyck's fascinating edition of the *Mwindo Epic*. Rureke mocks his scholarly and literate partner for his literalism, his pedantry, his demand for consistency, and his ignorance of the oral world. But he also begs him to use his new technology and technique to broadcast the great Nyanga story to the world, that it not be lost. Perhaps in this encounter we may see something of what must have happened when *The Iliad* was first written down, whether dictated by the final oral synthesizer of the poem, or by some gifted performer of it.

The form in which epic is passed back and forth between written text and oral performance itself suggests profound implications about how we became human. The paradox of individual active mortality and cultural passive immortality is right there in the relationship of performance and text. Performance dies upon the air but can push the story onward and upward into richer domains of universality, reflexiveness, and reference; text acts as the ratchet that preserves what is gained while mourning and celebrating the heroic acts of discovery and performance that made those gains. Perhaps we have here the cultural version of biological evolution, which similarly iterates the cycle of mutation (artistic originality), selection (audience response to live performance), and genetic inheritance, inscription in the genome (the ratchet of tradition). Whenever there is a change in the communicating and recording medium, this evolutionary feedback cycle attains a new level of reflexivity and self-reference.

Are epic poets in an age of literacy, like Milton and Kakuichi, necessarily blind (literally or metaphorically), so as to reignite this fertile evolutionary cycle? Might not this reflection suggest that one of the advantages of dictated text is that the scribe—like Milton's daughters—can read back to the poet what he has composed, so that the poet can become the audience for the oral performance of his own work, and so be able to revise and perfect it? Thus the poet could become the scribe, the scribe the performer. Vyasa, we may recall, is a member of the audience for Vaisampayana's performance of Vyasa's own *Mahabharata*. Further, if the scribe is, as is likely for a disciple and trainee, younger than the poet, the dark and beautiful shadow in the relationship is that the scribe will outlive his master and become his master's voice. A large part of our human evolutionary history as cultural beings is bound up in this relationship.

From Written to Printed

With a new medium, the old issues arise in a new way. The birth of myth out of muteness can itself be identified with the dawning of our consciousness of our own personal death and with the perception of the continuity of consciousness as itself a great mystery. With the origin of writing comes the pathos of reading words written by a dead hand, and words spoken by the dead re-performed by the living. Biological immortality in the form of offspring and a lineage—the second-best kind of immortality—is supplemented by the written record, the third-best kind of immortality, and the knowledge of one's actions becoming structures, part of an ongoing city.

Print also reawakens the ancient questions. Now the written record takes on the generative qualities of biological reproduction; like DNA, the written text can reproduce by being reprinted. It takes on a life of its own, not limited by the uniqueness of the manuscript. To be propagated it need not be performed out loud in a collective setting as with a purely oral recitation, but can be mechanically multiplied and then personally performed in the inner theater of a thousand readers' minds. The habit of silent reading at leisure, once known as the special gift of such master-scholars as Augustine, becomes the common skill of the citizen and the tool of his participation in the city's politics and future direction. The inner self, as R. Patton Howell has observed, is changed and reshaped by the possession of this inner text-based theater.[4] The survival of the text is much more reliable; its integrity as a pattern of words is more robust and accurate in detail; it rises from the ashes of every burned book but the last.

So a new wave of epics arises, to both re-explain the ancient anxieties and exploit the huge artistic opportunities offered by the medium. In China, for instance, *The Three Kingdoms*, a printed book (1552, revised and abridged c. 1660) based on old manuscript chronicles, reminds all Chinese readers of the appalling cost and mysterious value of Chinese national unity, and reconciles sectional loyalty with the solidarity of all those who use the Chinese characters. The *wen*, the written word, in which the epic is printed, implies a humanism and shared inner life that are in turn the birthplace of a compassion that transcends kin and home.

In Europe, the print publication of the 1455 Gutenberg Bible, Virgil's *Aeneid*, early printed vernacular translations of Homer, and the 1472 print publication of Dante's *Divine Comedy* initiated a popular craze for printed verse or prose narrative in the expanding literate population. Such works include Caxton's edition of Malory's *Morte D'Arthur* (1485), Camoens' *The Lusiads* (1572), Tasso's *The Liberation of Jerusalem* (1581), Spenser's *The Faerie Queene* (1590), Cervantes' *Don Quixote*

(1605–1615), Miklós Zrinyi's *The Peril of Sziget* (1651), and Milton's *Paradise Lost* (1668). Poets of other nations, seeing epic's astonishing unifying and identifying power for a national language and identity, followed with the *Kalevala* (1835), *Moby Dick* (1851), *Hiawatha* (1855), *Lacplesis* (1857–1861), *Martín Fierro* (1872), and *Aniara* (1956).

The printed epic brings with it a new set of opportunities and constraints that can tempt, limit, or liberate the author. One is the everyday ability of the author to speak directly, one-on-one, with the common reader in the communion of private silent reading. When epics exist only in manuscript, their audience is usually confined to two groups: literate scholars who have themselves been behind the scenes of literary composition, and who in closeted reading are the writer's colleagues; and illiterate listeners to publicly recited performances who are naïve about the inner workings of written composition, and perhaps easily impressed by the miracle of the rune or the glyph. When printed books (and thus literacy) are widespread, the normal contact of writer and reader becomes individual and private. Thus the writer loses some of the charisma of the lettered elite and the public event. The alphabetic or ideographic signs become commonplace, and have less inherent magic in themselves. But they also become more official, more associated with political authority, because of the filters of technological sophistication, the capital expense and civic dependency of the print shop, aristocratic patronage and subscription, church and state censorship and approval, and dictionaries. The ordinary reader is more likely to compare herself with the writer and wonder about the writer's political purpose and private ulterior motives, perhaps breaking the spell; but at the same time a more personal and empathic bond can be made between the reader and the hero (and even the reader and writer).

Wordsworth especially exploits this feature of the printed book, inviting personal friendship with the reader. Eliot and Pound (in *The Waste Land* and the *Cantos*) subvert or defy it by dazzling the reader with foreign vocabularies and orthographies, and by concealing their personal presence with incomplete syntax, odd diction, a variety of personae, a cognitively reader-hostile environment, and other devices. The charisma of the oracle is achieved, however, at a cost: the loss of the narrative connectivity that can carry a rich freight of imagery without exhausting the reader with hypothesizing about what is really going on.

The advantage of print is that it is fixed and thus relatively immortal. But it loses the immediate corrigibility of the oral presentation, which, like the stand-up comic's routine or the blue grass singer's set, can be changed with every performance according to the audience's reaction. So there is much less opportunity for on the job training in poetic technique, product testing, and refinement by continuous quality control, and a much greater danger that the writer will become self-indulgent, ride personal hobbyhorses, go on too long, and "flame," as they say in the Internet. Even the handwritten text offers the opportunity for revision every time a new copy is produced. But once a book gets into print its flaws tend to survive. Worse still, if the author repents of what he has written and publishes a second or third edition with important changes, as did Tasso and Wordsworth, he may very well end up blunting the freshness and vitality of the first version in the process, confusing the readership about which is the right version, and damaging the canonicity of the work as a whole. Thus the printed epic requires great discipline on the part of the author, and the observance of conventions, even inessential ones like in medias res, the division into "books," allusion to previous epics, and strict poetic form, becomes a real aid and control.

Print may resemble DNA in its power to reproduce itself. But unlike DNA (and unlike an oral performance tradition or even a recopied manuscript lineage) it cannot easily mutate and adapt. A heavily revised second edition of an epic poem does not so much resemble the adaptation of an organism to its environment as a genetic chimera produced by a bioengineer in a laboratory. It may be that the evolutionary advantages of the older means of transmission can be recovered by the freedoms and ample recoverable memory offered by the new media.

With print came the increasing dominance of prose over verse as the "natural" medium of storytelling. The emergence of prose can inspire or enable epics like *Don Quixote*, *The Three Kingdoms*, and *Moby Dick*, but it also presents a profound problem, which we must address in the final chapter. Printed prose is an excellent substitute for memory, an externalizing, a mechanizing of memory, a way of safely forgetting something while keeping it at hand. But epic in some way purports to embody and regenerate the internal memory and consciousness of the human race, and so far poetic verse is the best way we have found to linguistically embed a story in memory.

From Print to New Media

This book must, for the sake of coherence and relative brevity, limit itself to the verbal media. But it would be a pity to neglect the present-day implications of our observation that a wave of epics tends to follow each new breakthrough in the fundamental media of human expression and commemoration. As noted in the Introduction, epic is definitely back, in the world of youth culture. Perhaps we can already see the cultural shift that McLuhan prophesied, though it is already clear that the shift is not what he expected.

Critics of modernity as diverse as Matthew Arnold, Oswald Spengler, Theodor Adorno, and Jean Baudrillard bemoaned the disenchantment of the world—a disenchantment they regarded as a fact that, for the sake of intellectual integrity, it was necessary to acknowledge. The world is not inhabited by spirits, they said, nor even by the agents of a supernatural deity. But what seemed at the time the cutting edge of a new world was perhaps the last gasp of an old Enlightenment-period mistake. The mistake was made on good grounds: Descartes' identification of the mystery of self-consciousness as radically different from physical matter and Newton's demonstration that some parts of the universe at least were absolutely and uniquely determined by their own physical characteristics. If the universe was a machine running along the iron rails of mathematical physics, there was no room in it for spirits (and the enchantments they created by exercising their own will and caprice). The rational sacrifice required for the acknowledgement of this view as fact—required by intellectual honor—included, for instance, the need to regard animals as automata, human consciousness as an entirely alien phenomenon in the physical universe, value and meaning as illusions, and the future as eternally fixed.

In other words, the world was exactly like a book—an odd coincidence, given that the book at that time was the absolutely dominant medium of knowledge. A book is a fixed text whose physical existence is the result of mechanical processes, and whose meaning is alien and independent of its material composition. At any point in the reading of a book, the whole of its future already lies present in the pages yet to be read. The human consciousness of the reader hangs over it, not embodied in the dry pages. The meaning must be imputed to the pages by the reader, but is not inherent in them—one could burn the book and buy another copy without altering its meaning. Is it disingenuous to suggest that perhaps the model of knowledge storage had totally biased the knowledge itself—that the neat coincidence of worldview and information technology was no coincidence at all? What if the world is in many ways not like a book?

For the "facts" on which the modern successors of the Enlightenment based their bleak, courageous view of things have turned out to be simply false. The picture given by science since about World War II turns those facts upside down. Human self-consciousness is demonstrably generated by neurophysiological processes not much different from those of animals. We know that matter can think, because we can design machines that do so, at least on a level equivalent to the nervous systems of sea-slugs and the ganglia in our own brains that handle simple reflexes. Moreover, from quantum theory through chemical catalytic theory through evolutionary ecology through embryology through complexity theory, simple one-way one-result cause and effect has been shown to be rather rare in the universe, and achievable only under the equivalent of strictly controlled laboratory conditions (and in the quantum realm, not even then). Though all events have causes, the same causes can have many different effects, some coexisting with each other, others forever eliminating certain once possible trains of consequences. The world is made largely of autonomous self-organizing dynamical systems that regulate themselves by frankly computational means, combined with the exigencies of adaptation to an environment that they, in turn, can manipulate. Among those systems are ecosystems, animals and humans, which are clearly spirits in the full sense of the word, without requiring any supernatural dimension to provide them a home. So the world, despite our gloomy nineteenth-century impression of it, is not dead but alive, not determined but free, not a place in which we are aliens but our home, not populated by mechanisms so much as by organisms, not devoid of intentions but full of them. It is reenchanted. Our own little computational devices, our animal friends, and our own human companions, are all natural spirits.

Or so the younger generations evidently believe. Are they too deceived by the medium of the knowledge that they know—the live corrigible immaterial electronic multimedia environment in which we now live? Have they—and now increasingly we who were born before the end of World War II—simply exchanged one set of blinkers for another?

It would perhaps be more charitable to say that the blinkers of the printed book, though blinkers indeed if used as such, were also a valuable tool, an instrument for concentrating on and seeing a certain real and important aspect of the universe—basically classical mechanics and its implications. They thus isolated for us those parts of the world that we could put to work for us in making the machines that have been such an enormous and unprecedented boon to our species. That the blinkers could, used in this way, exclude other aspects of the universe (which the new electronic and bioelectronic information technology may now be better at handling) was probably necessary at the time so that scientists would not be distracted by the apparent mess of everything outside their tunnel vision. But when deterministic dialectical materialism in its various forms of communism, nazism, fascism, social Darwinism, racism, vulgar Freudianism, behaviorism, sexism, and so on proclaimed its authority over human life, something had to stop.

By extending the term "dialectical materialism," in this way I am underlining the pervasive scope of the assumption that the world is a foregone conclusion, that matter is all that exists, that causality operates uniquely and only from the bottom up and from the past to the future, that personal freedom is an illusion, that the book of the world is already published. Whether one's economic class, one's ethnic inheritance, the fitness of one's genes, one's race, one's early childhood experience, one's operant conditioning, or one's gender is seen as the sole cause of one's behavior and the determinant of value, the radical limiting of the human horizon is the same. Epic has always been the breaker of that horizon. As I put it in my *Genesis: An Epic Poem*:

> Would you prefer a novel, then? No space-travel,
> No adolescent fantasy, no risk
> Of obsolescence by the brute event?
> What would you pay? The characters must be
> What you would call believable; their acts
> Driven by some automatism you
> Can recognize, and being pictured, can
> Condone as human, psychological.
> How we twist, struggle, scrabble at the earth,
> Take any path that we might not be free.
> Freedom terrifies us. To be free
> Is to make, to love, to make all things new.
> Praise adolescence for at least the grace
> To fantasize the unbelievable,
> To row upstream against psychology,
> To play against our probability.[5]

The new media perhaps afford us a way to reclaim the epic mission as at the junctures of utterance and speech, speech and writing, writing and print. But need a book act, as I have suggested, as a set of blinkers? Not necessarily. To answer this question in a different way we might need to profoundly rethink many of our modernist and postmodernist preconceptions. What made books into a limitation on the nature of knowledge was a sort of idolatry of the form of the book itself: an insistence that its message conform to its medium, that it "should not mean but be," as Archibald MacLeish said of poetry.[6] If a novel's medium is psychological probability, ratified as psychological determinism by its preset and necessarily plausible denouement, its characters become psychological automata. "No ideas but in things," W. C. Williams' watchword,[7] could easily become "no motives for action but in things," "no action," no story. Edgar Allan Poe had already dismissed narrative poetry as essentially unpoetic. Yet as this study has argued, it is story that opens up the world, that truly represents the world as branchy, free, and full of surprises.

It was not the book as such that limited our purview but the idea that the material means of production should determine the meaning of an object. About the turn of the twentieth century the "serious" novel began to change from a window through which one could see the story—or even a door by which one entered it—into an object in itself. It was an object crusted with fine prose and wonderful verbal tricks, foregrounding its narrative innovations and critical sophistication, in which the plot itself was increasingly perceived as a scaffold for psychological or sociological erudition, political advocacy, or elaborate symbolic fireworks. As the author's freedom to elaborate the means of description increased, the autonomy of his or her characters invisibly diminished. And eventually the plot virtually disappeared under its rococo ornamentation. The portal into the story world—where anything can happen—became choked and impassable, and we were left with the book as a work of art, a collector's item, a connoisseur's pleasure, a critic's meat, a statement of the most recent and "novel" frame of reference and model for fashionable behavior.[8]

This development was paralleled in the visual arts by, for instance, Clement Greenberg, who praised modernist art for its flatness and its rejection of representation and narrative "kitsch."[9] It was paralleled in music by Schoenberg's rejection of melody (the narrativity of music), in drama by Brecht's alienation effect, in architecture by Bauhaus, "form follows function" and the increasing abstraction, dehumanization, and "denarrativizing" of the built environment. In each case, a sort of literalized existentialism—"existence precedes essence"—ended up fetishizing the medium of the artwork's production and confining its possible realm of meaning to what is socially acceptable—acceptable, of course, in the most correct, progressive, and "transgressive" social circles. Popular arts like rock and roll, science fiction, commercial graphics, and film blithely went on making stories notwithstanding. In any case, the book, which had been a portal to epic in the hands of a Tasso, a Lo Kuan-chung, a Milton, a Melville, could ossify into an obstacle if one took its form, as a model of a deterministic universe, too seriously. Nietzsche said: the spirit killeth, but the letter giveth life. St. Paul said: the letter killeth, but the spirit giveth life. If epic is to be believed, Paul was right.

Is there still a place for the epic that is also a book? This writer obviously believes that there is, having voted with his feet. But such a book must be wrested away from modernist and postmodernist aesthetics and must transcend its physical medium as a piece of spatialized and frozen fictional time. The medium is not the message, at least not in a crude literal sense.[10] Epic needs to recover its orality, its status as a real performance, its independence of the metaphysics of the book form. Like *Gilgamesh*, *The Divine Comedy*, the *Mahabharata*, and the *Popol Vuh* it can also be a text: but it is a text that the cicerone and audience walk through in a new way each time, taking the new branches of meaning and implication that the epic form allows and that this book has attempted to demonstrate. Can the new media fulfill these epic functions, while still preserving epic's mnemonic power? Again, we must postpone this issue to the last chapter.

Unification and Fixing of the National Language

As we have seen, epic can be triggered by and trigger new opportunities in the technology of the word. That technology can often mean a much greater dissemination and democratization of the foundational stories. It is thus no coincidence that epics often emerge precisely at the point where the establishment of a canonical national language can become possible, in which such things as spelling, grammar, and pronunciation divide themselves up into standard and dialect forms. As Plato remarks again and again in the Dialogues, Homer is not only a user of the Greek language but a maker of it. The same could be said of the way *The Aeneid* established a canonical Latin, of Dante's radical founding of the Florentine dialect as the official Italian language, of Camoens' distinctly unSpanish Portuguese, of the role of Shakespeare and Milton in establishing modern English on a London model, and so on. *Moby Dick* has played an analogous role in the United States, together with the dialect of the American epic Western.

A national poetry, with its flagship epics, may even have kept some languages alive that might otherwise have disappeared. This assertion could be argued in such cases as Hebrew, Hungarian, Armenian, Albanian, Mayan, Irish, Kurdish, and Serbian, where foreign overlords made determined efforts to replace the native tongue with their own. Without *Beowulf* and the revival of English as a heroic literary language by Chaucer and the Gawaine poet, might not English have gone the way of Gaelic and Welsh, and might we not now be speaking a dialect of Norman French? Would Katharevousa and modern Hebrew have become the official languages of Greece and Israel without the memory of their ancient epics?

But before we give too much credit to the uniqueness of national identity—with epic's role being, in Eliot's and Mallarmé's words, to purify the dialect of the tribe—some cautions are in order. Often, paradoxically, the epic composer needs to go to foreigners to find a template upon which to reorganize and grow his native language. It is often remarked that Milton refounded English grammar on Latin; less often is it observed that Shakespeare had already done so, though less obtrusively. There are Latinate elements in the national epics of Hungary and Lithuania, and Toltec Nahuatl elements in the *Popol Vuh*.[11] Dante went to Virgil's Latin; Virgil himself took Greek as his model. Kakuichi and the other *biwa hoshi* went to Mandarin Chinese for their grand template, and the Tamil poets went to Vedic Sanskrit. Melville famously echoes Milton and Shakespeare even as he forges an American classical dialect.

In taking this course epic composers are not merely borrowing the prestige of elder cultures or choosing the easy path of imitation over invention. The point is that the older language is already fixed (or even dead), and thus can serve as a firm foundation; and more important still, the appeal to a universally respected arbiter of correctness can overrule the factional loyalties of regional dialects within the poet's home language. The poet can claim to be disinterested even as he subtly weds his own dialect to the canonical grandeur of the elder tongue.

The language-building and language-standardizing project of the epic poet is, I believe, universal. Often it is quite explicit, as in the *Popol Vuh*:

> This is the beginning of the ancient word, here in this place called Quiché. Here we shall inscribe, we shall implant the Ancient Word, the potential and source for everything done in the citadel of Quiché, in the nation of the Quiché people.
> (Tedlock, 63)

Or in *Paradise Lost*:

> Sing heavenly muse, that on the secret top
> Of Oreb, or of Sinai, didst inspire
> That shepherd, who first taught the chosen seed,
> In the beginning how the heavens and earth
> Rose out of chaos: Or if Sion hill
> Delight thee more, and Siloa's brook that flowed
> Fast by the oracle of God; I thence
> Invoke thy aid to my adventurous song,
> That with no middle flight intends to soar
> Above the Aonian mount, while it pursues
> Things unattempted yet in prose or rhyme.[12]

Milton here seeks the aid of Moses and David, and the Hebrew language they spoke, though his greater linguistic debt is to pagan Rome. But the language-building ambition is quite clear. The Malinese griot puts it this way:

> . . . we are vessels of speech, we are the repositories which harbour secrets many centuries old. The art of eloquence has no secrets from us; without us the names of kings would vanish into oblivion, we are the memory of mankind; by the spoken word we bring to life the deeds and exploits of kings for younger generations.[13]

Economic Changes in the Media of Exchange

Another kind of communication is economic. The Austrian economists have shown us that the market, with its language of pricing, is a mode of discovery, of knowledge, and of the communication of knowledge. The Romans were wise when they made Mercury (the root of words like "mercantile," "commerce," "merchant," and "market" itself) not only the god of messages but also the god of merchants.

Any history of the emergence of the human species would necessarily include as central the elaboration of gift exchange and barter, the rise of local currencies, the consolidation of currencies into gold and silver, the birth of written or inscribed financial instruments including paper money, and the explosion of electronic and virtual forms of currency. Epic, as argued here, is the inner history of the emergence of the human race, and as such it is deeply interested in the origins and conflicts of these types of exchange.

This remark is not to be taken as the fairly standard "Theory" assertion that literature simply reflects the economic infrastructure of its time. We need not insult the intelligence of the epic composers by supposing that they were mere unconscious pawns of the then current discourse of knowledge, money, and power. Because their trade is to cut blazes and make words do new things, they are far less liable to be ideologically controlled than the most perspicacious of critics and theorists, who are necessarily bound to the vocabularies of their academies and professions; far more likely to be questioning the very currency of their own discourse. Nor need we insult the poets' ethics by supposing them to be shills, panderers, or enforcers of the economic interests of the hegemon. The injustice of the latter charge is especially piercing, since if anything is obvious about poets it is that they have always been the exposers of hypocrisy and manipulation, always been the voice of the underdog, always the first to be imprisoned or shot by tyrants and revolutionaries alike. True Thomas is in real danger when he speaks to the King or to the merchant (or even to the "fair ladye" who wants a rich and respectable husband). If anything, the Jeremiahs have almost too much fondness for the pit into which they are usually flung.

The interest of the epic poets in the evolution of economic value is both historical and critical. There is a tantalizing relation of similarity and difference between the meaning of a word and the value of a coin; between naming a thing and stamping a coin with an inscription; between meaning and means.[14] Epic poets can, as did Ezra Pound,[15] go seriously off the rails in their understanding of economics and currency; but their interest in it—no pun intended—is not misplaced. Just as the epic impulse is often renewed when a change in the medium of communication forces a reconsideration of our whole language for understanding the world, so epic often responds brilliantly to a change in the medium of economic exchange and the consequent reevaluation of our whole sense of value itself.

To explore this aspect of epic would take a book in itself. But a few examples of epic's play with the changing means of exchange may indicate the scope of the subject. One of the most striking examples is the Gilgamesh poet's deep interest in the inscription itself, which we have already explored in the context of the storytelling event and the technology of city wall building. Of course the origin of the cuneiform writing in which the poem comes down to us was in early Mesopotamian business contracts:

> Therefore, several major inventions follow each other in time: the cylinder seal is followed by the bulla, and finally the tablet and script appear together, as if one could not come without the other. In parallel with the third invention, writing on the surface of bullae began. . . . These innovations can be credited to the Uruk society considered in its entirety . . . .[16]

The cylinder seal is actually the first use of printing, in the sense of a duplicable sign: a carved stone cylinder was rolled over a clay surface to leave a unique image representing the ownership or authority of the seal owner. The use of the bulla (the same word is used for the Papal Bull as from the shepherd of the Christian flock) is exceptionally interesting. A contract between a landowner and a shepherd was created by placing a number of different shaped calculi or small stones—with different colors representing different types of sheep—into the hollow of a small round clay vessel and then sealing it shut. When the shepherd brings the sheep in from pasture, the two parties break the seal, revealing the exact numbers of the sheep at the outset, and thus any additions or losses to the flock; and so ending the contract. This system was extended to all sorts of merchant and trader contracts. After a time the contract was written on the surface of the bulla with the newly invented cuneiform autograph writing. Later, the tablet itself embodied the meaning of the bulla.[17]

So the tablets of the *Gilgamesh* text would have been necessarily associated in the mind of a reader with the storage and legal exchange of economic value, as if our stories were inscribed on coins or written on banknotes or composed in the form of property deeds. The epic is indeed a contract, even a bank or a treasury. The code of Hammurabi is thus both a formalization of this contract system and a logical analysis of the values implicit in the epic story. Even more radically, the Mesopotamian city was itself built of bricks, sometimes stamped with the city's seal, made of the same material as the bonds of exchange and the record of the great stories. The poets could not have missed the connection—the city is made of books, the bank-books of money; the book we read from is a building-block of a city and a bond in its currency reserve, and by reading the story we are setting the burnt clay bricks of the walls of the city into place and collecting the interest on its municipal bonds.

The Biblical epics themselves take on huge new significance in the light of this association. Noah's ark contains the token animals as a bulla contains the token sheep. Abraham, Isaac, Jacob, Joseph, and Moses are shepherds: Abraham is carrying out a shepherd's contract when he sets out to sacrifice his son on Mount Moriah, and the ram that God gives him instead is the calculus within the bulla, the sign instead of the reality. The son is to the ram as the ram is to the calculus in the bulla. God's mercy is to accept the token of the debt as payment of the debt itself, to commute the penalty for non-payment to the sacrifice of a ram, which he himself has provided. Jacob's contract with Laban is a story of how the landowner might substitute the wrong ewe for the one specified by the calculus inside the bulla. And on Mount Sinai Moses receives two tablets of stone inscribed personally by God using his finger as the stylus, containing the Law. The tablets are broken when the chosen people choose to make a golden calf, and the Law is reinscribed when the covenant is renewed. The ark of the covenant, then, is a portable contract seal between human shepherds and the divine landowner; and the ark, like a bulla, contains the scrolls of the epic of Exodus as Noah's ark contains the seeds of new life on Earth.

Another example of the promise for future scholarship along these lines is the currency crisis during the Heian period in Japan that helped to precipitate the Gempei Wars that the *Heike* describes. The reason why the samurai and the temples had so much power to reduce government to chaos was the *shoen* (manor) system of feudal land tenure, which virtually did away with money as such. In the absence of a government-issued currency, payment for goods and services came to be made in kind—in units of rice, for example, or lengths of silk—so that all economic exchanges became personalized as gifts. The result was the constant danger of misunderstanding and personal affront,[18] the fetishizing of objects of exchange, the substitution of social rank for earned financial wealth, and the ancestral rice field as the foundation of all value.[19] The *Heike* can be seen as a perceptive analysis of the tragic consequences. The *Heike* begins with two bad gifts that epitomize the economic collapse of the Heian period: the gift to the Emperor by

Tadamori, Kiyomori's father, of the Buddhist Tokujojuin Temple, and the Emperor's return gift to Tadamori of a province and of courtier privileges in the Palace, against precedent. The epic ends with the extermination of the Heike clan and the Emperor's direct lineage.

Composed in 1371, and recounting the events of the 1180s, the *Heike* reflects by implication the economic history that followed the triumph of the Minamoto and the reunification of Japan. Under the new regime Japan adopted the Chinese coinage, and an age of prosperity, trade, and technological advance followed. About the time the *Heike* appeared, Japanese coiners began to make imitations of the Chinese Song and Ming coins (which, however, were undervalued compared to the originals).[20] The *Heike* reads in this light as a rich and complex response not only to the tragedy of the civil war but to an epochal change in the means of economic value and exchange. Kakuichi revalues the often brutal, pragmatic, and unscrupulous actions of the poem's protagonists by setting them again and again in the context of the classical Chinese past (as Plutarch elevates his Roman magnates and warlords by pairing them with the classical Greek leaders in the *Lives*).[21] He recognizes sadly and ashamedly that Japan had failed, and had to recover its values by borrowing those of its ancient rival and mentor, China. At the same time, he yearns for a finer, more absolute, more perfect form of honor and commitment than could be found in his own more mercantile and econonomically leveled world of money exchange. And by implication the poem itself becomes a new gold standard, a new repository of value—and remains so in the Japanese imagination, as the epic films of Kurosawa attest.

A similar analysis of the *Popol Vuh* might focus on the curious role of cacao in the poem's intricate symbolism of resurrection.

> At the beginning of Part Three of the *Popol Vuh*, the authors introduce Hun Hunahpu, and his brother Vucub Hunahpu, asking us to drink to the Father of the Hero Twins. Tedlock interprets this as raising a calabash gourd of chocolate, the traditional drink of K'iche' "Masters of Ceremony" *nimchokoj* (possibly from K'iche' *chokola'j*, connoting the gathering of food and drink, specifically cacao, for a banquet). This symbolic drinking from the skull of Hun Hunahpu precedes the story of the origin of the calabash, and the story of Hun Hunahpu, which then unfolds. (Tedlock 1996, 249, 322)[22]

The point here is that the cacao bean was an important form of currency throughout the Maya lands.[23] So when the epic characterizes itself as a toast to the memory of the first hero, One Hunahpu, the vessel—the calabash—is his skull, and the drink is the unit of Mayan currency roasted and ground up to make a nourishing and stimulating drink. The drink itself is related to the liquid that the skull spits into Blood Moon's hand, which virginally impregnates her with the hero twins who will become the sun and moon of the first day. The roasting, grinding up, and dissolving of the cacao—making it no longer a unit of currency, realizing its value—are imaged in the burning, grinding, and drowning of the hero twins; they resurrect as catfish, and the iconology of Mayan myth associates the catfish shape with the shape of both the maize kernel and the innards of the cocoa bean. Here we have indeed a sacrament (or *chinjikijilu*), which unites the resurrected god-hero, the creation of humankind, the food staples of the society, and the common unit of currency; and the epic poem is the words that call the sacrament into being, the *hoc est enim corpus meum*.

When standardized Roman gold currency appears in northern Europe, the epic poets respond, as we have already seen,[24] with a searching symbolic analysis of its moral and social effects. Beowulf and the heroes of the *Nibelungenlied* and the *Volsungssaga* all contend with the dragon and his hoarded gold. Wagner is, I believe, right in interpreting the story of the Nibelungs as a warning against the concentration of value (and human obligation and human love) in unchanging metal. One of the great kennings for the action of the epic poet is to "unlock his word-hoard."[25] The danger of the dragon's hoard is that its value is not circulated; the response of the poet is to unlock the word-hoard, to give away something (words) that can be duplicated and owned by everybody in common. As the early medieval economy developed, powered by national gold currencies, great prosperity, cities, and alienation arose together; the epic poem, which is commonly owned, helps redress the moral loss.

In the Volsung saga, Regin is the smith who forges Sigurd's sword, but he is also the storyteller, the poet's alter ego. As Sigurd's mentor, he teaches him many languages and the runes of writing. Regin's brother Fafnir is the dragon who has deprived the storyteller of his inheritance. With Regin's advice Sigurd slays Fafnir and releases the treasure. But Sigurd is tempted by the gold, slays Regin and keeps the treasure for himself. This killing of the adviser/poet/smith turns the treasure into a curse. Further, we find out what is the meaning of the death of the dragon, lest we should be in any doubt about it: Fafnir's blood confers the classic poet's gift of being able to understand the language of the animals. Sigurd tastes it, and "when the blood from the serpent's heart touched his tongue, he could understand the speech of birds" (Brock, 66). The tragic equation is complex: the gold-hoard is a word-hoard as in *Beowulf*; if we try to keep it for ourselves, even if we have, as Regin has, a right to half of it, it will be our destruction; and Sigurd the dragon-slayer is a poet-slayer and will be destroyed in turn, because of the mutual jealousy of Gudrun and Brynhild over the gold ring of Odin, Andvaranaut (which is the divine supplement to the otter's ransom that completes the gold-hoard). The odd implication is that the poet who is telling this story is a ghost, who is haunting his murderer, but who redeems the curse of the gold by unlocking his word-hoard and circulating the currency of the poem.

In Shakespeare's *Henriad*, there is a profound and extended meditation on the means of economic exchange, especially in connection with the issue of sovereignty and its legitimation. By Shakespeare's time there was a robust metallic currency and the beginnings of currency standardization, theories of fiscal soundness, inflation and deflation, and the emergence of the issues of coining and counterfeiting.[26] Sir Thomas Gresham had already formulated his Law that bad money drives out good. Shakespeare's dramatic epic must find a way to "redeem from broking pawn the tarnished crown"[27] of England. I quote at length from my book *Shakespeare's Twenty-First Century Economics*, on the validity of coinage:

> But what if there is a serious question about the legitimacy of the stamp or inscription with which it is impressed? Who has the right to mint a coin? What if the king, whose image is on the coin, is not a legitimate king? What makes a king legitimate anyway? A sufficiently large number of counterfeit coins will debase a currency; a counterfeit king can debase a whole commonwealth. What if there were no legitimate city to return to after one's adventures in the forest? These problems cannot be handled in the mode of comedy; instead, they form the core of Shakespeare's great series of history plays, *Richard II*, *Henry IV* (parts one and two), and *Henry V*.
>
> In the Battle of Shrewsbury, which forms the climax of *Henry IV, Part One*, Henry IV uses a tactic that secures victory over the rebel armies arrayed against him, but which smacks of dishonor and symbolizes all too graphically the political problems of his regime. He has a number of his followers put on his own heraldry and coat armor, effectively disguising themselves as the King himself. Several of these fakes are killed by Douglas, his Scottish opponent. The King survives to see his enemies slain or captured; but the

rebellions continue, because the doubt as to Henry's legitimacy remains. Nobody can tell for sure which is the real king, and there are
many claimants to the throne. The problem lies in the history of
Henry's rise to power. Henry usurped the throne from Richard II,
and though Richard had himself been a weak, venal, and treacher-
ous king with royal blood on his own hands, and though Richard
had formally abdicated his throne, ceding it to Henry, nevertheless
the sacred chain of descent has been broken. Henry is a counterfeit
king.

This is not to say he is not a good king in many ways. He has the
mettle, discipline, and intelligence of a true king—his blood, in
Shakespeare's metaphor, is vigorous and potent. He has the right
metal to be king, but the inscription has been improperly acquired,
and thus his coinage, so to speak, is suspect. Shakespeare plays
with this idea throughout all four plays, punning on the colloquial
terms for the coins of the realm—"crown" (five shillings), "royal"
(ten shillings), "cross" (the inscription on the "tails" side of various
coins), and "sovereign" (one pound). How can the English monarchy, Shakespeare asks, recover its legitimacy? And how can its
economy regain its vigor and stabilize its currency, and so renew
the basic fertility of its soil, its productiveness, and its health in
the international markets (symbolized by participation in Europe's
great project of the Crusades)? The plays are full of references to
the financial instabilities of civil war economies. One can "buy land
now as cheap as stinking mackerel"; worse, one can "buy maidenheads as they buy hobnails, by the hundreds" (II.iv.362, 365). Hotspur, before the battle, puns on "crown" (the top of the head) and
"crown" (the coin):

> We must have bloody noses and cracked crowns
> And pass them current too.[28]

The implication is that to engage in rebellion is to use as legal ten-
der (pass current) a coin that is cracked and thus defaced and de-
valued.

All of these anxieties are summed up in Henry's first speech to his
lords in *Henry IV, Part One.*

> So shaken as we are, so wan with care,
> Find we a time for frighted peace to pant
> And breathe short-winded accents of new broils
> To be commenced in stronds afar afar remote.
> No more the thirsty entrance of this soil
> Shall daub her lips with her own children's blood,
> No more shall trenching war channel her fields,
> Nor bruise her flow'rets with the armed hoofs
> Of hostile paces. . . . Therefore, friends,
> As far as to the sepulcher of Christ—

Whose soldier now, under whose blessed cross
We are impressed and engaged to fight—
Forthwith a power of English shall we levy,
Whose arms were molded in their mother's womb
To chase these pagans in those holy fields
Over whose acres walked those blessed feet
Which fourteen hundred years ago were nailed
For our advantage to the bitter cross.[29]

The metaphor Henry uses for the soldiers' service to God in the Crusades is a mixed one. The soldiers are "engaged," a word like "mortgaged," implying the pledge of personal property or person itself as security for a sum of money. The passage also refers to the "impressing"—or we would say "press-ganging" of soldiers by forced conscription into an army, and the acceptance by the recruit of payment—the "cross" or the "king's shilling"—for his military service. And of course all this is based on the by now familiar process of pressing or stamping a coin, the British warrior shaped in the mold of the British womb and the cross of the British military uniform. In the ideal state of the kingdom, the "blood" to which Henry alludes so graphically at the beginning of his speech, the true wax or metal of England, must be properly molded and stamped with the cross of royal legitimacy if it is to carry value. But the poetic imagery of sacrifice—Christ's, the crusader's—implies that the only way the sacrifice of English blood in civil war can be stopped is paradoxically by more sacrifice. What sacrifice can redeem the pawned crown of England? This is the question, the poetic work that the plays set for themselves. . . .

Can the sovereign be merely the most recent winner in the political struggle? Surely not. Prince Hal must legitimately succeed to a crown that was not itself legitimately attained by succession. Though Hal is of kingly metal, the inscription or stamp of his sovereignty has been defaced. How does one make a counterfeit coin (made of genuine metal) into a true "crown" or "royal" or "sovereign" of the realm? . . .

The answer, when we express it in terms of coinage, is obvious: remelt the coin, and restamp it with a legitimate head of state. The answer is less obvious when we try to put it in terms of public policy and the necessary rituals of succession. Hal knows that the solution is not to join his father in the unscrupulous *Realpolitik* and treachery by which he maintains an uneasy seat on the throne. Hal seeks out an alternative father, one who is apparently free of all the hypocrisies of social power, and who embodies the ease and creativity of nature itself. He finds this alternative father in the fat highwayman Falstaff. Falstaff's solution to Hal's problem is that if nature has given a man kingly metal, the stamp doesn't matter:

"Never call a true piece of gold a counterfeit," says Falstaff to Hal; "Thou art essentially made, without seeming so" (II.iv.496). If Hal is a true piece of gold, he cannot be a counterfeit king. He is truly made out of sovereign essence and has no need to appear so. Ignore the stamp of rules and regulations, says Falstaff, live by gifts not earnings, thumb your nose at justice with its killjoy accountings; "we that take purses go by the moon and the seven stars, and not by Phoebus, he, that wand'ring knight so fair" (I.ii.14). Phoebus is Apollo, the god of daylight and reason—the Logos, the word, the inscription by which we impress nature and make it serve us. Who needs him, demands Falstaff, when we can have the Moon's perpetually borrowed light?

Falstaff is a misuser of the King's press, that is, someone who recruits soldiers in an illegal fashion for private profit, using the writ and seal authority of the monarchy. The word "press" itself alerts us to the deep relationship between the acts of minting and of conscription: both are ways to imprint, or impress, or stamp, the free material of nature for state use. The connection is underlined when Falstaff pretends to be dead on the battlefield in order to save his life. His defense against the charge of being a counterfeiter is that he is after all alive, and that life itself has a genuineness that trumps any kind of civilized, inscribed value, any such "trim reckoning" as honesty or honor (V.i.135). He argues that in denying the Apolline prerogative to stamp the raw material of life, he is himself genuine metal. The paradox is summed up in Falstaff's very name: he is a "false staff." Does this mean that he is the wrong kind of support for a king, or that he is no mere staff, but a caduceus or Moses-staff, that is also a living snake? Or both? To counterfeit a counterfeit is to be genuine. If, Falstaff points out, death is the counterfeit of life—a dead body is a mere simulacrum of a living one—to counterfeit death "is to be no counterfeit, but the true and perfect image of life indeed." Or is he a false caduceus, that is, a staff that would turn into a snake but could not turn back into a staff, like those of the Egyptian priests who competed in magic with Moses? . . .

At the Battle of Shrewsbury Henry Bullingbrook wears the coat of arms of the king of England, but though his metal is of the right bullion to do so, he is still a counterfeiter, his bull (or *bulla*) is false; we know this because he finds it necessary to outfit his base-metal followers in the same disguise. Imagine the heroic Henry V resorting to such subterfuges! Henry IV's plottings, machinations, image-manipulation, and legalistic hypocrisy are precisely what repels his son Hal and drives him into the arms of Falstaff.

. . . The theoretical solution to Hal's problem is to remelt the counterfeit coin of his inheritance and restamp it with a legitimate head of state. But this is in practice a long process—Hal must, for example, wait for his father to die. He cannot continue the defiling series of murders for the sake of power. Though he has already explicitly rejected his father's way, Hal's psychological coinage must take some shape in the meantime. In the deepest symbolism of the play, the placeholder head that is inscribed on Hal's coin is the Boar's Head, the sign of the tavern where he and Falstaff hang out. . . . Falstaff is the ritual King of the May, the Lord of Misrule, the embodiment of our animal nature. He is the boar, the sacrificial beast that must first be prepared for his role—the sins of the community heaped on his back—and then immolated for the health of the land.

The first step, then, in Hal's solution to the paradox of his inherited illegitimacy is to replace the King's head with the boar's head as his personal sign, replace the fake king with the authentic beast. Falstaff is authentic, in that he embodies the fundamental substance of the English national character—that substance that we find in Sir Bercilak (the jolly castellan in *Sir Gawain and the Green Knight*), in the Host and the Miller in the *Canterbury Tales*, in Dr. Johnson and Samuel Pickwick and even in Benny Hill. John Bull is the cartoon version of this mythic figure. Falstaff is invested by Shakespeare with all the imagery of traditional animal sacrifice festivals—the roasted Manningtree ox with the pudding in his belly, the Bartholomew boar-pig, the fat kine of Pharaoh's dream, the sow that has overwhelmed all her litter but one. These are images of great meat-feasts, of satisfied hunger, of carnival (literally, flesh-rites), of the fertility of the land that gives us such good things and provides us with a surplus to tide us over the winter. Falstaff is a huge relief from the starved dry politicking of the historical chronicle.

But of course so far Hal does not yet have a solution. We cannot have a man-beast for a king. The coin of the realm must have another stamp than the slavering and greedy snout of the boar. As soon as Falstaff is given the friendship of the Prince, he immediately abuses it, using it to commit highway robbery with impunity and to sell draft exemptions to the soldiers he has impressed into the king's service (another example, in the light of our discussion of Henry IV's proposed draft for the crusades, of Shakespeare's astonishing poetic economy). The problem with people who live like animals is that the big ones eat up the little ones; as Falstaff himself puts it, referring to one of the victims of his con games, "If the young dace be a bait for the old pike, I see no reason in the law of nature but I may snap at him."

But at least part of Hal's problem is solved. By consorting with Falstaff he has, as it were, reduced himself to a sort of Everyman; he has erased the stamp of his father and is now in the condition of Adam, with the potential to become anything he chooses:

I am now of all humors that have showed themselves humors since the old days of goodman Adam to the pupil age of this present twelve o'clock at midnight. (II. iv. 94)

The Boar's Head tavern is a place where Hal is liberated from his ordinary identity and can play any role he likes. It is, among other things, the space of theater art itself. In the course of the ensuing scene, Hal engages in a series of amateur theatricals, taking the parts of a bartender, a rich young drunk, the rebel Harry Hotspur, his own father the king, and himself as a dissolute young prince being scolded by his father. He is actually preparing himself to be the representative of all his people, since he has become, in play, each of them in turn.

Most important of all, he has thoroughly detached himself from his identity as an interested political party in the power struggle. He is thus in a position to "renormalize," as mathematicians say, the paradoxical situation in which he has been placed as the potential inheritor of stolen property. (To renormalize is to cancel out one mathematical absurdity with another, leaving an equation of finite real quantities that can be solved.) The manner in which this task is to be performed is explained symbolically in the episode of the Gad's Hill robbery. The Prince has agreed to help Falstaff and his companions rob some rich travellers on the Canterbury road. But by prearrangement Hal does not rendezvous with Falstaff; instead he waits until Falstaff has completed his holdup, and in disguise with his friend Poins he in turn robs the robbers, and turns the whole affair into a joke. Later he repays the money ("with advantage"—interest) to its proper possessors. It is just in this fashion that he will restore the legitimacy of the English throne: he must in some sense steal it from the thief (his father), commit a second crime to erase the first.

This act of counter-usurpation is in turn symbolized by the scene in which Hal encounters his father for the last time on Henry's deathbed. In error, Hal believes that his father is already dead, and pitying his father for the terrible burden of the crown that has destroyed him, Hal takes that same crown up from the pillow where it lies and tries it on himself, as if to wrestle with the antagonist that has defeated his father. But Henry is not yet dead; he awakens to find his son wearing the crown, and bitterly upbraids him for his unseemly haste. Hal apologises and they are reconciled at the end, but the act of counter-usurpation has been symbolically performed. And the symbolism is not empty, for throughout both *Henry IV* plays Hal has been psychologically and politically distanced from his father—so much so that at one point Henry wishes aloud that his son had been exchanged in the cradle with the chief rebel, Harry Hotspur. Significantly, when Hal comes to the throne, he discards the nickname "Hal," and adopts the name of the rebel, "Harry," as his familiar appellation. Hal has robbed the robber; or, to put it in terms of coinage, he has reminted the coin of sovereignty.

But Hal does not keep the money stolen from the travellers on Gad's Hill. The very name "God's Hill" connotes that the events that happen there, between London and Canterbury, the civil and the spiritual capitals of Britain, are of a ritual importance matching that of the martyrdom of the Archbishop Thomas a` Becket. Another Henry, the Second, had been the cause of Thomas' death in much the same fashion as Henry IV had been the death of Richard II. Hal has expiated the crime, but he must still, so to speak, make restitution, return the money. To whom does he owe the crown? The answer is, to the people of England. Hal now proceeds to pay it back, and the paying is the work of his reign. His royalty consists, so to speak, in the continuous paying of "royalties" to the people of the land, who are the authors of the authority over which he has copyright. The play in which Hal receives his true title, Henry V, is Shakespeare's vision of what a genuine king should be, that is, the leader whose constant work is the emancipation of his subjects. When Hal, now Henry V, wanders his camp on the eve of the battle of Agincourt, speaking incognito with the common soldiers and presenting himself as Harry Le Roy and the servant of England, there is a distinct premonition of the ideal role of the American president, the first citizen, the ruler as recycler of sovereignty back to the people. It is a reversal of Henry IV's stratagem of disguising his followers as himself. Instead of betrayal and execution, which are the fate of rebels against the counterfeit King Henry IV, the loyal soldier who challenges the disguised Harry gets a glove full of gold coins.

The restoring of the stolen property is a process, one that is never-ending, and one that constitutes the true function of sovereign rule.[30]

I have quoted this passage at length because the issues it addresses are implicit in all epic, and Shakespeare's incomparably acute analysis of them can act as a lens for viewing many other epics. When Ahab, for instance, nails the doubloon to the mast of the *Pequod* as his reward to the first sailor to sight the white whale, Melville is basically revisiting the same set of problems but in the light of the American experience. The doubloon, with its mystical incription, is a glowing symbol of sovereignty:

> On its round border it bore the letters, REPUBLICA DEL ECUADOR: QUITO. So this bright coin came from a country planted in the

middle of the world, and beneath the great equator, and named after it; and it had been cast midway up the Andes, in the unwaning clime that knows no autumn. Zoned by those letters you saw the likeness of three Andes' summits; from one a flame; a tower on another; on the third a crowing cock; while arching over all was a segment of the partitioned zodiac, the signs all marked with their usual cabalistics, and the keystone sun entering the equinoctial point at Libra.[31]

But what is sovereignty? After all, by offering the doubloon Ahab is usurping the "joint-stock" business legality of the voyage, substituting his own autocratic purpose for the democratic purpose of the *Pequod*. And when the offer is made it exposes nakedly the profoundly questionable nature of sovereignty itself. As each other member of the crew comes before the coin and interprets it, the meanings multiply into meaninglessness. If Melville has an answer, it is more, in the American spirit, like a question. If the autocratic and charismatic spirit of the old heroism can no longer serve the democratic regime, can sound business interest, combined with the brotherly charity he celebrates everywhere in his epic (and especially in Chapter 94, "A Squeeze of the Hand") make an adequate substitute? Ishmael is saved by his blood-brother's (and fellow-businessman's) coffin; can this "whale of a book" provide a new basis for sovereignty?

It is no coincidence that the date of publication of *Moby Dick*, 1851, falls exactly between two epochal events in the history of American currency, both in his lifetime. The first was the dissolution in 1836 by Andrew Jackson of the Second Bank of the United States. This act resulted in the issuance by about 1,600 local state-chartered private banks of private paper money currencies in over 30,000 varieties of design, which were very easily counterfeited. The resulting financial chaos, bank failures, and circulation problems, and the deflationary depression of 1837–1841, would have marked Melville's early manhood. Combined with the impending near-bankruptcy of the Federal Government, the banking collapse already constituted a crisis of financial sovereignty at the time *Moby Dick* was being written; the outbreak of the Civil War in 1861 and the printing of the Confederate dollar ratified the breakdown. Like the sailors on the *Pequod* who each have their own version of the meaning of the coin, the various colored banknotes constituted a cacophonous excess of significations. Ahab's autocratic gold is all that holds them together. The other great economic event in Melville's later life, but anticipated symbolically in *Moby Dick*, was the issuance in 1862 by the Federal Treasury of the first national gold-backed paper currency, the Greenback, which began to stabilize the system but which ushered in what Melville feared might become an imperial presidency.

Melville cannot have failed to recognize the implications of these economic changes for a writer of printed books. The technology and legitimacy of both minting and counterfeiting were now no different from the technology and legitimacy of epic-writing. Was his own currency good or bad? Was brotherhood on the large scale more properly federalism or confederacy? What made paper and ink valuable? Can a paper nation be valid? Can we all get back on the same page, and use the same dollar? Though in later life, as *The Confidence-Man: His Masquerade* attests, Melville's answers were more pessimistic, and the excess of significances more cacophonous, in *Moby Dick* the epic answer, the possibility of true refounding, is still open. Perhaps one reason for his later darker vision was the lack of response that his nation showed to his great epic novel, and to the failure of his verse epic *Clarel*. *Clarel* treats of a pilgrimage to the Holy Land that raises more pluralistic problems than it solves. It is very clear, though, what kind of questions Melville is asking. His pilgrimage plays the same role in *Clarel*, though at much greater length, that Henry IV's proposed crusade does in Shakespeare's play: the aborted search for a foundation or founding.

Epic, as many have noted, is an art of memory: literally in the first ages, when scops and guslers and blind *biwa hoshi* had to memorize their vast performances; more figuratively and more comprehensively, when written epic was the stored memory of a whole culture. So there is another deep relation between epic and money that this analysis indicates; for money, as we see from its origins in the bulla, is originally a way of keeping track of obligations when the numbers of participants in a market are too great to remember, the time between the sealing and consummation of a contract too long, the quantities and varieties of goods too complex to entrust to brain circuitry. Our bank account relative to the prices and to our needs is a precise memorial of the consensus of our society (including ourselves) of what our obligations are, what is our moral status as social beings, lest we forget our promises. Epic is the container, or rule-set, the bulla in which the moral calculi of our ethical lives lie undisturbed by fraud and natural bias—the ark in which the breeding-stock of our stories can safely ride out the flood. One might speculate, then, that the neglect and disfavor epic has suffered in the last hundred years or so in avant-garde circles is a grand cultural effort to throw off our responsibilities and lighten the ethical burden of our humanity. Like Falstaff, we "owe God a death" but would "be loath to pay Him before his day," as he says in his famous speech on the folly of honor.[32] We deny death, but if we do not honor our promises, we have broken the moral link between our past, present, and future selves, and so death—moral death, perhaps more weighty than physical death—is everywhere in our lives, not just at the end. And where, without epic, is the bulla or ark wherein our accounting lies safe?

Today we face a new set of challenges in the light of our economic technology: our currency is now basically cybernetic. Paper and coin are now just markers of our real wealth, which is a configuration of virtual ones and zeros preserved in optical and electronic circuitry and vouched for by a consensual illusion. We have recently (in 1987, 2001, and 2007) experienced three massive collapses in the sovereignty of our money—the savings and loan crash, the dot com[33] crisis and the mortgage meltdown. Meanwhile intellectual property and copyright have become battlegrounds, and we are becoming aware of how grievously we are in debt to the planetary ecosystem, having ignored our promises. Any epic composed today would necessarily take as one of its explicit or implicit goals to reground our economic exchange system, found a new one, or find a way to make it work without the need for any ground at all. And such an epic would inevitably exist at some stage of its composition and publication in the same ghostly medium as our money.

A New Religion

All these changes—in the means of publication, in the language, and in the means of exchange—that seem to trigger or be triggered by the composition of an epic, have ontological implications for the culture that achieves or suffers them. Often, perhaps always, they are accompanied by a transvaluation in our most fundamental beliefs and priorities. Whether the change in religion is explicit or implicit, conceived of as reform, liberation, revolution, replacement, or the rediscovery of fundamentals, it is a major feature of epic. We have already, perhaps, inferred through the analysis presented in this book that something of the sort is going on.

The religious earthquake at the heart of epic takes two different forms, sometimes (perhaps always) together. It can be finally digesting and ordering a religious transformation that has already taken place, as much as hundreds of years earlier; or it can be more or less explicitly enacting or even initiating a religious change in its own present moment of composition. Even if the religious change the epic depicts is an ancient one, however, it cannot but have implications for the present of the work.

A good example, as always, is the *Popol Vuh*. The poem clearly recounts two revolutions against older generations of gods.[34] The first is the revolution against the divine forces of brute nature such as Seven Macaw, Zipacna, and Earthquake (perhaps representing the old folk religions of Mesoamerica). The second is the revolution against the Lords of Death, who bear a striking resemblance to the gods of the Olmecs and Toltecs to the north, who had dominated the Mayan lands in pre-Classic times, and to those of their successors, the Aztecs, who were the current cultural threat in post-Classic times. The further implication of the poem—so claim some admittedly partisan scholars with a good deal of justification—is that the Mayans can throw off the death-cult of their new Christian conquerors as the Hero Twins threw off the death-cult of Xibalba.[35] In so doing, they may even claim to be recovering the true meaning of the Christian Book of Genesis.

As we have already glimpsed, a somewhat similar form of religious subversion can be found in the *Shahnameh*. Early kings battle with and overthrow the earthly demons, most especially the brain-eating wizard Zahhak, to establish the monotheism of the God of light; the same Persian culture that had been subjugated by the Arab form of Islam can perhaps likewise throw off its tyranny and establish the Persian form of Islam. The implication is that the ancient Persian cult of Ahura-Mazda may have been closer to true Islam than what the Arabs made of it, and Ferdowsi is rescuing the wisdom of the Prophet Muhammad from its misusers (as the *Popol Vuh* narrator rescues Genesis from the Spanish).

The emergence of a new religion from the old is almost universal in epic. The *Enuma Elish* celebrates the victory of the cult of Marduk over that of Tiamat. Exodus is about a religious revolution in which Jahweh replaces all the traditional local gods. The Greek epics presuppose the defeat of the Titans by the Olympians and the replacement of Typhon by Apollo at Delphi—and anticipate a future moment in which the wisdom of Athena will outshine the politicking of Zeus. The *Sundiata* celebrates the defeat of the animist nature religion of the wizard Soumaoro and the inception of the dynasty that was, under

Hajji Mansa Mousa, to establish Islam and build "houses in Mecca for pilgrims coming from Mali" (Niane, 83). The *Mahabharata* initiates the cult of Krishna in the Vedic tradition, implicitly critiques the Brahmanistic ritual, and anticipates the Buddhist meditative praxis. *The Journey to the West* integrates and synthesizes three religions. The *Heike* implicitly recognizes the contradiction between Samurai Shinto and monastic Buddhism, and seeks a new relation between them. *David of Sassoun* depicts a religious revolution; *The Aeneid* deifies imperial rule; *Njal's Saga* dramatizes the Christian conversion of Iceland; the crusader epics critique the practice of Christianity in the light of its challenge by Islam; in the Turkish *Battalname Destani* the hero Battal Gazi campaigns for Islam against the Crusaders.[36] *Parzifal* hints at the establishment of an exclusive Templar illuminati cult; *Faust* presents Goethe's new universal religion; *Moby Dick* seeks an American religious syncretism.

In *Henry IV* Part 1, Falstaff's robbery on Gad's Hill of the rich franklin from Canterbury recalls not only the conflict of Church and State between Henry II and the Archbishop Thomas à Becket, but also the seizure by Henry VIII of Church property that cemented the Protestant reformation in England. Henry VIII had in effect declared the church property to have been extorted from the people illegimately, on pain of a supernatural punishment it was not theirs to impose. In the complex economy of Shakespeare's play the franklin is an auditor, and he is carrying money from the pilgrimage center in Canterbury destined for the King's exchequer. What happens to the money? Hal, like Henry VIII, steals it from the thieves, and restores it to the national treasury, which will one day be his own. Hal, when he claims his title, gives as his attribute the role of debt-redeemer: "Who never promiseth but he means to pay."[37] Shakespeare must through the pageantry of his plays replace the old Catholic Divine Right of Kings; the State will control the Church and dispose of its revenues. But further problems arise at this point, which can only be solved by paying back to the people the value-stock it lent to the state, as Shakespeare suggests in the episode where Henry V pays his ransom—in gold "crosses"—to Williams to avoid having to fight and kill his own subject.

Both of my own epics predict profound religious changes: the account of the three-naved cathedral in *The New World* and the sermon of the Sibyl in *Genesis* explicitly expound a new religious perspective. At the time of writing these poems I had not consciously attended to the religious subversiveness of the epic as a genre: but the genre itself somehow compels its practitioner to touch that enticing and dangerous third rail—of heresy or prophecy. Religion—*religio*—is a tying-back, a binding again: the ligatures of the signature by which we bind ourselves to our moral selves. When religion itself rots and fails to bind, epic seeks further back, in our common history, for a sound tree whereon to tie back our valuations, and plaits a stronger cord of coherent narrative time to bind us. And sometimes epic must also seek prophetically forwards in time to find a higher vantage point from which that history can be better seen. This is, in retrospect, what I must have been trying to do in setting those poems in the future.

Notes

1. C. S. Peirce, *Peirce on Signs* (Chapel Hill, NC: The University of North Carolina Press, 1991); Ludwig Wittgenstein, *Philosophical Investigations* (Princeton, NJ: Prentice Hall, 1999); Willard V. Quine, *From Stimulus to Science* (Cambridge, MA: Harvard University Press, 1998).

2. Milman Parry, *The Making of Homeric Verse* (Oxford: Oxford University Press, 1987); Albert Lord, *The Singer of Tales* (Cambridge, MA: Harvard University Press, 2000).

3. E.g. Dennis Tedlock, trans. *Popol Vuh* (New York: Touchstone Books, 1985, 1996), 260–61.

4. R. Patton Howell, ed. *Beyond Literacy: The Second Gutenberg Revolution* (Dallas, TX: Saybrook Publishing Company, 1990), 171–76.

5. II.ii.98–113.

6. "Ars Poetica." In Archibald Macleish, *Collected Poems, 1917–1982* (Boston, MA: Houghton Mifflin, 1985), 116.

7. "A Sort of a Song." In W. C. Williams, *The Collected Poems of William Carlos Williams, Vol. II: 1939–1962* (New York: New Directions, 2001), 55.

8. Of course the behavior modeled was the latest in cool—bohemia in a bourgeois world, adultery in a married world, divorce in a family world, homoerotism in a heteroerotic world, apathy in a working world, unbelief in a believing world, perpetual youth in a dying world. But the coolness soon became lukewarm as a new fashion came along within the safe universe of socially constructed reality in the modern bureaucratic capitalist state. The result was the removal of the deep future, the narrativity of the world. That grand perspective is the epic perspective, which, paradoxically, requires grand commitments and makes possible the grand failures and successes that are truly, rather than fashionably, transgressive.

9. Clement Greenberg, *Art and Culture* (Boston, MA: Beacon Press, 1961).

10. Marshall McLuhan, *Understanding Media* (New York: Routledge and Kegan Paul), 1964.

11. E.g. Tedlock, 293, 315.

12. I. 6.

13. Niane, 1.

14. My book *Shakespeare's Twenty-First Century Economics: The Morality of Love and Money* (New York: Oxford University Press, 1999) explores these issues at some length.
15. See Canto XLV on "usura"; and Redman, Tim. *Ezra Pound and Italian Fascism* (Cambridge: Cambridge University Press, 2009).
16. Jean-Jacques Glassner, Zainab Bahraini, and Marc Van de Mieroop, *The Invention of Cuneiform: Writing in Sumer* (Baltimore, MD: Johns Hopkins University Press, 2003), 115–16.
17. Seals not unlike these are still used by dock authorities and businesses to ensure against theft or tampering, and equivalent quantum cryptographic seals are in the works for valuable electronic information.
18. In another tragic island epic, *Njal's Saga*, the law fails and violence erupts when Njal adds a cloak to the agreed monetary weregild for Hoskuld's death, a gift which Flosi, the recipient, takes as an insult to his manhood.
19. I. Morris, *The World of the Shining Prince; Court Life in Ancient Japan* (Oxford: Oxford University Press, 1964).
20. Currency Museum of the Bank of Japan.
21. Immediately following the initial invocation of the Gion Shoja temple bell, the comparison is made:

    > In a distant land, there are the examples set by Zhao Gao of Qin, Wang Mang of Han, Zhu Yi of Liang, and Lushan of Tang, all of them men who prospered after refusing to be governed by their former lords and sovereigns, but who met swift destruction because they disregarded admonitions, failed to recognize approaching turmoil, and ignored the nation's distress. (McCullough, 23)

22. Michael J. Grofe, *The Recipe for Rebirth: Cacao as Fish in the Mythology and Symbolism of the Ancient Maya*, <www.famsi.org/research/grofe/GrofeRecipeForRebirth.pdf>
23. John Bergmann, "The Distribution of Cacao Cultivation in Pre-Columbian America," *Annals of the Association of American Geographers* 59 (1969), 85–96.
24. In chapter 4, The Quest, section on Monsters.
25. "Him se yldesta andswarode, werodes wisa, wordhord onleac."—*Beowulf,* l. 258.
26. One of the charges against Shakespeare's friend and rival Christopher Marlowe in his trial for treason and heresy was that Marlowe had claimed that he had as much right to coin money as did the Queen. See Frederick Turner, "The School of Night," *Corona* 4 (1986).
27. *Richard II*, II. i. 293.
28. 1 *Henry IV,* II.iii.92.
29. I.i.1.
30. Frederick Turner, *Shakespeare's Twenty-First Century Economics: The Morality of Love and Money* (New York: Oxford University Press, 1999),103–11.
31. *Moby Dick,* 428.
32. 1 *Henry IV,* V.i.126–28.
33. The "m" in ".com" is our old friend the god Mercury.

34. Though, as with many religious revolutions, the appeal is to a more fundamental conception of deity than the elder gods themselves, to Maker and Modeler, who, as the poem implies, somehow stand alongside the new Christian religion: "We shall write about this now amid the preaching of God, in Christendom now" (63).

35. E.g. Sharonah Fredrick, "Fighting the Gods: The *Popol Vuh* (Or Why the Conquest of Mexico Could not Repeat Itself with the Maya)," *Revista de Humanidades: Tecnológico de Monterrey*, no. 014 (2003), 207–26.

36. I am indebted to my learned colleague Dr. Cihan Muslu for pointing me toward the Turkish epics of *Battalname* and *Dede Korkut*.

37. 1 *Henry IV*, V. iv. 43.

12

Conclusion: Epic Form and Epic Content

Meter and Mnemonics: The Epic Lyre

Epic, then, is an art of semantic, economic, moral, and religious memory. And Calliope, the epic muse (and of course the eldest of the muses) is not the only muse that is a daughter of Mnemosyne (memory). Modern critics, I believe, usually take the Greek myth rather condescendingly to mean that the Greeks overvalued the craftsmanship of artists who could memorize the old stories and the traditional artistic forms, and rhetorically fix their work in the popular memory. The epic epithet and repeated formula—swift-footed Achilles, the rosy-fingered dawn, the wine-dark sea—are crude and archaic blemishes, the underdrawing showing through, so to speak. Having experienced the glories of modern and postmodern originality, one might find the old pieties and devices of commemoration derivative, repetitive, and mechanical at best, and supportive of the hegemon at worst. And why imitate the past when you can create the future?

This book, as is clear, argues for the dynamic and transformative evolutionary role that epic has played in the history of human culture. So it may seem like a rhetorical question to ask how an art of memory (which surely, does it not, recapitulates the past?) can be so creative and innovative. But it is a good question. Any artist knows the strange sense of being possessed by something utterly strange and even frightening, which excitingly and addictively drives one to the pen, the chisel, the keyboard, or the paintbrush. That is the meaning of the muse—it's simply a name (common in many languages) for an absolutely unmistakable and recognizable experience that many, perhaps all, human beings have been through. How could the Greeks, so wise in so many things, have attributed that radical irruption, that literal inspiration—being blown full of (another's) breath—to fusty old tricks of memory?

Consider the possibility that what the myth of the muses says is simply, and humiliatingly, the case—that is, inspiration comes from the past and wells up when we are just trying to properly represent in traditional forms something that existed before and is still there. Shakespeare knew this well: in *A Midsummer Night's Dream* the fairies, who are also muses, are actually seen only by the "mechanical" bumpkin actors, and not by any of the more wittily original courtiers. The human character who gets the best glimpse—more than a glimpse—is Bottom the Weaver, the "Thomas the Rhymer" of the play. The point is that the actors are not trying to put on a cool new avant-garde conceptual piece. They are worrying about whether the prologue should be in tetrameters or ballad meter when the fairies, in grotesque animal forms, break into their rehearsal. They are trying to perform an ancient, classical, respectable, and traditional tragedy, and their attempts at verisimilitude, at representationality, at the classical meters, at the memorable phrase, are the very things that turn their play-within-the-play into the surreal, delightful, and magical thing that it is. In the sensori-motor regions of the brain, the human body is represented as a strange hunched Puck-like elf with huge hands, tongue and face, the so-called "cortical homunculus" of Wilder Penfield.[1] The default system by which we experience the world is already fantastical and odd; we have no need to try to be surreal.

Perhaps true originality is only arrived at as a by-product of the attempt to get things right, to put the work together in a craftsman-like way (and of course not usually even then). The wind of the spirit bloweth where it listeth, but it seems to especially like the chinks and crevices that result from our human attempt to fit what we have to say into the awkward framework of an ancient craft, to tell again an ancient content in a new context, to piously take on the voice of the ancestors, to paint an exact image of what is given to us by nature or history.

And Shakespeare will not let us get away with any kind of romantic assumption that it is the naïve innocence and spontaneity of the bumpkins that is responsible for their weird artistic success. To be more consciously knowledgeable of one's craft can make the chinks and crevices bigger, the draft more unsettling. At the end of the play, Puck explicitly identifies the "weak and idle theme"[2] of *A Midsummer Night's Dream* with the weak and idle theme of *Pyramus and Thisbe*; as Shakespeare was writing that play he was also writing *Romeo and Juliet*, whose plotline is identical to that of the bumpkins' chosen story. Shakespeare's verse is better than Quince's, certainly; but the bigger they come, the harder they fall. "The best in this kind are but as shadows," says Theseus, "and the worst are no worse if imagination amend them."[3] Shakespeare's unique and staggering expertise, his craftsmanship, his astonishing knowledge of the past, only make him better at making the kind of fool of himself that allows the muses, in all their terror and absurdity, into our closed little world.

Thomas the Rhymer becomes a fool when he becomes True Thomas, who cannot help telling the truth: and truth and rhyming—with all the technical skill and traditional tricks of it—are not opposites, as Plato maintained, but lovers. Rhyme forces us into the strange places in language—truths, though—where reason would not otherwise go. But if rhyme leads, reason can follow—"and grows to something of great constancy,/ But, howsoever, strange and admirable."[4]

Imagination may be only ever forced upon us by the need to connect the unknown—which rushes upon us time-bound beings at every moment—with the known and the remembered. Without memory the connection can never happen, imagination never be elicited. It is an awkward puzzle to neuroscientists who study memory and sleep that the hippocampus consolidates memory—which surely ought to be the most conservative, conscious, rational, and reliable of our mental faculties (it is so in the law)—in states of wild excitement, unconscious habituation, and during the rapid eye movement phase of our sleep when we dream. In the collective dream of ritual we actually reshape our brains.[5] In dreams we couple past memories to new experience and keep what sticks—the dendritic connections are myelinized and new pathways formed. And dreaming is the weirdest thing we do, as Shakespeare knew.[6] Memory is the organ of the imagination: the muses are daughters of Mnemosyne.

In the last few decades, two developments in the study of prosody have radically transformed the modernist view of verbal mnemonics. The first was the culmination of the research of Milman Parry and Albert Lord in the 1960s with the publication of *The Singer of Tales*, which established the mnemonic function of poetic meter in the composition and performance of oral epic.[7] The second was the work of Ernst Pöppel and myself in establishing the cross-cultural universality of the three-second poetic line and the neurophysiological and neurochemical basis of metrical form.[8] The repetitions of the metrical line and the rhyme sounds, so tiresome and sing-song to the sophisticated, turned out in our research to be what enable us to remember a poem. They are the instruments of that mysterious transubstantiation, the metamorphosis of brain contents into brain structure that enables us to reshape ourselves. The result was a renewal of interest among poets and readers of poetry in metered poetry after several decades of the hegemony of free verse.[9] Since then a whole field of research has sprung up applying the findings of neuroscience to oral poetic composition: David Rubin's *Memory in Oral Traditions: The Cognitive Psychology of Epic, Ballads, and Counting-Out Rhymes* (Oxford University Press, 1995), is a good example.[10]

Virtually all of the canonical epics composed before the advent of modernity (and most after it) are in verse. We have already, in Chapter 8, looked at the role of meter in the journey to the underworld. Meter is the protecting talisman of the poet, which guards him from the loss of memory that might leave him stranded down in the darkness of the past. It is both symbolized and accompanied by the Orphic lyre, the shamanic drum, the Albanian *lahuta* or *cifteli*, the Serbian *gusle*, the Finnish *cantele*, the Welsh *cwyth*, the Mandinka *kora*, the Hungarian and Scottish bagpipe, the Japanese *biwa*, the Nyanga rattle. It is the *terza rima* of Dante, the *sloka* couplet of Vyasa, the 7–5 *mora* line of Kakuichi, the octosílabo of Jose Hernandez, the Nibelungen line, the endecasílabo, the Eddic *fornyraislag*, the *laisse* of Turoldus, the *motaqareb* of Ferdowsi, the Homeric and Virgilian hexameter, the alliterative line of *Beowulf*, the iambic pentameter of Shakespeare, Milton, and Wordsworth.

Meter with its associated techniques of rhyme, alliteration, stanza form, etc., serves somewhat different mnemonic functions for the purely oral epic poet than it does for the epic poet who composes on the page for a reader. The oral poet needs meter as the vital device for remembering the next line and verse paragraph and for ad-libbing when memory fails or when local topicality or the occasion or inspiration demands an insertion. The literate poet, though he may still need meter to memorize the poetry for off-book performance, uses meter for something else as well—to preserve accurately the tone, cadence, emphasis and feeling of his own voice, so that it will live on in his death or absence.

To understand this point, we must examine the nature of the "metrical fiction." Poets almost never hew to the exact pattern of the metrical line they use, though there are craft rules that specify which departures from it will work, and which will so scramble the rhythm that the characteristic pulse of a given metrical form is lost. Take the iambic pentameter line of Shakespeare, Milton, and Wordsworth:

-/, -/, -/, -/, -/.

Usually there is a caesura somewhere in the line, depending on its grammar, and the placement of it gives the line a particular shape, such as:

-/-/-; /-/-/

or

-/-/-/; -/-/

or even

-/-; /-/-/-/

or

-/-/-/-/; -/.

Further, the iambic foot can be replaced by its opposite, the trochee (/-), at the beginning of a line or after a caesura, and spondees (//) or pyrrhics (--) can replace iambs as long as there are enough iambs in the neighborhood to keep the flow going.

The point is that each poet has a characteristic pattern of departures from the regular meter, and each poet uses different departures to indicate different feelings, moods, rhetorical positions, and strengths of logical inference. Early forms of script often lacked punctuation and lineation, so meter makes up for the prosodic loss of sense and meaning and intent—not so much by a characteristic rhythm, which would be monotonous, but by a characteristic *set of patterns of departure from* the regular metrical pulse. To illustrate this point, let us look at a few examples from the English epic poets.

Here is Shakespeare, straining the iambic line into a swift drumbeat of trochaic martial glory; I have indicated the stress by capitals and the caesura by the slash:

> ALL FURNished, /ALL in ARMS;
> ALL PLUM'D like ESTridges, /that with the WIND
> BATed like EAGles /having LATEly BATH'D,
> GLITT'ring in GOLDen COATS /like IMages,
> As FULL of SPIRits /as the MONTH of MAY . . .[11]

And here is Milton, with his slow, massive spondees, drawing out the sense variously from line to line in his "great argument":

> OF MAN'S FIRST DISoBEDience, /and the FRUIT
> Of THAT forBIDden TREE, /whose MORTal TASTE

BROUGHT DEATH into the WORLD, /and ALL OUR WOE,
With LOSS of EDen, /till ONE GREATer MAN
ReSTORE us, /and reGAIN the BLISSful SEAT . . .[12]

And now Wordsworth, with his musing, gentle voice, with many little pyrrhic scuds delicately weaving abstraction into feeling:

OH there is BLESsing /in this GENtle BREEZE,
A VISitant /that while it FANS my CHEEK
Doth SEEM HALF_CONSCious /of the JOY it BRINGS
From the GREEN FIELDS, /and from YON AZure SKY.[13]

Even when punctuation has gradually come to remedy the prosodic deficiencies of prose, and the abstract codification of grammar has given us templates for the proper tone and emphasis, the ability of regular metered poetry to convey the subtle raising and lowering of musical tone, the nuances of balanced emphasis, the push of excited language, even the melody of passionate speech, is unmatched. Thus epic poets use verse not only to help them remember the words, but to help their nation remember the sound and intention of the words.

There are exceptions to the rule, however—canonical classical epics as defined in this book that are not in verse. If epic is an art of memory, and verse is the preferred jog to the memory for the majority of epic composers, how do the exceptions manage the task of making their story memorable?

The question is of more immediate interest, because this book is concerned not just with what epic is and was, but also with whether epic can still be composed now and in the future. Can civilization even survive without epic or its equivalent? If our media of information have changed profoundly, as we have already surmised, and if epic treats such changes as opportunities, then how, other than in verse, can the mnemonic mission of epic be achieved? One might argue that the book itself—and any other exact medium of reproduction—renders memory obsolete. One can always get the book down from the shelf or google the poem on the Internet. But the point of epic is that it helps shape our brains themselves, those miraculously self-programming nonlinear non-Turing computers, and it cannot do so if it is not remembered. Our neurons are not calculating transistors or memory chips, but "memristors" that actively think by remembering and remember by thinking.

We do perhaps remember the plots of novels, and the memory theater of plot can do much; but unenhanced novelistic plot works, as we have seen, only to the extent that its normative psychological theory works, and epic, with its transgressiveness, may well be out to break and extend that theory itself. One advantage of novelistic plot is precisely that in the absence of meter after a year or so the plot becomes hazy in one's mind, and so one can read the book again with something of the same sense of suspense that one had the first time. But it is hard to forget epic poetry, and in any case the general plotlines of traditional epics are usually common cultural knowledge. It is not an ordinary suspense that one feels in experiencing great epic poetry, but more one of surrender to a beautiful and necessary and transformative ritual—a sort of initiation rite, ever-renewed. The suspense lies in the further depths that seem to open beneath one's feet as one retraces the known old path, the mists cleared by repetition so as to reveal strange vertiginous heights and new lands below.

The effect of meter, moreover, is not just to help us remember, but to help us remember particular kinds of things, things not paraphrasable in prose—those heights and depths not present in the chat and gossip of an ordinary novel. Meter allows us in the first place—before we have made judgments about what needs to be held in mind as relevant—to entertain and retain things that we would dismiss as silly or as annoyingly ambiguous in prose. The gates of horn are opened by the golden bough of meter, by the *terza rima* of Beatrice, but closed otherwise to the stranger in the wood. I myself "played it safe" by composing my epics in verse, as did my contemporaries Derek Walcott, Julia Budenz, John Gery, and Michael Lind.

But past epics that are loved and remembered have indeed foregone the aid of meter. A careful look at those exceptions may be revealing, and perhaps point to other solutions. The prose epic often resorts to a heightened and poetic kind of language, or to actual passages of poetry. *The Cattle Raid of Cooley* breaks from time to time into tightly metered poetic duets. Characters in the Icelandic sagas burst into poetry at extreme moments; *Egil's Saga* has many opportunities to do so, since the hero is himself a poet. Tolkien's *The Lord of the Rings* uses all sorts of poetic forms, introduced in a natural diegetic way without harming the narrative flow, as spells, war-chants, riddles, quotations from ancient legends, and the like. Other mnemonic techniques include the use of genealogy, a memory structure already shared by the audience in the case of such works as *Njal* and the *Laxdala Saga*:

the very clannish Icelanders would take note of an action performed by their great-great-great-great-great-grandfathers, and not forget it. Likewise an Israelite of the house of Levi or Benjamin, or a Mayan descendant of Noble Sweatbath or Nine Deer, or a d'Este descendant of Tasso's crusader.

James Joyce wrestled with the problem of memorability in *Ulysses* and *Finnegan's Wake*, since he knew well the role of epic in forging the uncreated conscience of one's race.[14] The famous Molly monologue is clearly poetry, and the wordplay of *Finnegan's Wake* is evidently an attempt to raise the novel to epic heights. Unfortunately, the poetic and the novelistic are at war in Joyce—the more fascinatingly novelistic he becomes, the more the grand epic themes recede, but the more poetic—in his own modernist poetic idiom—the more muddied the novelistic pleasures of suspense, identification with characters, and clear depiction of social reality.

Moby Dick, I believe, is more successful in creating epic prose, partly because of the larger-than-life, highly self-conscious, self-mythologizing, and intentionally cranky nature of his American characters. In Melville's time, every American (and immigrant to America) seems to have lived a second life, a rehearsed performance of the free democratic self-determining person, an audible reproach to the less conscious and more docile nations from which they came. Melville need not violate the novelistic canons of verisimilitude—people really did speak that way. Consider the epic grandiloquence of Civil War soldiers' letters home and newspaper reports. This passage, which I have rendered into good iambic pentameter blank verse simply by indicating line divisions, is famous:

> I leave a white and turbid wake; pale waters,
> Paler cheeks, where'er I sail. The envious
> Billows sidelong swell to whelm my track;
> Let them; but first I pass.
>
> Yonder, by ever-brimming goblet's rim,
> The warm waves blush like wine. The gold brow plumbs
> The blue. The diver sun—slow dived from noon—goes down;
> My soul mounts up! She wearies with her endless hill.
> Is, then, the crown too heavy that I wear?
> This Iron Crown of Lombardy. Yet is it
> Bright with many a gem; I the wearer,
> See not its far flashings; but darkly feel
> That I wear that, that dazzlingly confounds.

'Tis iron—that I know—not gold. 'Tis split, too—
That I feel; the jagged edge galls me so,
My brain seems to beat against the solid
Metal; aye, steel skull, mine; the sort that needs
No helmet in the most brain-battering fight![15]

Other epics not in verse throughout also resort to special cultural aids to repair the mnemonic deficit left by the absence of the metrical pulse. The *Popol Vuh*, as we have already seen (thanks to Tedlock's discerning research) supports the memory by reference to the singularly expressive, dramatic, and popular Mayan graphic tradition. The poem often reads as a tour of striking ritual cartoon images led by a magician-docent. Our visual/spatial memory—as Frances Yates and the ancient oratorical practitioners of the Memory Theater knew well—is very powerful. In the *Popol Vuh* it plays the role that meter plays for *The Iliad*, the *Mahabharata*, and *The Divine Comedy* (though they too use visual mnemonic cues, such as the shield of Achilles, the Vedic iconography of Krishna, and the memory theater of the cones, bolgias, ledges, and spheres in Dante's spiritual geography).

It has sometimes been remarked that China has no epic poem; but *The Journey to the West* and *The Three Kingdoms* are plainly epic in the terms this book proposes. I believe that, beyond the passages of poetry that both Wu Cheng-en and Lo Kuan-cheng include in their narratives, the special qualities of the Chinese ideographic script play an important mnemonic role. Chinese readers, so I am told by my excellent collaborators Deng Yongzhao, Daisy Guo, Wang Dongqing, Baomei Lin, and other Chinese scholars, see the written characters—especially the culturally central ones and those using the most important radicals—as pictures of ideas, with an unforgettable visual association. The massive repetition and collocation of such characters in the Chinese prose epics may well serve the purpose of imprinting the central plot points and philosophical themes in the memory of the reader.

I believe that this was what Ezra Pound was trying to do in the *Cantos*, with his use of Chinese characters and radicals; Baomei Lin argues this hypothesis tellingly in an unpublished PhD dissertation. But until there is a body of sophisticated English speaking poetic readers who are also familiar with Mandarin etymology, the mnemonic effect is lost. The free verse of the poem's form cannot help. The penchant of free verse is to avoid a pulse against which a personal voice and an intended significant emphasis can be made to stand out; and prosodically haphazard line-breaks, though they may make possible interesting syntactical ambiguities, tend to break up the narrative flow that establishes a memorable story. The result can, in the short lyric, produce delightful surprises and aperçus; but it cannot serve the large mnemonic ends of epic. A similar problem exists in W. C. Williams' *Paterson*.

Plot in itself is a mnemonic, but the novel must complicate plot to get its richest experiences and the suspense effect, and so loses memorability. The grand narrative of epic organizes plot hierarchically, as we have seen in the concentric and echoed structure of *The Odyssey*.[16] The single large action (as Aristotle put it) is divided into stories that are in turn arranged into micro-narratives that are then nested into parenthetical structures so that the oral poet and the experienced audience always know where they are. Plots exist in the spectrum that runs from the "one damn thing after another" model of perpetual (meaningless) surprise, through the garden of forking paths,[17] through the maze and the labyrinth, to the fully visualizable memory palace.[18] Epic must somehow combine all these, but the memory palace must contain and sum them all.

The repeated epithets and formulae, the preservation of a single poetic meter, and all the other classical devices of epic poetry, are not just props and tricks. They are at the core of the content itself. Any future drama, film, videogame, or virtual reality world of the future that aspires to epic must somehow find equivalent ways for engraving the human story into the circuitry of the brain. We are constituted by our cultural memory, our biosocial history. Epic's story is who we are.[19]

Epic Content: the Grand Narrative

As this book has argued, epic tells the story of our evolution as a species from the inside. In doing so it is not just stating in metaphorical terms the likely facts of our emergence on this planet, but also opening up the future to the continuance of our transformative tenure in the universe. It thus has an odd sort of normative force—odd, because if epic stories indicate anything, it is that clinging to old policies can stifle the process of growth and creation and oppress the freedom that is one of humanity's trademarks. What was needed for the heroic gest to happen was a free opening to the future; what is needed now, it is implied, is the same thing. How can there be a *policy* of openness to the future? The paradox is not, as epic shows, insoluble. Like the difference between the rules of Tictactoe and the rules of Chess, there are rule-governed systems that are closed, and rule-governed systems that are open, and epic seeks out the latter.

Milton claims that his poem will "justify the ways of God to Man," and if we really examine this challenge, something common to all epics emerges. To justify is to show the justice of something that has been done. If we take the words to mean "to justify to human beings the things that God has done" there is a certain chutzpah in Milton's claim; like Job, he is calling God to the witness stand to testify in His defense. What has He to justify? In the other sense of the phrase, it is to justify what God has done to human beings, i.e., sentenced them to death when they were formerly innocent and existentially exempt from mortality. *Paradise Lost* is a judicial review, a court of appeal where human beings can go to test the validity of the judge's verdict. To warrant a death sentence, a crime must be proven to have been committed, and to have been committed freely and intentionally; and the punishment must fit the crime. If the punishment is excessive, it should be reversed—"justify" in a third sense, to adjust something that was unjust so that it is now just. If Milton, as God's defense attorney, is forced to concede his opponent's case, he is obliged with the rest of the court to agree to fix and redress what was wrong, to take the sentence out of God's hands.

What was the crime? Choosing knowledge. To choose knowledge is to choose to be this species, *Homo sapiens*, Man the knower. There is no question that the crime was actually committed; anybody writing or reading this epic will already have opted for knowledge. So the issue now becomes: (1) Was the act done *freely*? and (2) Does knowledge deserve death?

Knowledge could only be chosen freely if there is indeed something called freedom. So the poem must, essentially, define what freedom is, and whether it could exist, and how it might have been created or generated in the first place. And it must distinguish between various senses of "free," ranging from absolutely random chaos, through the free play of ordered systems, to the nominal freedom of an animal to do what it wants (though it cannot choose what to want), to the truly culpable and laudable (and thus punishable) freedom of human beings. The latter senses of freedom presuppose the former senses: a totally unchaotic, ordered, deterministic universe could have no freeplay at all, animals are physical systems with degrees of freedom, and a world of animals without humans is thinkable, whereas a world of humans without animals is not (since humans are, among other things, animals). The crucial moment in this process is the step from involuntary intent to voluntary intent, from animal to human, from child to adult, from the innocent to the legitimately punishable: hence the recurrent motif of the beast-man and his fall.

Freedom is not just given but constructed, and rather elaborately so—not "constructed" in the snide deconstructive sense of being fabricated by people as an excuse for dominance, but really (self-?) assembled and stuck together piece by piece in a physical world and in our own bodies. Thus the poem must, by implication at least, explain the birth or originary necessity of chaos, the freeplay of ordered systems, the origin of intentionality, and the emergence of secondary (laudable or culpable) intentional *choice* of what to intend and choose. It must, then, be a documentation of the creation and/or evolution of the universe, including humans, and a demonstration that freedom in its highest punishable or praiseworthy sense can really emerge in it.

This, I take it, is part of the deep project of all epic. We do not need Milton's theology to recognize the universality and import of this basic epic theme (though perhaps Milton's struggle with the predestinarianism of his beloved Calvin may have helped sharpen the issue). The most fundamental judgment we make, and the basis of any moral action, is the discrimination of good will from ill-will, the praiseworthy from the punishable. Even if there were no god to do the actual punishing, it is enough—if we are to have a human society at all—that were such a god to exist, he would be justified in the praise or punishment. And free intent is the core desideratum of that judgment. Epic, whether it chronicles the Mayan gods' struggles to create freely knowing and choosing human beings, or the seduction of a wild man by a temple prostitute, or the dawning of personal responsibility in a raider of cities, or the choice of whether or not to draw one's bow against one's kin, or the death of a civilization through wanton impiety, is an aetiology of freedom. And more than this, perhaps, a recipe-book for freedom going forward.

It might be objected that fate is as pervasive a motif in epic as is freedom. But a moment's consideration would recognize that a being that is truly fated would have no use for an alternative for the way things are and the way things will be, nor any occasion to inquire about it. Freedom stories are always partly about fate. What else would a story that takes for its central theme the idea of human freedom choose as its necessary opponent, its fascinating villain, its stooge? Even if we are free only in our imaginations, we are free already, since our imaginations affect our actions. Could an unfree being even conceive of freedom, still less of fate as the opposite of it? To make fate into a subject, a theme, as it is in epic, is to recognize it as problematic and to be looking for loopholes. A nation is only ready to become a democracy when it has started to analyze and describe the nature of the monarchy under which it lives. Fate is to epic as the obvious solution to the identity of the murderer is to the detective story: Inspector Lestrade is essential, as he is going to be proved wrong by Holmes. Any *knowing* of fate, even fate in the abstract, already presupposes a world outside its writ where the observer (if free only as observer of his observerhood of fate) is free. So freedom can almost be defined as *knowledge of fate*. If there is one single characteristic of the epic hero that especially defines him, it is that at some point or other he knows his fate.

Beyond the first question—is human action free?—the other great question that epic must somehow answer is: does knowledge deserve death? The way epic answers it is always some variant of rephrasing the question, as: does knowledge *merit* death? Or even: is knowledge worth death? Or even, perhaps, is death worth knowledge? Epic must understand and analyze the nature of death itself in order to show the justice of the equation, which is why the hero so often takes a tour of the underworld of the dead. Death has two main features: it is the decisive limit of who and what we are, and it is a limit in *time*, which is otherwise open and limitless in the direction of the future. We are usually not much exercised by the fact that we are limited in space—except when we are parted from our beloved, or do not have the physical strength to do what we would, or cannot in an emergency be in two places at once. But the terminus to our time is something that does indeed, as Dr. Johnson put it, "marvelously concentrate the mind."

Knowing is always cumulative: the more one knows, the more one can know. Sooner or later the knower will encounter the observer effect and the bias of one's own perception and cognition; at that point knowledge begins to become self-knowledge. And knowledge essentially involves knowledge of limits: we only know an object by knowing where it stops and the rest of the world begins around it—that is, its shape. When we try to know the shape of our own knowerhood, we run across its limits, and of course the big limit is death. Every epic hero, one way or another, encounters that moment. Thus knowledge is, fundamentally, knowledge of death—the ability to imagine a world where we are not. In "Ode to a Nightingale" Keats says "thou wast not born for death, immortal bird." He knows perfectly well that a member of *Luschinia megarhynchos* turns up its little heels and drops from the twig at some point; he means that the significant element of death, what makes death death for us humans, is knowledge.

So if we like knowledge well enough, we might consider death to be a fair trade for it. It is in this sense not a case of punishment, but of proper payment for a purchase: the god might be accused of driving a hard bargain, but not of injustice. And after all, every bargain, hard or not, is a bargain—buyer and seller must both gain or there is no sale. Or is it a forced sale, an extortion? Remembering our exploration of freedom, is there another twist: can we choose but know? Are we forced by our very nature to know—*Homo sapiens*—and thus it's not a sale but a heist, a stickup? Your knowledge or your life? If we were made by a goddess, say Nature, why should she have designed into us that fatal curiosity? It's easy enough to bargain with an artificial intelligence if you built it and have already planted in its hardware and software an inclination to incur the obligation that comes with the unasked gift. The god's print is too fine to read until you have bargained away your immortality for a better pair of spectacles. If character is fate, where is our culpability, our freedom, our moral identity?

But there is a further twist yet, which appears when we run the thought experiment that all epics propose: what would it be like to have no limits at all? That, after all, would be the only way of escaping the terminus of our being, whether it be the shape of our body or the shape of our lifetime. We would have to be omniscient, omnipresent, omnipotent, and eternal. Epics have gods in them because a god is that thought-experiment. But if knowledge is knowledge of our own limits, a paradox emerges: such a god could not know anything, since he is limitless. He would not be able to check his own bias, could not see himself as others see him, could have no moral being, would have nothing to love, could have no freedom, because he would be totally determined by his own being and nature. He would have to be utterly alone, for any other agency or point of view or obdurate independent physical reality or genuine future would represent a limit and boundary beyond which his writ would not run—a boundary that would constitute death itself for such a being. Even his hand-puppets would have to have characteristics of their own to be entertaining at all. Perhaps Milton's God needs Satan to help him escape the tyranny of himself, to set him creatively free. One of the persistent themes in epic is the boredom and restlessness of the gods—but at least gods in the polytheistic plural have each other to disagree with, to be a little death for each other. They create humans to have a reality show to watch, with real surprises and plot twists.

The problem of knowledge and death is not just ours, then, but God's (or Nature's, in its first instance in contemporary cosmological physics as a single hot dense atom) as well. The primal god—Tiamat, Ymir, Chaos, the cosmic singularity—is utterly ignorant until it divides its agency, is torn apart, gains knowledge and self-knowledge, initiates a temporal sequence, experiences death in space or time. The creation of the universe is the way God falls, is incarnated, ruptures, and ruins himself in the primal sacrifice, a sacrifice repeated in the death of Osiris, of Jesus, of the avatars of Vishnu, of the Bodhisattvas—and of the heroes of epic. Such a view of creation is not outdated: the contemporary secular cosmogenesis itself identifies the origin of the universe, the first symmetry-breaking, the origin of time, the initiation of a series of temporal endings and spatial separations, and the origin of the "state of knowledge" of quantum systems as being essentially bound together. The universe expands, so to speak, to get a point of vantage from which it may experience and register itself into existence; it is a computer that must continually generate new hardware out of itself to keep track of its own expanding circuitry and software. It can do so only by freeing competitive reference frames and genetic algorithms to fight out the solutions among themselves, and thus letting its central control die. If God or Nature offers us a tricky bargain, it is one for which the offerer has already fallen.

And there is a further payoff for humans in (at least retroactively) confirming the purchase of knowledge at the expense of deathlessness. I settled earlier for a perhaps questionable definition of knowledge as the ability to imagine a world where we are not. That ability, to the extent that we can inhabit and experience that imagined world, would resolve the paradox that knowledge and limits are mutually constitutive. The very making of the bargain, of knowledge for death, initiates a process that constitutes a second life. This is the meaning of the epic hero's return from the underworld. Arjuna on the field of Kurukshetra, Hunahpu and Xbalanque in the oven of Xibalba, Achilles on the field of Troy, Gawain setting out for the Green Chapel, Roland refusing to blow the horn, the Princess Kenreimon in her final retirement, Ahab striking through the mask—all in different ways serve as our mentors into that second life, that enfranchisement. It is not that knowledge does not, after all, bring death, but that making the bargain of death for knowledge rightly and freely can make us *not mind* our own limits. We are as pleased by the existence of those others—around us in space and replacing us in the future—as we are with the existence of ourselves. Hunahpu and Xbalanque in their deaths become the sun and moon that will nourish the corn of human flesh. The Orphic lyre becomes the constellation, Lyrae, that still brightens our heavens.

Perhaps the deepest secret of epic is that the relationship between death and knowledge is misconceived. It is not that death is the punishment for knowledge, or even that death is the grievous price we are forced to pay for knowledge, which we value more than immortality; it is that death is the great prize, which we gain and purchase by going through the uncomfortable ordeal of coming to know. Death is the existence of everything other than ourselves, the fascinating presence of a natural world, of friends, enemies, loved ones, the future—all the things that make up what prevents us from being everywhere and everywhen. Our limits are the beginning of everything that might possibly make life worth living, suffering included. Knowledge is a cheap price to pay for death.

From these two basic themes—freedom and deathly knowledge—flow all the essential elements of epic with which we began: the hero, the quest, the natural man, the fall, the kin struggles, the deathworld journey, the city founding, and so on. The recipe for freedom-as-knowledge runs as follows:

First take a storyteller, a knower, the very fact that there is someone who knows something. Let that knower acknowledge the prior and independent existence of what is known, but become the voice of prior knowers of that known world, and of knowledge itself.

That storyteller must show how the various degrees of freedom, from simple temporal difference between what was before and what comes after, through involuntary animal intention to human conscious decision, emerged in the course of creation. This amounts to an implied or explicit history of the universe. The coherence and necessity of that history, its evolutionary intelligibility, the demonstrable failure of other ways to our condition, are the strength of the case the storyteller must make.

There must be a prototypical representative of the human race, the hero, who is part animal, part human, and part divine (or hero twins, who split these parts between them). He must embody authentically the human paradox of being both an exceptional and transgressive individual and the norm of his species, culture, and community. His birth is a mystery that can only be solved retrospectively, and whose solution leads to great dangers and rewards.

The hero must encounter some opening, a question or problem that cannot be solved in the terms that the status quo offers, and that affords an elusive goal that may change as the quest proceeds. This quest necessitates a journey, in which the hero is torn between nostalgia and the thrill of enterprise. The journey is full of conflicts in which the ability to turn life into a game is essential to survival and success, or at least to a significant and fitting end. We humans are born walkers, and thus born explorers; epic records the trials and prizes of that vocation. Human freedom, at least in part, is mobility itself; we know by going there and seeing for ourselves. The eye and the foot, as in Oedipus' name, are bound together in the paradoxes of knowledge and freedom.

Human beings are also the product of a unique kinship system, involving big brains, extended infancy, bonding of different kinds, marriage, in-laws, an incest taboo, adolescence, menopause, and longevity (especially female longevity). To know is also to know in the biblical sense. Kinship is itself a branchy and open-ended but rule-governed plan of classification, and is thus a paradigm and template of any free ordered system. The epic hero is usually embroiled in the complexities of this system, complexities that both hamper and help to define the achievement of meaning in the quest.

In the process of the quest, the three aspects of human life—the natural, the cultural, and the spiritual—are defined through action and story, and a quasi-legal language of covenant among them is postulated. The very fact of there being magisteria or regimes that are not reducible to each other is a primary prerequisite for freedom; there is always choice when there is the prior choice of which set of rules to obey. Of course having different masters is less comfortable than pure servitude, but here knowledge is a great solace at least. And one's voluntary loyalty in the presence of alternate allegiances may be rewarded.

The crucial leap in human evolution was from animals to human animals (not an outdated issue: it is currently being explored by a variety of scientific disciplines in the prehistoric caves of South Africa). That leap, by which we were enabled to look back at ourselves in the mirror of our language, is explored in epic through the paired stories of the battle with natural or animal man, and the natural man's fall from the natural state into culture and knowledge. With this step in the epic recipe a wealth of flavors is released, with subsidiary tales of sex, shame, clothes, drugs, technological invention, domestication of animals and plants, and the knowledge of death.

With the fall into knowledge comes death, and the epic hero must go through the experience of death in his journey into and back from the underworld. The games that gave him his "game face" in his heroic strife now return as part of the set of magics that enable him to enter the land of shades with some chance of return, a set that also includes a spirit guide, and a talisman that is often the musical instrument of the oral poet. In the underworld, the hero—now a hero-poet—speaks with the dead. The conversation establishes the essential communicative link between the dead and the living that enables humans, unlike all other animals, to accumulate knowledge rather than just fill up an inherited potential in every generation, as other advanced animals already do. It provides information about past history, prophecies of the future, assigned duties and the basic structure of the rituals of funeral that are universal among human societies. The hero is freed from death by death; the mystery of the human experience of time becomes a way to question death's finality.

The ground is now prepared for city-building, and the essential ground rules that make a city a city must be set in place: its walls and gates; its qualifications for belonging; a sacrificial system for building basic mammalian drives into higher, more abstract, and more voluntary moral vocabularies and laws; the founding of rituals such as marriages, funerals, food practices, and initiation rites; money; genealogies; a common language; geographical identifiers and locators; calendars; and legal systems. Home is where we are free, and where we know and are known: what are the constraints, what is the syntax of that condition of being at home?

The city has a history, and must free itself from the tyranny of myth while preserving its wisdom. The contradictions between rulership and herohood must be explored. National character and national destiny must be defined, so that collective cultural self-knowledge can correct for collective cultural choice of goals and aims.

The actions of the story must not simply be adventures—epic is not the same as picaresque. They must be significant, though not too obtrusively and univocally allegorical. The events of the story and the decisions of the hero must enlist both our natural sentiments and our judgments of consequential and logical entailment, so as to develop the core values of a working culture. Those value oppositions—good/bad, right/wrong, firstness/secondness, beautiful/ugly, playful/serious, etc.—must be distinguished from each other so as to allow a rich palette or scale or vocabulary for capturing important and decisive factors in making judgments. Here the moral value of free choice and the veridical value of discernment are united and integrated.

The epic as a whole must be made to refer back to its own medium of communication and to the history of that medium, as human expression emerged from muteness to speech, writing, print, and new media. It must, since it is concerned with the process of valuing itself, relate its story and literary form to the very currency of its society's economy, and to the fixing of the standard language. It must address not only in content but in form the establishment, reform, and transformation of the national religion (or suite of allowed religions).

Finally, in the presentation or "plating" of the epic feast, the key and guide must be memory and the arts of memorability, since the deepest freedom we have is the freedom to change ourselves, not just our actions; and memory is a physical change in the nature of our brains and bodies. Knowledge *is* memory. We must be able to change not only the contents of our thoughts but also the container of them. And it is only such changes that truly constitute knowledge. As humans our deepest pleasures, thanks to our evolution that gave us such rewards, are in just such transformations of ourselves. So indeed are our greatest pains: but the pleasures outweigh the pains.

Epic Magnitude

The colloquial use of the term "epic" by today's young is actually an important if obvious defining characteristic of the genre. An epic simply has to be *big*. Why?

One reason is that if epic is to become part of our memory it must be experienced as a place one has inhabited for a substantial amount of time, something we have imaginatively started to explore and move about in. It is not taken in to the mind as a precious acquisition, a jewel for the jewel box, as a beautiful lyric can be. Instead, *it* must take *us* in, make us feel at home in it, make us look out at the world from it, rather than be looked at and lovingly examined in its glass case. Time and familiarity themselves ingrain a thing into memory. We must live in epic country for a while for it to work its transformation on us.

A second reason for the magnitude of epic is that the genre purports to be comprehensive for its culture. It is about the parts of a culture, like any story, but it is also about the whole. The pervasiveness of lists in epic is no coincidence. When the *Heike* names all thirty leading members of the Heike who fled Kyoto in 1183 and all sixty-seven commanders of the Genji armies at the battle of Mikusa, or the *Cattle Raid of Cooley* names the seventy places that the armies of Medb and Aillill passed through in their invasion of Ulster, or *The Iliad* names all the Greek ships, or the *Popol Vuh* names all the ranks and titles of the Cauecs, the Greathouses, the Quichés and the Zaquics,[20] something beyond an obsession with details is going on. Part of the answer is that epic tries to include all the people and places where its writ is to run, it is inclusive, like a census. Nobody on the epic list can defect, because he is part of the story, is thus partly responsible for the way things are now, and shouldn't complain. He or his representative ancestor or place of origin chose this fate and has to live with it.

But further, epic tries to give a sense of the vastness, the cosmic scale, of its story. Such lists bury us deep in a huge fabric, out of sight of the center and far also from the edge of the world. Thus when we do come to its edge in the climactic scenes, we are fully aware of how massive, how weighty, is the shore we stand upon. All else has been summed up and comprehended; we have put all that behind us, but it backs us nevertheless. Nothing has been left out, so that when we do confront the nothing beyond the edge, it is genuine, not fake: we are truly in danger of being lost, because where we are is not in the list of all that we know.

Even a very big novel (unless it has crossed the epic threshold, like *Moby Dick*) does not give us that same sense of frightening comprehensiveness. In the novel the social world embraces us still. When the characters settle down from their youthful adventures, or give up their fight against the expected, or die, the waters of the social world, which after all has determined everything that has happened, close over their heads,

> Till human voices wake us, and we drown—[21]

and all is as it was before. Even the most horrific and cynical detective novel cannot, though it try, escape the conventions of class, psychological realism, worldly wisdom; every detective novel is a "cozy" at heart, even if Miss Marple has morphed into an alcoholic and suicidal Swedish left-wing charismatic loser cop. Epic, with its atrocious naivety, its huge flaws in respect of realism, its monstrous ambition, its eerie contacts with Nature and the Gods, is the old true magical realism that actually takes us to the edge of things.

With all its magnitude, however, epic must still respond to Aristotle's demand that the epic plotline must have a fundamental unity: an epic story depicts a single large action. That action can be—must be—broken up into many smaller actions and subdivided further into incidents and "beats." The term "action" itself can be stretched: the *Shahnameh* has many stories, many climaxes, but there is an underlying tragic current upon which floats the glory of Persia; the epic of the *Three Kingdoms* swarms with hundreds of characters and narratives, but still keeps its grand trajectory of the restoration of Chinese unity.

At this time of writing, it is "a truth universally acknowledged" that theory is dead, that the literary humanities are profoundly compromised and may even be irrelevant, that the appeal of literature is quixotic and anachronistic at best. In this book I have argued implicitly that there is life in the old dog yet. In the genre we set aside and dismissed, the oldest one of all, may be found the recrudescence of literary studies; and close by is the whole burgeoning, vital, and chaotic world of current popular epic, of big-screen action and fantastic cybernetic games, that sorely needs a rooting and a clarifying guide. That world makes a virtue of creative anachronism, and creative anachronism is the stock-in-trade of the epic world. The study of literature can perhaps revitalize itself by arranging and celebrating the marriage of the two worlds.

We live now in a global culture, and our probes and satellites have enabled us to see the world as a whole. Despite the fact that after our first foray to another world we seem to have fallen back into internecine concerns, the time is coming when we need to deal imaginatively, and in solidarity as humans and representatives of earthly life, with what is profoundly other. Epic may help us overcome the obscure diffidence or suppressed panic wherewith we turned back from the big quest. That quest will surely get us into trouble, as Odysseus got into trouble. But there is nowhere else to go.

Putting It All Together: *Mwindo*, a Test Case

This book celebrates other canons than the traditional "Western" classics, and rightly so. But what makes great works of literature great is that which makes them belong, not just to the canon of their own nation, but to the emergent human canon. *Mwindo* is a case in point. Certainly it is deeply rooted in the specific practices and ideas of the

Nyanga people of Zaire, a culture extremely "other" (on the surface) than that of our own tribe. But it is also hugely relevant to the titanic struggle of Africa as a whole for a humane and beautiful social order in the context of Africa's own characteristic cultural strengths and flaws. And beyond Africa it is one of the great pan-human documents, like all the major epics of the world, an account from the inside of how we humans became human. It has a rightful place in "our" canon.

Epic does many things. It defines the nature of the human storyteller; directly or indirectly it recalls the creation of the world and of the human race; it describes the paradoxical role of the hero as both the Everyman and the radical exception; it establishes the complex quest underlying all human action and tells the story of the journey that it entails; it gets to the bottom of the kin-strife that both blocks and inspires the quest; it distinguishes the three worlds of nature beneath us, society around us, and heaven above us; it recounts the tragic-comic Fall of our race from nature to culture, wild man to knowing man; it takes us shamanically into the underworld of death and back; it recounts the basic principles of the founding of a polity's laws and rituals and gives a representative history of its people; it provides by example a set of fundamental virtues, values, and vices; it embraces and understands the new medium of communication of its time; and it teaches us how to deal with the boundaries of the psychological, social and cosmological world, especially the mystery of time. All these elements are in *Mwindo*, many with a clearer and stronger articulation than are found in other epics.

Daniel Biebuyck's translation—or rather, his literal "trot" of the great storyteller Shekarisi Rureke's oral memorized version of the poem—is clearly the fullest and best version of the story to which a "Western" reader has access. That version is profoundly reflexive, in the sense that the storyteller, in playing out the part of the hero, is also himself performing a shamanic journey into the underworld. He is explicitly taking Biebuyck, the scribe, his helpers, and hearers—and ourselves, the readers he knows will read him—along for the ride. The exhaustion, thirst, and hunger he feels in this enormous recitation—and its astonishing intellectual and artistic effort—are openly introduced into the songs that Mwindo sings as he makes his great journey (a brilliant device that no other epic poet I know uses so directly and effectively). He takes on the paradoxical authority of the storyteller—he is only a servant, passing along a tradition he inherited from the Babuya lineage of Ihimbi whence the story-cycle came; but he is also himself a shaman, channeling the ancestral and divine beings of whom he tells. The hero's power comes from his songs; the singer's ordeal is itself a heroic journey.

The birth of the epic hero is almost always bizarre and marvelous. In telling the story of Mwindo's miraculous birth and his refusal to be destroyed by his father Shemwindo, Rureke is recapitulating in similar terms the Greek myth of the primal gods, who again and again attempt to eat or smother or abort their offspring and who are thwarted by the heroic intransigence of their spouses or their young themselves. In his journey, Mwindo encounters the great forces of the universe, the animal spirits, the sun, the moon, the rivers and storms—often embodied in the major characters he encounters. This is a cosmo-genesis, a myth of the hope of growth, of evolution, of new things breaking in on the old—the amazing ability of time to create a new moment every moment, of ability of life to give birth to new beings. We find it in the birth of the Chinese hero Tripitaka, the Mayan hero-twins, the Egyptian Osiris, Jumong the Korean hero, and Moses (who similarly escape an evil father-figure by floating down a river, a theme we have met in many world epics). Jesus escapes Herod's massacre of the innocents by leaving with his mother for the land of the Nile. The Malinese hero Sundiata escapes his own tyrants and goes into exile with his mother Sogolon, as Mwindo escapes his father by finding refuge with his beloved aunt Iangura. Time, and the human story, is an escape from the fixity or recycling of eternity. As Rhea saves Zeus from Cronus his father, Iangura offers sanctuary to her nephew, al-lowing the new time of his future regime to flow forth, to the rhythm of Mwindo's drum (and Rureke's recitation).

Like all epic quests, Mwindo's search for revenge on his father changes its goal and meaning radically as it brings the experience of the encounter with death and lived life. *Mwindo* is not only an epic but a *Bildungsroman*, a story of personal and moral formation and development. The hero finds that those who have most betrayed him and most deserve his wrath are also those most closely tied to all those he has loved; that the greater the offense to us, the more its revenge will damage us and our dear ones. He finds that his heroic ebullience and self-assertion—essential to being a person, a somebody, at all—must be humbled and chastened to really come into its own. Odysseus too, must hubristically challenge Polyphemus in order to make his name—literally to "get into Trouble"—but he must also learn patience and self-control so as to be able to regain his wife, son, and home. Mwindo's vaunting defeat of the nature-dragon Kirimu, who is dear to the lightning-god Nkuba, is like Odysseus' vaunting defeat of the nature-giant Polyphemus, who is dear to his father the sea-god Poseidon. Both heroes—as Parzifal, Cuchulainn, and Monkey (in *The Journey to the West*)—must repent of their hubris. Likewise, Gilgamesh's triumph over Humbaba leads to the death of his friend Enkidu, and his humiliation in the quest for eternal life is the very thing that makes him a good king and city-builder. In these archetypal moral equations, *Mwindo* is not just an epic but part of the eternal human epic, told again and again with a different dialect, but always in what Steven Pinker calls "Humanese."

Epic often recounts the tragic conflict of close kin as we as humans continually struggle with the paradoxes of the human kinship system: selfish care of our own genes versus unselfish sacrifice for the genes of our kin; blood kinship versus affinal love; father against son; female against male. The explicitness of *Mwindo*'s Oedipal theme is itself an important gloss on the many world epics in which the hero must contend for his existence and identity with a tyrannical male figure. Yes, basically men must struggle with their fathers (as women with their mothers) to find their own heroic stature—Cuchulainn with Conchobar, Sohrab with Rostam, Achilles with Agamemnon and Priam, Hamlet with Claudius, the Pandavas with the blind king Dhrita-Rashtra, Moses with Pharaoh. But usually the conflict is, in Freud's terms, more or less repressed and symbolically redirected; *Mwindo*, however, blurts it out. But what is truly remarkable about the poem is that Mwindo forgives his father. The truth-and-reconciliation ritual in which Shemwindo confesses his crimes, Mwindo refuses to accept his father's abdication and reinstates him as a king but under law, and embraces him as the father without whom he, Mwindo, could not be a true son, is a deeply moving solution of the Freudian problem. It is also an extraordinary political example to the whole continent of Africa, in which living ex-presidents free in their own country are extremely rare, and the transfer of power is almost always appallingly bloody. Mwindo always repents of the slayings that he as hero must perpetrate; and the greatest power of his *conga*, his caduceus or thyrsis, is not to kill but to bring back to life.

The central drama of all epic is the fall of the natural human being from the naked, innocent, deathless, simple, indigenous, and un-ashamed state of nature into the clothed, prurient, death-obsessed, wandering, conflicted, and self-conscious state of culture. We see

Mwindo grow from the naked natural baby, full of ebullient strength, unconscious boastful self-assertion, and oedipal passion for his aunt, into the wise, self-aware, well-traveled and fully clothed king/husband at the end, who, in Wordsworth's words, "hath kept watch o'er man's mortality." Mwindo achieves this transformation—as in different ways do Odysseus, Aeneas and Dante in the Italian epic tradition, and the Pandavas and the hero twins in the Hindu and Mayan epics—by means of the journey into the underworld of death. In contention with the lords of the underworld, Mwindo must himself submit to death but rise again through the power of his invincible *conga*; he must transcend death by internalizing it. His journey prepares him for marriage with Kahindo. Significantly, one of the marriage-tests imposed on him by her kin is to cultivate and harvest a crop of the staple food of the tribe (bananas) in one day. That is, to demonstrate the technology of post-lapsarian civilized culture (as Hunahpu and Xbalanque in the *Popol Vuh* must do, with an instant crop of corn, to be recognized as the true sons of the first pair of hero twins). In transferring his love from the mother-figure Iangura to Kahindo, Mwindo has achieved full human fallen adulthood. In his second great journey, with Nkuba/Lightning into the chilly realms of heaven, he shows himself to be not only the black shaman of the subterranean journey but the white shaman of the sky journey.

He returns, like Moses from Sinai, with the legal and moral laws of Nyanga polity and the liturgies and founding rituals of his society. His is to be a kingship bound by laws and limits and prohibitions, in which he is not the master but the servant of his people: his kingship is no more than the stamping feet of his people's assent. Why should not Africa, which has here perhaps the clearest of all definitions of the spirit of democracy, find here its own founding political myth?

Rureke himself is well aware that in transmitting his poem into the magic machines and alien medium of the recorded, written, and translated text he is joining myth to history. He simultaneously makes fun of the incomprehension and naivety of his European scribe, and acknowledges the profound new meanings that emerge from the transcription of his story into another universe and a future time.

Notes

1. Herbert Jasper and Wilder Penfield, *Epilepsy and the Functional Anatomy of the Human Brain*, 2nd ed. (W. Little, Brown and Co., 1954).
2. V. i. 434.

3. V. i. 214.
4. V. i. 26.
5. Crudely speaking, memories can be durably engraved into our brains either by sufficiently intense unique experiences, or by frequent repetition (or both). Memory has been classified by cognitive scientists into two basic types: procedural memory (know-how) and declarative memory (facts, including past events). Studies of brain damage, notably in the famous patient HM, both of whose hippocampi were surgically removed in order to reduce seizures, have demonstrated the robustness of this dichotomy, technically described as a "dissociation."

Thus ritual symbolism provides sensory experience that powerfully links autonomic activity with conscious thought, in a highly structured way relevant to important societal concerns. It induces physical responses that are experienced as complex emotions, which render particularly salient and memorable the conscious reflections or teachings made at the time that the ritual symbols are brought into play. The collective representations comprising a particular culture become embedded as neural representations in the brains of the participants. As such, they are embodied in enduring material changes in the structure and connectivity of brain tissue.

From an unpublished paper by Robert Turner (Max_Planck-Institute for Human Cognitive and Brain Sciences, Leipzig): "Ritual Action Shapes our Brains: an Essay in Neuroanthropology," delivered at COGNITION, PERFORMANCE AND THE SENSES, a Wenner Gren-sponsored workshop to develop anthropological theory, April 14–15, 2011, University of Sussex, Brighton, United Kingdom.

6. I owe some of the thoughts in the last two paragraphs to my excellent student Andrew Amato.
7. Milman Parry, *The Making of Homeric Verse* (Oxford: Oxford University Press, 1987); Albert Lord, *The Singer of Tales* (Cambridge, MA: Harvard University Press, 2000).
8. Frederick Turner, *Natural Classicism: Essays on Literature and Science* (New York: Paragon House Publishers, 1986). Reprinted in paperback, University Press of Virginia, 1991, 59–108.
9. Two connected poetic movements, the New Formalism and Expansive Poetry, emerged from this interest in the United States, and similar movements have arisen in Britain, France, Canada, Holland, Germany, Italy, and several other countries including Dubai, Albania, and Vietnam (where it may now be the dominant influence in Hanoi's dynamic poetic scene).
10. See also Elizabeth Minchin, *Homer and the Resources of Memory: Some Applications of Cognitive Theory to the Iliad and the Odyssey* (Oxford: Oxford University Press, 2001); Lisa Zunshine, *Why We Read Fiction: Theory of Mind and the Novel* (Ohio State University Press, 2006), examines the neuroscience of storytelling.
11. *Henry IV*, part 1, IV. i. 97
12. *Paradise Lost*, I. 1.
13. *The Prelude*, I.1.

14. *Portrait of the Artist as a Young Man*, Ch. 5.

15. Chapter 37.

16. Chapter 8, Section ix.

17. J. L. Borges, "The Garden of Forking Paths," *Ficciones* (New York: Grove Press, 1994).

18. A "garden of forking paths" in Borges' sense is in theory always open-ended, with an infinitely expanding set of possible destinations, though each branch or fork is traceable back to an origin. A maze has choices for the explorer, but is ultimately closed, and has only one destination. A labyrinth, regardless of its extreme complexity, and its incomprehensibility to the explorer of it, has only one path and one destination. A memory theater or palace can be complex but is closed, can be comprehended and memorized, and since all destinations within it are addressable, the dweller in it can move at ease from any part of it to any other without losing track of the sequence of significant objects it contains. Of particular interest in this context is the fractal self-similar structure, which can be bounded, infinitely deep and varied, yet accessed by simple Hamiltonian coordinates. It is extremely mysterious and extremely accessible (and beautiful); perhaps it is a good model for the ideal epic architecture.

19. Brian Boyd's *On the Origin of Stories: Evolution, Cognition, and Fiction* (Harvard University Press, 2009) makes a strong case for the neuropsychological evolution and human necessity of storytelling, very much in accord with the perspectives of this book.

20. *Heike*, 251, 299; *Cattle Raid of Cooley*, 18–21; *Iliad*, 2.492–759; *Popol Vuh*, 184–85.

21. T. S. Eliot, "The Love Song of J. Alfred Prufrock," last line.

A Bibliography of Epic Texts

NOTE: The following list provides bibliographical information about the texts and translations I have used in this book. If more than one text is given, the first is the one from which I have quoted, and any other text was used for reference or checking a point of translation or accuracy. When the title of the work in translation is different from the accepted title, I have given the accepted title first, and the translation's title second. There are often different spellings for proper names in foreign languages, and I have tried to follow the most common usage.

A study of this list will reveal something in itself: that lesser-known but profoundly important epic texts are often untranslated at worst, or revived in scanned versions by obscure small presses, or in abridged form only, or in editions obviously intended for young readers, or available only in digital form, or remnants of earlier short-lived bursts of personal enthusiasm. With untranslated texts I have had to rely on plot summaries in texts like Felix J. Oinas' useful *Heroic Epic and Saga* (Indiana University Press, 1978) and on various websites created by English-speaking enthusiasts. Many of the texts in translation are out of print and available only in libraries or used bookstores. Such texts are sometimes poorly proofread and unreliable in detail. This neglect is itself part of the larger impulse of this book, which is a critique of modernist and postmodernist critical fashion.

In any other kind of literary scholarship, my procedure—using translations and abridgements, and not citing the original in most cases—would be unjustifiable. But no human being on earth has mastered all the languages of the originals in this list, nor likely will in future, and I believe I have made a case that this conspectus is so worth doing that it is worth doing badly. The originals are themselves often in many versions, each of which is a genuine retelling of the story, including translations themselves. An epic is, strictly, all its retellings, so that the relationship of the text I have used to its "original" is not that of a mere paraphrase but that of a genuine part to an irretrievable whole.

There already exists excellent original-language textual scholarship on those works in this list that are both established classics and extant in a relatively invariant text. These obviously include the Homeric and Virgilian poems, and less obviously, works like the *Shahnameh*, the *Mahabharata*, and *The Three Kingdoms* (the latter, in my opinion, misnamed *The Romance of the Three Kingdoms*: it is not a romance but an epic). Here I have largely ignored issues that have already been covered by better scholars than I, and have used satisfactory translations.

My main focus has been on the forte of epic, that is, on narrative; and stories, and even the deep imagery and symbolism embodied in narrative action, survive translation and retelling with remarkable resilience. Using English-language versions in all cases means that we are at least comparing apples with apples. Obviously this gives English-language originals an apparently huge advantage, since the exquisite details of diction, etymology, homophony, and tone in the original are often blurred in the translation. On the other hand, acquaintance with many epics gives us a strong sense of the range of epic tones, so that though we may not understand the ethnic language of the original, we understand the literary language of the epic genre itself and can piece out what is missing in translation.

Texts Used or Referred to in this Work

Antar
Anonymous.
The Romance of Antar. Terrick Hamilton, trans., W. A. Clouston, ed. Dodo Press, 2008.

Battalname
No English translation from Turkish.

Beowulf
(Bilingual edition) Seamus Heaney, trans. Farrar, Straus, and Giroux, 2000.

Clarel: A Poem and a Pilgrimage in the Holy Land
Herman Melville. Northwestern University Press, 2008.

Davenport's Version: A Narrative Poem
John Gery. Portals Press, 2003.

David of Sassoun
Hovhannes Tumanian, trans. http://www.armeniapedia.org/index. php?title=Hovhannes_Tumanian:_David_of_Sasun.

Don Quixote
Miguel de Cervantes Saavedra. John Rutherford, trans. Penguin Classics, 2003.

Enuma Elish
The Babylonian Genesis: The Story of Creation. Alexander Heidel, trans. University of Chicago Press, 1974.

Faust (parts one and two)
J. W. van Goethe. David Luke, trans. Oxford World's Classics, 2008.

Genesis, an Epic Poem
Frederick Turner. Saybrook Publishers (a division of Norton), 1988: new edition, Ilium Press, 2011.

Gilgamesh
The Epic of Gilgamesh. N. K Sandars, trans. Penguin Classics, 1973.
The Epic of Gilgamesh. Andrew George, trans. Penguin Classics, 2003.

Hamlet
William Shakespeare. In *The Riverside Shakespeare*, ed. G. Blakemore Evans, 1974.

Iliad
Homer. Robert Fagles, trans. Viking, 1990.

Kalevala
Elias Lönnrot. Eino Friberg, George C. Schoolfield, trans. Kustannusosakeyhtio Otava, 1989.

King Dongmyeong of Goguryeo
Yi Kyu-bo. No English translation.

King Gesar
Anonymous.
The Warrior Song of King Gesar. Douglas J. Penick, trans. Mill City Press, 2009.

Lacplesis
Arthur Cropley, trans. Project Gutenberg eBook, http://www.gutenberg.org/cache/epub/17445/pg17445.html.

Laxdala Saga
Anonymous.
The Saga of the People of Laxardal. Keneva Kunz, trans. In *The Sagas of the Icelanders*, Penguin, 2000.

Mahabharata
Vyasa. William Buck, trans. New American Library, 1973.
The Mahabharata. Johyn D. Smith, trans. Penguin Classics, 2009.
The Bhagavad Gita. Juan Mascaró, trans. Penguin, 1973.

Manas
The Kyrgyz Epic Manas. Selections, trans. Elmira Köçümkulkïzï. Ebook. http://www.silk-road.com/folklore/manas/manasintro.html.

Manimekalai
Merchant-Prince Shattan. *Manimekhalai: the Dancer with the Magic Bowl.* Alain Daniélou & Iyer, trans. New Directions, 1965.

Moby Dick
Herman Melville. Modern Library, 1952.

Mwindo
Shé-kárisi Rureke.
The Mwindo Epic from the Banyanga (Zaire). Daniel Biebuyck, Kahombo C. Mateene, trans. University of California Press, 1989.
Oral Epics from Africa. John William Johnson, Thomas A. Hale, Stephen Belcher, eds. Indiana University Press, 1997.

The Magic Flyswatter: a Superhero Story of Africa. Trans. and abridged Aaron Shepard. Skyhook Press, 2008.

Njal's Saga
Anonymous. Penguin Classics, 2001.

Odyssey
Homer.
The Odyssey. Robert Fitzgerald, trans. Double day Anchor, 1963.

Omeros
Derek Walcott. Farrar, Straus and Giroux, 1992.

Oresteia: Agamemnon; The Libation Bearers; The Eumenides
Aeschylus.
Robert Fagles, trans. Penguin Classics, 1984.

Orlando Furioso
Ludovico Ariosto. Guido Waldman, trans. Oxford University Press, 2008.

Paradise Lost
John Milton.
John Milton: Complete Poems and Major Prose. Merritt R. Hughes, ed. Odyssey, 1957.

Parzifal
Wolfgang von Eschenbach.
Helen M. Mustard, Charles E. Passage, trans. Vintage, 1961.
Parzival and Titurel. Cyril Edwards, trans. Oxford World Classics, 2006.

Paterson
William Carlos Williams. New Directions, 1995.

Popol Vuh
Anonymous. Dennis Tedlock, trans. Touchstone, 1996.

Ramayana
Valmiki. R. K. Narayan, trans. Penguin, 2006.
The Concise Ramayana of Valmiki. Swami Venkatesananda, trans.
SUNY Press, 1989.

Shahnameh
Abolqasem Ferdowsi. Dick Davis, trans. Penguin Classics, 2006.

Silappathikaram
Merchant-Prince Shattan. Alain Daniélou, trans. Allen & Unwin,
1965.

Sir Gawaine and the Green Knight
The Pearl Poet. J. R. R. Tolkien, E. V. Gordon, eds. Clarendon Press,
1930.

Sundiata: An Epic of Old Mali
Anonymous. Djeli Mamoudou Kouyaté, oral storyteller. D. T. Niane,
G. D. Pickett, trans. Longmans, 2001.

Taghribat Bani Hilal
Anonymous. Lambert M. Tennoe, Mariam T. Henssonow, Susan F.
Surhone, trans. Betascript Publishing, 2010.
Oral Epics from Africa. John William Johnson, Thomas A. Hale,
Stephen Belcher, eds. Indiana University Press, 1997.

Tambuka
*Swahili Literature: Swahili Poetry, Utendi Wa Tambuka, Utenzi,
Mwana Kupona*. LLC Books, 2010.

The Aeneid
Robert Fitzgerald, trans. Vintage, 1984.
Virgil's Aeneid. Dryden, John, trans. Penguin Classics, 1997.
http://www.thelatinlibrary.com/verg.html.

The Alamo
Michael Lind. Houghton Mifflin, 1997.

The Book of Dede Korkut
Dede Korkut. Geoffrey Lewis, trans. Penguin Classics, 1974.

The Book of Exodus
The Book of Genesis
The New Oxford Annotated Bible. Herbert G. May, Bruce M.
Metzger, eds. Oxford University Press, 1973.

The Cantos of Ezra Pound
Ezra Pound. New Directions, 1996.

The Cattle Raid of Cooley
Anonymous. Translator unknown. Forgotten Books, 2007.

The Divine Comedy
Dante Alighieri. John Ciardi, trans. Three vols, Mentor Books,
1954.

The Faerie Queene
Edmund Spenser. Oxford University Press, 1966.

The Gardens of Flora Baum
Julia Budenz. Carpathia Press, Chelmsford, Massachusetts (in
press), 2011.

The Gaucho Martín Fierro
José Hernandez. Walter Owen, trans. Gordon Press, NY, 1977.

"The Henriad" (*Richard* II, *Henry IV* parts 1 and 2, *Henry V*)
William Shakespeare. In *The Riverside Shakespeare*, ed. G. Blakemore Evans, 1974.

The Journey to the West
Monkey. Wu Cheng-en. Arthur Waley, trans. Grove Press, 1958.

The Kossovo Epic
The Battle of Kossovo. Anonymous. John Matthias, Vladeta Vuckovic,
trans. Swallow Press, 1988.

The Liberation of Jerusalem
Torquato Tasso. Max Wickert, trans. Oxford University Press,
2009.

The Lusiads
Luis de Camoens.
The Lusiad of Camoens. Robert French Duff, trans. Chatto & Windus, 1880 (Kissinger Publishing's Legacy Reprint)

The New World
Frederick Turner. Princeton University Press, 1986: Twenty-Fifth Anniversary Edition, Ilium Press, 2011.

The Peril of Sziget
Miklós Zrinyi. Untranslated at the time of writing.
The Siege of Sziget. Laszlo Korossy, trans. Catholic University of America Press, 2011. (At the time of writing this text was not yet in print.)

The Poem of My Cid
Anonymous.
The Song of the Cid. Burton Raffel, María Rosa Menocal, trans. Penguin Classics, 2009.

The Poetic Edda
The Poetic Edda: The Mythological Poems. Henry Adams Bellows, trans. Dover Publications, 2004.
The Poetic Edda. Carolyne Larrington, trans. Oxford University Press, 2008.

The Prelude
William Wordsworth. Holt, Rinehart, 1954.

The Saga of the Volsungs
Jesse Byock, trans. University of California Press, 1990.

The Secret History of the Mongols
Anonymous.
The Secret History of the Mongols: The Origins of Chingis Khan. Francis Woodman Cleaves, trans., Paul Kahn, ed. Cheng and Tsui, 2005.

The Song of Hiawatha
Henry Wadsworth Longfellow. Adamant Media Corporation, 2000.

The Song of Roland
Turoldus. Patricia Terry, trans. Prentice Hall, 1992.

The Song of the Nibelungs
Anonymous.
Das Nibelungenlied: The Song of the Nibelungs. Burton Raffel, trans. Yale University Press, 2006.

The Tale of the Heike
Kakuichi. Helen Craig McCullough, trans. Stanford University Press, 1988.

The Three Kingdoms
Lo Kuan-chung.
The Romance of the Three Kingdoms. Two Volumes. C. H. Brewitt-Taylor, trans. Tuttle Publishing, 2002.

Toldi
János Arany. Untranslated to date.

General Bibliography

Alexander, Christopher, *A Pattern Language: Towns, Buildings, Construction* (Oxford: Oxford University Press, 1977).

Allums, Larry, *The Epic Cosmos* (Dallas, TX: The Dallas Institute Publications, 1992).

American Heritage Dictionary, 3rd ed. (Boston: Houghton Mifflin, 1992).

Bakhtin, M. M, "The Epic and the Novel: Towards a Methodology for the Study in the Novel," in *The Dialogic Imagination*, ed. Michael Holquist (Austin, TX: University of Texas Press, 1981).

Baudrillard, Jean, *The Illusion of the End* (Palo Alto, CA: Stanford University Press, 1994).

Benjamin, Walter, "The Crisis of the Novel" (review of Alfred Döblin's *Berlin Alexanderplatz*, 1930), in *Selected Writings*, vol. 2, ed. Michael Jennings (Cambridge: Belknap Press, 2003), 301.

Bergmann, John, "The Distribution of Cacao Cultivation in Pre-Columbian America," *Annals of the Association of American Geographers* 59 (1969): 85–96.

Besserman, Lawrence, ed., *The Challenge of Periodization: Old Paradigms and New Perspectives* (New York: Routledge, 1996).

Books LLC. *Paleoanthropological Sites: Zhoukoudian, Blombos Cave, Koobi Fora, Sibudu Cave, Pestera Cu Oase, Atapuerca Mountains, Olduvai Gorge, Qesem Cave.*

Borges, Jorge Luis, *Ficciones* (New York: Grove Press, 1994).

Bowra, C. M., *From Virgil to Milton* (London: Macmillan, 1948).

——, *Heroic Poetry* (New York: St Martin's Press, 1966).

Boyd, Brian, *On the Origin of Stories: Evolution, Cognition and Fiction* (Cambridge, MA: Harvard University Press, 2009).

Budenz, Julia, *The Gardens of Flora Baum*, 5 vols. (Chelmsford, MA: Carpathia Press, 2012).

Campbell, Joseph, *The Hero with a Thousand Faces* (Princeton, NJ: Princeton University Press, 1968).

Cavalli-Sforza, L. L., Paolo Menozzi, and Alberto Piazza, *The History and Geography of Human Genes* (Princeton, NJ: Princeton University Press, 1994).

Clarke, Arthur, *Childhood's End* (New York: Ballantine Books, 1953).

Coe, Kathryn, "Art: The Replicable Unit," in *Biopoetics: Evolutionary Explorations in the Arts*, ed. Brett Cooke and Frederick Turner (Lexington, KY: ICUS Books, 1999), 263.

Conrad, Joseph, *Heart of Darkness* (New York: Simon & Brown, 2010), 82.

Converse, Hyla S., and Arvind Sharma, "An Ancient Sudra Account of the Origin of Castes, *The Journal of the American Oriental Society* 114 (1994).

Cooke, Brett and Frederick Turner, *Biopoetics: Evolutionary Explorations in the Arts* (Lexington, KY: ICUS Books, 1999).

Corona: A Journal of Arts and Ideas (Published by Montana State University).

Cosmos: The Journal of the Traditional Cosmology Society (published by Edinburgh University Press).

Damasio, Antionio, *Self Comes to Mind: Constructing the Concious Brain* (New York: Random House, 2010).

Davidson, H. R. Ellis, *Gods and Myths of Northern Europe* (New York: Penguin, 1964).

Derrida, Jacques, *Of Grammatology* (Baltimore, MD: Johns Hopkins University Press, 1967).

———, *Writing and Difference*, trans. A. Bass (London: Routledge, 1978).

Dissanayake, Ellen, *What Is Art For?* (Seattle: University of Washington Press, 1990).

Douglas, Mary,. *Leviticus as Literature*. (Oxford: Oxford University Press, 2001).

———, *Purity and Danger: An Analysis of the Concepts of Pollution and Taboo* (London: Routledge, 1984).

Dumézil, Georges, *Mythe et Épopée* (Bibliotheque des sciences humaines) (Paris: Gallimard, 1995).

———, *Archaic Roman Religion* (Baltimore, MD: Johns Hopkins University Press, 1996).

———, *Gods of the Ancient Northmen* (Berkeley, CA: University of California Press, 1977).

Eibl-Eibesfeldt, Irenaeus, *Human Ethology* (New Brunswick, NJ: Aldine Transaction, 2007).

Eliade, Mircea, *Shamanism: Archaic Techniques of Ecstasy* (Princeton, NJ: Princeton University Press, 2004).

Eliot, George, *Middlemarch* (Oxford: Oxford University Press, 2008).

Eliot, T. S., *Selected Poems* (New York: Harbrace, 1964).

Emad, Parvis, *On the Way to Heidegger's Contributions to Philosophy* (Madison, WI: University of Wisconsin Press, 2007).

Foley, John Miles, *Homer's Traditional Art* (University Park, PA: Pennsylvania State University Press, 1999).

———, "Experiencing the Siri Epic," Folklore Fellows Communications, http://www.folklorefellows.fi/comm/rev/reviewffc264-266.html, 1999

———, *The Theory of Oral Composition: History and Methodology* (Bloomington, IN: Indiana University Press, 1988).

Fontenrose, Joseph, *The Ritual Theory of Myth]* (Berkeley, CA: University of California Press, 1971).

Foucault, Michel, (1969). *The Archaeology of Knowledge*, trans. A. M. Sheridan Smith (London and New York: Routledge, 2002).

Fox, Robin, *The Red Lamp of Incest: An Enquiry into the Origins of Mind and Society* (Notre Dame, IN: University of Notre Dame Press, 1984).

——, *The Tribal Imagination: Civilization and the Savage Mind* (Cambridge, MA: Harvard University Press, 2011).

Fraser, J. T., "Out of Plato's Cave: The Natural History of Time," *Kenyon Review* (Winter, 1980).

——, *Of Time, Passion, and Knowledge* (Princeton, NJ: Princeton University Press, 1990).

Frazer, James George, *The Golden Bough* (Old Saybrook, CT: Konecky & Konecky, 2010).

Fredrick, Sharonah, "Fighting the Gods: The *Popol Vuh* (Or Why the Conquest of Mexico Could not Repeat Itself with the Maya)," *Revista de Humanidades: Tecnológico de Monterrey*, no. 014 (2003): 207–26.

Freud, Sigmund, *Group Psychology and the Analysis of the Ego* (Eastford, CT: Martino Fine Books, 2010).

Girard, René, *Violence and the Sacred*, trans. Patrick Gregory (Baltimore, MD: Johns Hopkins University Press, 1977).

Gladhill, Charles William, *"Foedera": A study in Roman poetics and society*, PhD dissertation, 3313815 (Stanford University, 2008).

Glassner, Jean-Jacques, Zainab Bahraini, and Marc Van de Mieroop, *The Invention of Cuneiform: Writing in Sumer* (Baltimore, MD: Johns Hopkins University Press, 2003).

Gödel, Kurt, *On Formally Undecidable Propositions of Principia Mathematica and Related Systems* (Mineola, NY: Dover edition, 1992).

Gottschall, Jonathan. *The Storytelling Animal: How Stories Make Us Human* (Boston, MA: Houghton Mifflin, [2012]).

Gould, Steven Jay and Richard C. Lewontin, "The Spandrels of San Marco and the Panglossian Paradigm: A Critique of the Adaptationist Programme," *Proc. Roy. Soc. London B* 205 (1979), pp. 581-598.

Graves, Robert, *The White Goddess* (London: Faber & Faber, 1999).

Greenberg, Clement, *Art and Culture* (Boston, MA: Beacon Press, 1961).

Gregory, R. L., ed., *The Oxford Companion to the Mind* (Oxford: Oxford University Press, 1978).

Grofe, Michael J., *The Recipe for Rebirth: Cacao as Fish in the Mythology and Symbolism of the Ancient Maya*, http://www.famsi.org/research/grofe/GrofeRecipeForRebirth.pdf (accessed July 4, 2012).

Grosby, Steven, *Biblical Ideas of Nationality: Ancient and Modern* (Winona Lake, IN: Eisenbrauns, 2002).

Hooke, S. H., *Middle Eastern Mythology* (New York: Penguin, 1963).

Howell, R. Patton, ed., *Beyond Literacy: The Second Gutenberg Revolution* (Dallas: Saybrook Publishing, 1990).

Huizinga, Johan, *Homo ludens: A Study of the Play-Element in Culture* (Boston, MA: Beacon Press, 1971).

Jasper, H., and Penfield, *Epilepsy and the Functional Anatomy of the Human Brain*, 2nd ed. (New York: W. Little, Brown, 1954).

John Lukacs, *Historical Consciousness: The Remembered Past* (New Brunswick, NJ: Transaction Publishers, 2004), 118.

Joyce, James, *Portrait of the Artist as a Young Man*, (New York: Norton, 2007).

Jung, Carl, *The Portable Jung* (New York: Penguin, 1976).

Ker, W. P., *Epic and Romance* (Charleston, SC: Bibliolife, 2009).

Kerenyi, Karl, *Gods of the Greeks* (New York: Thames & Hudson, 1980).

———, *Dionysus: Archetypal Image of Indestructible Life* (Princeton, NJ: Princeton University Press, 1976).

Kinsella, Thomas, trans., *The Táin* (Oxford: Oxford University Press, 1969).

Larson, Gerald James, ed., *Myth in Indo-European Antiquity* (Berkeley, CA: University of California Press, 1974).

Lawler, Andrew, "Playing Politics or Just a Game," *Science* 328 (April 30, 2010): http://www.sciencemag.org

Leach, Maria and Jerome Fried, eds., *Funk and Wagnall's Standard Dictionary of Folklore, Mythology, and Legend* (New York: Funk & Wagtnalls, 1972).

Lewis, C. S., *A Preface to Paradise Lost* (Oxford; Oxford University Press, 1961 [1942]).

Lord, Albert, *The Singer of Tales* (Cambridge, MA: Harvard University Press, 2000).

Lorenz, Konrad, *On Aggression* (New York: Bantam 1967).

Lyle, Emily, *Sacred Architecture; In the Traditions of India, China, Judaism and Islam* (Edinburgh: Edinburgh University Press, 1992).

Lyotard, Jean-François, *La condition postmoderne: rapport sur le savoir* (Paris: Minuit, 1979).

Macleish, Archibald, *Collected Poems, 1917–1982* (Boston, MA: Houghton Mifflin, 1985).

Maslow, A. H., "A Theory of Human Motivation," *Psychological Review* 50, no. 4 (1943): 370–96.

McLuhan, Marshall, *Understanding Media* (New York: Routledge and Kegan Paul, 1964).

McNamee, Maurice B., S.J. *Honor and the Epic Hero* (New York: Holt, Rinehart and Winston, 1960).

Milton, John, and Merritt Y. Hughes, ed., *John Milton: Complete Poems and Major Prose* (New York: Odyssey, 1957).

Minchin, Elizabeth, *Homer and the Resources of Memory: Some Applications of Cognitive Theory to the Iliad and the Odyssey* (Oxford: Oxford University Press, 2001).

Morris, I., *The World of the Shining Prince; Court Life in Ancient Japan* (Oxford: Oxford University Press, 1964).

Murrin, Michael, *The Allegorical Epic* (Chicago and London: The University of Chicago Press, 1980).

Nagy, Gregory, *The Best of the Achaeans* (Baltimore, MD: Johns Hopkins University Press, 1980, 1997).

Nemoianu, Virgil, *Postmodernism and Cultural Identities: Conflicts and Coexistence* (Washington, DC: Catholic University of America Press, 2010).

O'Flaherty ,Wendy Doniger, *Other Peoples' Myths: The Cave of Echoes* (Chicago, IL: University of Chicago Press, 1995).

———, *Splitting the Difference: Gender and Myth in Ancient Greece and India* (Chicago, IL: University of Chicago Press, 1999).

Oinas, Felix, *Heroic Epic and Saga: An Introduction and Handbook to the World's Great Folk Epics* (Bloomington, IN: Indiana University Press, 1979).

Ozsváth, Zsuzsanna, and Frederick Turner, *Light within the Shade: Hungarian Poetry Over Eight Hundred Years.* Unpublished: forthcoming.

Parry, Milman, *The Making of Homeric Verse* (Oxford: Oxford University Press, 1987).

Peacock, W., *English Verse*, vol. II (Oxford: Oxford University Press, 1961).

Peirce, C. S., *Peirce on Signs* (Chapel Hill, NC: The University of North Carolina Press, 1991).

Pennisi, E., "Synthetic Genome Brings New Life to Bacterium," *Science* 330, no. 17 (December 2010): 1605.

Pinker, Steven, *The Blank Slate: The Modern Denial of Human Nature* (New York: Penguin, 2003).

Quine, Willard V. O., *Word and Object* (Cambridge, MA: MIT Press, 1960).

——, *From Stimulus to Science* (Cambridge, MA: Harvard University Press, 1998).

Quint, David, *Epic and Empire, Politics and Generic Form From Virgil to Milton* (Princeton, NJ: Princeton University Press, 1992).

Redman, Tim, *Ezra Pound and Italian Fascism* (New York: Cambridge University Press, 2009).

Ross, W. D., *The Right and the Good* (Oxford: Oxford University Press, 2002 [1930]).

Roth, Gerhard, and Ursula Dicke, "Evolution and Intelligence," *Trends in Cognitive Sciences* 9, no. 5 (May 2005).

Rubin, David, *Memory in Oral Traditions: The Cognitive Psychology of Epic, Ballads, and Counting-Out Rhymes* (Oxford: Oxford University Press, 1995).

Ruthven, K. K., *Myth* (London: Methuen, 1976).

Spencer, Herbert, *Spencer: Political Writings* (New York: Cambridge University Press, 1993).

Swift, Jonathan, *Gulliver's Travels* (New York: Penguin, 2003).

Tedlock, Dennis, trans., *Popol Vuh: The Definitive Edition of the Mayan Book of the Dawn of Life and the Glories of Gods and Kings* (New York: Touchstone, 1996).

Thomas Babington Macaulay, Review of Henry Neele's *The Romance of History. England* in *The Miscellaneous Writings and Speeches of Lord Macaulay* (London: Longmans, Green, 1889).

Thornton, Agathe, *The Living Universe: God and Men in Virgil's Aeneid* (Leiden: Brill, 1997).

Tolkien, J. R. R., *The Monsters and the Critics* (New York: HarperCollins, 1997).

Trout, Paul., *Deadly Powers: Animal Predators and the Mythic Imagination* (Amherst, NY: Prometheus Books, 2011).

Turner, Frederick, *Beauty: The Value of Values* (Charlottesville, VA: University Press of Virginia, 1992).

——, *Shakespeare's Twenty-First Century Economics: The Morality of Love and Money* (New York: Oxford University Press, 1999).

——, *Natural Classicism: Essays on Literature and Science* (New York: Paragon House Publishers, 1986. Reprinted in paperback, Charlottesville, VA: University Press of Virginia, 1991).

——, *Natural Religion* (New Brunswick, NJ: Transaction Publishers, 2006).

Turner, Robert, "Ritual Action Shapes our Brains: An Essay in Neuroanthropology," delivered at COGNITION, PERFORMANCE AND THE SENSES, a Wenner Gren sponsored workshop to develop anthropological theory, April 14–15, 2011, University of Sussex, Brighton, United Kingdom.

Turner, Victor W., *Schism and Continuity in an African Society* (Oxford: Berg Publishers, 1996).

——, *From Ritual to Theater: The Human Seriousness of Play* (New York: PAJ Publications, 2001).

——, *The Ritual Process: Structure and Anti-Structure* (New Brunswick, NJ: Aldine Transaction, 1995).

——, *The Forest of Symbols* (Ithaca, NY: Cornell University Press, 1967).

Vico, Giambattista, *The New Science of Giambattista Vico* (1744), trans. Thomas G. Bergin and Max H. Fisch (Ithaca, NY: Cornell University Press, 1948).

Weber, Clifford, "Metrical *Imitatio* in the Proem to the *Aeneid*," *Harvard Classical Review*, http://www.jstor.org/pss/311408

Western, Jessie, *From Ritual to Romance* (Mineola, NY: Dover, 1997).

Williams, W. C., *The Collected Poems of William Carlos Williams, Vol. II: 1939–1962* (New York: New Directions, 2001 [First Published 1944]).

Wilson, Edward O., *Consilience: The Unity of Knowledge* (New York: Vintage, 1999).

Wittgenstein, Ludwig, *Tractatus Logico-Philosophicus*, trans. C. K. Ogden (New York: Cosimo Classics, 2007).

——, *Philosophical Investigations* (Upper Saddle river, NJ: Prentice Hall, 1999).

Wright, Robert, *The Moral Animal: Why We Are the Way We Are* (New York: Vintage, 1995).

——, *Nonzero: The Logic of Human Destiny* (New York: Pantheon Books, 2000).

Yeats, W. B., and M. L. Rosenthal, eds., *Selected Poems and Two Plays of William Butler Yeats* (New York: Macmillan, 1962).

Zunshine, Lisa, *Why We Read Fiction: Theory of Mind and the Novel* (Columbus, OH: Ohio State University Press, 2006).

Index